Democracy in East Asia

A *Journal of Democracy* Book

•

SELECTED BOOKS IN THE SERIES

Edited by Larry Diamond and Marc F. Plattner

Liberation Technology: Social Media and the Struggle for Democracy (2012)

Poverty, Inequality, and Democracy (2012)
(with Francis Fukuyama)

Debates on Democratization (2010)

Democratization in Africa: Progress and Retreat (2010)

Democracy: A Reader (2009)

How People View Democracy (2008)

Latin America's Struggle for Democracy (2008)
(with Diego Abente Brun)

The State of India's Democracy (2007)
(with Sumit Ganguly)

Electoral Systems and Democracy (2006)

Assessing the Quality of Democracy (2005)
(Edited by Larry Diamond and Leonardo Morlino)

World Religions and Democracy (2005)
(with Philip J. Costopoulos)

Islam and Democracy in the Middle East (2003)
(with Daniel Brumberg)

Emerging Market Democracies: East Asia & Latin America (2002)
(Edited by Laurence Whitehead)

Democracy after Communism (2002)

Political Parties and Democracy (2001)
(Edited by Larry Diamond and Richard Gunther)

The Global Divergence of Democracies (2001)

Published under the auspices of
the International Forum for Democratic Studies

Democracy in East Asia
A New Century

Edited by Larry Diamond, Marc F. Plattner,
and Yun-han Chu

The Johns Hopkins University Press
Baltimore

9 8 7 6 5 4 3 2 1

Chapters in this volume appeared in the following issues of the *Journal of Democracy:* chapters 1, 5, and 6, January 2012; chapter 8, April 2010; chapter 9, October 2010; chapters 10, 11, 12, and 14, April 2012; chapter 13, October 2012; chapter 15, January 2013. For all reproduction rights, please contact the Johns Hopkins University Press.

The Johns Hopkins University Press
2715 North Charles Street
Baltimore, Maryland 21218-4363
www.press.jhu.edu

Library of Congress Cataloging-in-Publication Data

Democracy in East Asia : a new century / edited by Larry Diamond, Marc F. Plattner, and Yun-han Chu.
    pages cm. — (A journal of democracy book)
  Includes index.
978-1-4214-0968-9 (pbk. : alk. paper) — ISBN 978-1-4214-0969-6 (electronic) — ISBN 1-4214-0968-2 (pbk. : alk. paper) — ISBN 1-4214-0969-0 (electronic)
  1. Democracy—East Asia. 2. Democracy—Southeast Asia. 3. East Asia—Politics and government. 4. Southeast Asia—Politics and government—1945– I. Diamond, Larry Jay.

JQ1499.A58D46 2013
320.95—dc23
                                         2012038472

CONTENTS

ACKNOWLEDGMENTS

Although this is the second edition of *Democracy in East Asia,* it is composed entirely of new material. A great deal has changed in the region in the decade and a half since the publication of the first edition of *Democracy in East Asia* in 1998, and we have given this new edition the subtitle "A New Century" both to reflect the period that it covers and to clearly distinguish it from its predecessor.

The vast majority of chapters included here originated as papers prepared for a conference on "Democracy in East Asia and Taiwan in Global Perspective" held in Taipei on 24–25 August 2011. Funded by Taiwan's Ministry of Interior, the conference was intended as a celebration of the one-hundredth anniversary of the founding of the Republic of China. It was jointly organized by the Department of Political Science of the National Taiwan University (NTU) and the National Endowment for Democracy's International Forum for Democratic Studies. The idea of the conference was conceived by our good friend Yun-han Chu, professor of political science at NTU and a member of the Editorial Board of the *Journal of Democracy*. He proposed from the outset that the project should yield a new edition of *Democracy in East Asia*. This was a plan that we were delighted to endorse, especially given the quality of the attendees whom he suggested as potential invitees. And we were very pleased that Yun-han agreed to join us as a coeditor of this volume.

In addition to the contributors to this volume, the distinguished scholars who participated in the Taipei conference included Pippa Norris, Stephan Haggard, Tun-jen Cheng, Jih-wen Lin, Bridget Welsh, and Doh C. Shin. The chapters by Mark Thompson, Edward Aspinall, and Don Emmerson, along with a second chapter by Ben Reilly, were added later, but the core of the book remains the papers presented in Taipei. We wish to express our deep gratitude to the conference participants, to the Political Science Department of the NTU, to the Program for East Asia Democratic Studies of the NTU's Institute for Advanced Studies, and to the Ministry of Interior for their contributions to this project.

We are also grateful to our colleagues at the Johns Hopkins University Press (our book editor Suzanne Flinchbaugh, as well as Bill Breichner and Carol Hamblen of the Journals Division) for all their help in preparing this volume. Above all, however, we want to thank the members of the *Journal of Democracy* staff, who handled the extra editorial burden imposed by their labors on this volume with great efficiency and good cheer. Brent Kallmer handled the layout and production with his customary skill and determination. Phil Costopoulos and Tracy Brown edited most of the chapters, but our outgoing Assistant Editor Marta Kalabinski also helped with the editing, as did freelancer Justin Bonner. Our new Assistant Editor Nate Grubman provided significant assistance to Larry Diamond in drafting the Introduction, and Dorothy Warner once again did a fine job on the Index.

We cannot conclude without once again thanking the Lynde and Harry Bradley foundation for their longtime support of the *Journal of Democracy*. And we are happy to have still another opportunity to express our thanks to President Carl Gershman and the Board of Directors of the National Endowment for Democracy for the continuing moral and financial support that they have given to the International Forum for Democratic Studies and the *Journal of Democracy*.

INTRODUCTION

Larry Diamond

This is a book about the status and prospects of democracy in East Asia, a region of the world that encompasses seventeen countries containing 30 percent of the world's population. Although these countries are often considered as belonging to two separate regional groupings—the eleven countries of Southeast Asia (ten of which make up the Association of Southeast Asian Nations plus Timor-Leste) and the six countries of Northeast Asia (China plus Japan, the two Koreas, Mongolia, and Taiwan)—there is a logic to considering them as a single "region." With well over half the entire population of East Asia and its fastest-growing economy over the last thirty years, China casts a lengthening shadow of power, influence, and economic penetration over all of Northeast and Southeast Asia, and each of the region's sixteen other countries must take "the China factor" into account when framing policies and development strategies. In addition, most of these countries over the centuries and millennia have been significantly influenced by Chinese cultural traditions, and scholars have often cited their common Confucian traditions as a reason for the region's shared lack of democratic experience (or even democratic prospects). Many of them have significant ethnic-Chinese populations of their own, and more than a few have experienced military conflict with Chinese states at one time or another.

With the world's most powerful, dynamic, and self-confident authoritarian regime sitting at the geographic and demographic heart of the region, one would expect East Asia to be a place where democracy is weak and fragile. To be sure, East Asia is not among the world's most democratic regions: Only eight of its seventeen states currently count as electoral democracies (see Table 1 below), and these hold less than 30 percent of the region's population. Yet the proportion of democracies in East Asia is higher than the same proportion in South Asia, Sub-Saharan Africa, or the broader Middle East. Since the late 1980s, East Asia has gone from being the cradle and locus of "developmental authoritarianism," with Japan being the lone democracy—and a longstanding one-

TABLE 1—EAST ASIAN REGIMES, 1 JANUARY 2012

Liberal Democracy (FH 1–2.0)	Electoral Democracy (FH>2.0)	Electoral Authoritarian	Politically Closed Authoritarian
Japan (1,2)	Mongolia (2,2)	Malaysia (4,4)	Brunei (6,5)
S. Korea (1,2)	Indonesia (2,3)	Singapore (4,4)	Vietnam (7,5)
Taiwan (1,2)	Philippines (3,3)	Cambodia (6,5)	China (7,6)
	Timor-Leste (3,4)		Laos (7,6)
	Thailand (4,4)		Burma (7,6)
			N. Korea (7,7)

Principal source: Freedom House, 2012 Freedom in the World Survey, available at *www.freedomhouse.org.*

party–dominant system at that—to at least a mixed and progressing set of systems. Today, democracy seems to be on the move in East Asia, and the region may actually represent, even more than the Middle East, the next frontier for a significant wave of democratic transitions.

The late 1980s and 1990s were a period of significant democratic progress for East Asia. South Korea went from military rule to democracy, with the formal completion of the transition arriving in the form of the direct presidential election of December 1987. During the ensuing years, and particularly (as Yun-han Chu and Hyug Baeg Im explain in Chapter 7) during the second posttransition presidency of Kim Young Sam (1993–98), Korea proceeded to extend civilian control of the military and consolidate, reform, and deepen democracy in a number of respects. By then, the Philippines had already made a transition to democracy (in 1986), and the presidency of Fidel Ramos (1992–98) was also a period of at least modest democratic strengthening and reform. With direct presidential elections in 1996, Taiwan completed its extended transition to democracy, led from above by the long-ruling Nationalist Party or Kuomintang (KMT). Paralleling Korea's experience, Taiwan then underwent a gradual deepening and further liberalization of democracy, in a sense joining the "club" of advanced industrial democracies. For both Korea and Taiwan, further democratic thresholds were crossed when opposition parties won free and fair national elections, marking historic first alternations in power for Korea in 1997 and Taiwan in 2000. Today, these two countries rank with Japan as consolidated and liberal democracies. Comparative data on political rights, civil liberties, and the quality of governance confirm that all three are liberal democracies, though they could become better, more liberal ones by further enhancing the rule of law and civil liberties and by improving mechanisms of accountability and transparency to control corruption and political favoritism.

East Asia's merely electoral democracies have much further to go toward deepening and consolidating democracy. Shortly after the USSR's collapse in 1991, Mongolia made a historic transition to democracy, and since the early 1990s Freedom House has continually classified it as a "free" country, the only postcommunist country east of the Baltics to earn that designation. Yet in this phenomenally mineral-rich country the judiciary remains underdeveloped, the rule of law is weak, and corruption remains a grave problem, which is widely recognized by the public. Indonesia, since its transition to democracy in the 1999 elections, and especially during the first term of President Susilo Bambang Yudhoyono (2004–2009), has made progress toward institutionalizing democracy. The Philippines returned to democracy in 2010, when a free and fair election brought to the presidency Benigno "Noynoy" Aquino (son of the courageous democracy activist Corazon Aquino, who defeated the Marcos dictatorship in 1986). Yet semifeudal elites retain a strong hold on many Philippine provinces and constituencies, and their influence in the country's Congress has obstructed many needed reforms. In the World Bank's annual governance ratings, Indonesia and the Philippines rank in the bottom quartile of all countries in corruption control and not much better (the bottom third) in the rule of law. In 2010, among big (mainly G-20) emerging-market democracies such as Argentina, Bangladesh, Brazil, India, Mexico, South Africa, and Turkey, only Bangladesh did worse than the Philippines and Indonesia on these two indicators of the quality of governance.[1]

For many comparativists, Thailand is a puzzle. It has a per capita income and a human-development score roughly equivalent to those of Poland when it made its transition to democracy around 1990 (and not that much lower than what South Korea could boast in 1988). In terms of modernization theory, then, it seems well placed to become a stable democracy. But as Thitinan Pongsudhirak argues in these pages, Thailand has spent the past decade going through an "uneasy passage." Thais remain deeply polarized between a "red-shirt" camp (based in the countryside and among newer elites) that backs ousted premier Thaksin Shinawatra and a "yellow-shirt" camp (based in the urban middle class). The latter proudly wears the symbolic color of the monarchy and defends its preeminence. With the decisive opposition victory of the new Pheu Thai Party (led by Thaksin's sister Yingluck Shinawatra) in the May 2011 parliamentary elections, the political force that the military deposed in the 2006 coup has returned, and Thailand has become once again an electoral democracy, though an illiberal one still constrained by the monarchy and the military. Thailand faces a rocky road, as the stabilizing presence of long-reigning King Bhumibol (b. 1927) draws toward a close. If the end result is a weaker monarchy (and military), this might help to ease the country's intense polarization and create a more mature and securely institutionalized politics. At least the military seems to have learned from the political turbulence and polarization of the last decade that its direct intervention will not solve the country's political problems. If the 2006 coup does prove to be the last in Thailand's history, democracy will sink firmer roots over the coming decade as modernization further raises incomes and education.

In each of these four electoral democracies—Mongolia, Indonesia, the Philippines, and Thailand—at least three-quarters of citizens agree that "democracy may have its problems, but it is still the best form of government." In each, only about half the public is satisfied with the way democracy is working (save in Thailand, where it is three-quarters), but majorities in each country believe that democracy remains capable of solving their country's problems. One possible reason for this faith in democracy is suggested by the fact that wide majorities in each country (up to 76 percent in Mongolia and 80 percent in the Philippines) believe that the people retain the power to change the government through elections.[2]

With the exception of Timor-Leste, which achieved independence in 2002 as an electoral (though not very liberal) democracy, no new democracy has emerged in East Asia since Indonesia underwent its transition in 1999. Indeed, the past decade has seen oscillation rather than progress, with the Philippines and especially Thailand experiencing recurrent political crises and movements away from and back to electoral democracy. This lack of further democratic progress places East Asia within the global trend of a leveling-off and even a recession of democracy. In each year from 2007 through 2011, the number of countries around the world with declining freedom levels was at least twice the number of those with improving levels. Overall global levels of freedom and democracy have also been in retreat for a number of years now, and there has been a rising tide of democratic breakdowns.[3] When viewed against this overall trend, East Asia is actually not doing too badly.

If we count democracy by states rather than by the size of the populations involved, East Asia today is a bit below the overall international norm. Globally, slightly less than 60 percent of the world's states are democracies, while in East Asia that figure is slightly less than 50 percent. On the average of the two Freedom House scales of political rights and civil liberties, where 1 represents most free and 7 most repressive, East Asia had an average freedom score at the end of 2011 of 4.17, compared to 3.70 for all developing countries outside the West (and 3.30 for the world as a whole, including the Western democracies). In other words, East Asia is somewhat less free and less democratic than the world overall—and if we were to weight the regional figures by population, it would be substantially less free, due to the predominance within the region of China, with its huge populace and average Freedom House score of 6.5.

An important strand in thinking about East Asia argues that this democracy deficit grows out of Asian cultural values. As such, this analysis goes, the deficit is to be expected—and will most likely per-

sist. The idea is that East Asians value order over conflict, authority over freedom, and, by extension, development (with the material
prosperity it brings) over democracy.[4] And, so the argument goes, this
will not change with economic development. Survey evidence from
the East Asian Barometer provides some partial support for this argument, but also points to significant signs of contradiction. Certainly,
as Chong-Min Park and Yu-tzung Chang demonstrate in Chapter 4,
diffuse support for democracy has yet to become firmly entrenched
among the public throughout East Asia. And East Asians do choose
economic development over democracy (when forced to make a choice
in the survey question), but in a number of countries they also manifest reasonably high levels of support for democracy as a system of
government.[5] Moreover, a number of the findings from public-opinion
research do not fit with the "Asian values" thesis. For example, levels
of support for democracy are quite high in some of the less developed
East Asian countries, including Indonesia, the Philippines, and Thailand. While there is more skepticism of democracy (or more nostalgia
for authoritarianism) in Taiwan and South Korea, these two counties
(along with East Asia's other liberal democracy, Japan) manifest a
very broad and determined rejection of all authoritarian alternatives
to democracy, and they also evince stronger support than elsewhere
in the region for democratic norms such as individual freedom, the
rule of law, and checks on executive power.[6] The biggest challenge,
and perhaps the biggest puzzle, comes when we try to understand the
competitive authoritarian regimes of Singapore and Malaysia, where
large proportions of the public appear to support what Park and Chang
call "the regime in practice," but at the same time sizeable majorities
also express a preference for democracy.

Prospects for Further Democratization

It is by now widely appreciated that Singapore is by any standard a
massive anomaly. As we see in Table 2 below, Singapore is far richer
today than the other major "third-wave" countries were when they
made their transitions to democracy (this includes Spain and Greece,
which do not appear in the Table). Singapore is the most economically
developed nondemocracy in the history of the world. But Singapore is
changing, and this change will probably accelerate when the founding
generation of leaders, particularly Lee Kuan Yew (who is nearing 90),
passes from the scene. In the May 2011 parliamentary elections, the
ruling People's Action Party (PAP) recorded its weakest electoral performance since independence in 1965, winning "only" 60 percent of
the vote. Although the PAP still won (yet again) well over 90 percent
of parliamentary seats thanks to a highly rigged electoral system, the
opposition Workers' Party broke through for the first time to win a

TABLE 2—DEVELOPMENT LEVELS AND DEMOCRATIC TRANSITIONS

Country	Year of Transition	GDP per Capita, PPP$ (2009 international dollars)	HDI Score (year of transition)
Turkey	1984	6,316	-
Brazil	1985	7,596	0.687
Philippines	1986	2,250	-
South Korea	1988	9,086	-
Pakistan	1988	1,722	-
Hungary	1990	12,979	0.692
Poland	1990	8,376	0.683
Chile	1990	6,896	0.675
Bangladesh	1991	748	0.186
Thailand	1992	4,732	0.685
South Africa	1994	7,235	0.716
Taiwan	1996	19,938	-
Indonesia	1999	2,666	0.681
Mexico	2000	12,662	0.698
Ghana	2000	1,653	0.431
Ukraine	2005	6,037	0.696
Asia (Current)			
Singapore	-	56,522	0.866
Malaysia	-	14,670	0.761
Thailand	-	8,505	0.682
China	-	7,519	0.687
Vietnam	-	3,134	0.593
Laos	-	2,436	0.524
Burma	-	1,256	0.483

Notes: GDP per capita and Human Development Index (HDI) scores in the bottom index are for the years 2010 and 2011, respectively. All GDP per capita figures have been transformed into the value of constant 2009 dollar values using the GDP deflator.

Sources: For HDI, see *http://hdrstats.undp.org/en/tables/default.html;* for GDP per capita, see *www.imf.org/external/pubs.*

five-seat group constituency, and a total of six seats overall—a record for the Singaporean opposition. While a postelection survey failed to reveal a general increase in support for greater political pluralism since the last elections (in 2006), the expressed preference for a more competitive political system did increase dramatically in the youngest age cohort (21 to 29 years old), shooting up from 30 to 44 percent.[7] If Singapore remains in the grip of a half-century-old single-party hegemony, that hegemony now seems to be entering a more vulnerable phase. Opposition parties have new energy and backing, young people flock to social media to express themselves more openly, independent media provide a fuller range of news and opinions, and the ruling party feels compelled to ease censorship and other controls. Singapore, in other words, has now joined the ranks of the world's "competitive authoritarian" regimes—the class of autocracies in whose ranks democratic transitions are most likely to occur.[8]

Singapore's exceptionalism is widely known. Less well known is that Malaysia now also has a higher per capita income than most third-wave countries did when they made their transitions to democracy. In fact, among the prominent cases in Table 2, only Taiwan had a higher per capita income than Malaysia when it completed its democratic transition. Moreover, Malaysia's score on the UN Development Programme's Human Development Index—which, in measuring not only per capita income but also levels of health and education, is arguably a truer measure of development—is now significantly higher than the levels in Brazil, Chile, Mexico, and even Hungary, Poland, and Ukraine when they made their respective transitions to democracy. From the standpoint of modernization theory, then, Malaysia too is ripe for a democratic transition.

For more than a decade, Malaysia's competitive authoritarian regime has faced a much more serious challenge than anything that Singapore has so far seen. As the opposition has gained in unity, credibility, and mobilizing power, the long-ruling United Malays National Organization (UMNO) feels under increasing threat. Much of what is driving change in Malaysia is not only exhaustion with half a century of rule by one party (formally through a ruling coalition), but also a much better educated and more pluralistic society, with the attendant growth in independent organizations and the intense and innovative use of social media (including one of the most influential online newspapers in the world, *Malaysiakini*).

Alarmed by the upheavals that began sweeping the Arab world at the end of 2010, Malaysia's Prime Minister Najib Razak pledged to appoint a broad committee to review the country's electoral system and recommend reforms, and then vowed to repeal the draconian Internal Security Act. Many opposition and civil society leaders, however, saw these promises as empty, citing Razak's push to enact stiff new security laws in place of the old ones. After winning control of five of the thirteen states in 2008, opposition forces seem poised to do better in the next national elections. The new opposition alliance, Pakatan Rakyat, has been gaining momentum. The regime tried to destroy its leader, former deputy prime minister Anwar Ibrahim, with trumped-up charges of homosexual misconduct. These proved even less credible than when the ploy was first tried in 1999 (and resulted in a prison sentence of several years). In January 2012, a judge dismissed the charges against Anwar. To be sure, Malaysia's authoritarian establishment still has a lot of resources, but Razak's proposed reforms now seem "too little too late," as "cynicism still pervades the country."[9] A transition to democracy could happen at any time in the coming years through the familiar instrument that has brought it about in other competitive authoritarian regimes: the electoral process.

It is not only Southeast Asia's wealthier countries that are feeling

the winds of democratic change. As Burma's iconic democratic leader Aung San Suu Kyi has recently acknowledged, and as Min Zin and
Brian Joseph show in their contribution to this volume, that country's
political opening, launched falteringly amid widespread skepticism in
2008, suddenly seems quite serious. Labor unions have been legalized,
Internet censorship has been eased, and a number of political prisoners have been freed. Suu Kyi's National League for Democracy (which
won the aborted 1990 elections) swept the parliamentary by-elections in
April 2012, giving it a small but significant foothold in parliament. As
has happened with other authoritarian regimes that opted to liberalize
politically, Burma's authoritarian rulers seem to have been influenced
by democratic developments elsewhere in the world, as well as by the
prospective economic benefits—chiefly flowing from closer integration
with the global economy—that political liberalization might bring. As
an advisor to Burma's President Thein Sein noted in December 2011,
"The president was convinced about the global situation; he saw where
the global stream was heading."[10]

The Coming Change in China

Per capita income in China is still little more than half of what it is
in Malaysia, but it has been rising rapidly and now approaches the level
that South Korea could boast at the time of its democratic transition in
1987–88. In fact, by IMF projections, China could surpass that level
(about US$9,000 in 2009 Purchasing Power Parity [PPP] dollars) by
2013. In 1996, Henry Rowen predicted on the basis of data and projections regarding economic development that China would become what
Freedom House would call a Partly Free country by 2015, and a Free
one (with political-rights and civil-liberties scores as good as those of
India or Indonesia today) by 2025.[11] More recently, Rowen affirmed
that analysis, estimating that even if China's growth in GDP per capita
slowed to 5 percent annually starting in 2015, it would have by 2025 a
per capita income roughly equivalent to that of Argentina in 2007 (about
$15,000 in current PPP dollars—which is roughly where Malaysia is
today).[12] And if China's growth in per capita income were to slow immediately to 6 percent annually, it would still reach $13,000 in current
PPP dollars before 2020 —the level of Hungary in 1990 and Mexico in
2000 when they made their respective transitions to democracy.

It is not only modernization—the spread of democratic values and
capacities in tandem with rising incomes and information—that is feed-
ing the escalating pressure for democratic change in China. As Yun-han
Chu notes in Chapter 6, the growing density of ties between mainland
China and Taiwan—including direct access (through travel and satellite
television) to political news from the highly competitive and even rau-
cous democracy that is Taiwan—is serving as an additional stimulant to

the growth of democratic norms and aspirations in China. The irony of Communist China's relentless push for closer integration with Taiwan is that it may well begin to generate political convergence—but not in the way that the Communist leaders imagined.

Rowen's projections were a bit mechanical in assuming that economic growth would necessarily drive *gradual* political change toward democracy in China. Instead, it seems increasingly likely that political change in China will be sudden and disruptive. The leaders of the Chinese Communist Party (CCP) still show no sign of embarking on a path of serious political liberalization that might gradually lead to electoral democracy, as their counterparts in Taiwan's then-dominant KMT did several decades ago. Instead, the rulers in Beijing are gripped by a fear of ending up like the USSR's Mikhail Gorbachev, who launched a process of political opening in hopes of improving and refurbishing Soviet Communist rule, only to see it crumble and the Soviet Union itself end up on the ash heap of history. Torn by intense divisions within their own ranks and weakened by the draining away of power and energy from the center to the provinces and a congeries of increasingly divergent lower-level authorities, China's political leaders seem as frozen and feckless on the grand question of long-term political reform as they are brisk and decisive in making daily decisions on spending and investments. Although it is too soon to tell whether the next generation of Chinese leadership under new President Xi Jinping will be more flexible in allowing greater freedom, judicial independence, and political competition, the signs point to a continuation of conservatism and caution at the top of the system.

As Francis Fukuyama notes in Chapter 1, the lone flaw in the otherwise impressive institutionalization of Chinese Communist rule is its lack of adaptability. For a regime whose specialty is producing rapid economic change, such rigidity is a potentially fatal defect. With every month or year that ticks by while corruption, routine abuses of power, and stifling constraints on expression go unchecked, citizens' frustration mounts. Already, protests erupt with ominous frequency across tens of thousands of Chinese localities every year, while subversive and democratic ideas, images, and allusions proliferate online, despite the best efforts of fifty-thousand Internet police to purge Chinese cyberspace of "harmful content." As Minxin Pei has been arguing for some time and as he asserts again here in Chapter 5, the strength of the authoritarian regime in China is increasingly an illusion, and its resilience may not last much longer. As discontent with corruption, collusion, criminality, and constraints on free expression rise, so do the possibilities for a sudden crisis to turn into a political catastrophe for the CCP.

Beyond the ongoing frustrations with censorship, insider dealing, abuse of power, environmental degradation, and other outrages that can only be protested by antisystem activity of one sort or another, there are, as Fukuyama notes, the big looming social and economic challenges that China faces as the consequences of its one-child policy make themselves felt in a rapidly aging (and disproportionately male) population. Jack Goldstone reports that China's labor force stopped growing in 2010 and has begun shrinking at the rate of half a percent a year, which "will, by itself, knock 2.2 percentage points off China's annual economic growth potential." China, in other words, will get old before it gets rich. Urbanization, a key driver of productivity increases, is also slowing dramatically, and the growth of education "has clearly reached a limit," as the number of college graduates has expanded faster than the ability of the economy—even as it faces labor shortages in blue-collar industries—to generate good white-collar jobs.[13]

The Chinese economy will have to pay for rapidly rising wages and cope with industrial labor shortages even as it comes under pressure to finance pension, welfare, and healthcare benefits for the massive slice of the populace that is now moving toward retirement. Moreover, as it manages all this, China will need to address growing frustration among college graduates who cannot find jobs to match their expectations. If the suspected bubbles in the real-estate and financial markets burst as these twin generational challenges are gathering force, political stability in the world's most populous country may well become no more than a memory.

Increasingly, the CCP faces the classic contradiction that troubles all modernizing authoritarian regimes. The Party cannot rule without continuing to deliver rapid economic development and rising living standards—to fail at this would invite not gradual loss of power but a sudden and probably lethal crisis. To the extent that the CCP succeeds, however, it generates the very forces—an educated, demanding middle class and a stubbornly independent civil society—that will one day decisively mobilize to raise up a democracy and end CCP rule for good. The CCP, in other words, is damned if it does, and damned if it does not. The only basis for its political legitimacy and popular acceptance is its ability to generate steadily improving standards of living, but these will be its undoing.

To many readers at the time he published his essays, Henry Rowen's projections may have seemed rather optimistic. But today, as the need for a more open, accountable, and law-based regime becomes as obvious as the current leaders' inability to bring one about, it is no longer ridiculous to speculate that the end of CCP rule will come much sooner, quite possibly within the next ten years. Of course, a sudden collapse of the Communist system could give rise, at least for a while, to a much more dangerous form of authoritarian rule, perhaps led by a nationalistic military looking for trouble abroad in order to unify the nation at home. But this would likely represent only a temporary solution, for the military is incapable of governing a rapidly modernizing, deeply networked, middle-class country facing complex economic and social challenges.

Analyzing East Asia

The chapters that follow analyze East Asia's democratic trajectories and prospects from the perspective of both comparative analysis and country case studies. In Chapter 1, Francis Fukuyama begins by setting a broad historical and theoretical context, with a focus on the pattern of state development in China and elsewhere in the region over time. He argues that the historical sequence in which many East Asian states have developed could have powerful implications for democratic development regionwide. In China, a modern, centralized state emerged prior to any other in the world. Today, the Chinese state is more highly institutionalized than other authoritarian states, and its bureaucracy is comparatively modern, impersonal, and meritocratic. While Chinese officials lack any formal accountability to the people, they are held accountable to their superiors. Thus, Fukuyama maintains, they end up meeting popular demands more consistently than officials in other authoritarian regimes. While Fukuyama sees important flaws in the Chinese system that hinder its performance and limit its appeal, he believes the Chinese model is distinguished from that of other authoritarian states by its ability to cultivate professionalism and competence in governance.

Fukuyama argues further that this traditional Chinese model (which long pre-dates communism) remains influential even in societies that are not communist and now boast democratic governments. Historically, Japanese, Korean, and many Southeast Asian societies replicated this model, building strong bureaucratic states long before any democratic institutions capable of constraining such states ever made an appearance. Without democracy having arrived on the scene, these states enjoyed success in modernizing and industrializing their societies in order to pursue economic growth. Democracy was, so to speak, added onto all this, with the region's strong, effective bureaucratic states remaining fixtures. Democratic institutions that safeguard the rule of law and enforce accountability should enhance the performance of already high-functioning states. However, Fukuyama observes, East Asian citizens may worry that democratic checks on state power could also make complex national decisions more difficult to reach. In a region with a legacy of competent states, he argues, the most salient question is not how democratic institutions will perform in safeguarding the rule of law and enforcing accountability, but how these institutions (or their lack) will affect state performance. Regardless of the answer, China's shadow looms large.

Democratic performance in the region is also shaped by the design

of democratic institutions, argues Benjamin Reilly in Chapter 2. East
Asian democracies, Reilly observes, have largely adopted mixed-member majoritarian electoral systems that combine single-member districts
and national party lists but allot a greater proportion of seats to the former. This system has enouraged the formation of large political parties
or blocs. Within this broad trend, Reilly observes three subregional patterns. Northeast Asian democracies feature semipresidential constitutions, mixed-member electoral systems, and inchoate two-party systems.
In mainland Southeast Asia, where the Chinese model holds great sway,
ruling parties have established "semidemocracies." Maritime Southeast
Asia, on the other hand, features complicated electoral models, presidential or semipresidential executives, "fragmented" party landscapes,
and a penchant for experimental political engineering. These institutional arrangements should have predictable impacts on policy choices and
governance, Reilly suggests. By forcing leaders and parties to appeal to
the median voter, majoritarian institutional designs tend to drive policy
choices that fuel economic growth. Thus transitions from developmental
authoritarianism (where it still exists) to majoritarian democracy may
be relatively painless. Yet increasing polarization in countries such as
Taiwan, Thailand, and Mongolia illustrates the downside of letting winners take all.

During the past twenty years, a puzzling shift in policy priorities has
taken place in Taiwan, South Korea, and Japan, writes Joseph Wong in
Chapter 3. Before the 1990s, each of these states focused on delivering
economic growth. Most social spending stemmed from a top-down effort to raise the productivity of workers. Yet during the 1990s, when
global norms seemed to support a paring down of social-welfare states,
Japan, South Korea, and Taiwan shifted surprisingly in the opposite direction, from an emphasis on productivity to one on social welfare. Despite the absence of strong leftist parties or a labor movement, each of
these developmentally mature democracies began to drastically increase
spending on social programs aimed at helping vulnerable populations
rather than productive ones.

Economic troubles and a demographic shift that threatened to render
vulnerable a greater slice of the population help to explain this shift.
But Wong finds these causes insufficient. Rather, he argues that the increasing competitiveness of each country's democracy spurred the sharp
change in policy priorities. The decline of one-party dominance in each
country compelled political elites to heed growing concerns about the
quality and extensiveness of social-welfare measures; opened political
space in which legislators could press substantial policy changes; and
mobilized civil society groups to lobby more aggressively and challenge
traditional top-down models of reform. Although greater democratic
competition drove welfare-state expansion in these three democracies,
Wong questions how widely this model of policy change may apply to

other countries. Taiwan, South Korea, and Japan had the advantages of tremendous fiscal capacity and a history of equitable growth that limited the costs of redistributive programs. And the nonideological nature of their political parties allowed them greater latitude to shift course and pursue policies that elsewhere might have fallen under the purview of leftist or labor groups, narrowing their potential base of support.

In Chapter 4, Chong-Min Park and Yu-tzung Chang widen the comparative lens further to assess the political attitudes and values of citizens in East Asia's democracies and semidemocracies, as measured in the third-wave surveys of the Asian Barometer. The authors find that while citizens across the region generally rate democracy as superior to any alternative, many East Asians do not quite see democracy as a universal value. Democratic institutions such as popular elections and multiparty systems enjoy robust support. Yet support for the (classically) "liberal" norms that make for liberal democracy—such as checks and balances, the rule of law, and political pluralism—is more limited and shallow. This suggests that even citizens who support democracy in principle may prefer or be willing to accept illiberal practices. Furthermore, Park and Chang find citizens of the region's liberal democracies (Japan, Korea, and Taiwan) largely disenchanted with their governments. While public support in these countries for freedom and electoral competition is uniformly high, citizens perceive that these regimes are struggling to guarantee equality, accountability, and the rule of law. In most of the region's democracies, parliaments and political parties evoke cynicism. While support for democracy as a principle stems from trust in its minimalist institutions and some of its liberal norms (the rule of law, for example), support for democracy in practice depends more heavily on whether or not its institutions perform effectively. Given the shallow support for the region's liberal democracies illustrated by the Asian Barometer, Park and Chang conclude that democratic norms have yet to become fully entrenched throughout East Asia.

Northeast Asia

China's ruling Communist Party faces an array of potentially lethal challenges. If the CCP cannot overcome them (or at least manage them effectively), this failure could torpedo the Chinese model's appeal throughout the region. Will the Communist regime in China survive? In addressing this question in Chapter 5, Minxin Pei argues that the CCP's ability to survive until now should not be conflated with strength. On the contrary, he argues, "perceived authoritarian resilience is, in all likelihood, a temporary phenomenon that conceals fatal weaknesses." Nevertheless, the quality of an authoritarian state's survival strategy can affect its lifespan. In the case of China, Pei notes that effective use of repression, maintenance of a statist economy, and cooptation of emerging social groups have allowed the CCP to survive its most recent set of challenges. In wielding the most indispensable tool of any authoritarian government—repression—China has refined its strategy, limiting political rights and freedoms while conserving its resources by allowing citizens some agency in their private lives. Instead of lashing out at any threat, Pei explains, the government has targeted particular leaders and groups while being selective in using brutal means. Meanwhile, to preserve its ability to distribute rewards, the CCP has maintained a tight grip on state enterprises, which still account for almost 40 percent of China's annual GDP. In addition to maintaining control of the purse, with which it rewards its supporters, the Chinese state has both broadened and enhanced its base by reaching out to intellectuals, technocrats, and businesspeople, transforming itself from the self-proclaimed standard-bearer of workers and peasants into what Pei calls "a party of elites."

While these survival strategies have allowed the CCP to parry recent challenges, how well they will meet emerging ones remains unclear. Today, Pei observes, the CCP confronts a growing middle class whose fealty is costing ever more to buy, not to mention rising demands for better services, greater transparency, and more widely distributed prosperity. Moreover, recent survival strategies could inadvertently make these challenges more daunting. Selective repression has thwarted political opposition, but it has also invited corruption. Modernization has granted the party access to a growing number of elites, but the support of those elites is contingent on the party's ability to reward them materially—an increasingly difficult task as their numbers continue to grow. Preserving some degree of statist economic control has allowed the CCP to maintain control of the purse strings, but it has limited the private-sector growth necessary to expand employment opportunities for China's emerging cohorts of educated young people. The party's ability to manage these new stresses may tell us much about whether its survival in power to date has stemmed from inherent resilience or good but fleeting fortune.

As modernization challenges one-party authoritarianism in China, the CCP might do well to draw lessons from the gradual political opening engineered by the KMT in Taiwan. As Yun-han Chu explains in chapter 6, Taiwan and the People's Republic of China share much culturally, and their social and economic ties have grown increasingly strong in the last quarter-century. The CCP and KMT also share much history; each emerged in the early part of the twentieth century with a mission to rebuild and strengthen China, and both adopted Leninist methods and structures. While the CCP and KMT ultimately diverged markedly, Chu maintains that the CCP's current challenges resemble those that confronted the KMT in the 1970s and 1980s: replacing an outdated ideology with a new foundation for legitimacy, broadening the party's base, preserving hegemony over social and political organization despite emerging challengers, addressing the proliferation of mass media, and dealing with the growing demand for representation and participation driven by socioeconomic modernization. Ultimately, the KMT's transition to "a one-party–dominant regime" and its eventual loss of power could prove instructive to CCP elites. Chu points to two possible lessons. As the KMT's eventual electoral defeat illustrates, "developmental authoritarianism" creates stakeholders with growing demands for better governance and greater participation, and thus sows the seeds of its own demise. Yet a hegemonic party that initiates a drawn-out process of reform may stand a chance of prolonging its survival in power, as the KMT did for some time. Regardless of the conclusions that CCP elites draw from the KMT's evolution, Chu believes that Taiwan's past and present experience will help to shape discussion about China's political future.

Taiwan and South Korea are often considered East Asia's sturdiest third-wave democracies. According to Samuel P. Huntington, a democracy can be considered reasonably consolidated after it has undergone two peaceful and orderly turnovers of power by democratic means. In Chapter 7, Yun-han Chu and Hyug Baeg Im use Huntington's criterion as they consider how the democratic turnovers in South Korea and Taiwan have affected the quality of democracy in those countries. The authors conclude that indeed it was not until the second power rotation in each country that South Korea and Taiwan built robust support for democracy and overcame serious vulnerabilities. Interestingly, Chu and Im observe a similar trajectory of attitudes toward democracy in each country; during a difficult first democratic administration, confidence waned. Yet soon after the second democratic alternation, it rebounded. In each case, rotation in power brought significant political reforms while also confirming for dissatisfied elites that change could come in a timely and constitutional fashion through the ballot box.

Southeast Asia

When Indonesia embarked on a political transition following a regionwide financial crisis and the subsequent fall of President Suharto in 1998, it seemed as if a myriad of potential spoilers—Islamists, politically minded generals, ambitious local leaders—threatened to derail the prospective transition to democracy. Sidelining these spoilers in the decade and a half since, Indonesia has emerged as a somewhat surprising democratic success story. Yet the country's struggles to contain endemic clientelism and corruption have rendered its democratic success only a qualified one. In Chapter 8, Edward Aspinall delves into the roots of both Indonesia's democratic success and its democratic shortcomings. He finds them to be intertwined. Indonesia, he argues, has shown a remarkable ability to absorb would-be spoilers into its democracy rather than to marginalize or confront them. The military, for decades the key power source behind the longstanding dictatorship, was diverted from its political role, and a "new paradigm" of civil-military relations was ushered in. By devolving political power to local government, cutting peace deals with particularly restive regions, and redesigning an electoral system in order to encourage pluralism while barring locally focused parties from national politics, local leaders were convinced to buy into the idea of a coherent Indonesian democracy. Finally, Islamist political forces were absorbed into the system, contributing to their moderation and the stability of the country's democracy.

Yet as Aspinall points out, accommodating all these potential spoilers has had a cost. It has eased Indonesia's transition but limited the quality of its democracy. The spoilers have lowered their weapons but have not surrendered them. The generals no longer police domestic political movements, double as civil servants, or sit in legislatures. However, they still enjoy a "culture of impunity" and robust participation in the defense ministry, business, and other institutions that augment their power. Meanwhile, decentralization has increased opportunities for "predatory behavior" by local actors. Finally, while the participation of Islamists has perhaps moderated their goals, it has also contributed to a more Islamized state that could pose a challenge to pluralist democracy in the future. Ultimately, Aspinall argues, Indonesia's approach to potential spoilers has created for the near term a trade-off between the persistence and the quality of democracy. In the long term, however, the country's ability to address the shortcomings in the quality of its governance will have an impact on the strength and permanence of its democracy.

In the Philippines, the surprisingly orderly 2010 electoral defeat of President Gloria Macapagal-Arroyo by Benigno "Noynoy" Aquino III has restored many Filipinos' faith in their country's democracy and seemingly put an end to a period of democratic backsliding. Arroyo had been accused of electoral fraud and had pledged not to "[go] quietly." As Mark Thompson writes in chapter 9, the election brought into play the two narratives that have come to dominate political discourse in the Philippines: reformism and populism. The Philippines still faces many acute challenges, including generating shared prosperity, a workable physical infrastructure, and a rule of law that controls corruption and contains violence. Yet, as Thompson argues, the ability of a politician to win the battle of narratives can be just as critical to winning popularity as building a formidable patronage network or scoring tangible gains in meeting the country's challenges. Indeed, Noynoy's popularity stemmed from his skill at painting himself as a reformist and distinguishing himself both from his predecessor and from his populist opponents. In the Philippines, reformism has become a lasting ideology partially because it offers a contrasting approach to populism. While Noynoy's victory would seem to suggest that reformism enjoys greater support today, the election of his populist vice-president demonstrates that the contest is close. Whether President Aquino can leverage his popularity to bring about significant improvements in Filipinos' lives and their country's democracy remains unclear.

Even as the Philippines was climbing out of a modest democratic slump, Thailand spent the late 2000s in the throes of deepening polarization following a September 2006 military coup. In Chapter 10, Thitinan Pongsudhirak charts the contours of what he calls a "national stalemate." Removed from office and relegated to exile by the military, billionaire and populist ex-premier Thaksin Shinawatra has nonetheless remained the key figure in Thai politics. He now acts as a kind of shadow premier through his sister (who won the office at the polls in 2011) and a handpicked cabinet, having successfully defied years of efforts by establishment forces clustered around the military, the monarchy, and the bureaucracy to sideline him and blunt his movement's political appeal. Yet despite Thaksin's enduring popularity, says Thitinan, the former prime minister remains "synonymous with divisiveness" and has forged a legacy that is mixed at best.

Capitalizing on a post–Cold War order that has allowed reformers more room to maneuver, Thaksin reformed the bureaucracy, reached out to impoverished Thais excluded from recent economic gains, offered an appealing economic vision, and turned Thailand into a more assertive regional power. However, Thitinan refuses to overlook Thaksin's shady, authoritarian side and writes that Thaksin's "corruption, conflicts of interest, cronyism, human-rights violations, abuses of power, and other sins of misrule" have tarnished his record. Yet by clinging to outmoded Cold-War thinking and showing little interest in framing a democratic vision, Thaksin's opponents among the pro-monarchy "yellow shirts" have been no less responsible for the country's impasse. Thai society has changed fundamentally since Thaksin's election in 2001, and any opposition to Thaksin based solely on returning to a hallowed past is bound to fail. Thailand's democratic future depends on whether the monarchy and its supporters can reconcile themselves with a nation that will not recede in its desire for democracy, and whether Thai political leaders can build a brand of democracy that rises substantially above Thaksin's deep flaws.

In Malaysia and Singapore, hegemonic political parties—Malaysia's United Malays National Organization (UMNO) and Singapore's People's Action Party (PAP)—have claimed to be the linchpins of national order, stability, and prosperity. Democratization, say these parties, is a road to ruin. In Chapter 11, Dan Slater considers their argument and explores the effect that democratization might have on the capacity of the state to preserve order and prosperity. For Slater, clues to Singapore's and Malaysia's democratic future can be found in history—both their own and that of similar states that eventually made the shift to democracy. The distinctiveness of Singapore and Malaysia, he argues, lies in the prodigious strength of their respective state establishments and the conditions under which these strong states developed. In each country, today's ruling parties, who initially gained power through democratic means, inherited from British colonialism a strong state capable of enforcing order and collecting revenues. Ultimately, each built on this sturdy foundation.

Slater argues that similar cases of "strong-state democratization" seem to refute the justification for continued one-party rule and suggest that Malaysia and Singapore could proceed to democracy in an orderly fashion. South Korea and Taiwan have each democratized in recent decades without sacrificing state capacity, prosperity, or order. In each case, the ruling party's decision to lead the process allowed it to retain great influence and power. The moderate Korean and Taiwanese middle classes produced by modernization became bulwarks against destabilizing shifts. Most important, the strong state that once served an authoritarian government became the tool of a democratic one. Yet as Slater notes, while precedent suggests that Singapore and Malaysia's moderate middle classes and strong institutions would cushion the potentially destabilizing consequences of a ruling-party defeat, the very strength of the state in Malaysia and Singapore may lead the UMNO and the PAP to keep assuming that their grip on power is unassailable and that a transition is unnecessary. If the UMNO and the PAP fall into this trap, warns Slater, they will be missing what he calls a "historic shift." In both countries, he notes, radical-leftist and sectarian opposition movements have given way to moderate and multiethnic ones, leaving the field to broad and moderate opposition movements that could erode the ruling parties' legitimacy and hurt their chances of surviving a democratic transition if and when one arrives.

Despite adopting reform programs in the 1980s, ruling parties in Cambodia, Laos, and Vietnam have stuck to a similarly nondemocratic path, and as Martin Gainsborough observes in Chapter 12, a stubbornly illiberal political culture persists. For Gainsborough, the roots of this stagnation in all three countries lie in an elitist and paternalistic political culture and the growth of crony capitalism that has accompanied economic reform. The political culture characteristic of these countries, which share a French-colonial heritage and a customary closeness to the "Chinese model" of governance, features the idea that rulers should by and large be left to restrain themselves, thus rendering liberal institutions redundant or even distasteful. In this context, civil society is thought to serve little purpose, and elections act as confirmations of popular support rather than as channels of participation. Economic reform has failed to undermine this mentality because so much of the newly marketized economy in each country remains under state tutelage. In each country, marketization did not so much crowd out the state as augment it. Connections to political elites have grown in value, and public office has become a far more lucrative calling, making public officials and their cronies even more fervent stakeholders in the status quo. Gainsborough finds that these brakes on political opening have not been strong enough to halt the development of civil society. The emerging middle class in each country has increasingly engaged in backstage lobbying for limited reform. Yet the ties that bind the middle class to the political elite seem to moderate activists' aims. Barring the fall of the CCP in China, Gainsborough warns that the chances of regime collapse in Cambodia, Laos, and Vietnam are remote, though he holds out hope that evolving Southeast Asian societies could compel ruling parties to allow more political opposition.

Recent developments in Burma illustrate the unpredictability of democratization. Following decades of seemingly relentless authoritarianism and isolation, an opening emerged in March 2011 when newly elected president Thein Sein, a member of the military regime that has ruled Burma for half a century, delivered a speech calling for reform. In Chapter 13, Min Zin and Brian Joseph examine this political opening, the reasons for its emergence, the challenges it presents, and, ultimately, the potential it holds for promoting democratization in Burma—a country long ruled by one of the world's most rigid, brutal, and stubborn autocracies. Although Burma's transition "remains tension-wracked and far from complete," with an authoritarian, military-dominated regime still in place, Min Zin and Joseph argue that change is unmistakably underway. The drivers of this change include fear of overreliance on China, a desire to reengage with the West, the imperative to avoid another popular uprising like the one the military savagely put down only a few years ago, and a growing recognition that Burma has fallen behind its dynamic neighbors and the world generally.

When Burma's military leaders charted a roadmap to "discipline-flourishing democracy," they probably envisioned the endpoint as a more stable and prosperous Burma united under the leadership of a military-backed ruling party. Moving forward, the success of Burma's reform project may hinge on the decision of hard-liners to stay on the sidelines. To Min Zin and Joseph, constitutional guarantees of protection, coupled with an institutional arrangement that has set different elements of the regime against one another to some degree, have kept resistance to reform softer and more off-balance than it might otherwise have been. Burma's democratic forces, meanwhile, have played their hand well, staying united and embracing gradualism. Moving forward, the ability of Burmese democrats "to find and stick to the right mix of participation and contestation" will help to determine the success of their project. In addition, the Burmese state must emerge from reform better able to tackle the numerous challenges facing this impoverished country. As Min Zin and Joseph write, "The main chal-

lenge now, therefore, is less democratization per se than the building
of a state in which democracy can take root and grow." The 2015 elections, and the willingness of Burma's generals to accept their results,
will be critical.

In Chapter 14, Donald Emmerson examines the relationship between
democracy and good governance throughout Southeast Asia. The as-
sumption that they naturally go hand-in-hand, he writes, is faulty. While
governments in Timor-Leste and Indonesia are robustly democratic in
comparison to their neighbors, governance is not particularly strong either. This gap in performance, if it persists, could portend turbulence for
these democracies. Yet even if democracy is not a prerequisite for good
governance in the region, autocrats' competing claim that authoritarianism is the high road to good governance, stability, and growth also rings
hollow. Some of the region's most staunchly authoritarian regimes, such
as Burma (until very recently) and Laos, also have its worst governance
records. While Emmerson draws attention to democracies that are underperforming badly, he cautions that the gap between democracy and
governance is not necessarily an indicator of future instability. The decision of Burmese reformers to pursue democratic reform more vigorously than economic reform, Emmerson points out, seems to suggest that
democracy, regardless of its impact on governance, holds an intrinsic
appeal for many in the region.

In Chapter 15, Benjamin Reilly makes a second appearance in order
to ponder the puzzling pattern of democracy's presence or absence
across Southeast Asia. Indeed, the dearth of democracy in the region's
richest countries (Brunei, Malaysia, and Singapore), together with its
strength in the poorest (Indonesia, the Philippines, and Timor-Leste)
seems to defy the idea—so basic to modernization theory—that stable
democracy is fostered by economic development. The reason for this
seemingly anomalous situation, says Reilly, lies in the realm of history and geography. Reilly offers an alternative explanation noting
that most of the region's maritime states are democratic, while most of
its mainland states are autocratic and most of its "in-between" states
are semidemocratic. He therefore argues that physical proximity to
China and the traditional degree of Chinese influence (heavier on the
mainland, lighter on the offshore periphery) offer the best explanation
of how democracy is distributed across Southeast Asia. For centuries,
China forcibly drew its southern neighbors into a tributary system that
encouraged close ties. Even after this system unraveled, China continued to wield massive influence in countries such as Burma, Cambodia,
Laos, and Vietnam. In modern times, China has continued to play the
hegemon's role via pursuit of economic integration, support of Leninist parties, and military force or its threat. Just as nearness to China
and the weight of the undemocratic "Chinese model" can be seen to
act as drags on democratic prospects in the former tribute lands along

China's southern edges, so does the comparative weakness of Chinese influence in Indonesia and the Philippines help to explain why these poor societies have been able to build democracies despite their poverty. Once again, the fate of mighty China and its ruling Communist Party seems to remain a powerful contextual factor shaping democracy's prospects in East Asia.

A Coming Democratic Wave?

Political scientists generally have a poor track record of predicting major regime changes. One of their most powerful tools for doing so, modernization theory, is at best an imperfect guide. At worst, some argue, the theory is inapplicable to Asian authoritarian regimes like those in Singapore, Malaysia, China, and now Vietnam that are said to have found a more effective and enduring form of authoritarian governance, built on cultural foundations not suitable to democracy. However, if Asian cultures are not suitable for democracy, someone needs to explain why democracy has become consolidated and fairly liberal in Japan, Korea, and Taiwan, and why it has also taken root in Indonesia, Mongolia, and the Philippines as well. Moreover, if Asia is truly different—a region poised to resist international trends—we should find clear evidence of that in public-opinion surveys. While the data exhibit a complex pattern with many caveats, they show not so much defiance of global trends as a substantial and even growing desire for democracy and accountability in East Asia.

Whatever the specific scenario of change may be, China cannot keep moving forward to the per capita income, educational, and informational levels of a middle-income country without experiencing the pressures for democratic change that Korea and Taiwan did more than two decades ago. Those pressures are rising palpably now in Singapore and Malaysia. They will gather momentum in Vietnam as it follows China's path of transformational (even if not quite as rapid) economic development. In Thailand, continuing modernization over the next decade will change society in ways that will make democracy easier to sustain. All of this augurs well for East Asia's democratic future. Although the authors of this volume are somewhat mixed in their prognoses, it is not unreasonable to predict that, within a generation or so, most of East Asia will turn democratic, with profound consequences for democratic prospects globally.

NOTES

I am very grateful to *Journal of Democracy* Assistant Editor Nate Grubman for his subsantial and superb assistance in drafting this Introduction.

1. Worldwide Governance Indicators, the World Bank Group, 2011, *http://info.world-*

bank.org/governance/wgi/sc_country.asp. Indonesia and the Philippines were rated in the 27th and 22nd percentiles, respectively, on control of corruption and the 31st and 24th percentiles, respectively, on rule of law. South Korea, by contrast, was ranked in the 69th and 81st percentiles on these two measures.

2. Data are from Round III of the Asian Barometer.

3. Larry Diamond, "Democracy's Third Wave Today," *Current History*, November 2011, 299–307.

4. A classic and elaborate articulation of this argument can be found in Lucian Pye, *Asian Power and Politics: The Cultural Dimensions of Authority* (Cambridge, Harvard University Press, 1985).

5. As some of the papers of the Asian Barometer project have argued, it is somewhat hard to interpret these findings in countries like China and Vietnam, because not only do majorities say that democracy is the best form of government but they also consider that their current system is democratic. Thus if these data are to be believed, it is not clear whether people are supporting democracy as a system of government with popular sovereignty and limited, constitutional government, or rather their own authoritarian system that falsely claims the mantle of democracy.

6. Yun-han Chu et al., eds., *How East Asians View Democracy* (New York: Columbia University Press, 2008); and Yu-tzung Chang, Yun-han Chu, and Chong-Min Park, "Authoritarian Nostalgia in Asia," in Larry Diamond and Marc F. Plattner, eds., *How People View Democracy* (Baltimore: Johns Hopkins University Press, 2008).

7. "IPS Post-Election Survey 2011," Institute of Policy Studies, Singapore. My thanks to Tan Ern Ser for sharing a copy of the summary findings.

8. Stephan Ortmann, "Singapore: Authoritarian but Newly Competitive," *Journal of Democracy* 22 (October 2011): 153–64.

9. Ooi Kee Beng, "In Malaysia, Reforms Take a Staggered Path," *MalaysianInsider.com*, 3 December 2011, available at *www.themalaysianinsider.com/litee/opinion/article/in-malaysia-reforms-take-a-staggered-path*.

10. "In Myanmar, Government Reforms Win Over Some Skeptics," *New York Times*, 29 November 2011.

11. Henry S. Rowen, "The Short March: China's Road to Democracy," *National Interest*, Fall 1996, 61–70.

12. Henry S. Rowen, "When Will the Chinese People Be Free?" *Journal of Democracy* 18 (July 2007): 38–52.

13. Jack A. Goldstone, "Rise of the TIMBIs," *Foreign Policy.com*, 2 December 2011, available at *www.foreignpolicy.com/articles/2011/12/02/rise_of_the_timbis*.

I

Comparative & Institutional

1

THE PATTERNS OF HISTORY

Francis Fukuyama

Francis Fukuyama *is Olivier Nomellini Senior Fellow at Stanford University's Center on Democracy, Development, and the Rule of Law. His most recent book is* The Origins of Political Order: From Prehuman Times to the French Revolution *(2011). This essay originally appeared in the January 2012 issue of the* Journal of Democracy.

This essay begins with a simple premise. In order to understand the nature of democracy in East Asia, we must understand the nature of authoritarian government there. The contemporary problems of democracy in the region, and its ability to deal with future challenges, cannot be understood except in the context of a region whose largest player is a rapidly growing and relatively successful authoritarian regime—that is, China. In this essay, I am not considering this challenge as a matter of foreign policy, although I expect that accommodating a rising China will be an immense problem for the international system. Rather, it is a question of development models. East Asian democracy will be evaluated not in comparison to authoritarian regimes in Africa or the Middle East, but in comparison to China. We therefore need to understand the China model—both its strengths and weaknesses—as a prelude to discussing the future of democracy in Japan, Korea, Taiwan, and other countries.

The field of comparative politics has not developed an adequate conceptual framework for categorizing and understanding different forms of authoritarian government in comparison to the very rich vocabulary that we have for classifying democratic regimes. Put differently, we lack a language for describing the state, shorn of the institutions of law and accountability. We need to fill in this gap and develop an understanding of how the specific characteristics of East Asian government arise out of the historically determined development path that the region followed. There are as many similarities between democracies and nondemocracies in East Asia as there are between democracies in this region and democracies elsewhere. This constitutes both an advantage and a challenge for the future of democratic development there.

The core states of East Asia—China (both the People's Republic of China and Taiwan), Japan, and Korea—developed relatively high-quality, centralized bureaucratic states early in their histories and consolidated relatively uniform national identities on the part of ethnically homogeneous populations centuries before any of them developed countervailing institutions of law and accountability that would check and balance state power. As I argue in *The Origins of Political Order,* the first society to develop a modern state in the Weberian sense of the term—one based on impersonal recruitment, meritocratic bureaucracy, uniform administration, and the like—was China, which had accomplished this by the time of the founding of the Qin dynasty in 221 B.C.E.[1]

Modern liberal democracy is a combination of three sets of institutions: the state itself; the rule of law, which is a system of social rules regarded as binding on the actions of the de facto ruler; and mechanisms of accountability, which in the modern world are periodic multiparty elections. The state concentrates and uses power to enforce its will; the rule of law and mechanisms of accountability, by contrast, serve to constrain state power. The success of a liberal democracy depends on achieving a balance between strong state power and the checks and balances constituted by the legal and electoral systems. Unchecked state power is dangerous from any number of perspectives; at the same time, liberal democracies that are weak or paralyzed do not produce good outcomes for their citizens.

In contrast to other world civilizations, China never developed a rule of law. The legal codes of the Qin, Han, Sui, Tang, and Ming dynasties were all species of positive law, administrative enactments of the emperor. Needless to say, dynastic China also failed to create formal institutions of accountability. In Europe, state power was limited initially by the early emergence of law and then by the ability of certain well-organized social actors outside the state to resist state power and force states into a constitutional compromise. The precocious consolidation of a modern state allowed Chinese governments over the centuries to prevent the spontaneous emergence of new social actors that would challenge its power, such as a blood aristocracy, a commercial bourgeoisie, independent cities, religious institutions, or an organized peasantry.

This Chinese mode of governance then set the pattern for the rest of East Asia. Japan and Korea, and later the polities in Southeast Asia under Chinese cultural influence, inherited Confucian traditions of coherent centralized states and meritocratic bureaucracy. All of East Asia's traditional states were undermined, altered, and replaced in the process of confrontation with the West; but in the second half of the twentieth century, a powerful and highly institutionalized executive branch re-emerged in nearly all of them.

Unlike many new democracies in other parts of the world, where states were weak and lacking in capacity when they established rule-of-law and accountability institutions, East Asian democracies could presuppose the existence of a strong and coherent state. The problem of democratic development lay more on the side of society. For the most part, East Asian societies lacked strong and well-institutionalized social groups that could effectively resist state power, as well as a political culture that legitimated social protest and adversarial politics. With the onset of industrialization, new social actors such as a bourgeois class, trade unions, and students began to emerge, and in Japan, South Korea, and Taiwan the state was further checked by the international system (in the guise of the U.S. military). This permitted the development over time of democratic regimes in which indigenous social actors continued to evolve and became able to balance the state on their own.

A number of important consequences for contemporary development flowed from this particular institutional sequence. First and most important, almost all the recent examples of successful authoritarian modernization cluster in East Asia rather than other parts of the world. Hong Kong under British rule, Japan, Singapore, South Korea, Taiwan, Thailand, and of course China itself all developed rapidly in the second half of the twentieth century (in Japan's case, the process started a century earlier) under the stewardship of authoritarian governments that were only weakly constrained by democratic accountability. In contrast to the highly predatory states that emerged in the Middle East, South Asia, Latin America, and particularly sub-Saharan Africa, many of East Asia's authoritarian rulers preserved a developmental focus that created a stable platform for later democratization. Most of the arguments in favor of sequencing economic growth and law before a democratic opening are based on East Asian models.

A second consequence of this development pattern is that many East Asian states have been able to institute industrial policies to promote economic growth—policies which, in the hands of a less capable state, would result in a morass of rent-seeking and state capture. The final consequence is that the quality of liberal democracy is different in East Asia than in Europe, North America, or other parts of the West. Japan was the first Asian society to experiment with democracy, initially during the Taisho period in the 1920s and then more successfully under U.S. tutelage after 1951. Political sociologist Barrington Moore once suggested that Japan could successfully democratize because its social structure differed from that of China and other Asian agrarian societies. As in the West, power during the Tokugawa period (1603–1868) was diffused across a feudal aristocracy, and village communities possessed a degree of community and self-organization not present in China.[2]

Nonetheless, even now Japanese democracy looks and feels different from democracy in Europe or, particularly, the United States. First and most important is the domination of the political system by the Japanese state. A long tradition of analysis has noted that it was bureaucrats in alliance with the business community who, having usurped the role in determining policy normatively given to parliaments, were the principal decision makers.[3] (This dominance has faded since the end of Japan's high-growth period in the early 1990s, which partly reflects a decline in the bureaucracy's competence.) Second, a single hegemonic party (the Liberal Democratic Party) ruled Japan almost without interruption from 1955 to 2009; even today, when the country is led by the Democratic Party of Japan, it is not possible to say that Japan has made a transition to a stable two-party system with periodic alternation between government and opposition. And finally, Japan has never developed a Western-style adversarial political culture in which social discontents and demands for accountability are rapidly translated into political action. The Japanese public's grave dissatisfaction about the March 2011 Tohoku earthquake, tsunami, and nuclear disaster has resulted in surprisingly little political mobilization.

Other, newer East Asian democracies are actually more "Western" than Japan: South Korea, Taiwan, and Thailand have all seen more decisive shifts in power from government to opposition and a more adversarial political culture. Even so, there has been a strong undercurrent of support for a Japanese-style dominant-party system in South Korea and Taiwan, and in both countries the role of the central bureaucracy has been strong.

Authoritarian Government in East Asia

In many respects, the legitimacy and appeal of democracy in East Asia will depend not on how democratic countries in the region stack up on some global scale, but on how they are seen in relation to the region's dominant authoritarian country, China. Like Singapore before it, China represents a huge challenge because it has been so economically successful; the temptation to copy parts of the China model are strong both in the region and beyond. But before we can critique the model, we need to understand it, and here we face a major conceptual gap.

The field of comparative politics has developed a rich vocabulary for categorizing and analyzing liberal-democratic regimes, distinguishing their institutional features, and relating the latter to both political and economic outcomes.[4] The same cannot be said for the analysis of nondemocratic systems. Some recent attempts to establish taxonomies of regime types that extend from fully democratic to fully authoritarian have been made by Steven Levitsky and Lucan Way and by Andreas Schedler.[5] The primary contribution of this literature is to establish categories such as "competitive authoritarian" or "electoral authoritarian" to describe regimes that hold elections but are fundamentally in the grip of an authoritarian leader, like Vladimir Putin's Russia and Hugo

Chávez's Venezuela. The criteria used in establishing these taxonomic hierarchies are based on democratic best practice, with different degrees of authoritarian deviation from this norm. Indeed, one of Levitsky and Way's conclusions is that organizations such as Freedom House are too generous in rating countries as democratic.

These criteria seek to measure only the quality of institutions related to the rule of law and accountability, however. They do not include independent measures of the quality of the state. In this realm, there is a large deficiency in analytic categories: To the extent that we have a shared vocabulary, we revert to terms coined by Max Weber such as patrimonial, prebendal, sultanistic, and the like; alternatively, there is a literature expanding on the authoritarian-totalitarian distinction.[6] Indices like the Worldwide Governance Indicators developed by the World Bank Institute (WBI) try to capture some of the qualities of states in their measures of "government effectiveness," "regulatory quality," and "control of corruption." These, however, are not well thought-out concepts based on a theory of how a state should work; rather, they are convenient baskets in which WBI researchers aggregate existing quantitative governance measures. (It is not clear, for example, why "regulatory quality" should not be a subcategory of "government effectiveness" rather than a stand-alone measure.) There is no clear mapping between the WBI indicators and the older Weberian vocabulary. Contemporary measures of corruption do not, for example, distinguish between patron-client relationships within a bureaucracy and prebendalism, in which officials simply appropriate public resources for private use without any obligation to take care of clients. Nor do we have measures of the degree to which bureaucratic recruitment is merit-based or patrimonial.

There is a further respect in which our conceptual categories fail to take account of important distinctions between types of nondemocratic regimes. In the *Politics,* Aristotle develops a taxonomy of regimes based on two criteria: first, whether they are based on rule by the one, the few, or the many; and second, whether rule is based on the interest of the ruling group alone or on the common interest. Arraying these dimensions against one another leads to a six-fold categorization of regime types and allows Aristotle to distinguish between kingship, in which the rule of the one serves the common interest, and tyranny, in which it serves the tyrant's personal interest.[7]

As a matter of common sense, most people would allow for the possibility of benevolent dictatorship. There is a clear moral distinction between Singapore under Lee Kuan Yew, for example, and the predatory rule of Mobutu Sese Seko in Zaire or Kim Jong-Il in North Korea. Yet contemporary comparative politics has largely lost sight of the Aristotelian distinction between kingship and tyranny, and has no good way of categorizing nondemocratic regimes that nonetheless can be said to serve a broader public interest. The closest we come to such a term is the admission that some authoritarian states are "developmentally" minded—in other words, they seek to promote economic growth. And yet the view that a nondemocratic regime could promote common interests surely extends beyond questions of economics.

The term "accountability" has come to be associated almost exclusively with procedural accountability—that is, the presence or absence of free and fair multiparty elections. The idea that a regime can be procedurally unaccountable and yet morally constrained to act in response to perceived public interest is not one that receives much traction today. The failure to define accountability in terms of substantive outcomes rather than procedure is problematic on two grounds. In the first place, it is clear that many procedurally accountable democratic regimes are in effect unaccountable in terms of actual governance. Voters often fail to hold leaders accountable due to poor information, indifference, ethnic voting, patronage, or manipulation. The mere fact that the regime has put in place formal democratic procedures is no guarantee that substantive accountability will result.

The second problem is one that applies particularly to East Asia. Although dynastic China never developed either the rule of law or formal accountability mechanisms to limit executive discretion, moral accountability was central to the functioning of the system. This was the essence of Confucianism: It was an ethical doctrine designed to moderate the behavior of rulers and orient them toward the interests of the ruled. This moral system was institutionalized in a complex bureaucracy whose internal rules strictly limited the degree to which emperors, whose authority was theoretically unlimited, could act.[8] One of the important functions of that bureaucracy was to provide princely education and ensure that anyone who rose to a position of power understood that rule was not simply personal but a matter of fulfilling traditional duties.

There are, of course, any number of strong reasons to prefer procedural accountability over moral accountability. One basic problem with the latter concerns information. Even if a despot is benevolent, how does he or she know, in the absence of a free press and formal procedures such as elections that reveal preferences, what the common interest is? Moreover, in the absence of procedural accountability, how does one ensure a continuing supply of benevolent despots? In dynastic China, this was known as the "bad emperor" problem: Every now and then, a terrible tyrant would emerge and burst the boundaries of custom and accepted morality, doing enormous damage to the society.

Evaluating State Performance

This essay is not meant to lay out a comprehensive framework for analyzing state effectiveness that would close the gaps in the existing measures. A full measure would be extremely complex and probably sector-specific as well, since in most states the performance of some ministries and agencies is superior to the performance of others. Let us begin, however, by using three categories of state modernity as a starting point for analyzing China's authoritarian government. These categories are institutionalization, recruitment, and responsiveness.

Institutionalization. By institutionalization, I do not mean institutions as rules in the extremely broad sense used by Douglass North (a definition that encompasses both formal law and culture), but a thicker definition, drawn from Samuel P. Huntington's *Political Order in Changing Societies* (1968), in which institutions are "stable, valued, recurring patterns of behavior" that can be more or less complex, adaptable, autonomous, and coherent.

If we ask how well institutionalized China is, the answer would in most respects be "highly" when compared to almost all other authoritarian regimes. The ruling Chinese Communist Party (CCP) has evolved as a highly complex, adaptable, autonomous, and coherent organization, one that is run by an elite cadre system and is able to mobilize members across an extremely large society. Huntington was much criticized for arguing in *Political Order* that the former Soviet Union was highly developed politically, especially in light of communism's collapse in 1989. He was surely wrong in saying that the Communist Party was a mechanism for eliciting political participation. But his view that it represented a highly institutionalized organization was true.

The same can be said about the CCP. When compared to, say, the now-defunct Arab dictatorships of Mubarak in Egypt, Ben Ali in Tunisia, and Qadhafi in Libya, the Chinese regime is far more rule-bound. Leadership does not revolve around a single individual and his family; since 1978, the Party has developed a collective-leadership system that observes term limits and vests power in the Standing Committee of the Politburo. Leadership succession, one of the great weaknesses of many authoritarian regimes, is thus much less of a problem in China, nontransparent though the process is. Like all classic Leninist parties, the CCP has an elite structure that can transmit instructions from the hierarchy down to the neighborhood level. Its ability to enforce rules, from economic directives to control of political opposition, is much stronger than that of other authoritarian regimes.

The Party's greatest problem with regard to institutionalization is adaptability. Certainly an organization that shifts from being a doctrinaire communist party to one that includes businessmen and professionals (as under Jiang Zemin's "Three Represents") and fosters a capitalist economy is a model of adaptability. But there are also clear limits upon the CCP's ability to jettison ideological Marxist-Leninist baggage. Indeed, its paranoid response to the "Arab Spring" suggests a failure to envision a more liberalized form of dictatorship.

Recruitment. One of the hardest things to judge is the degree of patronage and corruption that exists within the Chinese political and administrative system. China has a poor reputation with regard to corruption. It ranks 78th out of 178 countries on Transparency International's 2010 Corruption Perception Index—close to Greece, Vanuatu, and Colombia.[9] This index, however, is singularly unhelpful in explaining the nature and extent of corruption in the Chinese system. The term *guanxi* means informal influence, and there are clearly factions and patronage chains that operate throughout the CCP's structure. Countless stories appear in the Chinese press or on microblogs about corrupt deals involving local officials, developers, and other elites. Periodically, one will erupt into a major scandal, such as the melamine-tainted infant formula of 2008 or the shoddy construction revealed by the Sichuan earthquake that same year. Selection of political leaders, including for the upcoming transition in 2012, is a totally nontransparent process.

On the other hand, when compared to the neopatrimonial politics of many other developing countries, China's system is far more impersonal and modern. Following a very ancient tradition, there are highly meritocratic features to the system, beginning with recruitment into the Party and state bureaucracy and promotion within these hierarchies. While *guanxi* may be necessary to open doors, one can stride through them only on the basis of a track record. Most stories of egregious corruption come from the lower levels of the party and government. Although high CCP cadres enjoy huge perks for themselves and their families, one does not get the sense that they are diverting massive sums of money to their own accounts on the scale of, say, senior Russian political figures. The informal vetting of new members of the Standing Committee of the Politburo is thorough; it is hard to be considered without having extensive administrative experience across a variety of provinces and economic sectors.

Again, one question for the future is whether, as Minxin Pei[10] suggests, this system is breaking down. The 2000s have seen the rise of a class of "princelings," whose family backgrounds and opportunities have propelled them into positions of power. As Martin Shefter notes, communist parties in their early days tended to exhibit relatively lower levels of corruption because they had to fight their way to power and had few resources to distribute.[11] Once securely in power, however, they tended toward repatrimonialization and the self-perpetuation of elites. It is, of course, difficult to measure the degree to which this has happened in contemporary China.

Responsiveness. There is virtually no formal downward political accountability in the Chinese political system. There are limited local elections, and Chinese citizens have the right to sue local government agencies for performance failures as in other Asian countries. Most observers contend, however, that these institutions do not confer any significant power on citizens to change government behavior. The press, which in democratic countries constitutes a critical check on state power, is strictly controlled.

Formal accountability in the Chinese system is entirely upward, toward the Party and the Party's higher decision-making echelons. In this respect, the current Chinese government replicates the structure, and revives the problems, of centralized government in dynastic times. Because lines of accountability flow upward through an enormous bureaucracy, the central problem for the senior levels of the government is how to monitor and control the behavior of the lower levels, a classic principal-agent problem. In dynastic China, there was a tendency to layer levels of hierarchical control on top of one another: The central bureaucrats in Luoyang or Chang'an or Beijing would monitor several layers of provincial bureaucrats; a corps of eunuchs would monitor the central bureaucrats; and a "eunuch-rectification office" would monitor the eunuchs.[12] This is not terribly different from the current situation of a party sitting on top of and monitoring a formal government bureaucracy.

The Party uses a number of techniques, some classic and some novel, to enforce accountability on lower-ranking officials. Local governments are rated on their economic performance, and local officials are made to compete against one another for resources and promotions. While corruption is prevalent at lower administrative levels, there are informal red lines that officials cannot cross; when they do, accountability can include a summary trial and execution.

The fundamental problem of any centralized hierarchy is one of information. Even if they do not concede the principle of democratic accountability, authoritarian governments will operate more effectively with greater knowledge of what is happening at the grassroots level. In principal-agent terms, there has to be some way of monitoring agent behavior that is not dependent on the agent's own reporting. This explains a couple of phenomena about contemporary China—the much expanded use of polling in government administration and the limited tolerance of online criticism of government performance.

The Chinese government's control and monitoring of the Internet is legendary and, with a reported fifty-thousand censors, much more extensive than in other authoritarian countries. As is well known, when the extensive microblogging and Internet discussions move toward criticism of government performance, they are usually shut down. But that several-hour window in which comments circulate allows the government not just to identify its critics, but also to listen to what they say. It is rumored that Hu Jintao receives regular reports of public opinion as expressed on Internet forums and Sina.com's Weibo (Twitter-like) service.

Through this kind of mechanism, the Party does not just shape public opinion, but seeks to stay on top of it enough to be able to respond to popular pressures before they erupt into violent acts of social protest. One can look at this cynically and say that the government is letting people blow off just enough steam to protect its own power and privileges; or one can regard it as a form of democratic mimicry by which rulers seek to be responsive to public opinion.

In a sense, Chinese authoritarian governance is structured like corporate governance in a modern Western firm. In both cases, formal accountability runs only upward, to the senior levels of the Party in the Chinese case and to the shareholders or board in corporations. Neither is downwardly accountable in formal terms, whether to citizens or to workers and customers. If the hierarchy fails to heed the wishes of these stakeholders, however, it will suffer.

In noting these features of the Chinese state, I am not arguing that the accountability of the Chinese government is in any sense comparable to that of democratic governments. The Party argues that it has a tacit authorization to rule China as it does, and there is some polling data that indicates that many Chinese believe the government is acting in their best interests.[13] But how will we ever know whether this is true in the absence of formal accountability mechanisms and freedom of speech?

Real democratic accountability is desirable, moreover, not just as a means of achieving economic growth, but as an end in itself. Every day the rights and dignity of ordinary Chinese citizens are ignored or denied by the government, and the wellspring of anger that this creates underlies the huge numbers of violent social protests that break out each year.

Nonetheless, the ability of the Chinese government to give citizens things that they want—in particular, security, jobs, and rising living standards—is clearly greater than for most authoritarian regimes. Unless we understand this, we will not understand the challenge that China poses to democratic practice in the region and further afield.

Democracy and the Future of the State in East Asia

Several countries in East Asia are heirs to a Chinese-style centralized state, which lies at the core of their economic success. Japan, South Korea, and Taiwan have all had highly competent developmental states that pursued ambitious industrial policies during their high-growth phases, and only later added the rule of law and democratic institutions to serve as checks on executive power. Instead of asking the typical question of how the democratic institutions will fare in and of themselves, we need to examine how the presence or absence of the rule of law and democratic institutions will affect the performance of the state in East Asia. I believe that this is a legitimate question, since democracy will be judged in large measure on how it affects economic performance and other outcomes of state behavior.

The rule of law and democratic accountability are important to high-quality state performance. If governments are not rule-bound and predictable, if they do not protect property rights, then they will constitute obstacles to economic performance. And if they are not democratically accountable, there will be no way of removing bad leaders or giving them feedback on their performance. The Chinese government's recent refusal to permit public discussion of the causes of the July 2011 high-speed rail accident does not bode well for the future of rail safety in the country.

Yet it is possible to have so many checks and balances in a democratic system that the costs of making decisions become excessive and the process bogs down. An example would be the reported inability of Japan's national government to override a legal prohibition on the helicopter airdropping of critical supplies during the recent Fukushima Dai-ichi nuclear-reactor crisis. Obviously, the problem is more severe when institutional separation of powers is supplemented by what Gary Cox and Mathew McCubbins call "separation of purpose"—that is, strong disagreements on policy issues within the electorate.[14] Japan, South Korea, and Taiwan have all been suffering from what one might label a crisis of increasing separation of purpose over the years, as democratic politics has increasingly become polarized around parties that have been more interested in gaining tactical advantage than in making difficult decisions about national issues. This has led to stasis on important issues such as economic reform in Japan and national defense in Taiwan.

An important empirical question that I have never seen systematically addressed is the impact of democracy on bureaucratic quality in East Asia. I noted earlier that East Asian democracies were built around strong states and relatively weak organized social actors. This balance has been shifting rapidly. Powerful interest groups have emerged, as tends to happen during long periods of peace and stability.[15] A common analysis of the Japanese inability to act on a variety of fronts—from trade liberalization to agricultural modernization—points to the ability of relatively small interest groups to block significant reform. One of the hallmarks of classic postwar Asian governance was the state's ability to discipline private-sector actors when necessary—or, as Stephan Haggard and Robert R. Kaufman put it, a lower propensity for rent-seeking and state capture compared to other regions.[16] Anecdotally, it would seem that this is less characteristic of East Asian democratic governments now than it was forty years ago.

All countries in East Asia, whether democratic or authoritarian, will face certain large problems in the coming two decades that will test their political systems. It is worth speculating as to whether the region's authoritarian or democratic systems will be better able to handle them.

One issue concerns the shift out of an export-driven growth model, which all countries in the region employed to a greater or lesser extent, to a more balanced system in which exports are supplemented by strong domestic demand. Raghuram Rajan has pointed out that the Japanese effort to do this has been a notable failure: Although Japanese leaders have recognized the need to move toward a domestic demand-based system at least since the signing of the Plaza Accord on currency markets in 1985, relatively little progress has been made in increasing levels of consumption or reducing the productivity gap between export-oriented industries and the rest of the economy.[17] The reasons for this are at least partly political. The stimulus efforts undertaken since Japan's asset bubble burst in the early 1990s have been highly inefficient, being directed toward interest group–driven infrastructure projects that yielded little in terms of increased productivity while putting Japan on a fiscally unsustainable path.

Will authoritarian China be able to do better in this regard? The Chinese government has recognized the need to stimulate domestic demand for some years now and has committed substantial sums toward the development of poorer inland areas. We do not yet know enough about the efficiency of those investments to predict whether or not they will have the desired long-term effects. Clearly, there are interest groups that have an impact on Chinese decision making, if for no other reason than because many Chinese officials have gotten rich from collaborating with a variety of developers, industrialists, and the like. Is the Chinese authoritarian system strong enough to resist the blandishments of coastal export interests, or has it already been captured? This is an empirical question whose answer is not currently clear.

A second important long-term issue concerns the necessary renegotiation of the social contract as a result of falling birthrates and increased longevity. As is well known, Japan has been a leader in this regard, but all states in East Asia—democratic and authoritarian alike—will suffer the same fate during the first half of the twenty-first century. China's birth rates have not fallen as dramatically as those of Japan, Singapore, South Korea, or Taiwan, but even with a lifting of the one-child policy it will start down this road with perhaps a fifteen-year delay. Increasing dependency ratios will entail a number of painful decisions, including higher taxes on the smaller future cohorts of workers; cuts in pension and health-care benefits; higher retirement ages; and possibly the rationing of medical procedures.

As is clear from the mounting fiscal woes of nearly all developed democracies, these are not decisions that they make easily or well. Superficially, it might appear obvious that an authoritarian system would have an easier time forcing painful tradeoffs on a population without formal means of protesting. But here we get to one of the great advantages of a democratic system based on consent of the governed: Precisely because democratic systems consult and require the consent of more social actors, decisions once taken enjoy much greater support. As Cox and McCubbins might put it, democracies trade decisiveness for resoluteness. While an authoritarian system such as China's may force unpopular decisions on an unwilling populace, it risks generating a social explosion in response when the sacrifices are as draconian as the ones envisioned here.

NOTES

    1. Francis Fukuyama, *The Origins of Political Order: From Prehuman Times to the French Revolution* (New York: Farrar, Straus and Giroux, 2011).

2. Barrington Moore, Jr., *Social Origins of Dictatorship and Democracy: Lord and Peasant in the Making of the Modern World* (Boston: Beacon, 1966), 228–313.

3. See Gerald L. Curtis, *The Logic of Japanese Politics: Leaders, Institutions, and the Limits of Change* (New York: Columbia University Press, 1999).

4. On the economic side, see Torsten Persson and Guido Tabellini, *The Economic Effects of Constitutions* (Cambridge: MIT Press, 2003).

5. Steven Levitsky and Lucan A. Way, "Elections Without Democracy: The Rise of Competitive Authoritarianism," *Journal of Democracy* 13 (April 2002): 51–65; Andreas Schedler, *Electoral Authoritarianism: The Dynamics of Unfree Competition* (Boulder, Colo.: Lynne Rienner, 2006); and Schedler, "Elections Without Democracy: The Menu of Manipulation," *Journal of Democracy* 13 (April 2002): 36–50.

6. This distinction was originally made in Carl J. Friedrich and Zbigniew Brzezinski, *Totalitarian Dictatorship and Autocracy,* 2nd ed. (Cambridge: Harvard University Press, 1965). One of the more comprehensive efforts to characterize such states is Juan J. Linz, *Totalitarian and Authoritarian Regimes* (Boulder, Colo.: Lynne Rienner, 2000).

7. Aristotle, *Politics* III.v.1. Marc Plattner noted the utility of this taxonomy in making distinctions among authoritarian regimes in a presentation to the Draper Hills Summer Fellows at Stanford University, 2011.

8. For examples of how constrained Chinese emperors were in the Ming Dynasty, see Ray Huang, *1587, A Year of No Significance: The Ming Dynasty in Decline* (New Haven: Yale University Press, 1981).

9. See *http://transparency.org/policy_research/surveys_indices/cpi/2010/results.*

10. Minxin Pei, "China and East Asian Democracy: Is CCP Rule Fragile or Resilient?" *Journal of Democracy* 23 (January 2012): 27–41.

11. Martin Shefter, *Political Parties and the State: The American Historical Experience* (Princeton: Princeton University Press, 1993), 30–31.

12. See Fukuyama, *Origins of Political Order*, ch. 21.

13. See Tianjian Shi, "China: Democratic Values Supporting an Authoritarian System," in Yun-han Chu et al., eds., *How East Asians View Democracy* (New York: Columbia University Press, 2008), 209–37.

14. Gary W. Cox and Mathew D. McCubbins, "The Institutional Determinants of Economic Policy Outcomes," in Stephan Haggard and Mathew D. McCubbins, eds., *Presidents, Parliaments, and Policy: Political Economy of Institutions and Decisions* (Cambridge: Cambridge University Press, 2001), 21–63.

15. See Mancur Olson, *The Rise and Decline of Nations: Economic Growth, Stagflation, and Social Rigidities* (New Haven: Yale University Press, 1982).

16. See, for example, Stephan Haggard and Robert R. Kaufman, *The Politics of Economic Adjustment: International Constraints, Distributive Conflicts and the State* (Princeton: Princeton University Press, 1992).

17. Raghuram G. Rajan, *Fault Lines: How Hidden Fractures Still Threaten the World Economy* (Princeton: Princeton University Press, 2010).

2

PARTIES, ELECTORAL SYSTEMS, AND GOVERNANCE

Benjamin Reilly

Benjamin Reilly *is professor of political science in the Crawford School of Public Policy at the Australian National University. His books include* Democracy and Diversity: Political Engineering in the Asia-Pacific *(2006). He has been a Reagan-Fascell Democracy Fellow at the National Endowment for Democracy and a visiting professor at the Johns Hopkins School of Advanced International Studies (SAIS) in Washington, D.C.*

One of the patterns familiar to students of comparative politics is the clustering of specific forms of democracy in different world regions. Thus, continental Europe is typified by the combination of parliamentary government and proportional-representation (PR) electoral systems, Latin America is almost entirely presidential but with PR legislative elections, and the Anglosphere is mostly parliamentary (the rather large exception of the United States aside) but also determinedly majoritarian in using plurality or majority electoral systems (with the somewhat less large exception of New Zealand).

The democratization of East Asia is producing a similar effect, with a distinctive form of electoral majoritarianism emerging in the region's new democracies. However, there is strong subregional variation between Northeast and Southeast Asia, and increasingly between mainland and maritime Southeast Asia as well. Thus the "third wave" Northeast Asian democracies of Mongolia, South Korea, and Taiwan are distinguished by their combination of (semi)presidential government, mixed-member electoral systems, and nascent two-party politics. In Southeast Asia, by contrast, two countervailing clusters prevail: one-party-dominant parliamentary systems in the "semidemocracies" of Cambodia, Malaysia, Singapore, and possibly Thailand; and more complex electoral models and fragmented party systems in the presidential or semipresidential Southeast Asian democracies of Indonesia, the Philippines, and Timor-Leste.

A foundational insight of political science is that different institutional formats will have direct and important consequences for the operation of political systems. Thus, majoritarianism in the English-speaking world has long promoted two-party systems formed along a basic left-right political cleavage and making corresponding policy appeals, while the predominance of PR in continental Europe has allowed for a multiplicity of parties based on other kinds of social cleavages, as well as much greater minority representation.[1] In Latin America, the "difficult combination" of PR and presidentialism has been blamed for recurring problems of executive-legislative deadlock and weak governments.[2]

How do these arguments apply to East Asia, which evidences a combination of presidential, parliamentary, and semipresidential government? As I have argued elsewhere, the transition to democracy in many East Asian countries over the past two decades also has spurred a distinctive institutional evolution. It has given rise to a characteristic model of electoral *governance* based on mixed-member majoritarian (MMM) systems, in which part of the parliament is elected from local districts by plurality rules and another part from a nationwide party list by PR rules, with no linkage between the two. Distinctively, Asian examples tend to emphasize local districts over national lists, with an average of three-quarters of all seats chosen from districts, and a much smaller proportion from a party list. Electoral outcomes have reflected this majoritarian slant, with larger parties of government predominating and, in some cases, nascent two-party systems appearing to take root.

Despite increasing country-level variation, recent years have seen a continuation and in some ways a deepening of trends toward a regionally distinctive form of electoral governance across democratic East Asia. These tendencies, however, are increasingly being mediated by other factors—most notably, geographic proximity, regime type, and internal sociopolitical dynamics—on a subregional level. As a result, the broad cross-regional trend toward more majoritarian democracy has been tempered by the emergence of identifiable subregional reform clusters in Northeast Asia, and a growing division between mainland and maritime Southeast Asia.

In Northeast Asia, the preference for majority-enhancing electoral governance has continued apace—with the MMM model pioneered by Japan's 1994 parliamentary reforms having spread to the semipresidential systems of South Korea, Taiwan, and, most recently, Mongolia. The combination of MMM elections with semipresidential systems of government represents something of a challenge to political-science orthodoxy, which sees semipresidentialism as a dubious constitutional choice for new democracies in particular.[3] However, other aspects of the Northeast Asian experience are more confirming of democratic theory. Along with Japan (East Asia's only longstanding democracy), South Korea and Taiwan are the entire region's most economically developed states, and thus constitute the East Asian cases most in step with the expectations of the comparative political-science literature on democratization, which typically sees democratic change in the context of modernization theory.

A similar approach to electoral governance has also been apparent in Southeast Asia, with both Thailand and the Philippines adopting similar mixed-member electoral system designs as part of their transitions to democracy. Indeed, Thailand has been arguably the most enthusiastic exponent of 'political engineering' to be found anywhere in Asia, promulgating successive constitutions aimed at reshaping Thai politics.[4] But this institutional approach to political reform also makes for something of a cautionary tale: Thailand's reformist 1997 "People's Constitution" contained so many incentives for cohesive parties and strong government that many see it as having aided the rise of Thaksin Shinawatra and his Thai Rak Thai (TRT) party.[5] The 2006 coup removed Thaksin from power and revoked many of these incentives for strong parties and stable government. In Thailand's latest bout of institutional tinkering, however, the 2011 electoral law reverted for the most part to the 1997 MMM model in a move that helped Thaksin's younger sister Yingluck and the TRT's successor party to victory in the 2011 elections.

Elsewhere in mainland Southeast Asia, autocracy or one-party-dominant quasi-democracy remains the order of the day. Laos and Vietnam remain standout examples of the "China-lite" model of closed and nominally communist political systems with relatively open market economies. Cambodia practices partly competitive elections and could at a stretch be considered a member of the majoritarian quasi-democratic club, especially since the ruling Cambodian People's Party abandoned the last vestiges of parliamentary power-sharing and consolidated its single-party rule in 2006. Burma's flawed but nonetheless marginally competitive 2010 parliamentary elections and subsequent political loosening raise the prospect of a more democratic future—although its constitutional structure retains a privileged place for the military and seems to be inspired by Suharto-era Indonesia more than anyplace else.

By contrast to this uncertain picture, today it is in *maritime* Southeast Asia that we find the region's only genuine electoral democracies: Indonesia, the Philippines, and Timor-Leste.[6] The relative success of democracy in "island Asia" is surprising, given the socioeconomic characteristics of these three countries, which are among Asia's most diverse and least developed states. Maritime Southeast Asia is also much more threatened by the spread of militant Islam than anywhere else in East Asia outside southern Thailand. Yet the current regional division of Southeast Asia between the (mostly) autocratic mainland and the (mostly) democratic maritime realm is unmistakable. Even the resilient semidemocracies of Singapore and Malaysia, located at the intersection of Southeast Asia's mainland and maritime realms, support this correlation between geography and regime type.

Distance from China is one obvious if insufficient explanation for what could be called the region's "geography of democracy." There are a range of explanations for this pattern, from the deep historical legacy of China's "tribute-gathering" relations with its southern neighbors to its support for communist revolutions and Leninist political structures in contemporary Laos and Vietnam. Today, the so-called CLMV states (Cambodia, Laos, Myanmar, and Vietnam) see their political and economic futures tied to China far more than to maritime Southeast Asia. ASEAN has also been increasingly dividing along the mainland–island fault line over the last decade, as China has progressively drawn into its orbit the polities and economies of the mainland states. The varying responses to Burma's military regime are one example of this, with Indonesia and the Philippines much more outspoken than mainland states. Democratization has thus become a wedge issue that highlights a growing economic, political, and security divergence between Southeast Asia's maritime and mainland realms.

Maritime Southeast Asia is also anomalous in other ways. As in Northeast Asia, maritime Southeast Asia's three genuine democracies are all presidential or semipresidential, despite the well-known warnings from Juan Linz and other scholars about the "perils of presidentialism" in new democracies.[7] Moreover, Indonesia and Timor-Leste also combine their presidential or semipresidential systems with PR-based electoral systems, an arrangement that has been identified as especially problematic for effective governance.[8] Along with the Philippines they also possess highly fragmented party systems, in contrast to the dominant one-party or emerging two-party systems to be found elsewhere in East Asia. Forging stable party politics amid great social diversity and regional disparities is a common challenge, as evidenced by the vigorous efforts to limit separatism and reward nationally oriented parties that have occurred in Indonesia.[9]

Southeast Asia's three democracies have also engaged in a great degree of political experimentation in recent years, much of it unwise. Indonesia, for instance, has adopted an "open" party list for lower-house elections—a move that promotes accountability but weakens political cohesion. Indonesia's 2009 election, in contrast to those of 1999 and 2004, was a contest more of candidates than of parties, as victory hinged on personal rather than party vote totals. This move, the result of a constitutional-court decision, has increased internal party fissures and undermined incentives for party-building in Indonesia. In the Philippines, party-list seats representing "sectoral interests" and marginalized groups such as youth, labor, the urban poor, farmers, fishermen and women were introduced at the 1998 election. However, the party-list seats have not worked as intended, in part because of a restriction limiting each

TABLE 1—GEOGRAPHIC CLUSTERS AND REGIME TYPE IN EAST ASIA

Cluster 1 – Northeast Asia	Cluster 2 – Mainland Southeast Asia	Cluster 3 – Maritime Southeast Asia
Presidential or semi-presidential democracy	Parliamentary semi-democracy	Presidential or semi-presidential democracy
Taiwan, South Korea, Mongolia	*Singapore, Malaysia, Cambodia, Thailand*	*Indonesia, Philippines, Timor-Leste*

group to no more than three seats in Congress, and the whole concept of sectoral representation remains highly controversial. Finally, in Timor-Leste, regional representation has been abolished altogether, and the country now elects its entire parliament from one national constituency—a curious move for an agrarian society where demands for constituency service and local representation are paramount.

Explaining the Patterns

To sum up the key argument so far: East Asia's divergent institutional reforms have resulted in subregional "clusters" of electoral democracies which to a significant extent follow the region's basic geographic divisions—a striking and in some ways surprising outcome. While advocacy of stronger political parties, majority-enhancing elections, and stable governments remains common, actual institutional choices display significant divergence not just between Northeast and Southeast Asia, but also within Southeast Asia's mainland and maritime realms. This is most obviously the case when we consider the distinctions among the presidential, parliamentary, and semipresidential forms of government. Indeed, when we look at the region through a system-of-government lens, there is less cross-regional convergence and more subregional clustering on a geographic basis (see Table 1 above). In combination with regime type, this divergence is likely to translate into increasingly divergent political outcomes across the region in the future.

What explains this pattern? I think there are several processes at work.

First, historical legacies are clearly relevant, particularly when it comes to metaconstitutional choices. Just as former British colonies tended to replicate the form if not the substance of the Westminster system, the colonial influence of the United States in the Philippines, of the Netherlands in Indonesia, and of Japan in Taiwan and Korea is still apparent in constitutional and electoral systems, although again the link is often more one of form than of substance. The nature of electoral authoritarianism in postwar Southeast Asia has also had a crucial impact, not just on formal institutions but also on the development of the region's party systems.[10]

In the contemporary era, regional isomorphism has been similarly important. The introduction of MMM electoral systems across East Asia is the result, in part, of intraregional borrowing. Japan's adoption of an MMM system influenced Taiwan, and was also cited by Thai reformers during their constitutional debates in 1997.[11] More recently, Mongolian electoral reformers looked to the example of Korea, while Timor-Leste's switch to pure PR brings its political system more into line with that of Portugal, its former colonial master, as well as Indonesia's. The "demonstration effect" of neighbors and former colonists remains a key influence determining the menu of reform choice.

Another reason why majority-enhancing reforms have been popular is their conformity to both elite and mass opinion across much of Asia, particularly its Sinitic societies. Elite opinion, derived in part from the political thinking of Sun Yat-sen and Chiang Kai-shek, recognizes political pluralism and the need for a competitive party system, but also attempts to limit the expression of pluralism to a two-party system in the name of unity, stability, and good governance.[12] This same thinking is likely to prevail in China itself should it ever undergo democratic transition. Outside the Sinitic world, statements by contemporary political leaders in countries such as Indonesia have also expressed a firm desire to limit what are seen as the negative consequences of political fragmentation and an excessive number of political parties.[13]

At the mass level, Asian publics tend to see democracy through an instrumental lens, focusing on the ability of the system to deliver economic development rather than to adhere to more abstract liberal ideals.[14] Survey research from across the region suggests that Asian public opinion is also less open than that of other regions to minority-rights guarantees. Opinion polls in seven East Asian nations found higher support for majoritarian democracy than more "pluralist" models that included legal protections for minorities. Those countries with the highest support for democracy also had the lowest support for pluralism, prompting the survey's authors to conclude that a distinctive feature of East Asian democracy is the lack of public support for pluralistic values and minority-rights guarantees.[15] East Asia's electoral majoritarianism thus appears to reflect, at some level, the attitudes held by a significant number of its citizens.

A final explanation for East Asia's distinctive reform patterns may lie in the nature of the region's party systems. Asia's semidemocracies tend to rely on dominant political-party machines for their ongoing rule. Certainly this is true in Cambodia, Malaysia, and Singapore. The long-lasting primacy of ruling parties has enabled them to tilt the electoral playing field in their favor. In the genuinely competitive democracies, by contrast, where competitive multiparty systems are the order of the day, this is more difficult. Electoral politics in democratic Southeast Asia continues to be characterized by fluid and shifting party systems. Indonesia, despite a sharp drop in overall party numbers, still has a

TABLE 2—CONSTITUTIONAL, ELECTORAL, AND PARTY SYSTEMS IN
DEMOCRATIC EAST ASIA

Country	Constitutional System	Electoral System	Party System	Subregional Cluster
Japan	Parliamentary	MMM	Two-party	Northeast Asia
S. Korea	Presidential	MMM	Two-party	Northeast Asia
Taiwan	Semipresidential	MMM	Two-party	Northeast Asia
Mongolia	Semipresidential	MMM	Two-party	Northeast Asia
Singapore	Parliamentary	FPTP	One-party dom.	Mainland SE Asia
Malaysia	Parliamentary	FPTP	One-party dom.	Mainland SE Asia
Cambodia	Parliamentary	PR	One-party dom.	Mainland SE Asia
Philippines	Presidential	MMM	Multiparty	Maritime SE Asia
Indonesia	Presidential	PR	Multiparty	Maritime SE Asia
Timor-Leste	Semipresidential	PR	Multiparty	Maritime SE Asia

Note: The table omits Thailand and Burma, where political arrangements were in flux at the time of writing.

fragmented multiparty legislature, and even Timor-Leste, which began life as a two-party system, has become more fragmented over time (see Table 2).

Why It Matters

Variations in political constellations across the region are important for several reasons. First, they point to the difficulties that political elites face in building consolidated democratic governments in very different kinds of societies. These variations also affect governmental performance and public policy, subjects of increasing interest to both scholars and policy makers. This is the topic to which I now turn.

Because of the different incentives they create for vote-seeking politicians, we should expect different electoral and party systems to generate clear variations in governmental policy and performance. To simplify a large and complex literature: In competitive one-party-dominant or two-party systems, parties must seek support across a range of social groups, and therefore need to provide benefits to society at large in the form of public goods to maximize their chances of gaining and keeping office. In multiparty systems, by contrast, it may take only a relative handful of votes to win a seat. Parties in such systems are therefore drawn to more "narrowcast" campaign strategies focused on providing benefits to supporters rather than public goods to the electorate as a whole. These differing electoral incentives mean that vote-seeking politicians in fragmented multiparty systems are pushed to deliver more private goods than would be either necessary or possible under a more consolidated party system. Such private goods can include the fruits of nepotism, cronyism, and corruption, all problems of long standing in Asia.

These findings have particular relevance for East Asia's democracies, where the quest for more programmatic parties has been linked to concerns about economic development. One consequence of Asia's shift toward electoral majoritarianism is the need for politicians to appeal to broader swaths of voters. With both elite and public opinion focused on the need for "prodevelopment" politics, there has been an active effort to promote more nationally focused party politics, whether through electoral-system reform (as in Japan), as part of a new constitution (as in Thailand and the Philippines), or directly via political-party laws (as in Indonesia). All these reforms have flowed in part from a quest for more cohesive parties capable of boosting political stability and (so it was thought) delivering better governance. In Japan, for example, former Liberal Democratic Party secretary-general Ichiro Ozawa argued that reformed electoral laws and a two-party system were necessary for the country's long-term survival.[16] Similarly, former Indonesian president Megawati Sukarnoputri and other national leaders argued that limitations on party proliferation were necessary to protect Indonesia's national integrity.[17] Thai reformers made similar claims.[18]

One of the most immediate impacts of these reforms across East Asia has been a change in party systems, as smaller parties have been winnowed out and larger parties have increasingly dominated. As Duverger's Law would predict, electoral systems dominated by single-member districts have encouraged the development of two-bloc (if not quite two-party) systems, particularly in those countries which adopted the full "Asian model" of oversized executive leadership, MMM systems, and limits on party fragmentation. In some cases, the outcome of these reforms has been a rapid political realignment. Japan, Taiwan, and Mongolia have all moved from situations of one-party dominance to party systems that resemble in form if not substance classic two-party models (see Table 3 below). Indeed, these three Asian democracies are today purer examples of two-party systems than those found in classic Westminster democracies such as the United Kingdom (which currently has 2.57 effective parliamentary parties), Australia (2.95), Canada (3.15), or New Zealand (2.78).

In Thailand and the Philippines, party structures remain fluid, although both appear to have converged upon a "two-ish" party system in recent years. For example, following the overwhelming victory of Thaksin's Pheu Thai Party (PTP) in the 2011 elections, Thailand now has a two-and-a-half-party system, with the PTP commanding slightly more than half the seats in parliament (53 percent) and the opposition split between the Democrats (32 percent) and a handful of others. However, following what has become the norm of government formation in democratic

TABLE 3—ASIA'S NEW "TWO-BLOC" PARTY SYSTEMS

	Historical Mean ENP	Current ENP
Japan	3.43	2.1
South Korea	2.83	2.9
Philippines	4.90	1.9
Thailand	5.03	2.6
Taiwan	2.56	2.2
Mongolia	1.31	2.0

Note: ENP stands for "Effective Number of Parliamentary Parties."

Southeast Asia, new prime minister Yingluck Shinawatra moved quickly to bring several smaller parties into government following her victory, increasing her majority to 299 of 500 seats and providing a sizeable parliamentary buffer against any defections. A similar process occurred following the election of Benigno "Noynoy" Aquino as Philippine president in June 2010. [19]

Table 3 sets out the current state of play for the region's party systems, comparing the historical average in terms of effective numbers of parliamentary parties with the result as of the most recent election in each country (as of 2011).

Electoral reforms that privilege programmatic policy offerings and the related impact of a shift toward two large parties competing for the middle ground should, in theory, have profound governance implications. As discussed above, economists argue that countries with centralized executives, majoritarian elections, and limited party systems should economically outperform those with PR and fragmented executive and party systems. Given the electoral premium that majoritarian institutions place on capturing the political center and appealing to the median voter, we should therefore begin to see clear policy consequences flowing from these shifts in electoral and party systems. This is a fundamental conclusion of Stephan Haggard and Robert Kaufman's analysis of democratic transitions, and has also been supported by several recent case studies from individual Asian countries. [20]

One example from this volume is Joseph Wong's chapter detailing the evolution of welfare states as a response to the demands of centrist electoral competition in Taiwan, Korea, and Japan. Other scholars have tracked the movement from particularistic politics toward more programmatic policy offerings in Japan as shifting electoral incentives have led to a decline in particularism;[21] in Taiwan as the Nationalist Party's pursuit of the median-voter strategy on the national-identity question has reshaped politics there;[22] and, most recently, in Thailand as regards health policy.[23] All these studies lend credence to the theoretical insight that institutional reforms to electoral systems should lead to direct, and

predictable, policy consequences as incentives for political elites to deliver particularistic politics are supplanted by the need for public goods
that appeal to the median voter.

The most comprehensive comparative investigation of this subject to date is Michael Rock's. He tested the implications of moves
toward "developmental democratic states" in Indonesia, Malaysia, the
Philippines, Singapore, South Korea, Taiwan, and Thailand. Using
regression analysis, Rock found that states following the "East Asian
model" of political reform detailed above faced no tradeoff between
growth and democracy. Rather, those that adopted majoritarian
institutions grew even faster than was the case under authoritarian rule
(thus contradicting the often-heard observation about the link between
autocratic rule and rapid growth in East Asia), while those that instead
adopted more consensual political models enjoyed no such growth
boost. As Rock summarizes:

> Democratic governments in the East Asian newly industrializing econo-
> mies have constructed a particular set of democratic institutions—mixed
> member majoritarian electoral systems, cross ethnic political coalitions,
> party systems that are less fragmented and polarized than elsewhere, and
> oversized cabinets—that encourage politicians to appeal to broad groups
> of the electorate by providing the public goods and policies necessary to
> get growth going. As a result, the political shift from developmental au-
> tocracy to majoritarian democracy in these polities has occurred without
> a significant slowdown in economic growth.[24]

Questioning the "Asian Model"

Rock's analysis strengthens my argument that there is a distinctive
"Asian model" of electoral democracy, but there have also been some
valuable critiques of this idea. Critics have questioned three key tenets
of the "Asian model" argument by asking whether Asia's electoral
governance is as distinct from those of other regions as I have claimed;
whether these diverse societies have had experiences that match one
another closely enough; and whether the idea of Asian institutional
convergence holds up to sustained empirical inquiry. These are all
serious questions.

The first critique, questioning the distinctiveness of Asia's electoral
and governance model, came from Matthew Shugart when he reviewed
my book *Democracy and Diversity* in the second issue of the journal
Democratization for the year 2008. "While the basic arguments for the
region's distinctiveness are convincing," Shugart wrote, "at times the
book exaggerates that distinctiveness. Reilly's emphasis on the majoritarian 'mixed-member' systems of the region neglects to note how common this model is in the former communist countries." Although this
may have been true in the 1990s, when a number of postcommunist

democracies briefly adopted MMM systems, today this model prevails
in only one postcommunist country, the Central Asian republic of Ta-
jikistan. Elsewhere, the Seychelles is the only other electoral democracy to use an Asian-style MMM system—that is, a noncompensatory
plurality-PR model in which most seats come from districts rather than
a list. In reality, democratic East Asia increasingly stands alone in its
adoption of this model, and as a result the region has become more, not
less, distinctive in global terms.

The second critique comes from regional specialists such as Dirk
Tomsa and Daniel Lynch, who question how successful political
engineering has been in practice.[25] Both rightly stress that the results of
this kind of engineering in countries such as Indonesia, Thailand, and the
Philippines have been mixed at best. Nonetheless, the recent experience
of these states shows how electoral reforms have generated majoritarian
outcomes across East Asia. After Suharto fell in 1999, the Indonesian
government's task force on reform proposed a classic "Asian model": a
mixed system with 420 seats elected from single-member districts and
75 from a national list. Although this proposal failed, the majoritarian
impulse behind it has remained evident. Indonesian reformers have
shrunk the element of electoral proportionality by sharply reducing
district magnitude (in 1999, some districts had more than sixty seats;
a decade later most had only three to ten). In keeping with this, the
number of political parties in parliament has gone from twenty in 1999
to just nine today.

Thailand similarly adopted a classic "Asian-style" MMM system as
part of its 1997 reforms, with 80 percent of the seats elected from single-
member districts and 20 percent from a nationwide list. Under the military regime that seized power in 2006, however, the country reverted to
a hybrid form of the old system, with bloc voting in three-member districts and several regional lists rather than a single nationwide list. This
departure from the Asian model was meant to dilute the voting power
of the northern provinces where Thaksin's support was strongest.[26] Yet
the scheme proved short-lived. For the crucial 2011 elections, won
overwhelmingly by the pro-Thaksin party, the 1997 system was rein-
troduced, although this time with 25 percent of the seats coming from
a nationwide list. In South Korea, the cognate figure is 18 percent, in
the Philippines it is 19 percent, in Taiwan it is 30 percent, and in Japan
it is 37.5 percent—a testament to the isomorphic nature of East Asian
electoral reform.

A final and more substantive critique of the "Asian model" idea
comes from Aurel Croissant and Teresa Schächter's analysis of
institutional patterns in Asia's young democracies, which finds little
evidence for any clear "pattern of democracy in East Asia"[27] However,
the very breadth of their research design makes this conclusion less
than compelling. Their framework takes them well beyond my focus

on electoral and party systems to include federalism, judicial review, central banks, and interest groups among a host of other variables, while their eclectic collection of Asian democracies similarly goes well beyond East Asia to include Bangladesh and Nepal, while excluding Malaysia, Singapore, and Timor-Leste. Unsurprisingly, different research designs yield different conclusions.

Given perceived links between "stable" democracy and development, elite and mass-level suspicion of minority rights and representation, and heightened worries about particularism, the normative value accorded to majoritarian democracy in Asia has continued to rise. Where it suits the interests of political incumbents, the need for more "stable and aggregative" political systems has become a commonplace reform aim, as in Indonesia. Elsewhere, this objective has been abandoned, sometimes by the same elites who once championed it, as in Thailand. Of course, there remains a huge gap between the normative aspirations and preferences of Asian publics and the short-term decisions taken by politicians, as in all democracies. Nonetheless, I think the relationship between elite and mass opinion as well as partisan political calculation and a desire to keep up with regional governance trends can explain many of Asia's recent institutional choices.

Lasting Regional Distinctiveness

Asia's evolution toward a distinctive regional model of electoral governance is important not just for Asianists, but also for comparative political science. In recent years, a persistent alternative (indeed competing) argument to the isomorphic model of electoral governance has come from political scientists who argue that models of electoral governance are in fact converging on a *global* basis. In terms of the academic literature on electoral systems, for instance, Bernard Grofman highlights "a well known proposition that the general trend in electoral system change has been in the direction of greater proportionality."[28] Similarly David Farrell states that globally "since the early 1990s, the trend has been away from plurality and toward proportional systems."[29]

Perhaps the most persistent advocate of this line of argument in recent years has been Josep Colomer, who argues that there is "a general trend toward proportional representation over time" when electoral systems are chosen or reformed.[30] Colomer argues for an evolutionary tendency toward more inclusive and proportional electoral institutions and more representative outcomes in all democracies, regardless of region. He claims that there has been an evolution from indirect elections to direct elections by majority rule and from these to mixed systems and finally to PR, as "more and more countries tend to adopt electoral systems with multi-seat districts and proportional representation rules . . . it seems that a kind of 'invisible hand' in the field can be identified."[31]

Despite its intuitive appeal, this teleological model finds little support in East Asia. It is true that the replacement of single-nontransferable or bloc-vote systems with mixed models in Japan, the Philippines, South Korea, Taiwan, and Thailand introduced an element of PR in the form of party-list seats. Yet these have not led to more proportionality in electoral outcomes. Instead, because the list seats comprise such a small share of each legislature, each of these countries actually experienced a marked *decline* in the proportionality of election outcomes after reforms were made. As discussed above, the shift toward two-bloc politics in Japan, Mongolia, and Taiwan, as well as electoral reforms in Cambodia, Indonesia, and Thailand, has strengthened this trend.

But while the claim for a teleological progression toward ever-greater proportionality cannot be sustained, it is also the case that the determinedly majoritarian cast of politics in democratizing East Asia may itself have some unexpected and possibly unwelcome political consequences. The theoretical and empirical *policy* payoffs from more programmatic and policy-focused parties have yet to be accompanied by more centrist *political* offerings. Indeed, recent elections have seen a surge in political tensions and electoral violence in some of Asia's most promising young democracies, including Taiwan, Thailand, and Mongolia. The bitter partisan polarization that both accompanied and reinforced the emergence of two-bloc party systems in each country suggests that the classic scholarly critique of majoritarian democracy—a critique which claims that concentrating power and limiting representation is an inherently flawed and dangerous model for plural societies and a poor choice for new democracies in general—may still have relevance for Asia.

NOTES

1. Arend Lijphart, *Democracies: Patterns of Majoritarian and Consensus Government in Twenty-One Countries* (New Haven: Yale University Press, 1984).

2. Scott Mainwaring, "Presidentialism, Multipartism, and Democracy: The Difficult Combination," *Comparative Political Studies* 26 (July 1993): 198–228.

3. See Benjamin Reilly, "Semi-Presidentialism and Democratic Development in East Asia," in Robert Elgie, Sophia Moestrup, and Yu-shan Wu, eds., *Semipresidentialism and Democracy* (London: Palgrave Macmillan, 2011).

4. Björn Dressel, "Thailand's Elusive Quest for a Workable Constitution, 1997–2007," *Contemporary Southeast Asia* 31 (August 2009): 296–325.

5. See, for example, Erik Martinez Kuhonta, "The Paradox of Thailand's 1997 'People's Constitution': Be Careful What You Wish For," *Asian Survey* 48 (May–June 2008): 373–92.

6. According to Freedom House rankings over the past decade.

7. See Juan Linz, "The Perils of Presidentialism," *Journal of Democracy* 1 (Winter

1990): 51–69; Juan Linz and Arturo Valenzuela, eds., *The Failure of Presidential Democracy,* 2 vols. (Baltimore: Johns Hopkins University Press, 1994).

8. See Mainwaring, "Presidentialism, Multipartism, and Democracy." See also Jih-Wen Lin, "The Rules of Electoral Competition and the Accountability of Semipresidential Governments," in Elgie et al., *Semipresidentialism and Democracy.*

9. Benjamin Reilly, *Democracy and Diversity: Political Engineering in the Asia-Pacific* (Oxford: Oxford University Press, 2006).

10. Dan Slater, *Ordering Power: Contentious Politics and Authoritarian Leviathans in Southeast Asia* (New York: Cambridge University Press, 2010); Allen Hicken and Erik Martinez Kuhonta, "Shadows from the Past: Party System Institutionalization in Asia," *Comparative Political Studies* 44 (May 2011): 572–97.

11. See Willy Jou, "Electoral Reform and Party System Development in Japan and Taiwan: A Comparative Study," *Asian Survey* 49 (September–October 2009): 759–85.

12. See David Lorenzo, *Conceptualizing a Chinese Democracy: Sun Yat-sen, Chiang Kai-shek, Chiang Ching-kuo and Democratic Learning* (Baltimore: Johns Hopkins University Press, 2012).

13. As discussed in Ben Hillman, "Political Parties and Post-Conflict Transition: The Results and Implications of the 2009 Parliamentary Elections in Aceh," Canberra: Centre for Democratic Institutions Policy Paper 1/2010, 2010.

14. Yun-han Chu et al., "Asia's Challenged Democracies," *Washington Quarterly* 32 (January 2009): 143–57.

15. See Robert Albritton and Thawilwadee Bureekul, "Social and Cultural Supports for Pluralist Democracy Across Seven Asian Nations," paper presented to the annual meeting of the International Studies Association, Honolulu, 2005.

16. Takayuki Sakamoto, "Explaining Electoral Reform: Japan versus Italy and New Zealand," *Party Politics* 5 (October 1999): 419–38.

17. Hillman, "Political Parties and Post-Conflict Transition," 2.

18. See Dressel, "Thailand's Elusive Quest," and Kuhonta, "The Paradox of Thailand's 1997 'People's Constitution.'"

19. This represents something of a challenge to conventional political science expectations such as the 'minimal winning coalition' theory formulated by William Riker, which predicts that winning parties will seek to govern alone or with the smallest number of coalition partners necessary to maintain government, only including others if they are needed to guarantee a legislative majority. However, in Asia, the opposite appears to be true: Asian democracies typically employ "oversized" rather than "minimal winning" cabinet formations, often with many more parties than numerically needed. See Reilly, *Democracy and Diversity,* ch. 7.

20. Stephan Haggard and Robert Kaufman, *The Political Economy of Democratic Transitions* (Princeton: Princeton University Press, 1995).

21. Gregory W. Noble, "The Decline of Particularism in Japanese Politics," *Journal of East Asian Studies* 10 (May–August 2010): 239–73.

22. John F.S. Hsieh, "The Political Consequences of Electoral Reform in Taiwan," in I. Yuan, ed., *Cross-Strait at the Turning Point: Institution, Identity and Democracy* (Taipei: National Chengchi University, 2008), 39–58.

23. Joel Selway, "Electoral Reform and Public Policy Outcomes in Thailand: The Politics of the 30-Baht Health Scheme," *World Politics* 63 (January 2011): 165–202.

24. Michael Rock, "East Asia's Democratic Developmental States and Economic Growth," paper presented at the annual meeting of the Association for Asian Studies, Honolulu, April 2011, 29.

25. Dirk Tomsa, "What Type of Party? Southeast Asian Parties between Clientelism and Electoralism," in Dirk Tomsa and Andreas Ufen, eds., *Party Politics in Southeast Asia: Clientelism and Electoral Competition in Indonesia, Thailand and the Philippines* (London: Routledge, 2012); Daniel Lynch, "Democracy, Security and Regionalism in Asia," *Asia Policy* 10 (July 2010): 189–95.

26. Thitinan Pongsudhirak, "Thailand Since the Coup," *Journal of Democracy* 19 (October 2008): 140–53.

27. Aurel Croissant and Teresa Schächter, "Institutional Patterns in the New Democracies of Asia: Forms, Origins and Consequences," *Japanese Journal of Political Science* 11 (2010): 173–97.

28. Bernard Grofman, "Foreword," in Josep M. Colomer, ed., *Handbook of Electoral System Choice* (New York: Palgrave Macmillan, 2004), xiv.

29. David Farrell, *Electoral Systems: A Comparative Introduction* (New York: Palgrave Macmillan, 2001), 19.

30. Josep M. Colomer, "Institutional Design," in Todd Landman and Neil Robinson, eds., *The SAGE Handbook of Comparative Politics* (Thousand Oaks, Calif.: Sage, 2008), 562.

31. Colomer, "Institutional Design."

3

FROM DEVELOPMENTAL STATES TO WELFARE STATES

Joseph Wong

Joseph Wong is professor of political science at the University of Toronto, where he holds a Canada Research Chair. He directs the University's Asian Institute, and is author of Healthy Democracies: Welfare Politics in Taiwan and South Korea *(2004) as well as* Betting on Biotech: Innovation and the Limits of Asia's Developmental State *(2011).*

Over the past two decades, the East Asian postwar developmental state has undergone a major transformation. Celebrated for their economic miracles (the postwar period of remarkable economic growth), countries such as Taiwan, South Korea, and Japan have also deepened their commitments to social-welfare reform. High-growth developmental states—onetime welfare-state "laggards" that focused solely on the economic goal of aggregate growth through industrial upgrading—now place a higher priority on inclusive and universal social policy. Since the beginning of the 1990s, social spending has risen in all three countries. The scope of social-policy programs has increased, with new reforms being implemented and coverage expanded. Moreover, the political and economic pressures of globalization, which have led to the retrenchment of existing social-protection schemes elsewhere, have been successfully resisted in these East Asian cases. Indeed, in Taiwan, Korea, and Japan, the idea of redistributive social-welfare policy and the normative imperative of mitigating socioeconomic inequality have become mainstream, as opposed to radical and politically marginal reform agendas.

It is puzzling that the welfare state took root in these countries during the 1990s, precisely at the time when the political economy of globalization and the supposed "race to the bottom" would have predicted otherwise. That the governments in these countries have developed both new and increasingly redistributive social-policy measures in the absence of strong programmatic leftist parties or particularly cohesive labor movements runs counter to conventional theories of the welfare state. The fact that they have effectively overcome the legacies of the high-growth developmental state and the postwar belief that the welfare state was inimical to economic growth poses an important empirical puzzle. In order to solve these puzzles, we must examine closely the politics of East Asian democracy.

The Social-Spending Story

The characterization of the Taiwanese, Korean, and Japanese post-war developmental states as welfare-state laggards was not unfounded. Social spending among the three was comparatively low (and essentially nonexistent in Taiwan and Korea) before the 1980s. Though a crude measure of social-welfare provision, particularly when considered alone, overall social-spending figures illuminate governments' financial commitment to social policy as well as changes in that commitment over time. The data tell us, for instance, that social spending in Taiwan and Korea was extremely low during the early part of the postwar period and aimed primarily at education rather than social-protection programs. In Japan, social-policy expenditures spiked during the 1970s when the ruling Liberal Democratic Party (LDP) expanded its social-policy regime, but leveled off during the next decade when the government trumpeted the idea of the "Japanese-style welfare society"—political rhetoric for welfare retrenchment. In the 1980s, Japan's relatively low levels of social-policy spending made it an outlier among advanced OECD countries.[1] It was not until the 1990s that there was a significant jump in overall social spending in Japan, as well as in Taiwan and Korea.

In addition to spending levels, the design of policy instruments also matters. Taking a cue from the Bismarckian welfare state, Japan's social-policy regime was based on the social-insurance model. Taiwan and Korea also adopted social-insurance schemes after the Second World War. Unlike welfare programs that are financed through general tax revenues, such as the archetypal welfare state in Nordic Europe, social insurance is intended to place responsibility for insurance premiums upon the individual. Depending on the extent to which social-insurance schemes pool financial contributions and risk among enrollees, social insurance tends to be less redistributive.

In Taiwan, Korea, and Japan, insurance schemes were decentralized, limiting their pooling effects and thus their redistributive potential. They tended to benefit the relatively well-off, the healthier, and the young. The vulnerable were excluded, highlighting the absence of any meaningful notion of social rights and social citizenship. Because social-insurance systems in Taiwan, Korea, and Japan were work-based, only those employed in the formal sector benefited. This system most adversely affected Korea and Taiwan, where nearly half the working population was either self-employed or worked in the informal sector.

In the early 1980s, less than half the populations of Korea and Taiwan were enrolled in any social-insurance program. Private coverage was not financially feasible for most. Social-assistance programs for those in need were means-tested, resulting in many poor people being excluded; for those who qualified, benefits were minimal. The majority of citizens in all three countries tended to rely on family and kinship networks to provide social protection and social security in old age, leading many to conclude that the provision of social welfare in Asia was shaped by Confucian norms and values. East Asians were believed by some to be culturally resistant to the idea of the modern welfare state.[2]

This does not mean, however, that *no* social policies were implemented in East Asia in the postwar period. For instance, a labor-insurance scheme was created in Taiwan during the early 1950s, although coverage was extremely constrained—exclusively to government employees, military personnel, and workers in large, often state-owned firms. In the 1970s, the Korean government introduced a voluntary medical-insurance program, though the uptake was slow and limited to a handful of large conglomerate firms. Efforts during the 1960s to put into place limited social-insurance schemes in Korea lacked political will and consequently failed. To the extent that any significant social-policy measures were implemented prior to the 1990s in Taiwan and Korea, they tended to protect the industrial worker and other political constituents of the state.

Social policies in East Asia, according to Ian Holliday, were thus "productivist" in nature, intended to bolster economic growth and subsumed within broader economic and industrial policy goals. Extremely high levels of education spending were a reflection of the imperative to upskill workers in order to fulfill the labor demands of industrial upgrading rather than of the importance placed on social rights per se. Aggregate economic growth, it was believed, provided the best social safety net, and social policies were designed to facilitate such growth. As Japan's full-employment strategy of "income doubling" during the 1960s demonstrates, social protection in industrializing East Asia was ultimately a function of earned wages. In the East Asian developmental state model, Holliday concludes, "minimal social rights" were "linked to productive activity" and "directed towards growth."[3]

The extension of social policy by the East Asian developmental state adhered to a strategic political logic. Kent Calder's analysis of Japan's political economy shows how, for instance, the expansion of social-policy coverage, including universal medical insurance and pensions during the 1960s and 1970s, was a reactive compensatory strategy used by the LDP to quell mounting opposition during moments of political crisis.[4] Despite the creation of medical and old-age-income insurance schemes, the LDP was hardly a social-democratic party. Rather, it was an effective catchall party that maintained its electoral dominance by skillfully and selectively compensating important political constituents. Calder's crisis-and-selective-compensation model was even more apparent in the authoritarian developmental states of Taiwan and South Korea. Limited social policies targeted specific political and economic constituencies, such as workers in large firms, government officials, and the military. As in postwar Japan, the periodic expansion of social-protection schemes coincided with moments of political crisis for the ruling regime. Selective piecemeal social-policy reform was motivated by the authoritarian state's instincts for political survival, rather than by a normative political commitment to social welfare. The absence of strong political parties on the left in Japan—and in the case of Taiwan and Korea, the absence of democracy altogether before the late 1980s— meant that the East Asian developmental state was insulated from political pressure to legislate more thorough social-policy reform. Rather, the state steered social-policy reform from the top-down to meet its political and economic goals.

Toward More Inclusive Policies

Something happened during the 1990s, however, that set the East Asian developmental state on a new course toward welfare-state deepening. Spending increased markedly. As a percentage of GDP, social-security spending in Japan nearly quadrupled between 1960 and 2000, with the largest increase occurring during the 1990s. In Taiwan, total social-security spending tripled between 1980 and 2000, while expenditures in South Korea increased eightfold during that same period. In 2000, social-security spending accounted for 28 percent and 21 percent of government spending in Taiwan and Korea, respectively. Even after these rapid and substantial increases, spending was still low when compared to other, more established welfare states, but it nonetheless demonstrated a growing commitment in East Asia to social welfare.

Growth in spending in Taiwan, Korea, and Japan was a function of the expansion of pre-existing social programs as well as the introduction of new ones. The Korean government instituted universal medical insurance in 1989. A national pensions program was legislated around the same time and implemented in the late 1990s. The Korean government also introduced new unemployment protections. By 1999, government spending on unemployment benefits was sixty times higher than it had been in 1996, just three years earlier.

In Taiwan, the Kuomintang (KMT) government implemented in 1995 the National Health Insurance (NHI) program, which featured an integrated-risk and financial-pooling mechanism that redistributed resources across income and occupational groups. More generous old-age income-security measures were introduced shortly thereafter. Social-welfare reform in Japan followed a similar trajectory during the 1990s, though this was a little less dramatic given that many of Japan's social-insurance programs had been introduced earlier on. Beginning in the late 1980s, income-security benefits were expanded to include women and were eventually extended to all citizens.

Elderly care, which in Japan began with the means-tested 1989 Gold Plan, was made universal with the implementation of the 1997 Long Term Care Insurance (LTCI) program, which was partly government funded. Publicly subsidized child care was introduced with the 1994 Angel Plan. Taiwan and Korea established similar state-subsidized social-care systems. In Korea, for instance, government spending on children and the elderly increased more than tenfold between the early 1990s and early 2000s. Along with the passage of tougher regulations governing gender equality in the workplace, income-maintenance policies targeting women, particularly those working in the informal sector or employed as casual laborers, were implemented in all three countries.

Most significant is the fact that social-policy reform during the 1990s and 2000s targeted new constituents and especially vulnerable populations that had previously been excluded. For example, wage earners in the precarious informal sector, many of whom are women, were provided protection. Benefits that were once exclusive to employed industrial workers were also extended to the self-employed. Dependents, such as children and the elderly, were similarly integrated into the evolving and increasingly universalized social-policy regimes in Taiwan, Korea, and Japan.

Unlike in years past, when limited coverage in social-policy programs benefited those who were already relatively privileged, the introduction of a more universal welfare state in all three places during the 1990s was in fact intended to protect, by right of social citizenship, precisely those vulnerable populations that were economically unproductive. Put another way, beginning in the 1990s welfare-policy reform was intended to be more inclusive and more redistributive across disparate risk and income groups, rather than merely supportive of, and subsumed within, the overriding objective of economic growth. Having evolved beyond the productivist social-policy goals of the developmental state toward a more sincere commitment to social rights and citizenship, the *institutional purposes* of social-welfare policy had been fundamentally transformed in Taiwan, Korea, and Japan.[5]

What prompted this transformation? The context in which the nascent welfare state developed in East Asia provides some insight regarding this important question. First, Taiwan, Korea, and Japan experienced economic instability and uncertainty during the 1990s. Japan's economy, as is well known, slowed to a grinding halt after its bubble economy burst. Taiwan's industrial base was being hollowed-out by cheaper competitors in late-developing countries, most notably in China. And South Korea was hit especially hard by the 1997 Asian financial crisis. Unem-

ployment was on the rise in all three countries, and economic recovery
was not at all a given. Socioeconomic vulnerabilities were exposed, and
thus the need for effective social protection became more acute. Related to this, socioeconomic inequality was on the rise as the income
gap between the haves and have-nots grew. The full extent of the gray
economy was revealed, as the distance between reported household incomes and unreported wealth increased, thus exacerbating inequality.
The postwar miracle of growth with equity in Taiwan, Korea, and Japan
was being undone, and new social-policy measures were required to
mitigate the consequences.

The functionalist imperatives of social-welfare deepening extended
to social factors as well. For example, Taiwan, South Korea, and Japan
were—and continue to be—in the midst of a major demographic shift,
which has put pressure on policymakers to address the emergence of
new vulnerable groups. All three societies have rapidly aging populations. By the 1990s, demographic projections indicated that the elderly
(people over 65) in East Asia were expected to make up a growing and
significant portion of the total population. In the case of Japan, for example, nearly a quarter of its citizens are projected to be older than 65
by 2020.

Meanwhile, fertility rates began to decline rapidly in the 1980s, and
by the 1990s they had fallen far below the population-replacement rate.
Korea's fertility rate, for instance, decreased from 5.6 (per household)
during the early 1960s to 1.5 by the mid-1990s and just 1.17 in 2003,
making the country's future demographic challenges especially pronounced. Japan and Taiwan face a similar situation. The demographic
shift, apparent already by the early 1990s, meant that the cost of social protection, particularly for the elderly, continued to increase, while
the economically productive proportion of the population—those who
can pay for social programs—shrank, thus requiring more government
investment in social welfare, especially for intergenerational transfers
typical of pay-as-you-go social-security systems.

Finally, compounding the functionalist challenges to the welfare state
were changing norms in East Asia regarding traditional family-centered
measures for social protection. For example, the number of three-generation households, which had historically provided care for dependents
such as children and the elderly, decreased rapidly in Japan between
1980 and 2000. Meanwhile, the number of single-person households,
many headed by young working women, increased significantly. The
pace of social change was even more pronounced in Korea and Taiwan,
where the number of three-generation households shrank by nearly half
from 1990 to 2000.

Divorce rates were also on the rise, doubling in Taiwan and Japan
between 1980 and 2000, and increasing sixfold (to 36 percent) in Korea during that same period. Female participation in the labor market

consequently grew quickly. The effect of this sociocultural change with respect to gender norms and gender relations was the rapid decline in the salience of the family-centered model of social protection, particularly as it had been women who tended to provide care in what used to be the male, single-breadwinner household. Simply put, by the 1990s, traditional safety nets in Taiwan, Korea, and Japan were wearing thin. From a functionalist point of view, then, the state had little choice but to step in.

But did it? The contextual factors that I have outlined here, which seemed to have encouraged welfare-state expansion in East Asia, are entirely reasonable. And yet the empirical record suggests that they are also a bit too deterministic, a bit too functionalist. After all, economic uncertainty, rising inequality, the demographic challenges of aging societies and the changing structure of families and households are hardly unique to these Asian societies. These sorts of structural changes are common in many places. But social-policy reforms in other countries have not been nearly as thorough as in Taiwan, Korea, and Japan during the 1990s. As Stephan Haggard and Robert Kaufman explain, prospective welfare states in other countries have been stymied by the economic pressures of globalization, weak fiscal capacity, and state mismanagement, as well as by the lack of political will among policymakers.[6] Why, then, do we see welfare-state deepening in Taiwan, Korea and Japan? More specifically, what was the *political logic* that facilitated welfare-state expansion, if pressing functionalist imperatives alone cannot fully explain this transformation? The answer, I contend, rests in the political relationship between East Asian democracy and social-welfare reform.

The Impact of Democracy

The deepening of the welfare state in Taiwan, Korea, and Japan coincided with major political changes in each country. In Taiwan, the opposition Democratic Progressive Party (DPP) formed in 1986 and martial law was lifted a year later. Taiwan's first full legislative elections took place in 1992, followed by its founding presidential election in 1996, the year after the ruling KMT had implemented the National Health Insurance (NHI) program. Although the DPP lost both elections, it nonetheless appealed to Taiwanese voters and thus forced the KMT's hand in initiating a new reform agenda, including healthcare reforms that the ruling party had eschewed a decade earlier. During local elections in 1993, both KMT and DPP candidates promised to increase old-age benefits. This not only ratcheted-up expectations regarding the government's commitment to social welfare, it also demonstrated how the dynamics of competitive elections effectively deepened the pension-reform agenda. A decade later, the DPP government legislated a comprehensive old-age income-security scheme. Monthly allowances for pensioners expanded during the legislative debate as the KMT proposed and then counterproposed even more generous benefits than initially had been included in the DPP bill.

A similar process occurred in Korea. In the summer of 1987, Roh Tae Woo, the handpicked successor to authoritarian ruler Chun Doo Hwan, unexpectedly initiated a democratic transition when he announced that a direct presidential election would be held later that year, followed by full National Assembly elections in 1988. In the run-up to the balloting, important compromises over new electoral rules were struck between Roh and Korean opposition leaders, somewhat leveling the electoral playing field. It was at this time that the Roh government legislated a national-pension scheme and a universal medical-insurance program. Nearly a decade later, in the wake of the 1997 Asian financial crisis, perennial opposition leader Kim Dae Jung successfully ran on a so-cial- and economic-policy platform that resulted in reforms to corporate governance as well as efforts to integrate what were then decentralized medical-insurance funds. Kim's healthcare reform increased redistribu-tion across different occupational and income groups. In both Taiwan and Korea, the transition to democracy and, more important, the institu-tionalization of relatively competitive elections were critical in sparking social-policy reform.

Unlike Taiwan and Korea, Japan was a democracy throughout the postwar period. Yet it had been governed by only one party, the LDP, which remained undefeated in elections until the early 1990s. A catchall party that had engineered Japan's postwar economic miracle, the LDP continually delivered economic growth, for which it was consistently rewarded at the polls. As time wore on, however, the LDP became in-creasingly mired in internal party scandals and was blamed for Japan's sluggish economy.

In 1993, the party experienced its first electoral defeat. The LDP was put on the defensive as new political parties proliferated (more than twenty new parties formed after the 1993 election). For the first time in the postwar period, Japan's democracy featured competitive electoral contests, as viable alternatives to the LDP mobilized voters. And though the LDP did regain power later in the decade, it was only through the formation of various coalitions with other parties. The LDP-led govern-ing coalitions of the late 1990s reprioritized social-policy reform, such as expensive programs in child care and long-term care for the elderly, and abandoned the party's welfare-retrenchment plan of the 1980s. As in Taiwan and Korea, competitive elections in Japan shaped the social-policy agenda.

The introduction of competitive elections in Taiwan, Korea, and Ja-pan during the late 1980s and early 1990s institutionalized a new politi-cal logic that was very simple: Contending parties needed to *win* elec-toral support, which meant that they also needed to articulate winning platforms that appealed to voters. No longer could ruling parties simply suppress dissent as they had in authoritarian Taiwan and Korea. Nor could dominant parties such as Japan's LDP continue simply to presume its catchall appeal to voters. Political incentives had changed with the introduction of competitive elections. Parties needed to be more politically entrepreneurial. They had to differentiate themselves from one another, and to do so they had to cultivate new and broader coalitions of electoral support by mobilizing voters around social cleavages; as a result, welfare policy emerged as a winning issue in Taiwan, Korea, and Japan during the 1990s. Polling data in all three places reveal that social-policy reform and concerns about socioeconomic inequality were important priorities for voters. While economic growth continued to be a key priority for voters, it was no longer the only one.

Political change in the 1990s not only altered the incentives of the political (democratic) game, it also restructured the policymaking process. Within the state apparatus, for instance, the earlier omnipotent power of the bureaucracy in the developmental state began to give way to a more assertive legislature. Individual legislators and legislative committees increasingly steered the social-policy reform agenda. Alternations in power and the continual reconfiguration of the legislature in Taiwan, Korea, and Japan weakened the preexisting ties between the legislative and bureaucratic branches, thus transforming the national assembly from its former role of rubber stamp into a viable institutional check on bureaucratic power. More and more, interest groups began to lobby legislators rather than bureaucrats. Weak party discipline, endemic in all three places, also meant less cohesion within parties, which resulted in the ad hoc formation of interparty coalitions when it came to social-policy reform. Elite survey data collected in Taiwan and Korea during the late 1990s suggest that legislative influence in policymaking increased after democratic transition.[7] Changes were as significant in Japan. According to T.J. Pempel, the LDP's defeat in 1993 was tantamount to a major "regime shift" in how Japan's state apparatus functioned.[8] Political change during the 1990s opened up the *political space* within which political entrepreneurs could operate.

This political space extended to civil society as well. Democratic transition in Taiwan and Korea was initiated by societal mobilization from below, and the institutionalization of democratic rules of the game ensured that civic groups and social movements remained important actors thereafter. Civil society organizations in Japan emerged most forcefully in the early 1990s. Before then, civic groups tended to be local and usually formed in reaction to some specific grievance; civil society mobilization at the time was not national in scope, and civic groups were not proactive policy agenda-setters.

By the 1990s, however, civil society groups had become important and effective social-policy reform advocates in all three countries. In

Korea, groups such as the Citizens' Coalition for Economic Justice (CCEJ) and Peoples' Solidarity for Participatory Democracy (PSPD) were critical in shaping Kim Dae Jung's social- and economic-reform agendas during the late 1990s. Taiwan's National Health Insurance Coalition successfully fought back against the KMT government's efforts to privatize the management of the NHI program. And in Japan, groups such as the Women's Committee for the Improvement of Aged Society (WCIAS) pressured the government to create a universally inclusive long-term-care insurance program during the mid-1990s; in fact, the WCIAS's influence was so strong that it was a member of the Ministry of Health and Welfare's policy advisory body.

In Taiwan, Korea, and Japan, the effects of political change during the early 1990s—such as the institutionalization of competitive elections, the empowerment of national legislatures, and the mobilization of civil society groups—reconfigured prevailing practices in the setting of social-policy agendas and in social policy making. The *political logic* of social-policy reform was altered. No longer was social-welfare policy made from the top-down, nor was social-policy reform subsumed within a broader economic-growth agenda, as it had been in the hierarchical developmental states. Instead, such reform had become a winning agenda in and of itself, and the processes by which social policies were made had become considerably more inclusive.

Conditions of the Democratic Transformation

Democratic transitions in Taiwan and South Korea and newly competitive elections in Japan during the early 1990s entailed a different political logic. It was the new political-incentive structure inherent in democratic politics that initially sparked the deepening of the welfare state in these three countries and subsequently shaped its course. Democracy was an important variable, but the installation of democracy alone does not guarantee the emergence of the welfare state, especially in late-developing countries. Places such as Taiwan, Korea, and Japan have in many ways become an aspirational model for social-policy reform, with many countries attempting to emulate the East Asian experience. Emulation elsewhere, however, has been difficult—not because the causal connection between democracy and welfare described above is spurious, but because these particular East Asian cases benefited from other enabling factors that made the transition from developmental state to welfare state more socially, politically, and economically viable. Three enabling factors stand out.

Fiscal and economic capacity. The most common refrain from social-policy advocates in other parts of the world upon learning about the East Asian experience in welfare-state deepening is that Taiwan, Korea, and Japan are rich, while many countries in the non–Anglo-European world are not. And they are right. The political logic of democracy and welfare expansion requires that states have the fiscal capacity to implement reform and that citizens, in turn, have the available economic resources to contribute, especially to social-insurance programs. During the 1990s, GDP per capita in Taiwan and Korea was much higher than in their Latin American counterparts, and Japan's GDP per capita was among the highest in the world. East Asians were, quite simply, comparatively richer than those living in many other parts of the world. Their governments were also richer.

Interregional variation in state fiscal capacity was just as pronounced, particularly among late-developing economies. For instance, during the 1990s, Latin America's large economies were-running chronic deficits and carried major debt burdens, most equaling over half of GDP. Debt service burdens were also very high, ranging from about a quarter to nearly 50 percent of the value of exports. By contrast, during the same period Taiwan and South Korea ran minimal (to zero) budget deficits, debt was comparatively low, and debt service to export ratios were less than 11 percent.[9] The East Asian developmental states were relatively healthy in fiscal terms and able to afford social-welfare expansion during the 1990s. Simply put, being (comparatively) rich and democratic facilitated the deepening of the welfare state in Taiwan, Korea, and Japan.

Growth with equity. That Taiwan, Korea, and Japan sustained, on average, around 8 percent growth per year between the 1960s and 1980s is noteworthy. What is even more laudable, perhaps even miraculous, is that rapid economic growth in those countries was accompanied by tremendous socioeconomic equity. Taiwan's and Japan's Gini coefficients consistently hovered around 0.30 throughout the postwar high-growth period; in South Korea, the Gini ranged between 0.30 and 0.40. Contrast these measures with the average Gini coefficient in Latin America in 1980, which was approximately 0.50, and it is clear that East Asia's industrializers were more in line with the egalitarian economies of northern Europe. Growth with equity was in part motivated by political concerns. Japan's LDP was concerned early on about challenges from socialist and communist parties. In Korea, prior to the authoritarian rule of General Park Chung Hee during the early 1960s, student and worker movements ensured that the developmental state there was similarly mindful of distributive outcomes. In Taiwan, the KMT promoted socioeconomic equity as a way of mitigating potential ethnic tensions between Chinese mainlander émigrés and ethnic Taiwanese, particularly as the mainlander-based KMT and its supporters were in the minority.

But growth with equity was not only a political strategy; it was also

an important part of East Asia's industrialization strategy. Poverty alle-
viation was a priority in Taiwan, Korea, and Japan, though one that was
embedded in the larger aims of aggregate economic growth. In the early
postwar period, land reform in all three places helped to jumpstart agricultural and industrial development and narrowed the distance between
social classes. To facilitate continual industrial upgrading, the developmental state invested heavily in human-capital development, most notably through an emphasis on universal and accessible education. By the
early 2000s, high school enrollment rates in all three places were near
100 percent. Universal education not only ensured a skilled labor force,
it also facilitated social mobility, which in turn resulted in greater socioeconomic equity. Policymakers in Taiwan, Korea, and Japan also pursued the dual objectives of growth and equity through a full-employment
strategy—for example, Japan's income-doubling plan of the 1960s, the
heavy and chemical industries drive in Korea during the 1970s, and the
promotion of small and medium-sized enterprises (SMEs) in Taiwan to
facilitate greater social mobility and more entrepreneurial opportunity
and to narrow the gap between worker and manager.

The *legacies* of growth with equity in Taiwan, Korea, and Japan,
were important in establishing the larger social, economic, and political
context in which social-policy debates were mediated during the 1990s,
when the nascent welfare state emerged in the region. Social-welfare
policy is fundamentally about redistribution, meaning it is technically
a zero-sum arrangement that creates winners and losers. The extent to
which conflict between potential winners and losers can be mitigated
and interclass compromises formed in large part determines the likelihood of effective redistributive social policy. In this respect, the legacies of growth with equity in East Asia favored social-welfare reform by
lowering the economic, political, and social costs of introducing redistributive social-welfare policies. The experience of growth with equity
in Taiwan, Korea, and Japan simply made it easier for political entrepreneurs to pursue equity-enhancing social-policy reform.

First, relative income equity through the 1980s and into the 1990s
lowered the *economic costs* of redistributing wealth across wage groups
and disparate (in terms of income) households. The distance between
the richest and poorest was narrower in Taiwan, Korea, and Japan—
due to an existing distribution of income that was relatively egalitarian—meaning the costs of redistribution were lower and the prospects
of welfare deepening were much less constrained. The potential winners
in the social-welfare bargain did not win big, and those who lost did
not lose that much. In Latin America, by contrast, economic growth has
been accompanied by extreme socioeconomic inequality. The economic
costs of transferring wealth from the richest to the poorest there are
much higher, as the prospective losers in redistribution would lose a
great deal more.

Second, the legacies of growth with equity in Taiwan, Korea, and Japan mitigated the *political costs* of redistribution. Again, the contrast between these East Asian cases and developments in Latin America is instructive. In places such as Brazil, Chile, and Mexico, class politics are intensely divisive. Unlike in democratizing Latin America, however, in Taiwan, Korea, and Japan class conflict did not become deeply entrenched in the formal political-party system. Distributional battles were fought in East Asia. Yet because such battles were not fought among programmatic and ideologically left or right parties, the political costs of pushing (or resisting, for that matter) a social-policy reform agenda were considerably lower. To be supportive of social-welfare expansion, for instance, was not politically costly, provided that public opinion and broad cross-class electoral coalitions supported such an initiative, which was the case in industrial East Asia. Moreover, the threat of alienating electoral support from those most likely to lose in redistributive social-welfare arrangements—that is, higher-income earners and the wealthy—was considerably reduced because the gap between the rich and poor was less pronounced. The prospects of constructing winning cross-class coalitions were, politically speaking, more likely. Simply put, the political costs of supporting welfare reform were less severe, and during the 1990s in particular, such support often yielded political gains.

Third, growth with equity in the East Asian developmental state lowered the *social costs* of redistributive social welfare by blunting the perception of distinct class divisions within society. For instance, most Japanese throughout the postwar period considered themselves to be a part of the "middle mass." The vast majority of South Koreans who benefited from the developmental state's growth-with-equity strategy also saw themselves as part of the middle class. Similarly, Taiwan's society was perceived to be "classless."[10] This did not mean that class divisions did not exist or that they did not animate politics in these East Asian societies. For example, the *minjung* movement in Korea, which fostered democratic transition during the late 1980s, was formulated in part along socioeconomic class lines. Yet we also know that soon after Korea's transition the *minjung* coalition fell apart, leaving the ideological leftists marginalized from mainstream politics while the majority of middle-class activists gravitated back toward a more politically conservative position. It was the overwhelming social perception of "middle class-ness," a legacy of growth with equity, that tempered the potentially divisive politics of social-policy reform. Yasusuke Murakami's observation that in Japan "people of the new middle mass do not see the issues around them in ideological terms of class conflict or of revolution" captures this perception.[11] The stakes, both real and perceived, between social policy's winners and losers were not prohibitively high for social-policy reformers seeking to deepen the welfare state in Taiwan, Korea, and Japan

Ideological flexibility. A relatively unique feature of these East Asian democracies was the seemingly nonprogrammatic nature of their political-party systems. Unlike in the established democracies of Europe or the more recent transitional democracies in Latin America and Southern and Eastern Europe, party systems in East Asia were (and are) not well institutionalized in terms of the left-right ideological continuum. Party identification among voters was (and continues to be) weak. Parties were inconsistent in their electoral platforms. And intraparty cohesion was ephemeral, with splinter and factional parties breaking off quite regularly. Part of this can be explained by the historical dominance of catchall ruling parties—the KMT in Taiwan, the Democratic Justice Party (DJP) in Korea, and Japan's LDP—that basically crowded out competitors along the ideological spectrum, leaving little programmatic space for potential challengers. Part of this can also be explained by the legacies of the Cold War, which essentially forclosed any partisan affiliation with the left.

In the eyes of many observers, the nonprogrammatic nature of the party systems in Taiwan, Korea, and Japan suggests that multiparty democracy is not well institutionalized there, and that the quality of democracy has suffered as a result. Moreover, the absence of a strong leftist political party, according to the conventional wisdom among welfare-state scholars, means that the prospects for social-welfare deepening are not promising. The lack of cohesion among unions and their failure to attach themselves to any political party (such as a programmatic social-democratic party) would also imply a weak link between East Asian democracy and the prospects for social-policy reform. And yet, given what has happened in terms of social-policy reform in Taiwan, Korea, and Japan, an argument can be made that the nonprogrammatic nature of their party systems during the 1990s actually facilitated rather than hindered the development of the welfare state in the region. In other words, the absence of ideological rigidity in the party system in fact favored the politics of welfare-state deepening.

The introduction of democratic competition during the late 1980s and early 1990s in Taiwan, Korea, and Japan institutionalized a new set of incentives for parties to become more politically entrepreneurial. In the face of new (or renewed) electoral competition, political parties were incentivized to exploit new cleavages, articulate winning platforms, and assemble winning electoral coalitions. Social-welfare policy emerged as a winning issue. Unlike in other democracies where political parties tend to be more ideologically programmatic, however, social-policy reform in Taiwan, Korea, and Japan was not understood to be the exclusive ideological domain of the partisan left.

Put another way, social-policy reform—be it in health care, pensions, public assistance or social care—was not experienced by parties and voters as an ideologically leftist or distinctly social-democratic agenda. After all, it was the incumbent authoritarian party in Korea, the DJP, that universalized medical insurance by expanding coverage to nearly half the population in the late 1980s. The same notionally conservative political party legislated a national pensions program in 1988 and currently campaigns on a platform of policies promoting shared growth. In Taiwan, it was the authoritarian-turned-democratic KMT, and not the opposition DPP, that started developing a national health-insurance program during the late 1980s and implemented it in 1995. Likewise, in the 2000s it was the opposition KMT that pressured the DPP government to increase old-age income allowances and not to raise health-insurance premiums. Similarly, in the late 1990s in Japan, the nominally conservative LDP, and not the opposition, prompted state investments in new social-protection schemes for child care and elderly care, as well as new income-security measures.

Politically entrepreneurial parties such as the DJP, the KMT, and the LDP crafted winning electoral coalitions around social-policy reform not because they were committed leftists but because they could win elections by running on such issues. But these parties were not constrained ideologically in doing so. Their efforts to articulate a pro-social-welfare agenda were not seen as illegitimate or ideologically inconsistent. Indeed, it was precisely the ideological flexibility and "free space" inherent in the nonprogrammatic party systems of democratic Taiwan, Korea, and Japan that allowed the social-democratic reform agenda to be there for the taking. Ideological and partisan flexibility, as opposed to programmatic rigidity, prevented political and ideological deadlock over social-policy reform.

Looking Ahead

Whether or not Taiwan, Korea, and Japan are substantive welfare states is debatable. Certainly, when compared with the "gold standard" of welfare states such as Sweden, the East Asian cases examined here fall short (although Sweden today would likely fall short as well). What is less debatable is that Taiwan, Korea, and Japan have moved beyond the singularly focused high-growth model of state-led economic development toward much more comprehensive social-policy regimes. Beginning in the 1990s, social spending in all three places increased manifold. Existing social-protection programs were expanded and in many cases universalized. Since then, all three countries have also created programs to reach new constituents and protect previously unprotected vulnerable populations. The purposes of social policy have evolved beyond the productivist logic of the developmental-state era to become more inclusive as well as redistributive.

Looking forward, one should expect that the current social-welfare policy trajectory will more or less stay the present course. It is unlikely, for instance, that we will see these social-insurance regimes become fully government-financed welfare states, such as those in postwar Europe where tax revenues were redistributed by the state for the purposes of social protection. The costs of breaking from existing social-policy institutions in East Asia would be prohibitive; thus a wholesale restructuring is unlikely. For similar path-dependent reasons, however, it is equally improbable that Taiwan, Korea, and Japan would significantly retrench their current social-policy regimes. People have come to expect a modicum of egalitarianism—a normative expectation rooted in part in the legacies of postwar growth with equity and reinforced by the expansion of social welfare in the 1990s. Efforts to retrench existing programs have met with tremendous resistance and by and large have been unsuccessful. Indeed, as Asian populations continue to age rapidly, it is expected that the social safety net in democracies such as Taiwan, Korea, and Japan will broaden.

Democratic politics and the mobilization of voters have ensured that vested interests in, and normative expectations about, the current social-policy regimes in all three countries have become more fixed over time. Citizens have not blamed economic downturns or uncertainty in the region on the growing costs of social protection. Rather, it seems that the once-powerful postwar idea that social welfare is inimical to economic growth no longer resonates in mainstream political and policy debates, which is perhaps the most convincing indicator that the postwar-developmental state has indeed been transformed in ways that have come to accommodate, if not embrace, a redistributive welfare state.

NOTES

1. For a spirited and convincing rebuttal to this claim, see Gregory J. Kasza, *One World of Welfare: Japan in Comparative Perspective* (Ithaca: Cornell University Press, 2006).

2. Catherine Jones, "Hong Kong, Singapore, South Korea, and Taiwan: Oikonomic Welfare States," *Government and Opposition* 25 (October 1990): 446–62.

3. Ian Holliday, "Productivist Welfare Capitalism: Social Policy in East Asia," *Political Studies* 48 (September 2000): 708.

4. Kent E. Calder, *Crisis and Compensation: Public Policy and Stability in Japan, 1949–86* (Princeton: Princeton University Press, 1988).

5. See Ito Peng and Joseph Wong, "Institutions and Institutional Purpose: Continuity and Change in East Asian Social Policy," *Politics and Society* 36 (March 2008): 61–88.

6. Stephan Haggard and Robert Kaufman, *Development, Democracy, and Welfare States: Latin America, East Asia and Eastern Europe* (Princeton: Princeton University Press, 2008).

7. Joseph Wong, *Healthy Democracies: Welfare Politics in Taiwan and South Korea* (Ithaca: Cornell University Press, 2004).

8. T.J. Pempel, *Regime Shift: Comparative Dynamics of the Japanese Political Economy* (Ithaca: Cornell University Press, 1998).

9. Haggard and Kaufman, *Development, Democracy, and Welfare States,* 192.

10. Michael Hsin-Huang Hsiao, ed., *East Asian Middle Classes in Comparative Perspective* (Taipei: Institute of Ethnology, Academia Sinica, 1999).

11. Murakami Yasusuke, "The Age of New Middle Mass Politics: the Case of Japan," *Journal of Japanese Studies* 8 (Winter 1982): 45.

4

REGIME PERFORMANCE AND DEMOCRATIC LEGITIMACY

Chong-Min Park and Yu-tzung Chang

Chong-Min Park *is dean of the College of Political Science and Economics and professor of public administration at Korea University. He directs the Asian Barometer Survey in South Korea.* **Yu-tzung Chang** *is associate professor of political science at National Taiwan University. He is co-principal investigator and program manager of the Asian Barometer.*

Compared to other regions, the track record of "third-wave" democratization in East Asia has been largely mixed.[1] East Asia's first third-wave democracy emerged in the Philippines in 1986 when the People Power Revolution overthrew the country's longstanding dictatorship. South Korea's transition immediately followed with the adoption of a democratic constitution and founding election in 1987. Taiwan, whose transition began that same year with the lifting of martial law, held its first presidential election almost a decade later, in 1996. Mongolia made a rapid transition to democracy in 1990, abolishing one-party communist rule and holding its first multiparty parliamentary elections in more than sixty years.

Cambodia's transition from one-party communist rule began in 1991, but democratization was halted by the 1997 coup. Thailand's transition to democracy began in 1992, but democratic consolidation was interrupted by a 2006 military coup. Indonesia embarked on the transition to democracy in 1998 with the forced resignation of longtime autocrat Suharto and the holding of open, multiparty parliamentary elections in 1999. Most recently, beginning in 2011 Burma, a longtime military dictatorship, began taking steps toward political liberalization.

Yet many countries in the region have remained immune to the global wave of democratization. Singapore and Malaysia, puzzling anomalies, have preserved pseudodemocracies characterized by controlled or uneven multiparty competition. China, Laos, North Korea, and Vietnam have maintained one-party communist rule, and Brunei is a "sultanistic" regime. The transformation of autocracies into democracies in the region has stalled for over a decade.

With this background in mind, this chapter examines public support for democracy as an idea and public evaluations of the regime-in-practice across the democratic and pseudodemocratic countries of East Asia. How do East Asians orient themselves toward democracy as an idea? Do they believe in the legitimacy of democracy? How strong is their adherence to the norms and institutions associated with liberal democracy? Apart from support for democracy as an idea, how do they orient themselves to their regime-in-practice? How supportive are they of the prevailing system of government? To what extent do they believe that the regime-in-practice reflects the institutions and mechanisms of democracy? How much trust do they have in representative institutions of the regime-in-practice? And, most important, what shapes orientations toward democracy as an idea and evaluations of the regime-in-practice? By addressing these and other related questions, we seek to understand the patterns of citizen orientations to political regimes, both ideal and real, across East Asia.

In order to do so, we have used public-opinion data drawn from the third wave of the Asian Barometer Survey (hereafter, ABS III) conducted in nine countries between 2010 and 2012. The sample countries are divided into three groups according to regime type: liberal democracies (Japan, South Korea, and Taiwan), electoral democracies (Indonesia, Mongolia, the Philippines, and Thailand), and pseudodemocracies or competitive authoritarian regimes (Malaysia and Singapore).[2]

Conceptual Framework

David Easton's theory of political support serves as our starting point for analyzing citizen orientations to democracy and evaluations of the regime-in-practice.[3] Easton described political support as something that flows from an individual's evaluation (whether favorable or unfavorable) of a given political system. He distinguished among three levels of such systems: the political community ("a group of persons bound together by a political division of labor"), the regime (the system of government and its principles or justifications), and the authorities (incumbents in authority roles). He further differentiated three components within the regime: values, norms, and the structure of authority. The regime values "serve as broad limits with regard to what can be taken for granted in the guidance of day-to-day policy." The regime norms are the "procedures that are expected and acceptable in the processing and implementation of demands." The structure of authority refers to the "formal and informal patterns in which power is distributed and organized with regard to the authoritative making and implementing of decisions."[4] Hence, political support at the regime level includes attitudes toward the values, operating norms and procedures, and institutional arrangements of a political regime.

Much of the empirical research on support for democracy builds on this conceptual distinction between different aspects of the regime. For instance, Russell J. Dalton distinguishes between three objects of regime support: principles, norms and procedures, and institutions. He further differentiates between two modes of orientation: affective and evaluative. The former represents "adherence to a set of values," and the latter reflects "judgments about political phenomena."[5] Pippa Norris classifies three objects of regime support: principles (the core values of a political system), performance (the functioning of a political system), and institutions (actual state institutions such as parliament, courts, the police, political parties, and the military).[6] Similarly, John A. Booth and Mitchell A. Seligson differentiate between three dimensions of regime legitimacy: core regime principles, regime performance, and regime institutions.[7]

Despite conceptual clarification and theoretical distinction, researchers have had difficulties distinguishing empirically between different types or modes of political support. Nonetheless, a multidimensional or multilevel conceptualization of political support is useful for disentangling citizen orientations toward a political system. By specifying the targets of support, we should be able to better understand the nature of political discontent, its sources, and its consequences.

Following prior theory and research, we distinguish between three aspects of the regime: values, norms and rules, and institutions. Moreover, we distinguish between support for democracy as an idea (democratic support) and support for the regime-in-practice (regime support), which varies depending on the political setting. In democracies, support for the regime-in-practice may reflect practical support for democracy. In autocratic settings, however, support for the regime-in-practice indicates practical support for autocracy.

In breaking down the various kinds of support for democracy, we focus on three specific notions reflecting commitment to democracy. The first aspect of democratic support refers to general orientations toward democracy as a whole. In public-opinion surveys, this aspect of democratic support is often measured by agreement that democracy is the best (or most preferred) form of government. Likewise, in this study it is measured by both preference for democracy over its alternatives (especially authoritarian regimes) and acceptance of democracy as the best form of government. The second aspect of democratic support encompasses orientations toward specific norms and procedures of democracy. In this study, it is measured by adherence to certain liberal norms, such as checks and balances, the rule of law, and social pluralism. The last aspect concerns orientations toward specific institutions of democracy, such as popular elections and a multiparty system.

Similarly, in analyzing regime support we look at three factors reflecting the endorsement of the regime-in-practice. The first aspect of

TABLE 1—DIFFUSE SUPPORT FOR DEMOCRACY

	Preference for Democracy over Its Alternatives	Acceptance of Democracy as Best Form of Government	Both	(N)
Liberal Democracy				
Japan	63	90	61	(1,880)
South Korea	66	83	58	(1,207)
Taiwan	51	87	48	(1,592)
Electoral Democracy				
Indonesia	58	77	52	(1,550)
Mongolia	49	86	47	(1,210)
Philippines	55	76	46	(1,200)
Thailand	68	89	66	(1,512)
Competitive Authoritarianism				
Malaysia	74	87	69	(1,214)
Singapore	47	79	44	(1,000)

Note: Entries are percentages. Missing data not reported.
Source: ABS III

regime support pertains to citizens' overall evaluation of the regime-in-practice. In public-opinion surveys, satisfaction with the workings of democracy is often used to measure this aspect of regime support, although its meaning is contested.[8] Here, we measure regime support using both pride in and "loyalty" to the prevailing system of government. The second aspect of regime support evaluates the performance of political institutions. We measure this by the extent to which the regime-in-practice embodies the values and institutions of democracy. The last aspect involves evaluation of specific institutions of the regime-in-practice. Our indicators are trust in representative institutions—parliament and political parties.

Orientations Toward Democracy

Diffuse democratic support. To ascertain support for democracy in general we selected two questions. One asked respondents to choose from the following three statements the one that best described their feelings: 1) "Democracy is always preferable to any other kind of government"; 2) "under some circumstances, an authoritarian government can be preferable to a democratic one"; and 3) "for people like me, it does not matter whether we have a democratic or a non-democratic regime." The other question asked respondents whether they agreed or disagreed with the statement "Democracy may have its problems, but it is still the best form of government." We consider affirmative responses to both questions to indicate diffuse support for democracy.

As Table 1 shows, among the region's democracies Thailand displayed the highest level of preference for democracy over its alternatives. It was closely followed by South Korea and Japan. In these countries, roughly two-thirds of respondents considered democracy always to be preferable. In contrast, Mongolia displayed the lowest level of preference for democracy, with Taiwan placing slightly ahead of it. In these two countries, only half of respondents (49–51 percent) expressed unconditional preference for democracy. The two competitive authoritarian regimes exhibited sharply contrasting patterns: Malaysia (74 percent) had a higher level of preference than all its democratic neighbors, whereas Singapore (47 percent) had a lower level than all the democracies.

Acceptance of democracy as the best form of government turned out to be far more widespread. An overwhelming majority (83–90 percent) in most democratic countries agreed that "Democracy may have its problems, but it is still the best form of government." Surprisingly, in the two competitive authoritarian regimes agreement was even higher (79–87 percent) than in some democratic countries. In every sample country, acceptance of democracy as the best form of government was higher than the preference for democracy over its alternatives. The difference was striking especially in Mongolia, Taiwan, and Singapore.

By looking at the percentage of respondents who answered in the affirmative to both questions, we ascertained the level of diffuse democratic support. Among the region's democracies, Thailand displayed the highest level of diffuse democratic support (positive answers to both questions). Japan and South Korea were close behind, followed by Indonesia. Only in these countries (and Malaysia) did a majority express unconditional adherence to democracy.

The East Asian model of economic success under authoritarian rule seems to sustain a skeptical view of democracy as a universal value. No matter which conception of democracy ordinary people may have, democracy has yet to be seen as "the only game in town" in much of the region.

Support for liberal democratic norms. Freedom and equality are often considered the foundational values of liberal democracy. These values are to be achieved through the institutions and mechanisms of limited government, which include the separation and balance of government powers, the rule of law, and a pluralist civil society. How supportive are East Asians of these liberal democratic norms?

To measure acceptance of the norm of checks and balances, we have used two agree-disagree statements: "When judges decide important cases, they should accept the view of the executive branch" and "If the government is constantly checked by the legislature, it cannot possibly accomplish great things." Surprisingly, none of the East Asian countries surveyed enjoyed majority support for the norm of checks and

TABLE 2—SUPPORT FOR LIBERAL DEMOCRATIC NORMS

	Support for Checks and Balances	Support for the Rule of Law	Support for Social Pluralism
Liberal Democracy			
Japan	47	42	31
South Korea	48	31	42
Taiwan	27	55	24
Electoral Democracy			
Indonesia	30	35	23
Mongolia	28	17	15
Philippines	13	31	15
Thailand	39	11	14
Competitive Authoritarianism			
Malaysia	25	35	13
Singapore	25	25	25

Note: Entries are the percent of those giving prodemocratic responses to a pair of questions. Missing data not reported.
Source: ABS III

balances as indicated by disagreeing with both statements (see Table 2). In South Korea and Japan, ranking first and second, respectively, slightly less than half subscribed to the norm. The Philippines displayed the lowest level of support, lower even than Singapore and Malaysia. In Taiwan, Mongolia, Indonesia, and Thailand, only a minority (27–39 percent) was supportive of the norm. Support for executive power unconstrained by the legislature or the judiciary—a hallmark of autocratic rule—retains broad support in the region, even among its newer democracies.

Second, we measured support for the rule of law, which is considered essential for protecting liberty and equality from the arbitrary exercise of state power. To measure acceptance of this norm, we selected two agree-disagree statements: "When the country is facing a difficult situation, it is okay for the government to disregard the law in order to deal with the situation" and "If we have political leaders who are morally upright, we can let them decide everything." Table 2 shows the percentages disagreeing with both statements.

According to these two measures, only Taiwan enjoyed majority support for law-based governance. The second highest level of support was in Japan, where only two in five were supportive of this norm. In South Korea, the Philippines, and Indonesia, only about one in three (31–35 percent) favored law-based governance, and the proportion was much lower in Thailand and Mongolia (11–17 percent). In competitive authoritarian regimes, only a minority subscribed to the norm. In South Korea, Mongolia, and the Philippines, rejection of rule by "good leaders" was far weaker than rejection of arbitrary rule, indicating mixed attitudes toward the liberal conception of rule of law. Overall, the prevailing conception of good governance in the region still seems to reflect the traditional value of rule by leaders who are virtuous and benevolent.

Finally, we examined support for the liberal value of social pluralism and its related implicit value of societal freedom with two agree-disagree statements: "Harmony of the community will be disrupted if people organize lots of groups" and "If people have too many different ways of thinking, society will be chaotic." There was no country surveyed where a simple majority of citizens supported this norm (by disagreeing with both items). The country with the highest level of support was South Korea, where 42 percent endorsed the norm. In other countries examined, only a small minority (14–31 percent) was supportive of the norm. In particular, Thailand, Mongolia, and the Philippines displayed very low levels of support.

Overall, public adherence to liberal norms associated with the idea of limited government proved to be shallow across the region, suggesting that the cultural foundation of liberal democracy remains superficial. Diffuse support for democracy is not accompanied by commitment to specific liberal democratic norms, suggesting either a radically different view of what democracy is or that much of the avowed support for democracy may be mere "lip service."[9]

Support for democratic institutions. Trust in existing political institutions is often used to ascertain support for democratic institutions. It makes little sense, however, to use this trust as an indicator of idealistic support for democratic institutions. In autocratic settings, high trust in political institutions clearly cannot be taken to indicate high support for democracy. Even in democratic settings, people may be supportive of democracy and, at the same time, critical of their actual regime's institutions.

To measure support for democratic institutions, we chose two forced-choice questions asking respondents to indicate the kind of government that they would prefer. The first asked them to choose between two statements: "Political leaders are chosen by the people through open and competitive elections" and "Political leaders are chosen on the basis of their virtue and capability even without election." The second also asked them to choose between two statements: "Multiple parties compete to represent political interests" and "One party represents the interests of all the people." The first set of questions captures a preference for popular elections and the second, a preference for a multiparty system. Both are essential institutions for minimalist democracy.

Support for popular elections was high regardless of regime type (see Table 3). In every sample country, at least two-thirds of respondents wanted their political leaders to be popularly elected through

TABLE 3—SUPPORT FOR INSTITUTIONS OF MINIMALIST DEMOCRACY

	Popular Elections	Multiparty System	Both
Liberal Democracy			
Japan	80	78	67
South Korea	81	73	64
Taiwan	79	81	67
Electoral Democracy			
Indonesia	77	53	47
Mongolia	75	79	63
Philippines	68	57	41
Thailand	72	68	56
Competitive Authoritarianism			
Malaysia	69	28	22
Singapore	80	70	59

Note: Entries are percentages. Missing data not reported.
Source: ABS III

open and competitive elections. Even in the competitive authoritarian regimes, democratic elections were widely favored. By contrast, support for a multiparty system differed across the regime types. In all three liberal democracies and two of four electoral democracies (Mongolia and Thailand), at least two-thirds supported it. In the other electoral democracies (Indonesia and the Philippines), only a simple majority supported a multiparty system. Overall, support for the institutions of minimalist democracy varied. In Japan, Taiwan, South Korea, and Mongolia, nearly two in three (67–63 percent) favored both popular elections and a multiparty system. Indonesia and the Philippines, unlike their democratic neighbors, showed low support—fewer than half of respondents (47–41 percent) favored both democratic institutions. Interestingly, in Thailand the political turmoil that has surrounded elections did not translate into widespread rejection of popular elections and a multiparty system. Finally, a majority in Singapore favored both democratic institutions, whereas in Malaysia less than a quarter did.

Despite low levels of public adherence to liberal norms, public preference for democratic institutions turned out to be high across much of the region. It should be noted, however, that there existed cross-national differences in the gap between diffuse support for democracy and preference for democratic institutions. In all three liberal democracies (Japan, South Korea, and Taiwan), one electoral democracy (Mongolia), and one competitive authoritarian regime (Singapore), support for democratic institutions was higher than diffuse support for democracy. In particular, the gap was greater in Taiwan, Mongolia, and Singapore, suggesting that ambivalence toward democracy as a whole in these countries does not indicate disapproval of minimalist democratic institutions. By contrast, in Indonesia, the Philippines, and especially Thailand and Malaysia, the preference for democratic institutions was lower than diffuse support for democracy, casting doubt on the authenticity of citizen beliefs in democratic legitimacy.

Overall, popular elections and a multiparty system—the hallmarks of minimalist democracy—remained widely accepted in much of the region, although certain liberal norms associated with limited government were not widely embraced. This finding suggests that diffuse support for democracy, while not yet based on liberal democratic norms, is nonetheless generally accompanied by support for minimalist democratic institutions.

Evaluations of the Regime-in-Practice

Having analyzed East Asian views on democracy, we now turn to citizen evaluations of the regime-in-practice, examining three components: support for the regime-in-practice as a whole, evaluation of the performance of political institutions, and trust in existing representative institutions.

Diffuse regime support. To ascertain general support for the regime-in-practice, we selected two agree-disagree statements: "Thinking in general, I am proud of our system of government" and "I would rather live under our system of government than any other that I can think of." The first reflects pride in the current system of government, whereas the second reflects loyalty to it. We consider affirmative responses to both questions to reflect diffuse regime support (see Table 4).

Among the region's democracies, there was a sharp divergence. Thailand displayed the highest level of pride: More than four in five were proud of their system. This was followed by Indonesia, where two-thirds of respondents took pride in their system. In South Korea, Japan, and Taiwan, only a minority (29–40 percent) expressed pride in their system. Despite living in one of the most successful democracies in the region, South Koreans displayed the lowest level of pride in their system (less than a third). Nine in ten Singaporeans and eight in ten Malaysians were proud of their system, suggesting low popular disaffection with the ongoing political order of competitive authoritarianism.

A similar pattern was found in response to the question about loyalty to the system, which was greater than pride in the system in every sample country except for Singapore. Japan and Taiwan displayed a larger gap (26 and 21 percent, respectively) while Mongolia, the Philippines, and South Korea exhibited a smaller gap (11–14 percent), indicating that in the former countries the prevailing system of government was viewed more as "a lesser evil" than in the latter countries. This finding suggests that low pride in the system may not necessarily indicate preference for "exit" from the system, perhaps because of no viable alternatives.

TABLE 4—DIFFUSE SUPPORT FOR THE REGIME-IN-PRACTICE

	Pride in the System	Loyalty to the System	Both
Liberal Democracy			
Japan	36	62	30
South Korea	29	43	23
Taiwan	40	61	34
Electoral Democracy			
Indonesia	69	75	61
Mongolia	45	56	36
Philippines	46	60	34
Thailand	83	87	77
Competitive Authoritarianism			
Malaysia	80	83	74
Singapore	92	89	85

Notes: Entries are percentages. Missing data not reported.
Source: ABS III

By combining responses to both questions, we ascertained the level of diffuse regime support. Among the region's democracies Thailand, again displayed the highest level of regime support (about three-quarters), followed by Indonesia (three-fifths). South Korea exhibited the lowest level of diffuse regime support, followed by Japan, Taiwan, the Philippines, and Mongolia. In these countries, only minorities (23–36 percent) expressed diffuse support for the regime-in-practice. It is noteworthy that Singapore and Malaysia maintained a huge reservoir of diffuse regime support, suggesting that the ongoing political order may weather short-term public dissatisfaction with policy outputs.

Overall, most East Asian democracies seemed to fall short of citizen aspirations, illustrating higher levels of public discontent with the democracy-in-practice. More notably, in Japan, South Korea, and Taiwan, the regimes-in-practice failed to engender even simple majority support, indicating widespread public disaffection with the actual functioning of liberal democracy.

Evaluation of institutional performance. Since institutional performance is a multidimensional phenomenon, it is necessary to distinguish between its different aspects and to ascertain public evaluation of each dimension. In this study, we focus on five dimensions associated with a high-quality democracy: freedom, equality, the rule of law, electoral competition, and accountability.[10] The initial two pertain to substantive aspects, whereas the last three are procedural. The public's evaluation of institutional performance indicates the extent to which the prevailing system of government is seen to embody the values and institutions of liberal democracy.

Freedom is one of the foundational values of liberal democracy. To measure the public's evaluation of regime performance on this dimension, we selected two agree-disagree statements: "People are free to speak what they think without fear" and "People can join any organization they like without fear." Table 5 shows the percentage of those who agreed with both statements. Among the region's democracies, Thailand registered the highest level of public approval, followed by Indonesia and Taiwan. In these three countries, more than two-thirds (68–77 percent) of respondents felt that they enjoyed both freedoms. South Koreans, Japanese, and Mongolians were more critical—only about half (47–53 percent) affirmed both statements. Surprisingly, Malaysia returned higher scores: Three in four believed they enjoyed both freedoms. As expected, Singapore displayed the lowest level of affirmation (44 percent).

To measure citizens' evaluation of regime performance on equality, we again selected two agree-disagree statements: "All citizens from different ethnic communities are treated equally by the government" and "Rich and poor people are treated equally by the government." Once more, as Table 5 shows, Thailand displayed the highest level of affirmation (84 percent) among the region's democracies, followed by Indonesia (62 percent).

Public assessments of equality were more severe in the other democracies, ranging from 12 percent in Korea to 34 percent in Mongolia. Competitive authoritarian regimes fared better. A majority in Malaysia and Singapore considered both types of equality provided. In most sample countries, perceptions of unequal treatment of the economically disadvantaged were more conspicuous than perceptions of unequal treatment of ethnic minorities, suggesting that economic disparities constitute a major source of political disaffection across much of the region.

Another foundational value, the rule of law, is essential for securing not only liberal democracy but also good governance. To measure evaluation of regime performance on this dimension, we selected two questions. One asked, "How often do government leaders break the law or abuse their power?" and the other, "How widespread do you think corruption and bribe-taking are in the national government?" The two most favorable replies in each case were taken as signs of positive regard for the rule of law. Public evaluation of regime performance regarding this value was largely unfavorable except in Singapore (75 percent). Even in Japan, which displayed the highest level of approval among the region's democracies, only half of respondents had a favorable judgment. In Thailand, one in three considered public officials to be law-abiding. In Mongolia, less than a tenth of respondents felt that their society was governed by the rule of law. In the other democracies, only a small minority (15–22 percent) gave a favorable evaluation. Yet in competitive authoritarian Malaysia, a third did.

TABLE 5—EVALUATION OF POLITICAL INSTITUTIONAL PERFORMANCE

	Freedom	Equality	Rule of Law	Electoral Competition	Accountability
Liberal Democracy					
Japan	50	19	49	46	22
South Korea	47	12	19	52	21
Taiwan	68	20	22	58	30
Electoral Democracy					
Indonesia	74	62	17	47	33
Mongolia	53	34	6	54	6
Philippines	63	20	15	39	29
Thailand	77	84	34	54	28
Competitive Authoritarianism					
Malaysia	74	59	35	56	39
Singapore	44	62	75	47	37

Notes: Entries are the percent of those having favorable responses to a pair of questions. Missing data not reported.
Source: ABS III

Electoral competition, another plank of liberal democracy, pertains to the degree to which the electoral process is free, fair, and competitive. One question here asked respondents to evaluate the freeness and fairness of the most recent national election. The other asked them whether they agreed or disagreed with the statement "Political parties or candidates have equal access to the mass media during the election period." In four of the seven democracies (South Korea, Mongolia, Thailand, and Taiwan), a majority (52–58 percent) considered the electoral process to be free, fair, and competitive (see Table 5). The Philippines displayed the least favorable evaluation, followed by Japan and Indonesia. In these countries, only a minority (39–47 percent) considered the electoral process to be free, fair, and competitive. Surprisingly, the competitive authoritarian regimes fared well: Evaluations in Malaysia were more favorable than those in every democracy except for Taiwan, and Singaporeans evaluated elections more favorably than did Japanese and Filipinos.

Lastly, we measured accountability, which pertains not only to the relationship between citizens and government leaders (vertical accountability) but also the relationship between branches of government (horizontal accountability). Our measures were again the responses to two agree-disagree statements: "Between elections the people have no way of holding the government responsible for its actions" and "When the government breaks the laws, there is nothing the legal system can do." Public evaluations of accountability in the democracies were largely negative; only in Indonesia did even a third evaluate accountability favorably. The two competitive authoritarian regimes fared much better. The findings illustrate the strengths and weaknesses of regimes across East Asia in the eyes of their publics. If we consider a favorable evaluation of a third or less as a failing mark of institutional performance, then South Korea, Taiwan, and the Philippines failed on three dimensions (equality, rule of law, and accountability); Japan and Mongolia failed on two (equality and accountability for Japan, and rule of law and accountability for Mongolia); and Thailand and Indonesia each failed on one (accountability for Thailand and the rule of law for Indonesia). Thus in every democracy examined—liberal or electoral—citizens perceived common problems in the rule of law and accountability and, somewhat less pervasively, a lack of equality. By contrast, the two competitive authoritarian regimes had no below-the-failing-mark evaluations.

If we consider majority public-approval level a minimum threshold for good performance, Thailand had a passing grade on three such dimensions (freedom, equality, and electoral competition), and Taiwan, Mongolia, and Indonesia had two passing marks. In Japan, South Korea, and the Philippines, however, respondents perceived good governance on only one such dimension (electoral competition in South Korea, and freedom in Japan and the Philippines). In six of the seven democracies surveyed, freedom received an approval level above the minimum threshold, whereas in four of the seven democracies electoral competition surpassed such a level. Both of these are hallmarks of "thin" democracy. Surprisingly, competitive authoritarian regimes fared better in the eyes of their publics, with the Malaysian system being evaluated well on three performance dimensions (freedom, equality, and electoral competition) and the Singaporean system on two (equality and the rule of law).

Overall, the prevailing systems of government surveyed in the region were viewed as deficient in controlling government corruption and official abuses of power. Moreover, they were also viewed as weak in nonelectoral popular control of government. Although electoral autocracies with a façade of controlled multiparty elections fared better on many dimensions, they too were viewed as deficient in nonelectoral accountability. In contrast to expert-based assessments, citizens of the three liberal democracies in East Asia do not view their prevailing systems of government as high-quality democracies.

Trust in representative institutions. In democratic settings, trust in political institutions may be used to indicate support for democratic institutions.[11] Since our study includes not only democracies but also competitive authoritarian regimes, we consider this measure to reflect support for the institutions of the regime-in-practice. In public-opinion surveys, the targets of trust include various public institutions such as parliament, courts, political parties, the armed forces, the police, and the civil service. In order to focus on representative political institutions,

TABLE 6—TRUST IN INSTITUTIONS

	Parliament	Political Parties	Both
Liberal Democracy			
Japan	11	9	5
South Korea	11	12	8
Taiwan	19	14	9
Electoral Democracy			
Indonesia	50	42	34
Mongolia	28	17	11
Philippines	43	35	25
Thailand	49	35	27
Competitive Authoritarianism			
Malaysia	70	54	49
Singapore	83	69	67

Notes: Entries are percentages. Missing data not reported.
Source: ABS III

here we have selected the parliament and political parties as the objects of trust (see Table 6).

Among the region's democracies, Indonesia displayed the highest level of trust in parliament, followed closely by Thailand. In these countries, about half the electorate expressed trust in parliament. In the Philippines, a large minority (43 percent) expressed some degree of trust in Congress. By contrast, only small minorities (11–28 percent) in Japan, South Korea, Taiwan, and Mongolia expressed some degree of trust in their legislatures. The Japanese and South Koreans were most cynical; only about one in ten trusted parliament. Competitive authoritarian regimes fared far better, with large majorities in Malaysia and Singapore expressing trust in parliament.

In most democracies, trust in political parties was even lower. There was no democracy surveyed in which a majority had trust in political parties. Indonesia displayed the highest level of trust (42 percent), followed by Thailand and the Philippines (35 percent in both). In these three countries, only a large minority trusted political parties. In the more advanced democracies of Japan, South Korea, and Taiwan, as well as in Mongolia, only small minorities (9–17 percent) had trust in political parties. In sharp contrast, more than two-thirds of respondents in Singapore and more than half in Malaysia trusted political parties.

By combining responses to both questions, we ascertained the level of trust in current representative institutions. In Japan, South Korea, and Taiwan, less than a tenth (5–9 percent) had trust in both institutions. Mongolia fared only a little better (11 percent). Other electoral democracies registered somewhat higher levels of trust in parliament and parties: In the Philippines, Thailand, and Indonesia, more than one in four (25–34 percent) trusted both institutions. By far the highest levels of political trust, however, were in Singapore (67 percent) and Malaysia (49 percent), suggesting that these regimes are resilient. Overall, ordinary citizens in East Asian liberal democracies appear highly cynical about parties and politicians. This finding should not be taken as a rejection of democratic institutions, however. As noted earlier, large majorities (73–81 percent) in the same countries support a multiparty system. Moreover, large majorities (80–83 percent) disagreed with the statement "We should get rid of parliament and elections and have a strong leader decide things." Similarly, a larger majority (87–91 percent) disagreed with the statement "Only one political party should be allowed to stand for election and hold office." These findings show a wide discrepancy between trust in current regime institutions and support for democratic institutions, suggesting the prevalence of "critical citizens" in East Asian liberal democracies. These critical citizens are supportive in general of democratic values and institutions but cynical about their actual political institutions.[12]

Sources of Political Support

Citizen support for a political regime is considered one of the critical conditions for regime stability. This is especially so for a democracy, which cannot be sustained without popular consent to its values, norms, and institutions. Hence, prior research has sought to understand what shapes citizen support for a political regime. Two competing explanations have emerged. The instrumental account emphasizes performance-driven political support. Within this account, some theorists emphasize economic performance[13] while others consider political performance to be more influential.[14] Unlike the instrumental account, the intrinsic view asserts that values and norms acquired through political socialization matter more than short-term performance.

Considering both views, we may divide sources of political support into three broad clusters: 1) normative commitment to the norms and institutions of democracy; 2) evaluation of political institutional performance; and 3) evaluation of policy performance. The first cluster includes four variables: checks and balances, the rule of law, social pluralism, and minimalist institutions.[15] The second cluster includes five variables: freedom, equality, the rule of law, electoral competition, and accountability.[16] The third cluster includes four variables: national economy, personal economy, basic welfare, and public safety.[17] In addition to these clusters, we have added one set of variables to represent demographic controls: age, educational attainment, and income.[18] We employed pooled cross-sectional data from the countries of each regime type for multivariate analysis.

TABLE 7—SOURCES OF DIFFUSE SUPPORT FOR DEMOCRACY

	Liberal Democracy	Electoral Democracy	Competitive Authoritarianism
Norms and Institutions			
Checks and balances	.045(.009)***	.035(.008)***	Ns
Rule of law	.018(.009)*	Ns	Ns
Social pluralism	.033(.008)***	Ns	-.065(.013)***
Minimalist democratic institutions	.210(.017)***	.086(.017)***	Ns
Institutional Performance			
Freedom	.109(.008)*	.019(.008)*	.024(.012)*
Equality	Ns	.017(.007)*	Ns
Rule of law	.043(.009)***	.039(.009)***	Ns
Electoral competition	.025(.009)**	.041(.009)***	.031(.015)*
Accountability	Ns	Ns	Ns
Policy Performance			
National economy	-.039(.012)***	Ns	Ns
Household economy	Ns	Ns	Ns
Basic welfare	Ns	Ns	Ns
Public safety	Ns	.048(.016)**	Ns
Demographic Controls			
Age	.026(.008)***	.041(.008)***	.045(.013)***
Education	.083(.016)***	.055(.014)***	.060(.023)**
Income	Ns	.060(.013)***	Ns
R-square	.127	.077	.059
(N)	(3,340)	(3,426)	(1,350)

Note: *p<0.05 **p<0.01 ***p<0.001
Source: ABS III

Diffuse democratic support. Table 7 shows the results of the multivariate analysis for diffuse support for democracy. For this dependent variable, we found that two institutional-performance variables—freedom and electoral competition—had the most frequent significant effects regardless of regime types. The effects of other key variables, however, do differ depending on regime type.

In liberal democracies, all four commitment variables—checks and balances, rule of law, social pluralism, and minimalist democratic institutions—had significant effects. The more that people are committed to liberal norms and minimalist institutions of democracy, the more likely they are to be supportive of democracy. Three of five institutional-performance variables had significant effects. Favorable evaluation of freedom, the rule of law, and electoral competition encouraged support for democracy. Notably, equality and accountability had no effects. Only one of the four policy-performance variables—national economy—had significant, albeit negative, effects. Neither basic welfare nor public safety had effects. Of the demographic variables, age and education had significant effects: Older people and the more educated were more supportive of democracy than younger people and the less educated, a common finding in this type of research.

In electoral democracies, two of four commitment variables had significant effects. The more that people are committed to checks and balances and minimalist institutions of democracy, the more likely they are to be supportive of democracy. In contrast, four of five institutional performance variables—freedom, equality, the rule of law, and electoral competition—had significant effects. The only exception was accountability. Only one policy-performance variable—public safety—contributed to diffuse support for democracy. All demographic variables had significant effects: older people, the more educated, and the affluent were more favorably disposed to democracy than younger people, the less educated, and the poor.

In competitive authoritarian regimes, only one of four commitment variables—social pluralism—had significant (albeit negative) effects. Oddly, the more that people are committed to social pluralism, the less likely they are to be supportive of democracy. Even adherence to minimalist institutions of democracy had no effects. Two of five institutional-performance variables—freedom and electoral competition—had significant effects. Yet none of the policy-performance variables had effects. Of the demographic variables, age and education had significant effects: Older people and the more educated were more supportive of democracy than younger people and the less educated.

As the coefficient of determination (R^2) indicated, our model was not successful at accounting for diffuse support for democracy at the individual level. Yet it should be noted that the model worked better in liberal democracies than in other types of regimes. The effects of commitment variables were more frequently found in liberal democracies than in electoral democracies. In contrast, the effects of institutional-performance variables were found more often in electoral democracies than in liberal democracies. This finding suggests that in electoral democracies diffuse support for democracy is more performance-based than in liberal democracies. Notably, neither norms nor performance mattered much in competitive authoritarian regimes.

In democratic settings, we would expect people to be more supportive of democracy when they consider regime performance to be satisfactory. In nondemocratic settings, however, better regime performance would not necessarily encourage support for democracy because there would be no reason for people to entertain democracy as an alternative if they found their regime's performance satisfactory. Perhaps this is why regime performance played little role in engendering diffuse support for democracy in competitive authoritarian regimes. Another notable find-

TABLE 8—SOURCES OF DIFFUSE SUPPORT FOR THE REGIME-IN-PRACTICE

	Liberal Democracy	Electoral Democracy	Competitive Authoritarianism
Norms and Institutions			
Checks and balances	-.045(.018)*	Ns	-.062(.024)**
Rule of law	Ns	Ns	Ns
Social pluralism	Ns	Ns	-.068(.023)**
Minimalist democratic institutions	Ns	.076(.036)*	Ns
Institutional Performance			
Freedom	.061(.016)***	.054(.017)**	.061(.020)**
Equality	.121(.018)***	.213(.015)***	.152(.020)***
Rule of law	.145(.018)***	.139(.018)***	.081(.019)***
Electoral competition	.134(.018)***	.112(.019)***	.178(.026)***
Accountability	.043(.015)**	Ns	Ns
Policy Performance			
National economy	.134(.024)***	.209(.028)***	.292(.038)***
Household economy	.100(.029)***	Ns	Ns
Basic welfare	.122(.029)***	.141(.026)***	.275(.046)***
Public safety	.138(.031)***	.156(.033)***	Ns
Demographic Controls			
Age	.093(.016)***	.061(.018)***	.048(.023)*
Education	Ns	-.151(.029)***	Ns
Income	Ns	Ns	-.161(.035)***
R-square	.206	.253	.331
(N)	(3,291)	(3,431)	(1,362)

Note: *p<0.05 **p<0.01 ***p<0.001
Source: ABS III

ing is that policy performance mattered little, regardless of regime type.

Diffuse regime support. Having analyzed the sources of diffuse democratic support, we now turn to the sources of diffuse support for the regime-in-practice—democratic or autocratic (see Table 8). In liberal democracies, only one of the four commitment variables had significant, albeit negative, effects. The more that people are committed to checks and balances, the less likely they are to be supportive of the prevailing system of government, suggesting that their democracy-in-practice was viewed as short of this element of limited government. By contrast, all five institutional-performance variables had significant effects. Moreover, all four policy-performance variables had significant effects. Of the demographic controls, only age had a significant effect, indicating that older people were more supportive of the regime-in-practice than younger people.

In electoral democracies, only one of the four commitment variables had significant effects: The more that people are committed to institutions of minimalist democracy, the more likely they are to be supportive of the regime-in-practice. Yet, four of the five institutional-performance variables (the exception being accountability) had significant effects. Of the four, equality was the strongest predictor. Similarly, three of the four policy-performance variables had significant effects. Among them, the national economy was the strongest predictor. Of the demographic controls, age had positive effects while education produced negative effects. Younger people and the more educated were more critical of the regime-in-practice than older people and the less educated.

In competitive authoritarian regimes, two of the four commitment variables had significant but negative effects: The more that people are committed to checks and balances and social pluralism, the less likely they are to be supportive of the regime-in-practice. At the same time, four of the five institutional-performance variables had significant effects. In particular, the impact of electoral competition was most notable. Two of the four policy-performance variables—the national economy and basic welfare—had significant effects. The more that people are inclined toward favorable evaluations of the national economy and the provision of basic welfare, the more likely they are to be supportive of the regime-in-practice. Of the demographic controls, age had a positive (albeit weak) effect, while income had a negative effect. The better off were far more critical of the ongoing political order than the worse off.

As the coefficient of determination (R^2) indicated, our model was relatively successful in accounting for diffuse support for the regime-in-practice at the individual level, especially in competitive authoritarian regimes, where the entire set of variables accounted for a third (33 percent) of the variance in diffuse regime support.

Unlike diffuse support for democracy, diffuse support for the regime-in-practice was largely shaped by political and socioeconomic performance. Significant performance variables differed among regime types. In liberal democracies, there was no single dominant performance variable, although the rule of law seemed slightly more important. By contrast, in electoral democracies equality and the national economy emerged as the most important predictors. In competitive authoritarian regimes, the national economy and basic welfare emerged as stronger predictors. Equality, electoral competition, the national economy, and basic welfare turned out to be consistent predictors of diffuse support for the regime-in-practice, regardless of regime type. Accountability, one of the key procedural dimensions of democracy, played little or no role. One of the most notable findings is that adherence to liberal norms had negative, if any, effects, suggesting that the ongoing political orders—democratic or autocratic—fall short on some standards of limited government in the eyes of their citizens.

In liberal democracies, institutional performance played a limited role in engendering support for democracy but a notable role in fostering support for the regime-in-practice. Adherence to liberal norms contributed to diffuse support for democracy but undermined diffuse support for the regime-in-practice, suggesting that the spread of liberal democratic norms may have something to do with the phenomenon of democratic deficit.[19]

In electoral democracies, institutional performance contributed to both support for democracy and support for the regime-in-practice. Policy performance, however, contributed little to support for democracy, but it did encourage support for the regime-in-practice. This finding suggests that satisfactory institutional performance would help to further democratic consolidation, but satisfactory policy performance may not contribute to democratic deepening.

In competitive authoritarian regimes, neither institutional performance nor policy performance contributed much to support for democracy. They did, however, increase support for the regime-in-practice, suggesting that satisfactory regime performance may help to strengthen regime stability. Poor performance may weaken support for the prevailing system of government, but may not strengthen support for democracy. What would undermine support for the autocracy-in-practice would be the spread of liberal norms such as checks and balances and social pluralism.

Overall, what emerged from the analysis is that institutional performance made a negligible contribution to diffuse support for democracy but a notable contribution to diffuse support for the regime-in-practice. Policy performance hardly encouraged support for democracy, but it did facilitate support for the regime-in-practice. Adherence to liberal norms encouraged support for democracy but contributed little to support for the regime-in-practice. Diffuse support for democracy is hardly performance-based, while diffuse support for the regime-in-practice is largely performance-based. Hence, good performance may strengthen support for the ongoing political order but may not necessarily encourage support for democracy. It is commitment to liberal norms and basic institutions of democracy that fosters support for democracy.

Seven Key Points

Using cross-national survey data drawn from ABS III, we have described here how East Asians orient themselves toward political regimes. Building on David Easton's theory of political support, we have distinguished between three levels of citizen orientations toward regimes—values, norms and rules, and institutions. Furthermore, we differentiated between orientations to democracy and evaluations of the regime-in-practice. In order to ascertain possible discrepancies between idealistic orientations and realistic evaluations, we contrasted support for democracy as an idea with evaluation of the regime-in-practice.

Seven key points emerge from our study. First, the analysis shows that diffuse support for democracy—as measured by both the preference for democracy over its alternatives and the acceptance of democracy as the best form of government—has yet to be firmly entrenched across much of East Asia. Even in the three liberal democracies surveyed, those both preferring democracy to any alternatives (especially authoritarian regimes) and considering democracy to be the best form of government have yet to reach a two-thirds majority.

Second, support for liberal norms associated with limited government was fairly weak—far weaker than diffuse support for democracy, indicating that avowed support for democracy is not rooted in specific liberal norms and procedures. This finding suggests that a considerable number of East Asians could be indifferent to illiberal or delegative democracy.

Third, support for minimalist institutions of democracy such as popular elections and a multiparty system remains firm in much of East Asia. In fact, preference for these institutions was more robust than adherence to liberal norms. In this regard, it is no wonder that rejection of strongman or single-party rule was overwhelming in much of the region. Yet support for minimalist democratic institutions was lower than diffuse support for democracy in some sample countries, suggesting that varying conceptions of democracy are held by ordinary citizens.

Fourth, diffuse support for the regime-in-practice remained low in most democracies examined. Pride in the system was generally much lower than loyalty to (rather than exit from) the system, indicating the prevalence of a realist view of democracy-in-practice as "a lesser evil." It is notable that diffuse regime support was much higher in competitive authoritarian regimes than in most democracies, suggesting that the former faced weaker pressure for regime change from ordinary people.

Fifth, evaluation of institutional performance varied depending on its dimension. Evaluation of freedom was largely favorable across most of the region, and evaluation of electoral competition was fairly favorable in much of the region. In contrast, East Asian democracies, liberal or electoral, all suffered from a public perception of weakness in rule of law and poor accountability. Equality was another perceived failing in the eyes of citizens of many East Asian democracies. Despite lacking the institutions and mechanisms of democracy, the two competitive authoritarian regimes fared better on almost every dimension in the view of their citizens, especially in the area of law-based governance.

Sixth, public trust in parliament and political parties, the hallmarks of representative democracy, remained low across most of the region except for the competitive authoritarian regimes. In particular, political cynicism ran deeper in liberal democracies than in electoral democracies, reflecting a global phenomenon of critical citizens who have little trust in parliament and political parties but still favor democratic institutions and processes.

Lastly, citizen support for democracy was based more frequently on adherence to minimalist institutions and some liberal norms. Citizen support for the regime-in-practice, however, was based largely on evaluation of regime performance. In liberal and electoral democracies, institutional performance proved to be more relevant than policy performance. In competitive authoritarian regimes, by contrast, policy performance mattered more than institutional performance. The growth of popular support for democracy seems to require adherence to liberal norms and minimalist democratic institutions, whereas the growth of popular support for the regime-in-practice appears to depend on the institutions and practices of good governance as well as satisfactory policy outcomes.

Each regime type in East Asia appears to face its own political challenges. Liberal democracies face publics whose orientations toward democracy tend to be more favorable than their evaluations of the regime-in-practice, and these democracies are thus likely to be under public pressure to reform the prevailing system of government to achieve "thick" democracy. Meanwhile, electoral democracies face publics whose evaluations of their regime-in-practice tend to be as favorable as their orientations toward democracy, and these regimes are thus likely to experience slow or faltering democratic consolidation or progress. Finally, the two competitive authoritarian regimes face publics whose evaluations of the regime-in-practice tend to be far more favorable than their orientations toward democracy, and these regimes (especially Singapore) are thus likely to remain resilient in the midst of global democratization.

NOTES

1. Yun-han Chu et al., eds., *How East Asians View Democracy* (New York: Columbia University Press, 2008); Doh Chull Shin, "The Third Wave in East Asia: Comparative and Dynamic Perspectives," *Taiwan Journal of Democracy* 4 (December 2008): 91–131; Larry Diamond, "China and East Asian Democracy: The Coming Wave," *Journal of Democracy* 23 (January 2012): 5–13.

2. For the concept of competitive authoritarianism, see Steven Levitsky and Lucan A. Way, *Competitive Authoritarianism: Hybrid Regimes After the Cold War* (Cambridge: Cambridge University Press, 2010).

3. David Easton, *A Systems Analysis of Political Life* (New York: Wiley, 1965); David Easton, "A Re-Assessment of the Concept of Political Support," *British Journal of Political Science* 5 (October 1975): 435–457.

4. Easton, *A Systems Analysis of Political Life*, 177 and 193.

5. Russell J. Dalton, *Democratic Challenges, Democratic Choices: The Erosion of Political Support in Advanced Industrial Democracies* (Oxford: Oxford University Press, 2004), 5–9 and 22–25.

6. Pippa Norris, "Introduction: The Growth of Critical Citizens?" in Pippa Norris, ed., *Critical Citizens: Global Support for Democratic Governance* (Oxford: Oxford University Press, 1999), 9–13.

7. John A. Booth and Mitchell A. Seligson, *The Legitimacy Puzzle in Latin America: Political Support and Democracy in Eight Nations* (New York: Cambridge University Press, 2009), 49–55.

8. Damarys Canache, Jeffery Mondak, and Mitchell Seligson, "Meaning and Measurement in Cross-National Research on Satisfaction with Democracy," *Public Opinion Quarterly* 65 (Winter 2001): 506–28.

9. Christian Welzel and Ronald Inglehart, "The Role of Ordinary People in Democratization," *Journal of Democracy* 19 (January 2008): 126–40.

10. See, for example, Joe Foweraker and Roman Krznaric, "Measuring Liberal Democratic Performance: An Empirical and Conceptual Critique," *Political Studies* 48 (September 2000): 759–87; Larry Diamond and Leonardo Morlino, "The Quality of Democracy: An Overview," *Journal of Democracy* 15 (October 2004): 20–31.

11. See, for example, Ola Listhaug and Matti Wiberg, "Confidence in Political and Private Institutions," in Hans-Dieter Klingemann and Dieter Fuchs, eds., *Citizens and the State* (Oxford: Oxford University Press, 1995), 298–322.

12. See, for example, Norris, *Critical Citizens*.

13. See, for example, Seymour Martin Lipset, "Some Social Requisites of Democracy: Economic Development and Political Legitimacy," *American Political Science Review* 53 (March 1959): 69–105; Peter Kotzian, "Public Support for Liberal Democracy," *International Political Science Review* 32 (January 2011): 23–41.

14. See, for example, Geoffrey Evans and Stephen Whitefield, "The Politics and Economics of Democratic Commitment: Support for Democracy in Transition Societies," *British Journal of Political Science* 25 (October 1995): 485–514; Richard Rose, William Mishler, and Christian Haerpfer, *Democracy and Its Alternatives: Understanding Post-Communist Societies* (Baltimore: Johns Hopkins University Press, 1998); Michael Bratton and Robert Mattes, "Support for Democracy in Africa: Intrinsic or Instrumental," *British Journal of Political Science* 31 (July 2001): 447–74.

15. Each variable was constructed by simply adding the scores of its two constituent indicators. The resulting scores of the first three variables ranged from 1 to 7, while those of the last variable ranged from 1 to 3.

16. Each variable was constructed by simply adding the scores of its two constituent indicators. The resulting scores of each variable ranged from 1 to 7.

17. To measure evaluation of the national economy, we asked, "How would you rate the overall economic condition of our country today?" We also asked, "How would you rate your economic situation today?" Responses to each question were coded as follows: very good=5, good=4, not good or bad=3, bad=2, and very bad=1. To measure evaluation of basic welfare, we selected one agree-disagree question: "People have basic necessities like food, clothes, and shelter." Responses were coded as follows: strongly agree=4, somewhat agree=3, somewhat disagree=2, and strongly disagree=1. To measure evaluation of

public safety, we asked "How safe is living in this city/town/village?" Responses were coded as follows: very safe=4, safe=3, unsafe=2, and very unsafe=1.

18. Age was coded as 17–29=1, 30–39=2, 40–49=3, 50–59=4, and 60+=5. Educational attainment was coded as less than high school=1, high school=2, and some college+=3. Income was substituted with subjective income adequacy, which was measured by asking the following question: "Does the total income of your household allow you to satisfactorily cover your needs?" Responses were coded as follows: "our income covers the needs well, we can save"=4; "our income covers the needs all right, without much difficulty"=3; "our income does not cover the needs, there are difficulties"=2; and "our income does not cover the needs, there are great difficulties"=1.

19. For a systematic attempt to account for the democratic deficit, see Pippa Norris, *Democratic Deficit: Critical Citizens Revisited* (Cambridge: Cambridge University Press, 2011).

II

Northeast Asia

5

IS CCP RULE FRAGILE
OR RESILIENT?

Minxin Pei

Minxin Pei *is the Tom and Margot Pritzker '72 Professor of Government and director of the Keck Center for International and Strategic Studies at Claremont McKenna College. He is the author, most recently, of* China's Trapped Transition: The Limits of Developmental Autocracy *(2006). This essay originally appeared in the January 2012 issue of the* Journal of Democracy.

The continuing survival of authoritarian regimes around the world and the apparent resilience of such regimes in several major countries, particularly China and Russia, have attracted enormous scholarly interest in recent years.[1] Analysts have put forward various theories to explain the success and durability of these regimes. Some theories focus on authoritarians' capacity to learn from mistakes (their own as well as those made by other authoritarians) and adapt accordingly. Others center around an observed correlation between high natural-resource rents and regime survival. Still others identify the repressive capacity of authoritarian regimes as the key to their durability, while a final group of explanations pays special attention to the capacity of authoritarian regimes to institutionalize their rule.

These theories may provide tantalizing explanations for the endurance of authoritarian regimes, but they suffer from one common weakness: They are ad hoc and inductive. Moreover, they have a selection-bias problem resulting from small sample sizes (limited by the number of surviving autocracies). As a result, when supposedly invulnerable autocracies crumble in the face of mass protest and popular uprising, the explanations of authoritarian resilience largely break down. The series of popular revolts in 2011 that toppled autocracies in Tunisia and Egypt, triggered a civil war in Libya, and sparked prolonged and bloody anti-regime protests in Syria and Yemen provide a humbling lesson for those who had viewed those regimes as "robust" and "resilient."

In terms of authoritarian resilience, the People's Republic of China

(PRC) stands out as exemplary. Not only did the ruling Chinese Communist Party (CCP) survive the turbulent spring of 1989, when millions of protesters nationwide nearly toppled its rule and it put down demonstrations in Beijing's Tiananmen Square with dramatic violence, but it has since thrived. The ruling elites coalesced around a new strategy that joined the promotion of rapid (mostly export-led) economic growth to the preservation of one-party rule through selective political repression. The rapid growth of the Chinese economy in the post-Tiananmen era has lent the CCP popular legitimacy and the resources to defend its political monopoly. The party has demonstrated remarkable tactical sophistication, a knack for adaptation, and a capacity for asserting control. It has succeeded in maintaining unity within the elite cadres, resisted the global tide of democratization, and prevented the revolution in communications technologies from undermining its grip on the flow of information. It has also manipulated nationalism to bolster its support among the young and better educated, eliminated any form of organized opposition, and contained social unrest through a combination of carrots and sticks.

The CCP's ability to consolidate authoritarian rule even as a wave of democratic openings swept much of the world after 1989 raises several important questions. Does the Chinese case validate any of the theories of authoritarian resilience advanced by scholars who specialize in the study of other regions? What are the explanations for authoritarian resilience in China, and what evidence supports them? Are these explanations theoretically robust? Is authoritarian resilience in China a passing phenomenon, or is it something more durable?

Explaining Authoritarian Resilience

Theories of authoritarian survival all share a common feature: They turn theories of democratic transition upside down. Specifically, they attempt either to identify the *absence* of factors normally favorable to democratic transition or to pinpoint the *presence* of unfavorable factors associated with the prevention of democratic transition. Among all these explanations, three stand out.

The first focuses on matters of political economy. Generally speaking, authoritarian regimes that are dependent on natural-resource rents tend to be more durable. Such regimes are able to buy off the population with high welfare spending and low taxation. Resource-based rents also allow autocratic regimes to escape political accountability and maintain a strong repressive apparatus. Authoritarian regimes with significant control over economic resources, such as state-owned enterprises, have greater survival capabilities because such control allows rulers to keep their key supporters loyal through patronage and to reassert their influence over the economy.

The capacity to adapt to new social and political challenges is a second variable associated with authoritarian resilience. For example, a number of authoritarian regimes have managed to stay in power by manipulating elections. The long-ruling one-party regimes in Malaysia and Singapore stand out for the sophistication of their political institutions. During its 71-year reign, Mexico's Institutional Revolutionary Party (PRI) was said to have maintained a "perfect dictatorship" featuring highly developed political institutions that managed leadership succession and generated popular support.[2] Resilient authoritarian regimes adapt by learning to differentiate between the types of public goods that they provide. More sophisticated autocracies typically supply welfare-enhancing public goods such as economic growth but limit "coordination goods" such as the freedom of information and association, in order to reduce the opposition's ability to organize.[3]

The third explanation concerns the balance of power between the regime and opposition. Despite its obvious importance, the role of repression in the survival of autocracies has received surprisingly little attention. Yet a simple and persuasive explanation for authoritarians' longevity is that they are ready, willing, and able to use the coercive power necessary to suppress any societal challenge. More than anything else, it is effective repression that has sustained the Middle East's autocracies.[4] As long as this balance of power favors autocratic regimes, their survival is guaranteed by the application of repression. Of course, if the military refuses support, as happened in Tunisia and Egypt in early 2011, the balance of power shifts decisively and the regime is doomed.

In the Chinese context, the discussion about authoritarian resilience has centered around three themes—regime institutionalization, organizational learning and adaptation, and organizational and administrative capacity. Regime institutionalization—the process through which important norms and rules of the game are formulated and enforced—is thought by some to be the key to the CCP regime's durability. Since 1989, the CCP supposedly has greatly improved the procedures governing political succession, defined functional responsibilities, and promoted elites on the basis of merit. These and other measures, according to Andrew Nathan, have greatly increased the degree of institutionalization within the CCP, enabling it to survive and succeed.[5] In Steve Tsang's view, the post-Tiananmen regime has evolved into a distinct and more resilient form of Leninist rule by adopting a mixture of survival strategies that focus on governance reforms (to preempt public demands for democratization), greater capacity for responding to public opinion, pragmatic economic management (considerations of socialist ideology take a back seat to the need for growth), and appeals to nationalism. Tsang calls this "consultative Leninism."[6]

Those who stress the second theme—organizational learning and adaptation—note that authoritarian elites are motivated by an urge to survive and can draw useful lessons from the demise or collapse of their counterparts in other parts of the world. As a result, a regime may adopt new policies that contribute to its longevity and power. David Shambaugh argues that the collapse of the USSR taught the CCP valuable lessons, leading it to implement effective policy responses to post–Cold War challenges both at home and abroad.[7]

The third theme stresses that, compared to other developing-world autocracies, China's organizational and administrative capacity is exceptional. Since 1989, the CCP has undertaken further measures to strengthen the capacity of the Chinese state in revenue collection and regulatory enforcement. By building state capacity, the CCP has made itself more resilient.[8]

These explanations of the Chinese regime's durability leave several important questions unanswered. For example, is regime survival the same thing as regime resilience? Scholars studying the persistence of authoritarian rule in China rarely make a conceptual distinction between the two. Yet the mere fact of regime survival does not necessarily indicate regime resilience; survival is an empirical measurement, whereas resilience is a subjective concept. Thus authoritarian regimes that survive are not necessarily resilient.

If it lacks strong opposition or employs brutal repression, even a decrepit autocracy—that is, one without a high degree of institutionalization or performance-based legitimacy—may hang on for a long time. It would, for example, be a definitional stretch to label the personalistic dictatorship of Zimbabwe's elderly Robert Mugabe a "resilient autocracy." What, after all, constitutes the resilience of a regime? Longevity is perhaps the most-used criterion, and by that standard, the regimes of Burma, Cuba, and North Korea would be considered resilient. But because the word "resilience" implies inherent strengths and the capacity to endure and overcome adversity, regime survival reflects only one aspect of resilience, not others. In fact, these regimes appear to live under perpetual siege and in a permanent state of crisis and insecurity, making it hard to call them resilient. Even for the more successful authoritarian regimes—China and, to a lesser extent, Russia—their degree of resilience is debatable. In the case of China, for example, the CCP faces daily instances of defiance and disturbances, ranging from hundreds of local protests to accidents and disasters caused by corruption and incompetence. It is forced to devote massive resources to maintaining domestic order.

Authoritarian resilience, however defined, may result from tried-and-true survival tactics rather than the adoption of innovative political strategies. Although many studies have focused on autocrats' use of semicompetitive elections to legitimize their power and on authoritarian regimes' successful management of succession and promotion of regime elites,[9] the more critical variables are economic patronage, political cooptation, and ruthlessly effective repression. For all their current success and perceived strengths, authoritarian regimes have not been able to address effectively the systemic and well-known weaknesses that imperil their long-term survival and limit their policy choices in responding to public demands. Such weaknesses include political illegitimacy; endemic corruption caused by lack of political accountability and misalignment of interests between the regime and its agents; political exclusion of the middle class; and predatory state policies that victimize and alienate disadvantaged social groups. As long as such systemic weaknesses persist under authoritarian rule, autocracy is unlikely to remain resilient.

To be sure, some authoritarian regimes have helped their survival chances by improving internal rules governing succession and promotion, learning useful lessons from the success or failures of other authoritarian regimes, strengthening the administrative capacity of the state, and managing to restrict the provision of coordination goods. Such autocracies are undeniably more sophisticated in institutional and tactical terms than garden-variety dictatorships in developing countries. But an explanation of the survival of "resilient" authoritarian regimes must take into account the additional factors that enable them to maintain power and the underlying forces that threaten their long-term survival. Such a comprehensive analytical approach is likely to yield more useful insights into the political dynamics of regime survival and demise in contemporary autocracies.

In particular, we should consider simpler and more straightforward explanations for the survival of authoritarian regimes—economic performance, for example. Everything else being equal, empirical research shows that authoritarian regimes that manage to perform well economically tend to survive longer.[10] Obviously, autocracies gain political legitimacy if the standard of living rises as a result of sustained economic growth. Autocratic regimes can use the resulting rents to coopt the middle class and redistribute the benefits from growth among the ruling elites, thus avoiding internecine struggles over a more or less fixed set of spoils. Sustained economic growth in an authoritarian regime also allows ruling elites to finance and maintain an extensive repressive apparatus to suppress political opposition.

Another straightforward explanation is that the greater the range of a regime's survival strategies—the more diversified its "portfolio" of methods for staying in power—the more likely it is to endure. Force alone may sustain some authoritarian regimes, but heavy use of repression can be costly. Moreover, large military and internal-security forces will consume resources that might otherwise be spent on nonrepressive survival strategies such as cooptation and patronage. Highly repressive regimes are also unlikely to instill confidence in private entrepreneurs or to create business opportunities for them. Robert Barro has found that heavy repression depresses economic growth, while moderate repression may have a positive impact.[11] In autocracies that rely solely on repression, economic performance tends to be abysmal, sowing the seeds of social discontent and sapping regime legitimacy.

Even if a regime's economic performance has been satisfactory and its survival strategies and tactics sophisticated, it must still contend with autocracy's inherent flaws—the absence of procedural legitimacy, a narrow base of social support, gross misalignment of interests between the regime and its agents, and systemic and pervasive corruption—all of which threaten its long-term durability. Thus, perceived authoritarian resilience is, in all likelihood, a temporary phenomenon that conceals fatal weaknesses.

The Keys to CCP Survival

The three keys to the CCP's survival are refined repression, economic statism, and political cooptation. Proponents of the authoritarian-resilience theory have downplayed or overlooked their role. Although autocracies may use other, sometimes more sophisticated, means of keeping power, the most important is the use of violence against political opposition. No autocracy has survived without in some way resorting to repression. The difference between more successful autocracies and less successful ones lies mainly in how they use repression. The more successful autocracies do so more selectively, efficiently, and effectively while the less successful ones typically repress opposition in cruder, more wasteful, and less productive ways.

Since the early 1990s, China has shifted toward "smart repression." The CCP has narrowed the scope and shifted the focus of its repressive actions. While the CCP continues to restrict people's political freedoms and civil rights, it has almost completely withdrawn from their private lives and stopped meddling in lifestyle issues. At the same time, the regime has drawn a clear line against organized political opposition, which is not tolerated in any form.

Selective repression, such as brutally suppressing the quasi-spiritual group the Falun Gong or targeting leading dissidents, avoids antagonizing the majority of the population while achieving the objectives of political decapitation and preventing organized opposition from emerging. This approach also conserves the regime's repressive resources and utilizes them more efficiently. The CCP regime has become more selective in its application of harsh crackdowns both because it learned lessons from the 1989 experience and because of the party-state's institutional decentralization. China's multiple levels of authority allow the regime to avoid either using excessive repression or making needless concessions in dealing with popular resistance.[12]

The regime's repressive tactics have also grown more sophisticated, even as the Party remains ruthless in defending its political monopoly. It now favors a less brutal approach, forcing top dissidents into exile abroad, for example, rather than sentencing them to long prison terms. Routine harassment of human-rights activists and political dissidents has taken on softer forms: Inviting them to have tea with the police is a favorite tactic. The regime's methods for dealing with rising social unrest have likewise become more sophisticated. Confronted with hundreds of collective protests and riots each day, the party-state has shown a considerable capacity to deploy highly effective measures such as quickly arresting and jailing protest leaders to decapitate local unrest, disperse crowds, and pacify the masses.[13]

The regime's efforts at manipulating public opinion have also become more complex—a mix of harsh censorship and campaigning for popular support. Rather than simply relying on old-fashioned ideological indoctrination, the CCP's propaganda department has, in recent years, learned to influence the social agenda by showcasing the Party's success in addressing social issues such as rising housing prices and declining access to healthcare. Although this approach has not been entirely successful, it is a telling example of the CCP's growing tactical sophistication.

Through its massive investment in manpower, technology, and training, the CCP has greatly improved the operational capabilities of its already well-funded, well-equipped, and well-trained security forces. The CCP has dealt with the emergence of new threats, such as information and communication technologies, with relatively effective countermeasures that include both regulatory restrictions and technological fixes. In this manner, the regime has contained the political impact of the information revolution, although it has had to adopt new tactics in order to do so. Instead of losing its grip on the flow of information, the CCP's propaganda operations have grown more sophisticated, helping to guard the CCP's political hegemony.

The Party's operational capabilities with regard to emergency management have also improved during the last decade. In 2003, with the SARS outbreak, China faced its first major public-health crisis since the end of the Cultural Revolution. The government's initial response was incompetent and ineffective. After replacing key leaders, however, the regime quickly turned the situation around. Natural disasters, major accidents, protests, and the like are frequent in China. Because of better emergency response, however, such periodic shocks have not inflicted serious damage on CCP control.

The CCP fully understands the inseparable link between political survival and control over the country's economic resources. Without its ability to hand out economic rents, the Party would surely lose the loyalty of its supporters and its ability to retain power. Thus the CCP keeps extensive and tight control over China's state-owned enterprises so that it can dole out political patronage.[14] This means that the Party is inherently incapable of implementing market-oriented reforms beyond a certain point, since they will ultimately undermine its political base. China's stalled economic reform in recent years has vindicated this view. Indeed, the Party has not only publicly announced its intention of retaining state control of key economic sectors such as finance, energy, telecom services, and transportation, but has also successfully defended these monopolies or oligopolies from domestic and international competition. State-owned firms dominate these industries, while private firms and foreign competitors are kept out. Such policies have slowed the pace of privatization but enabled the state to remain the country's most powerful economic actor.

Even after three decades of economic reform, firms owned or controlled by the party-state account for close to 40 percent of China's GDP. The regime's domination of the economy rose to a new level after the government used aggressive fiscal and monetary policies to maintain high rates of growth following the 2008 global economic crisis. With a fiscal-stimulus package of nearly US$700 billion and $2 trillion in new bank loans, the Chinese state further strengthened state-owned enterprises at the expense of the private sector.[15]

While the economic-efficiency losses caused by the state's continuing and deep involvement in the economy are huge, the political benefits of this strategy are clear. The Party retains the power to appoint top officials in state-owned firms and the capacity to distribute lucrative economic rents to its key constituents (bureaucrats and businessmen with ties to the ruling elites). For members of these groups, the Communist Party's patronage pays. One study shows that politically connected firms often have higher offering prices when their stocks are listed on China's equity markets.[16] Economic patronage thus serves a dual function: It is both a critical instrument for influencing economic activities and a source of incentives to secure and maintain the backing of the regime's key political supporters.

In addition to keeping a strong hand on the levers of the economy, authoritarian regimes can help to extend their lives by expanding their social bases. Since the early 1990s, the CCP has been working successfully to do just that, building an elite alliance through cooptation. Elevating the political status of the intelligentsia and the professional class and improving their material benefits—while simultaneously using regulations and sanctions to penalize and deter intellectuals who dare to challenge the regime—are the most important elements of this strategy.

The Party has systematically campaigned to recruit the intelligentsia and professionals into its fold and to award them important technocratic appointments. This effort has succeeded both in raising the CCP's technocratic capacity and in extending its base into the intelligentsia, an elite social group that was at odds with the Party in the 1980s over the issue of political reform.[17] The much-publicized effort to recruit private entrepreneurs into the Party has done less to expand its social base, since the majority of private owners of nonagricultural firms were already Party members who had used their power to convert state-owned assets into private property. Nevertheless, numerous studies have concluded that the CCP has been relatively successful in coopting private entrepreneurs. Some scholars have even called Chinese private entrepreneurs "allies of the state."[18] One case study finds that local officials who are supportive of the private sector have proven to be more effective in incorporating private businesspeople into local power structures.[19]

The CCP's strategy of political cooptation has been unexpectedly successful, leading some observers to argue that China's emerging middle class mainly favors the status quo. In addition to pacifying the middle class, the CCP has managed to transform its own membership base. During the Mao era, it was predominantly a party of peasants and workers; now it is a party of elites. According to official figures released in 2010, roughly 10 percent of the Party's 78 million members at the end of 2009 were workers and 20 percent were farmers. The remaining 70 percent were bureaucrats, managers, retired officials, professionals, college students, and intellectuals. Particularly noteworthy is the high proportion of well-educated individuals in the CCP—36 percent were either college graduates or had received some college education, and 15 percent were management, technical, and professional personnel and college students.[20] By comparison, less than 8 percent of China's total population is college-educated. In short, political cooptation has turned the Party into an elite-based alliance. The incorporation of key social elites into an authoritarian regime generates significant political benefits for the rulers. Among other things, it denies potential opposition groups access to social elites and makes it much harder for lower-status groups to organize and become effective political forces.

Behind the Façade of Authoritarian Strength

There is a sharp and intriguing discrepancy between how strong autocracies seem to outsiders and how insecure the rulers themselves feel. Autocrats are constantly on guard against forces that pose even the slightest threat to their rule, expending tremendous resources and taking excessively harsh and repressive measures in the process. But if authoritarian regimes really were so strong, then such costly measures motivated by insecurity would be self-defeating and counterproductive: They would be unnecessary and, by wasting a regime's scarce resources, would undermine its long-term survival. So why is there this discrepancy? The answer is quite simple: The authoritarian strength that outsiders perceive is merely an illusion. Insiders—the authoritarians themselves—possess information about the regime's weaknesses that outsiders know little about. These weaknesses make authoritarians feel insecure and prompt them to act accordingly.

The resilience of China's authoritarian regime may be a temporary phenomenon, fated to succumb eventually to autocracy's institutional and systemic defects. These defects are inherent features of autocratic systems and therefore uncorrectable. Thus the measures that the CCP has taken since the early 1990s to strengthen its rule (regardless of how effective they may have been) merely serve to offset somewhat the deleterious effects that these flaws have on regime survival. In the long run, China's authoritarian regime is likely to lose its resilience.

Ironically, an authoritarian regime's short-term success can imperil its long-term survival and effectiveness. Success, defined in terms of suppressing political opposition and defending a political monopoly, makes it more likely that authoritarians, unrestrained by political opposition, free media, and the rule of law, will engage in looting and theft, inevitably weakening the regime's capacity for survival.

Authoritarian regimes tend to breed corruption for a variety of reasons. A principal cause is the relatively short time horizon of autocrats, whose hold on power is tenuous, uncertain, and insecure. Even where the rules of succession and promotion have improved, as they have in China, such improvement is only relative to the previous state of affairs. Succession at the top remains opaque and unpredictable in China. Although the top leadership has managed to reach compromises through bargaining, thereby avoiding destabilizing power struggles, succession politics continues to be mired in intrigue and factionalism. In the case of promotion, the only objective rule appears to be an age requirement; all the other factors that are supposedly merit-based can be gamed. The fact that many officials resort to bribery to gain promotions indicates that personal favoritism continues to play an important role in internal Party promotions.[21]

All this renders uncertain the political future of members of the CCP hierarchy and thus encourages predatory behavior. There is evidence that corruption has worsened in China in recent years despite periodic anticorruption campaigns launched by the CCP.[22] More important, because of the deep and extensive involvement of the Chinese party-state in the economy, the combination of motives (driven by uncertainty) and opportunity (access to economic rents) can create an ideal environment for regime insiders to engage in collusion, looting, and theft.

Corruption endangers the long-term survival of authoritarian regimes in several ways. It can hinder economic growth, thus reducing the regime's political legitimacy and capacity to underwrite a costly patronage system and maintain its repressive apparatus. Corruption also contributes to rising inequality by benefiting a small number of well-connected elites at the expense of public welfare, thus further fueling antiregime sentiments and social tensions. Corruption creates a high-risk environment, making it difficult to enforce regulations governing the workplace, food and drugs, traffic, and environmental safety, thereby increasing the risks of accidents and disasters and the likelihood of mismanaged government responses to them.[23]

The Limits of Political Cooptation

By nature, autocracies are exclusionary political coalitions. Although the incorporation of social elites can generate short-term benefits for rulers, it is a costly and ultimately unsustainable strategy because the modernization process produces social elites at a faster rate than authoritarian rulers can coopt them. Eventually, the regime will be unable to afford to coopt so many social elites, thus creating a potential pool of opposition leaders.

A key test of the CCP's capacity for coopting new social elites is the employment of college graduates. Since the late 1990s, college and university enrollment in China has shot upward. In 1997, Chinese tertiary educational institutions admitted a million new students; in 2009, they admitted 6.4 million. The number of college graduates soared in the same period. In 1997, students graduating from college numbered 829,000; in 2009, that figure was 5.3 million.[24]

For all its focus on coopting social elites, however, the CCP has been able to recruit into its own ranks only a small percentage of China's college graduates. In 2009, the CCP recruited 919,000 new members with a college degree (roughly 30 percent of the Party's annual new recruits).[25] In other words, so far the CCP has been able to absorb each year only about a fifth of the net increase in the college-educated population. This implies that the CCP leaves out the vast majority of newly minted college graduates. Because Party membership confers enormous material benefits, college graduates who are rejected by the CCP are bound to be frustrated politically and socially.[26] Because of the difficulty that graduates of second- and third-tier colleges have experienced in finding employment in recent years, the prospect that this group will form an antiregime force has become ever more likely.[27]

The long-term effectiveness of political cooptation is also limited by the questionable loyalty of those social elites being targeted for recruitment into the Party and its patronage system. To the extent that these individuals join the Party or support its policies chiefly out of pecuniary interests, the CCP may not be able to count on their loyalty if its ability to satisfy their material interests declines, due to poor economic performance or constraints on the state's fiscal capacity. In a crisis, when these opportunistic supporters might be called on to risk their lives or property to defend the Party, it is doubtful that a majority would stick with a regime in danger of collapse.

For the most part, however, authoritarian regimes adapt and make adjustments in times of crisis. The CCP adopted many of its regime-strengthening measures in response to the challenges posed by the Tiananmen crisis in 1989 and the collapse of European communism that followed soon thereafter. These measures have largely been effective in addressing the challenges stemming from these twin crises: reviving the country's stagnant economy through greater liberalization and opening to the outside world; ending international isolation; placating the intelligentsia; and boosting the confidence of the business community. But the measures that helped to keep the regime in power during the tumults of the late twentieth century are not necessarily working as well in the postcrisis era.

Activist Opposition

Today, after two decades of rapid economic growth, China's political landscape and socioeconomic environment have radically changed. New threats to the CCP's hold on power have emerged, while the dangers of the early 1990s—the threats that the Party's current adaptive survival strategies were designed to meet—have disappeared or dissipated. The Chinese government no longer faces international isolation or a mass antiregime movement led by the intelligentsia.

Instead, the CCP regime now faces an entirely new set of challenges. Rapid economic growth has greatly expanded China's middle class. Although most members of that middle class have remained politically acquiescent, some have become more active in civic affairs, such as environmental protection and charity work. While regime repression has effectively destroyed the political-dissident community, opposition to the regime has taken more innovative forms. Activists today challenge the CCP on issues that can connect them with ordinary people—labor rights, forced evictions, land disputes, environmental protection, and public health. The CCP's single-minded focus on GDP growth has led to a systemic degradation of the Chinese state's capacity for providing such essential public goods as health care, education, and environmental protection. Rising official corruption and an unbalanced economic-development strategy that has depressed the growth of household income and consumption have also fueled a rapid increase in income inequality.

Most of the countermeasures that the Party has taken since Tiananmen are ill suited to dealing with these issues. If the CCP is to address these challenges effectively, it will have to abandon many key components of its post-Tiananmen strategy. Economically, it needs to find a different development model that is less investment-intensive and socially costly. Politically, it may have to replace repression and cooptation with some form of political liberalization to gain a broader base of social support. But the leadership of the Hu Jintao administration has shown no sign that the Party is ready or willing to embrace such fundamental policy shifts. This means that the CCP is now at risk of falling into the trap of "adaptive ossification"—applying an outdated adaptive strategy that no longer works. The result can be, ironically, an accumulation of tensions and risks during the period of perceived authoritarian resilience. Just when the party-state has come to be viewed as resourceful and supremely skilled at hanging on, it may in fact have entered a time of stagnation and dwindling dynamism.

Is the PRC's authoritarianism resilient or decaying? The answer to this question will depend on whether the CCP's post-Tiananmen strategy of relying on economic growth and political repression continues to prove effective despite social and economic conditions that have changed drastically during the past two decades. Proponents of the resilience school are expecting the CCP's adaptive capacity to be equal to the challenges that lie ahead. Skeptics, meanwhile, are pointing to the institutional flaws inherent in any autocracy and expressing doubt that the CCP will manage to frame and implement a substantially different survival strategy that can help it to maintain its political monopoly and gain new sources of legitimacy.

I side with the skeptics in rejecting the argument that the post-1989 regime has made itself resilient through fundamental institutional and policy innovations. Instead, the principal reasons for the CCP's survival since Tiananmen have been robust economic performance and consistent political repression. Although it is true that the CCP may have improved its political tactics, its survival for the last two decades would have been unthinkable without these two critical factors—economic performance and political repression.

In the future, economic performance and political repression may remain important factors for the CCP's survival, but their contribution is likely to decline for several reasons. First, the deleterious effects of authoritarian decay will offset the positive impact of economic growth. Second, political repression is likely to be less effective in defending the regime's political monopoly, as opposition groups and figures equipped with novel methods and technologies will acquire greater capabilities to challenge and delegitimize CCP rule. Finally, the probability of splits in Party ranks will rise as the CCP's fortunes fall and the choices confronting it become harder. Ironically, those at the top of the Party's hierarchy may prove the least firmly bound to it, whether by ideological commitment or political loyalty. As regime decay sets in and "crises of order" begin to increase in frequency and severity, top players within the party-state itself will be tempted to exploit the opportunities thereby presented for boosting their own power and advantages. Open factionalism will not be far behind. Splits within the rulers' highest inner councils, we should recall, are typically a prime condition for democratic transition.

NOTES

1. For representative works on the theme of resilient authoritarianism, see Olga Kryshtanovskaya and Stephen White, "The Sovietization of Russian Politics," *Post-Soviet Affairs* 25 (October 2009): 283–309; Andrew Nathan, "China's Changing of the Guard: Authoritarian Resilience," *Journal of Democracy* 14 (January 2003): 6–17; Marsha Pripstein Posusney, "Enduring Authoritarianism: Middle East Lessons for Contemporary Theory," *Comparative Politics* 36 (January 2004): 127–38; Eva Bellin, "The Robustness of Authoritarianism in the Middle East: Exceptionalism in Comparative Perspective," *Comparative Politics* 36 (January 2004): 139–57; Jason Brownlee, "Low Tide after the Third Wave: Exploring Politics under Authoritarianism," *Comparative Politics* 34 (July 2002): 477–98; Bruce Bueno de Mesquita and Alastair Smith, "Political Survival and Endogenous Institutional Change," *Comparative Political Studies* 42 (February 2009): 167–97.

2. Chappell Lawson, "Mexico's Unfinished Transition: Democratization and Authoritarian Enclaves in Mexico," *Mexican Studies* 16 (Summer 2000): 267–87.

3. Bruce Bueno de Mesquita and George W. Downs, "Development and Democracy," *Foreign Affairs* 84 (September–October 2005): 77–86.

4. See Bellin, "Robustness of Authoritarianism in the Middle East"; and Louay Abdulbaki, "Democracy and the Re-Consolidation of Authoritarian Rule in Egypt," *Contemporary Arab Affairs* 1 (July 2008): 445–63.

5. Nathan, "Authoritarian Resilience."

6. Steve Tsang, "Consultative Leninism: China's New Political Framework," *Journal of Contemporary China* 18 (November 2009): 865–80.

7. David Shambaugh, *China's Communist Party: Atrophy and Adaptation* (Berkeley: University of California Press, 2008).

8. Dali Yang, *Remaking the Chinese Leviathan: Market Transition and the Politics of Governance in China* (Stanford: Stanford University Press, 2004).

9. See Steven Levitsky and Lucan A. Way, "Elections Without Democracy: The Rise of Competitive Authoritarianism," *Journal of Democracy* 13 (April 2002): 51–65.

10. Adam Przeworski et al., *Democracy and Development: Political Institutions and Well-Being in the World, 1950–1990* (New York: Cambridge University Press, 2000).

11. Robert J. Barro, "Democracy and Growth," *Journal of Economic Growth* 1 (March 1996): 1–27.

12. Yongshun Cai, "Power Structure and Regime Resilience: Contentious Politics in China," *British Journal of Political Science* 38 (May 2008): 411–32.

13. See Murray Scot Tanner, "Chinese Government Responses to Rising Social Unrest," Testimony presented to the U.S.-China Economic and Security Review Commission, 14 April 2005.

14. See Richard McGregor, *The Party: The Secret World of China's Communist Rulers* (New York: Harper, 2010).

15. Barry Naughton, "China's Economic Policy Today: The New State Activism," *Eurasian Geography and Economics* 52 (May–June 2011): 313–29.

16. Bill Francis, Iftekhar Hasan, and Xian Sun, "Political Connections and the Process

of Going Public: Evidence from China," *Journal of International Money and Finance* 28 (June 2009): 696–719.

17. Cheng Li, "The Chinese Communist Party: Recruiting and Controlling the New Elites," *Journal of Current Chinese Affairs* 38, no. 3 (2009): 13–33.

18. Jie Chen and Bruce J. Dickson, *Allies of the State: China's Private Entrepreneurs and Democratic Change* (Cambridge: Harvard University Press, 2010).

19. Björn Alpermann, "'Wrapped up in Cotton Wool': Political Integration of Private Entrepreneurs in Rural China," *China Journal* 56 (July 2006): 33–61.

20. Xinhua News Agency, 28 June 2010.

21. The practice of paying bribes for appointments and promotions is widespread in China. See Yan Sun, "Cadre Recruitment and Corruption: What Goes Wrong?" *Crime, Law and Social Change* 49 (January 2008): 61–79; Jiangnan Zhu, "Why Are Offices for Sale in China? A Case Study of the Office-Selling Chain in Heilongjiang Province," *Asian Survey* 48 (July–August 2008): 558–79.

22. Andrew Wedeman, "Anticorruption Campaigns and the Intensification of Corruption in China," *Journal of Contemporary China* 14 (February 2005): 93–116.

23. For a survey of the consequences of corruption in China, see Yan Sun, *Corruption and Market in Contemporary China* (Ithaca: Cornell University Press, 2004).

24. *Statistical Yearbook of China* (Beijing: Zhongguo tongjinianjian chubanshe, 2010), 756–57.

25. Xinhua News Agency, 28 June 2010.

26. For a study of the privileges enjoyed by CCP members, see Bruce J. Dickson and Maria Rost Rublee, "Membership Has Its Privileges: The Socioeconomic Characteristics of Communist Party Members in Urban China," *Comparative Political Studies* 33 (February 2000): 87–112.

27. A 2009 online survey of 21,057 new college graduates found that only half had found jobs. In 2007 and 2008, the percentage was 56 and 52 percent respectively; see *http://edu.QQ.com*, 30 July 2009.

6

CHINA AND
THE TAIWAN FACTOR

Yun-han Chu

Yun-han Chu *is Distinguished Research Fellow at the Institute of Political Science at Academia Sinica (Taipei) and professor of political
science at National Taiwan University. He is coeditor (with Tse-Kang
Leng) of* Dynamics of Local Governance in China during the Reform
Era *(2010). This essay originally appeared in the January 2012 issue
of the* Journal of Democracy.

If the People's Republic of China (PRC) moves toward democracy, it is
likely to be in no small part due to the influence of the Republic of China
(ROC or Taiwan). This influence comes not only from the direct impact
of Taiwanese political and social actors in promoting change, but also
from Taiwan's being the first and only democracy yet to be installed in a
culturally Chinese society. In addition to demonstrating the compatibil-
ity of democracy and Chinese culture, Taiwan's successful democratic
transition illustrates a possible exit strategy that the Chinese Communist
Party (CCP) could follow if it seeks to move away from one-party authoritarianism. It is very uncertain, of course, whether China will take
this path, as the CCP is also subject to a wide range of other influences
and pressures that might push it in an altogether different direction.

Geographically separated from mainland China by the Taiwan Strait,
the island of Taiwan has been politically separate since the end of the
Chinese Civil War in 1949, when the Nationalist Party, or Kuomintang
(KMT), retreated to the island. In 1987, Beijing and Taipei lifted the
mutual ban on travel and trade. Since then, the trickle of cross-Strait
economic and cultural exchange has become a massive flow. By 2003,
mainland China had overtaken the United States as Taiwan's most important trading partner. In 2010, Taiwanese travelers made more than
six-million visits to mainland China, and there are now close to a million Taiwanese expatriates living and working in the PRC. Taiwanese
companies and businessmen have invested more than US$150 billion
in mainland China and have reinvested the bulk of their profits to ex-

pand their operations. With more than 70,000 business projects across the mainland, Taiwanese firms have penetrated into China's remotest corners.

The geographic proximity and cultural affinity between the two Chinese societies, along with increased economic exchange and social contacts, make Taiwan a plausible social and political model for the PRC. While most PRC residents learn about Taiwan via state-controlled and government-censored news media, many urban dwellers access Taiwan-based news and entertainment programs via satellite TV and the Internet. Some PRC-based websites copy and paste articles from Taiwan's leading newspapers, thereby circumventing the ban on those papers' sites. The reach of Taiwan-based mass media and popular culture has been intensively felt not only in the PRC's urban centers, but throughout Chinese-language cyberspace. During 2011, two of the top three media stars with the most "followers" (almost nine million) on Sina Weibo (China's version of Twitter) were from Taiwan.[1]

Taiwanese political commentators, political comedians, and talk-show hosts have become household names in China. Some of Taiwan's best-known social critics have blogs that attract large numbers of Internet users ("netizens") from mainland China. The PRC's urban middle class closely follows and discusses all the major twists and turns in Taiwanese politics. When mainland Chinese visitors come to Taiwan for the first time, they often stay up late into the night, glued to the television, watching political talk shows and satires. On the evening of Taiwan's 2008 presidential election, an estimated 200 million mainland Chinese viewers watched the ballot counting via satellite TV or the Internet. One of the hottest online discussion topics in mainland China today is about the implications of major political events in Taiwan.

Just as Taiwan's mass media have been instrumental in spreading news about Taiwan's democratic experience, many Taiwan-based social actors have contributed to China's political liberalization with information, ideas, and practical knowledge. Taiwanese NGOs working on a broad range of social issues—from the environment to consumer rights to assisting battered wives—have developed extensive networks with like-minded organizations throughout China. For instance, Taiwan-based religious groups have played a key role in reviving the traditional religions, in particular Buddhism and Taoism, on the mainland, paving the way for official recognition of the legitimacy of Buddhism by the PRC.[2] Other NGOs, meanwhile, have helped to spread the ideas and practices of civic action. In 2007, the Tzu Chi Foundation, Taiwan's largest Buddhist charitable organization, became the first overseas religious organization officially to be registered in the PRC, and it has developed the most extensive private charity network to date in mainland China.

Taiwanese entrepreneurs have also helped to lead the social transformation that has been taking place in China over the last two decades. In addition to being investors, employers, and providers of modern managerial know-how and access to international markets, they have played a significant role in shaping local governance, especially in the areas of regional planning and industrial development. There are hundreds of Taiwanese chambers of commerce across China, and they engage with local governments on a range of policy issues. Taiwanese experts and businessmen have helped to develop industrial, science, and trade zones in many provinces, including Fujian, Guangdong, Hubei, Jiangsu, and Shanghai. Taiwanese advisors and entrepreneurs have transformed Kunshan, a rural town in Jiangsu, into the world's premier production center for computer and telecommunications equipment, and all medium-sized Chinese cities aspiring to become high-tech hubs now emulate the "Kunshan model."

Taiwan has also become a critical source of know-how for developing a modern law-bound state, a prerequisite for liberal constitutionalism. PRC experts and bureaucrats have carefully scrutinized every aspect of Taiwan's legal system. Because Taiwan's legal system is based on German code law rather than on Anglo-Saxon common law, it has had greater influence than Hong Kong on the revamping of China's legal system. Taiwanese legal scholarship has been the greatest overseas source of ideas in China's recent efforts to overhaul its civil and criminal codes, litigation and bankruptcy procedures, and regulatory frameworks. Lee & Li, one of Taiwan's leading law firms, collaborates closely with two top Chinese law schools—Tsinghua University Law School and Zhejiang University Law School—holding a joint graduate seminar on business and law each year and sending its senior partners to both schools as guest lecturers.

Cross-Strait exchange and cooperation between academics and professionals have also increased in recent years—most notably, in the fields of finance and banking, public administration, management science, local governance, and survey research. Many former Taiwanese government officials and scholars specializing in public administration have helped the senior cadres of various Chinese ministries to better understand the mechanisms of internal control and horizontal accountability that are built into Taiwan's state bureaucracy in such areas as budgeting, auditing, administrative procedures, and civil-service exams. When the PRC's Ministry of Civil Affairs revised the rules and procedures for China's local elections, officials looked to Taiwan's election laws and procedures and sought the input of Taiwanese experts.

Taiwan's government has played only a limited role in fostering the cross-Strait engagement. In fact, under presidents Lee Teng-hui (1988–2000) and Chen Shui-bian (2000–2008), the Taiwanese government created a number of obstacles to cross-Strait exchange that impeded Taiwan-based social actors from unleashing their full potential in China. The 2008 presidential election, won by the KMT's Ma Ying-jeou, ushered in a new era of cross-Strait rapprochement. Recognizing the importance of Taiwan's soft power yet knowing that conventional public diplomacy could provoke China into taking countervailing measures, President Ma's government has refrained from taking an explicit role in coordinating cross-Strait cultural exchange. Spontaneous private initiatives enjoy more room for maneuver, as they are seemingly less offensive, intrusive, and threatening.

Similar Challenges

The leaders of the CCP have closely observed and drawn lessons from Taiwan's democratic transition and particularly from the collapse of the KMT's hegemony after its electoral debacle in 2000.[3] Many in the party elite see strong parallels between the fate of the KMT and the possible future of the CCP. The genesis and early organizational development of the two parties were not only strikingly similar but also intimately intertwined.[4] Both emerged in the early twentieth century with the aims of rebuilding state and society out of the ashes of imperial China and saving the nation from predatory imperialist powers. Each adopted a Leninist configuration—clandestine, organized by cells, vanguard-led, presumably mass-based, and committed to the principle of democratic centralism. With self-proclaimed (and competing) historical missions—a nationalist one for the KMT and a socialist one for the CCP—both parties superimposed themselves onto the state and society, achieving institutional hegemony.

After 1949, the KMT evolved quite differently than did its communist rival. Nonetheless, the one-party authoritarian regime installed by the KMT on Taiwan conformed to many of the organizational and operational characteristics of classic Leninist parties in terms of the centralization of power in the paramount leader, the symbiosis between party and state, and the way in which the party-state penetrated society.[5] Moreover, for more than thirty years the KMT (much like the CCP) organized the society that it governed, structured the political arena in which it operated, and articulated a worldview that lent substance and coherence to its political domination.[6]

The postwar KMT regime differed in key ways from its Marxist-Leninist counterparts, however. First, the KMT was closely linked to the West ideologically, as well as through a security alliance and an economic partnership. Second, the party recognized private-property rights, supported a market economy, and partially institutionalized the rule of law. Third, the KMT attracted the support of a distinctive development coalition based on the country's export-led industrialization. Paradoxically, since China opened up to the West in the late 1970s and embarked on a path of market-oriented reform, the CCP has similarly deviated

from the classic Leninist model. With its epic transition from totalitari-
anism to developmental authoritarianism, the CCP has drawn closer to
the KMT's political trajectory.

After presiding over more than three decades of rapid economic
growth and social transformation, the CCP now faces a set of five major political challenges to its hegemony similar to those faced by the
KMT in the late 1970s and early 1980s. Taiwan's ruling party responded
to these challenges with a series of strategic and institutional adjustments that might have appeared incremental or even cosmetic, but were
in fact quite consequential. The first challenge was how to replace a
bankrupt guiding ideology and discredited revolutionary mandate with
a new foundation for regime legitimacy. The second-generation KMT
leadership under Chiang Ching-kuo (CCK), the son of founding president Chiang Kai-shek and president himself from 1978 to 1988, shelved
the mission of "recovering the mainland and reunifying China" and replaced it with "building up Taiwan" and "shared affluence" (*junfu*). The
leadership worked to realize this new vision through ambitious projects
for modernizing the island's infrastructure and upgrading its industrial
sector. The KMT regime also boosted its legitimacy by adopting a populism anchored in a compassionate, approachable, and public-spirited
leadership that exemplified the Confucian virtues of unselfishness, fru-
gality, and self-discipline.

In recent years, the PRC has adopted similar approaches for tacking
this first challenge. President Jiang Zemin's (1993–2003) vision of the
"well-off society" (*xiaokang shehui*) and his successor Hu Jintao's call
for a "harmonious society" and for China's "peaceful rise" represent the
CCP's latest efforts to redefine the regime's *raison d'être* in a way that
will resonate with a majority of the people. Other parallels to the Taiwanese approach include President Hu's adopting the populist motto of
the "New Three People's Principles" (*sange weimin*),[7] and PRC premier
Wen Jiabao's amiable leadership style, which is strikingly similar to
that of CCK, who often visited villagers and workers and immediately
rushed to areas devastated by natural disasters.

The second challenge faced by the KMT and later by the CCP was
how to reestablish the party's social foundation as new social forces
emerged outside its organizational scope. The KMT's second-generation
leadership tried to transform it from a vanguard into a catchall party and
from a revolutionary to a ruling party. The KMT vigorously recruited
new members not just from its old constituencies (including mainlanders,
the military, public-sector employees, teachers, and members of farmers'
and fishermen's associations), but also from the expanding entrepreneurial, professional, and urban middle classes that had benefited from the
state's export-led industrialization strategy. More specifically, CCK tried
to rejuvenate the party's old and fading membership with younger technocrats, foreign-educated scholars, and talented native Taiwanese groomed

through the party's academy. At its peak in the mid-1980s, party member-ship reached almost 18 percent of the entire adult male population.

In 2004, the CCP leadership decided to broaden its party base, just as the KMT had a few decades earlier. With a new guiding principle known as the "Three Represents," enshrined in the PRC's constitution that year, the CCP cast its lot with the beneficiaries of its economic reform. No longer a vanguard party of the "three revolutionary classes" (peasants, workers, and soldiers), the party now claims to represent advanced pro-ductive forces, advanced culture, and the fundamental interests of the great majority of the Chinese people (the "Three Represents"). While this effort to coopt private business owners, intellectuals, and profes-sionals is often derided as window dressing, it reflects the party's ef-forts to adapt itself to the changed economic and social environment in China.[8]

Dealing with a More Plural Society

The third challenge was how to safeguard the party's monopoly on organized social life from the encroachment of autonomous social movements and bottom-up civic organizations. As early as the 1950s, the KMT party apparatus had incorporated business and professional associations, labor unions, farmers, state employees, journalists, the intelligentsia, students, and other targeted groups into state-sponsored corporatist organizations. During the 1960s and 1970s, these organiza-tions functioned as private-sector arms of both the state bureaucracy and the party. But with the growing importance of private enterprise, the KMT had to formally recognize the economic might of the private sector. Beginning in the early 1980s, the existing business associations became functional conduits for soliciting policy input and coordinat-ing industrial policy. In particular, representatives from the "big three" national organizations—the Federation of Industry, the Federation of Commerce, and the blue-ribbon National Council of Industry and Com-merce—were elevated to the party's top echelon and granted member-ship on the KMT Central Standing Committee.

The KMT leadership adopted a two-pronged approach for dealing with the emergence of autonomous labor and environmental move-ments, consumer-rights groups, and other public-interest advocacy or-ganizations outside the existing corporatist structure. First, it enacted the Civic Organization Law (1989) to register and regulate these volun-tary groups. And second, it elevated the bureaucracies in charge of la-bor affairs, the environment, and consumer protection to ministry-level agencies and selectively coopted moderate leaders of social movements into the new ministries' advisory bodies. As the legal space and mobi-lizing power of grassroots NGOs expanded, the reach of the party-state into associational life necessarily receded.

The CCP today is reigning over a society undergoing epochal transformation, and as state-society relations evolve, the level of the state's
control over its citizens declines. All kinds of new actors, especially
foreign-trained professionals, have emerged in key areas such as the
state bureaucracy, the export sector, and higher education. This has
transformed the ruling establishment and created a more plural society,
along with new forms of political discourse and political participation.
It has also necessitated new legal, regulatory, and market structures.
In order to absorb newcomers into the party and government, the CCP
has had to introduce new organizational rules—largely merit-based or
market-based—that have replaced the old hierarchical structure of the
socialist command economy.[9]

The CCP regime is also dealing with waves of social protest. Beneath the veneer of rapid economic growth and political stability, there
are myriad simmering social grievances against the government. These
stem from the widening gap between rich and poor, legal discrimination
against uprooted migrants from the countryside, corruption and abuse of
power by local officials, land expropriation without proper compensation, and environmental degradation. Like the KMT in the early 1980s,
CCP leaders have shown adaptability, and at times even tolerance, in
dealing with popular protest. The regime has adjusted its national fiscal priorities in order to mitigate the negative consequences of uneven
development, has improved the state's administrative and regulatory
capacities to deal with emerging social problems and market failures,
and has instructed local authorities to handle incidents of social unrest
carefully in order to prevent them from escalating.

The CCP regime must also contend with an explosion of associational life in China.[10] Grassroots NGOs, which typically evade regulation by
declining to comply with difficult registration procedures, have proliferated, posing a significant challenge to the party-state's once-omnipres-
ent control over organizational space. Likewise, an increasing number
of underground religious sects and even organized criminal gangs have
undermined the state's governance capacity. Nevertheless, the regime
has had some success in maintaining ties with certain key constituencies
(workers, youth, women, businessman, scientists and engineers, and lit-
erary and art circles)—by reinvigorating existing mass organizations.
At the same time, the party has put other segments of society, such as
underground religious movements, dissident intellectuals, human-rights
lawyers, and independent labor movements, on a tighter leash.

The most notable development is the rapid expansion of intermediary
organizations between the state and the private sector. With the party's
approval, business and industrial associations such as the All-China
Federation of Industry and Commerce were established alongside their
government-agency counterparts and formally assimilated into the hierarchy of state-sanctioned organizations. Both private and state-owned

enterprises have become involved in a tug of war with government agencies and with each other to gain policy advantages, often setting the agenda, providing alternative options, and pressing for favored outcomes.

The fourth challenge that has confronted both the KMT and the CCP is how to contain and harness the rise of demand-driven mass media and alternative sources of information that compete with official organs. During the 1970s and early 1980s, the KMT still imposed rigorous censorship over mass media, films, and publications. It stopped issuing new licenses for newspapers and restricted the maximum number of pages that newspapers were allowed to publish. Nevertheless, the growing demand for independent news and critical opinion steadily eroded the KMT's monopoly on the supply of information and ideas. Party-owned newspapers gradually lost readers to KMT-affiliated but privately owned newspapers, which often evaded monitoring agencies in order to gain wider circulation. Independent publishers constantly played hide-and-seek games with law enforcement and found ways to turn decent profits off reprints of banned books and magazines. Despite granting some leeway to independent print media, however, the KMT still kept a tight grip on radio and television and managed to foster a broad consensus supporting orderedly and incremental political change.

Similarly, the CCP today is grappling with the political consequences of the rapid commercialization and internationalization of the media in China, and like the KMT it fiercely guards its ownership of electronic media. The CCP faces a much greater challenge than did the KMT of the late twentieth century, however, as the CCP's policing power has been overwhelmed by the explosion of online social media. In December 1997, China had about 670,000 Internet users; by December 2010, this number had shot up to 457 million. As Yang Guobin put it, "[T]his communication revolution is a social revolution because the ordinary people assume an unprecedented role as agents of change."[11] Every day a torrential flow of information and opinion passes through cyberspace, as billions of messages are transmitted wirelessly. In its attempts to police China's netizens, the regime is fighting an impossible battle against time and technological innovation.

The fifth major challenge to the one-party state in both Taiwan and China has been how to deal with contending economic interests and with the rising popular demand for political representation and participation engendered by socioeconomic modernization. Of all the institutional adjustments that the KMT leadership introduced during the 1970s and early 1980s, none had a greater impact than allowing limited popular elections for national representative bodies. Under the pretext of a protracted civil war, the KMT had suspended national elections for almost a quarter-century and extended indefinitely the tenure of incumbent representatives elected on the mainland in 1948. A series of devastating

diplomatic setbacks in the early 1970s compelled the KMT to introduce
a limited electoral opening in 1972, which was then expanded in 1980
and again in 1989. Each time, more seats in the Legislative Yuan and the
National Assembly were decided by popular election.

This historic opening did not seem risky at the time. After all, the
KMT had developed a proven formula for controlling limited popular
elections at the local level: The party had introduced elections at the
township, city, and county levels as early as 1950 and for the Taiwan
Provincial Assembly as early as 1954, seeking to incorporate the na-
tive Taiwanese elite into the party-building process and provide the
authoritarian system with a modicum of democratic legitimacy. At the
grassroots level, the KMT incorporated existing patron-client networks
into the party structure. Within each administrative district below the
provincial level, the KMT kept at least two competing local factions
striving for public offices and rents. The fierce competition among these
factions effectively blocked the entrance of opposition candidates into
local elections. On top of this, the central leadership could enjoy an
overall electoral victory that was delivered by disparate local factions.
Thus for almost three decades, the KMT faced a weak and unorganized
opposition consisting primarily of defiant local factions that had no national political ambitions and posed little threat to the KMT's dominant
position.

Yet the gradual opening of the national representative bodies set in
motion the regime's demise, as Taiwan's socioeconomic development
had already made the island ripe for a democratic opening. In the second half of the 1970s, a loose coalition formed of anti-KMT independent candidates with national political aims, which came to be known
as *dangwai* (literally "outside the party"). *Dangwai* candidates used the
electoral process to foster popular aspirations for democratic reform and
a separate Taiwanese identity. Emboldened by their electoral success
in the 1977 provincial-assembly and county-magistrate elections, the
dangwai coalition steadily moved closer to becoming a quasi-party, and
in 1986 finally founded the Democratic Progressive Party (DPP) in open
defiance of martial law.

Chiang Ching-kuo's decision to tolerate the formation of the DPP and
his announcement a week later that he intended to lift martial law and
many other longtime political bans essentially sealed the fate of the authoritarian regime. This incumbent-initiated political liberalization was
intended to be the first part of a guided transition, or "democratization
in installments."[12] With a multistage constitutional-reform process, the
KMT managed to ensure an orderly sequencing of democratic openings
and to extend the transition period to almost a decade. It was able to
do so in part because the DPP lacked the capacity to impose its reform
schedule and agenda on the incumbent regime. The KMT's socioeco-
nomic-development program had been broadly based, and the party had

already locked in the support of key constituencies, thereby limiting the range of mobilization and confrontation strategies available to the opposition.

As a result, the KMT was able to engineer a transition from a one-party authoritarian regime to "a one-party-dominant regime" (a system best exemplified by Liberal Democratic Party rule in Japan), making Taiwan perhaps the only case among the third-wave democracies in which a quasi-Leninist party not only survived an authoritarian breakdown but turned the crisis to its advantage. Had a political cleavage over national identity not emerged and led to an intraparty split, the KMT might possibly have kept power for much longer after the democratic transition.

The CCP leadership today recognizes that China's rapid socioeconomic transformation has already brought about a growing demand for accountability, representation, and participation. It feels compelled to lower the barriers for various kinds of stakeholders to join the policy-making process and to make the system more responsive to the increasingly diverse demands of Chinese society.[13] Before long, China's urban sector will demand further political opening. Taiwan's "democratization in installments" could be a useful model for the next generation of CCP leaders, who will be under increasing pressure to find a viable exit strategy. The island's experiences have demonstrated that it is possible for a hegemonic party to engineer a peaceful and gradual transition away from one-party authoritarianism on the basis of a successful record of economic modernization.

Although there are numerous parallels between the rocky political terrain that the second-generation KMT leaders encountered during the late 1970s and early 1980s and the delicate political situation that the CCP leadership finds itself in today, the strategic options available to the two sets of incumbent elites are not identical. Much more than the Chinese party-state, the KMT regime was severely constrained by three structural vulnerabilities. First, the KMT was vulnerable to the influence and pressure of foreign actors. Taiwan had been highly dependent on the United States for access to markets, security guarantees, and meaningful participation in international organizations such as APEC and WTO. Before its transition, Taiwan had been a relatively small and strategically insecure society that needed to democratize in order to regain international legitimacy and maintain the support of its most vital ally, whereas the PRC today is a rising global power and a strategic rival to the United States.[14]

Second, the ideological foundation of the KMT's postwar authoritarian order was intrinsically shaky, anchored as it was on the disputed claim that the ROC government remained the sole legitimate government representing the whole of China. The mainlander-dominated KMT leadership had been fighting an uphill battle—defending its extraconstitutional arrangements (martial law) amid a global wave of democra-

tization, insisting on the "One China" principle when almost all major
nations had shifted their diplomatic recognition to the PRC, and upholding a Chinese identity in opposition to an emerging Taiwanese identity.
Toward the second half of the 1980s, it became increasingly difficult for
the KMT to deny the necessity of redistributing power from the mainlander elite to native-Taiwanese citizens through democratic means.

Third, the KMT was constrained by its own ideological and institutional commitments. The ROC's 1947 Constitution embraced democratic norms and upheld the right to dissent and to open political contestation, at least in principle. The KMT had defended Taiwan's postwar
authoritarian arrangements on the grounds that the country was under
imminent military threat from its communist rival across the Strait. Authoritarian rule was founded on a system of extraconstitutional legal
arrangements and emergency decrees that replaced or superseded many
important provisions in the 1947 Constitution. The cross-Strait détente
of the early 1980s began to soften the people's siege mentality, however, and undermined the regime's rationale for maintaining a state of
emergency. It became increasingly difficult and costly for the KMT to
suppress the popular demand for returning to constitutional "normality."
Yet the KMT remained strong because of its ability to engineer electoral
dominance and because it had a unified political coalition behind its
development strategy, which had impressively addressed issues both of
growth and equality. Therefore, the option of peacefully transforming
authoritarian rule was readily available.

The CCP's Freedom of Action

The structural conditions that Hu Jintao's generation inherited are
in many respects less stringent than those of Taiwan two decades ago.
First of all, the CCP regime is unencumbered by the kind of ideological
or institutional commitments that had constrained the KMT. The CCP
has committed itself to the development of "socialist democracy," not
Western-style liberal democracy. The party's monopoly on power is still
enshrined in the PRC's constitution, which precludes public contestation for power. In addition, while Chinese nationalism turned out to be a
liability for the KMT elite, it remains the CCP's most valuable political
asset. Hu Jintao's vision of China's peaceful rise, which addresses the
popular yearning for China's preeminence on the world stage, serves as
an important pillar of legitimacy for the regime.

Furthermore, in terms of ideology, Western ideas and values have yet
to establish themselves, especially in the face of two strong ideological
counterweights: First, the CCP's socialist legacy has been reinvigorated
by the so-called New Leftists, who are critical of neoliberal economics,
characterize U.S. democracy as a plutocracy, and advocate a stronger
role for the state in addressing inequality, regional disparities, and the

rampant corruption and injustice brought on by privatization. Second, there has been a resurgence, with the support of the regime, of Chinese cultural identity, philosophy, and worldviews—notably, Confucianism, which is presented as a compelling alternative to Western liberalism as the country retreats from communism.[15]

Of all the world's transitional societies, China—due to both its size and its history of anti-imperialist struggle—is the least susceptible to the sway of the United States or any of the industrialized democracies. On the contrary, China enjoys a growing strategic and economic capacity for creating a more hospitable external environment, especially within its own orbit of political and economic influence in Asia. Moreover, the world today is vastly different than the one in which Taiwan began its transition. The global tidal wave of democratization has receded, giving way in the developing world to what Larry Diamond has dubbed a "democratic recession."[16] Even the advanced Western democracies, long admired by China's liberal-minded intellectual elite, are steadily losing their attractiveness as the European fiscal crisis deepens and the political paralysis that has gripped Washington since 2008 lingers.

At the same time, the limited electoral pluralism that the CCP has allowed at the local level has not yet reached the critical point where it could set in motion the self-propelling dynamics of institutional evolution that Taiwan experienced. Yes, village elections have become a normal feature of grassroots political life, and they represent an important step forward in China's quest for a more accountable political system. But the impact of village-level democracy within an overarching authoritarian environment is limited.[17]

The local and national People's Congresses—the representative bodies that are entrusted with the formal power to enact laws, pass the budget, and elect top executive officials at all levels of government—are perhaps more promising. The pluralization of economic interests and deepening social stratification in China have already had an impact on elections for the local People's Congresses, as well as on the role that their deputies have played in setting policy priorities and drafting laws and regulations. China's emerging business-owning and professional class, however, is not yet the kind of autonomous social force that incubated Taiwan's political opposition, however. China's economic structure today is far more state-centric and state-dominated than was Taiwan's twenty years ago. China's state-owned enterprises still occupy the commanding heights of the economy, and most private firms rely on state actors to ease the resource constraints of China's regulated markets. In addition, state involvement in decision making at the firm level, especially in the areas of corporate governance, labor relations, and finance, remains a core feature of China's state-guided capitalism. Furthermore, a majority of private capital holders are inextricably linked to the agents and institutions of the party-state.[18] As a result, for the foreseeable future the CCP will still be able to exert its supremacy over the local and national People's Congresses and keep today's limited political pluralism in check.

There are two starkly different lessons to be drawn from Taiwan's transition experience with regard to China's democratic future. On the one hand, the eventual demise of the KMT's one-party regime suggests that developmental authoritarianism, despite its organizational capacity and adaptability, will eventually become the victim of its own success. A highly resilient developmental authoritarian regime may find ways to slow or mitigate the corrosive effect of rapid socioeconomic modernization on its political hegemony, but there is no way to stop it.

On the other hand, a well-entrenched hegemonic party such as the CPP can drag out the process of gradual political liberalization over a long period of time. This is likely to be even truer for the CCP than it was for the KMT, as China is far more powerful than was Taiwan and is thus operating in a less restrictive external environment. If the CCP can avoid an irreparable intraparty split (which often results from power struggles over succession under authoritarianism), sustain the momentum of economic growth, and adequately address China's growing regional disparities and economic polarization, it is not inconceivable that the CCP could retain its hegemonic status in China for quite a while yet.

In order to do so, the party would have to adopt the right balance of coercion and materialist payoffs, along with a blend of populism and nationalism; it must rebuild the state's governing capacity and adapt the existing representative institutions and consultative mechanisms to accommodate an increasingly complex economy and pluralistic society; it will have to combine eclecticism and pragmatism in dealing with socioeconomic issues; and it must selectively coopt emerging social forces and constantly replenish its pool of talent. This was largely how the second-generation KMT leaders stretched out Taiwan's political-liberalization process and concomitant authoritarian weakening over almost two decades (from the early 1970s to the late 1980s) amid rapid socioeconomic change and a deterioration of its international standing.

No matter how the CCP elite sizes up its strategic options, Taiwan's democratic trajectory still constitutes a crucial and illuminating social experiment in the eyes of mainland Chinese citizens. Competing interpretations of Taiwan's democratic experience will continue to shape the parameters of public discourse on the mainland as the intellectual debate over China's political future gains momentum.

At the same time, Taiwan-based political, economic, and social actors are potentially powerful catalysts for democratic change in China. Taiwan's transformative power lies not just in its experience with economic modernization, social pluralism, and democratic development, but also in its "Chinese-ness." The people of Taiwan in their daily lives have preserved and practiced Chinese social customs; dietary habits; conceptions about the body and health; notions of life, death, fate, and the supernatural; and family-based ethics. The elements of modernity embodied in the Taiwanese model are inspirational, while the island's shared linguistic and cultural heritage with China makes Taiwan's way of life relevant, comprehensible, and accessible. On Taiwan, modernity and tradition have combined to form a vibrant and constantly evolving society.

The improvement in cross-Strait relations since March 2008 has accelerated the flow of exchange and deepened social ties between the two sides. As more and more mainland Chinese visitors and exchange students set foot on the island for the first time, Taiwan's influence on the PRC grows. If the island is to have a real impact on the mainland, however, it must first improve the overall quality of its young democracy and make its citizens proud of their political system. Over the long run, Taiwan can maximize its political leverage if its next generation of leaders is willing to engage with China about the long-term prospect of a reunified political community founded on democratic principles and rules. The tail can wag the dog only if the tail is still attached to the dog.

Maximizing the island's soft power of democracy is the best and perhaps the only strategy available to Taiwan for protecting its long-term interests. Doing so will enhance the ROC's capacity to steer the future course of cross-Strait relations despite the growing imbalance between the two sides in hard power. This strategy will also allow Taiwan to become a significant and constructive player in East Asia and on the world stage. If Taiwan fails to seize this critical opportunity, it risks becoming increasingly vulnerable, irrelevant, and marginalized.

NOTES

1. The two TV stars are *Xiao* (Junior) S and Tsai Kang-yung.

2. Taiwan-based Buddhist organizations were the principal sponsors of the inaugural meeting of the World Forum on Buddhism. This meeting, which was endorsed by the Chinese government and held in Hangzhou in 2006, was widely regarded as a watershed event.

3. In fact, following Taiwan's historic power rotation in 2000, the CCP's Central Party School (CPS) commissioned a special research project to determine what lessons the Party should draw from the KMT-directed political opening and its eventual fall from power. I was invited by the China Reform Forum, an offshoot of the CPS, to give a presentation in front of the CPS's vice-president and senior research staff about what caused the KMT's eventual fall from power.

4. Bruce J. Dickson, *Democratization in China and Taiwan: The Adaptability of Leninist Parties* (New York: Oxford University Press, 1997), ch. 1.

5. For the quasi-Leninist features of the postwar KMT, see Yun-han Chu, *Crafting Democracy in Taiwan* (Taipei: Institute for National Policy Research, 1992), ch. 2, and Tun-jen Cheng, "Democratizing the Quasi-Leninist Regime in Taiwan," *World Politics* 41 (July 1989): 471–99.

6. Yun-han Chu, "The Legacy of One-Party Hegemony in Taiwan," in Larry Diamond and Richard Gunther, eds., *Political Parties and Democracy* (Baltimore: Johns Hopkins University Press, 2001), 266–98.

7. On 18 March 2003, a day after assuming the presidency, Hu Jintao proposed the "New Three People's Principles" (*xin sanmin zhuyi* or *sange weimin*): to use the power for the people (*quan weimin shuoyong*), to link the sentiments to the people (*qing weimin shuoji*), and to pursue the interest of the people (*li weimin shoumo*).

8. Bruce J. Dickson, "Dilemmas for Party Adaptation: the CCP's Strategies for Survival," in Peter Hays Gries and Stanley Rosen, eds., *State and Society in 21st-Century China: Crisis, Contention, and Legitimation* (London: RoutledgeCurzon, 2004), 141–58.

9. Edward S. Steinfeld, "China's Other Revolution," *Boston Review*, July–August 2011.

10. Shaoguang Wang and Jianyu He, "Associational Revolution in China: Mapping the Landscapes," *Korea Observer* 35 (Autumn 2004): 485–533.

11. Guobin Yang, *The Power of the Internet in China: Citizen Activism Online* (New York: Columbia University Press, 2009).

12. This concept was coined by Masahiro Wakabayashi in *Taiwan—Bunretsu kokka to minshuka* [Taiwan: democratization in a divided country] (Tokyo: University of Tokyo Press, 1992), 17.

13. Andrew Mertha, "'Fragmented Authoritarianism 2.0': Political Pluralization in the Chinese Policy Process," *China Quarterly* 200 (December 2009): 995–1012.

14. Larry Diamond, "Why China's Democratic Transition Will Differ from Taiwan's," in Bruce Gilley and Larry Diamond, eds., *Political Change in China: Comparisons with Taiwan* (Boulder, Colo.: Lynne Rienner, 2008).

15. Daniel Bell, *China's New Confucianism: Politics and Everyday Life in a Changing Society* (Princeton: Princeton University Press, 2008).

16. Larry Diamond, "The Democratic Rollback: The Resurgence of the Predatory State," *Foreign Affairs* 87 (March–April 2008): 36–48.

17. Thomas P. Bernstein, "Village Democracy and Its Limits," *Asien* 99 (April 2006): 29–41.

18. Christopher A. McNally and Teresa Wright, "Sources of Social Support for China's Current Political Order: The 'Thick Embeddedness' of Private Capital Holders," *Communist and Post-Communist Studies* 43 (June 2010): 189–98.

7

THE TWO TURNOVERS
IN SOUTH KOREA AND TAIWAN

Yun-han Chu and Hyug Baeg Im

Yun-han Chu *is Distinguished Research Fellow at the Institute of Political Science at Academia Sinica (Taipei) and professor of political science at National Taiwan University. He is the coeditor (with Tse-Kang Leng) of* Dynamics of Local Governance in China during the Reform Era *(2010).* ***Hyug Baeg Im,*** *professor of political science and international relations at Korea University (Seoul), is dean of Korea University's Graduate School of Policy Studies and director of its Institute for Peace Studies.*

Korea and Taiwan (ROC) have become widely recognized as the two most successful "third-wave" democracies in Asia.[1] For more than a decade, citizens of these two countries have chosen the heads of their executive branches and members of their legislatures through regular, free, and fair elections. Moreover, in the last decade, both have peacefully undergone two power rotations—in Korea, between the Grand National Party and its opposition parties, and in Taiwan, between the Kuomintang (KMT) and the Democratic Progressive Party (DPP). According to Samuel Huntington's "two-turnover test," the two nascent democracies were "consolidated" as of 2008.[2] Passing this artificial threshold, however, tells us little about the kinds of long-term impacts and consequences that the two peaceful power rotations have had in their respective democracies. It only shows strong evidence for the contending elites' acceptance of the rules of democratic competition.

In this chapter, we examine the multifaceted impacts and consequences of the two peaceful power rotations in Korea and Taiwan in five analytical domains: 1) avoiding democratic breakdown; 2) avoiding democratic erosion; 3) completing democracy; 4) deepening democracy; and 5) organizing democracy.[3] For the sake of relevance and space, in each domain we select only the most important and meaningful issues for closer examination. Our analytical framework is intended to be context-specific and historically relevant rather than comprehensive and cross-nationally

TABLE 1—REPUBLIC OF KOREA (SOUTH KOREA) PRESIDENTS
SINCE THE DEMOCRATIC TRANSITION IN 1987

	Tenure	Party	Power Rotation
Roh Tae Woo	1988–1993	Democratic Justice Party/ Democratic Liberal Party	No
Kim Young Sam	1993–1998	Democratic Liberal Party/ New Korea Party/ Grand National Party	No
Kim Dae Jung	1998–2003	National Congress for New Politics/ New Millennium Democratic Party	Yes
Roh Moo Hyun	2003–2008	New Millennium Democratic Party/ Open Uri Party/ United New Democratic Party/ United Democratic Party	No
Lee Myung Bak	2008– incumbent	Grand National Party/ Saenuri Party	Yes

generalizable. We also take caution not to commit the fallacy of over-attribution, because not all the observed changes in political institutions and organizations or evolution in behaviors and attitudes of both the elites and masses were attributable to the two power rotations. Many other forces and dynamics were at work during the same period.

Korea and Taiwan in Comparative Perspective

As part of our effort to develop a context-sensitive framework for analyzing the implications in Taiwan and Korea of two peaceful power rotations, we must identify some important similarities and dissimilarities in the trajectories of their regime evolutions. First, unlike most of the third-wave democracies of Latin America and Eastern Europe, in both cases the political openings were not triggered by any major socioeconomic crisis or external market shocks, nor were they accompanied by popular demands for major socioeconomic reforms. Support for the old regime's development program in the two newly industrializing East Asian countries was much more broadly based than in many Latin American countries with comparable levels of industrialization. Indeed, the very effectiveness of the development program during the authoritarian era has meant that ties to the old regime were not entirely a liability for the incumbent elite. Nor was the political coalition behind this development program one whose cohesion could be easily disrupted. As a consequence, in both cases the incumbent elites enjoyed substantial political leverage—especially in the case of Taiwan—over the process of democratic transition and the crafting of new constitutional and electoral arrangements.

TABLE 2—REPUBLIC OF CHINA (TAIWAN) PRESIDENTS SINCE THE INTRODUCTION OF DIRECT ELECTIONS

	Tenure	Party	Power Rotation
Lee Teng-hui*	1988–2000	Kuomintang	No
Chen Shui-bian	2000–2008	Democratic Progressive Party	Yes
Ma Ying-jeou	2000–incumbent	Kuomintang	Yes

*Lee Teng-hui's first directly, elected term began in 1996. Prior to that he served out the term of the deceased President Chiang Ching-kuo, whose vice president he had been.

Coincidentally, both countries settled on a constitutional design that features semipresidentialism, a first-past-the-post rule for electing the president, and insufficient (if not flawed) mechanisms for breaking executive-legislative gridlock under divided government. In both cases, the ruling elite of the old regime managed to survive the founding election and refurbish its governing position with democratic legitimacy.

Both young democracies inherited a wrenching security environment, as each is part of a divided nation and faces an enormous military threat from the other side. Both were burdened by widespread nostalgia for the seeming effectiveness and efficiency of the authoritarian era. At the same time, both countries benefited from favorable socioeconomic conditions—including a well-educated citizenry, a sizeable middle class, a dynamic market economy, and a vibrant civil society—that facilitated democratic consolidation much more so than in the majority of other third-wave democracies. Democracy has never collapsed in a country with the level of per capita income that Korea and Taiwan now enjoy.

Despite all the shared characteristics, there are at least two significant differences between the two cases. First, Korea's democratic transition was from a military regime while Taiwan's was from the rule of a hegemonic party. The Korean military regime had never institutionalized its rule and had been politically fragile, ideologically hollow, and organizationally shallow since its inception. In contrast, Taiwan's one-party authoritarian regime had institutionalized its hegemonic presence in society well before the island became industrialized and was equipped with an established pattern of elite recruitment and a massive party apparatus with organizational links to key social constituencies and local factions.

Given the Korean military regime's seeming shortcomings, the first power transfer from the military elite to the opposition could have occurred as early as 1987 had opposition leaders Kim Young Sam and Kim Dae Jung not run against each other, splitting the opposition vote. On the other hand, Taiwan's KMT could have extended its lease on political control even longer had KMT rivals Lien Chan and James Soong not run against each other in 2000 (the latter on a the ticket of a breakaway party), allowing DPP candidate Chen Shui-bian to win the 2000 presidential election with 39.7 percent of the popular vote. Korea's first real power turnover, with Kim Dae Jung's electoral victory in 1997, was in a sense long overdue, while the DPP probably came to power before its time in 2000.[4]

Second, the transition in Taiwan called into question not only the legitimacy of the regime but the legitimacy of the state itself—its claims to sovereign status, its territorial boundaries, and the compass of its citizenship. The polarized conflict over national identity in Taiwan is emotionally much tenser, politically more divisive, and structurally more intractable than the regionalism engulfing Korean society. By the same token, the clash between Taiwan's so-called Pan-Blue and Pan-Green camps over cross-Strait relations has also been more acute and explosive than the schism between the conservative bloc and the progressive bloc over inter-Korean relations. As a result, the politics of polarization has been a far more serious hindrance to the consolidation of democracy in Taiwan than in Korea. In a nutshell, the two power rotations yielded many similar opportunities and challenges but also a few country-specific problems.

Meanings and Consequences of the Two Power Rotations

Kim Dae Jung's victory in Korea in 1997 and Chen Shui-bian's victory in Taiwan in 2000 were both landmark events by any measure. In both cases, this first real power rotation established a series of new precedents and reinforced popular belief in the legitimacy of the new democratic institutions. With the election of Kim Dae Jung, Korea became East Asia's first third-wave democracy to attain a peaceful rotation of power. Kim Dae Jung's victory was historic because it broke a longtime stereotype of East Asian democracies ruled by "a dominant, corporatist party that tolerated a limited opposition but never ceded power."[5] The DPP's victory in Taiwan in 2000 put an end to the KMT's 55 years of continuous rule over the island. It opened up a historic opportunity to deal with the holdovers from the authoritarian past and tackle the young Taiwanese democracy's lingering deficiencies and weaknesses.

In both cases, the first power rotation was preceded by reform-minded presidents who were tied to the old governing party but at the same time were independent enough to push for further democratization, making progress in some sensitive areas such as asserting civilian control over the military and setting up special commissions to deal with the issue of "transitional justice." In the case of Taiwan, President Lee Teng-hui went much further. He engineered a revamp of the constitutional design, marginalized the KMT's old-timers (mainlander elites), and reoriented the KMT's core commitment from upholding Chinese nationalism to constructing a separate Taiwanese identity. Both Kim Young Sam and

Lee Teng-hui should be given credit for laying the groundwork for each country's first peaceful power turnover.

In both cases, the new governing elites frequently suffered political paralysis and failed to live up to the popular expectation of extensive political reform. In both cases, the new era under these novice elites did not last long and was brought to an abrupt end by a humiliating electoral defeat.

Avoiding Democratic Breakdown

When analyzing Korea and Taiwan's ability to avoid democratic breakdown, we must ask whether these two young democracies have faced even a remote threat of illegal or pseudolegal overthrow by antidemocratic forces and whether the two power rotations helped to further neutralize and eliminate that possibility. Both do face a remote possibility of "sudden death" caused by outright military aggression from their communist rival. In addition, early in their respective democratic transitions, Korea had to overcome its praetorian legacy while Taiwan had to neutralize its military, which had long been loyal to the KMT.

Korea's democratic transition was characterized as a "transition by pact"—that is, by compromise between soft-liners within the authoritarian regime and moderate opposition members.[6] As a result, both reformers in the regime and the moderate opposition had critical interests in protecting the transition process by avoiding violent confrontation and accelerating the constitution-making process. Regime reformers abstained from using repressive power apparatuses to quell civil unrest after then–presidential candidate Roh Tae Woo's 29 June 1987 declaration offering compromise with prodemocracy forces. In return, the moderate opposition refrained from rallying the masses to the streets to press the regime for more substantive democratic reforms. Likewise, in response to the "Great Workers' Struggle" in which a million workers waged more than 3,400 strikes from July to early September 1987, regime reformers did not resort to police force to squash the strikes and allowed the striking workers and management to resolve their conflicts through dialogue and negotiations. For their part, the moderate opposition abstained from politicizing the workers' outburst to gain political advantage.

In addition to their abstention strategy, both sides worked to speed the drafting of the new constitution in order to preempt both hard-liners and the radical opposition from exploiting the unrest and instability created by the massive workers' protests. Three leaders of the democratic transition (Roh Tae Woo, Kim Young Sam, and Kim Dae Jung) agreed on a minimalist constitution-drafting process. Instead they would revise the indirectly elected presidential system into a directly and popularly elected five-year, single-term presidential system without touching many substantive issues such as the neutrality of the military in politics, workers' rights to participate in the management and distribution of profits, and the protection of universal human rights. They drafted the new constitution in just two months, finishing on 18 September 1987. It was approved by popular referendum on October 27. The founding election was held on 19 December 1987, less than six months after the democratic breakthrough in June. By accelerating the birth of a new democratically elected government, transition leaders prevented the antidemocratic forces who tried to exploit the instability, turmoil, violent street mobilizations, and populist upheavals during the transition period from inflicting "sudden death" on the new democracy.

After constituting the new democratic government, the main potential forces that could overthrow the new democratic government were politicized military officer groups inside the government and retired military officers. Guillermo O'Donnell and Philippe Schmitter called the military the queen of the democratic chess game who "may simply sweep the opponents off the board to kick it off and start playing solitaire."[7] Since the Korean War in 1950, Korea has been one of the most militarized countries in the world, and even after the democratic transition establishing civilian supremacy over the military was a highly risky job. To make matters worse, the first popularly elected president, Roh Tae Woo, lacked the credentials to persuade politicized military officers to return to the barracks because he was himself a former general who had been deeply involved in the May 1980 military coup.

It was not until the Kim Young Sam presidency that the military was comprehensively purged from politics. Kim Young Sam, the first civilian president in thirty years, called his government a "civilian government" (*munminjungbu*) and launched a massive project of demilitarization and civilianization of Korean politics. Upon his inauguration, Kim Young Sam took decisive and quick actions to disband the Hanahoe Club, a politicized clique of military officers that had occupied key strategic posts in the military and national-security apparatus under the Chun Doo Hwan and Roh governments. Immediately after disbanding the Hanahoe Club, Kim Young Sam purged most of the Hanahoe members from the military and national-security apparatus.[8]

Kim Young Sam even prosecuted the two former presidents, Chun and Roh, on charges of corruption, military mutiny, treason for staging the December 1979 coup, and the massacre of civilians during the Kwangju uprising in 1980.[9] With the quick and thorough purging of the politicized military-officer group, President Kim averted the possibility of a sudden breakdown of the new democracy by coup-plotting officers. Moreover, he removed the "reserved domain" for the military in Korean politics. The military and the national-security apparatus were deprived of their privileged status and prerogatives outside the control of democratically elected civilian representatives.[10]

Unlike Korea, Taiwan's young democracy did not face any meaning-ful internal threat of illegal or pseudolegal overthrow by antidemocratic forces after its founding election. Lee Teng-hui had already politically tamed the military—which was a mainlander-dominated power bloc within the KMT—by forcing out former general Hau Pei-tsun from the premiership in 1993. On Lee's instruction, two days after the 20 March 2000 election, Chief of the General Staff Tang Yao-ming quelled any lingering anxiety about the resistance of the military and security estab-lishment to a DPP takeover by publicly pledging the allegiance of the armed services to the newly elected president. Chen Shui-bian and the DPP elite, however, still harbored a deep suspicion about the loyalty of the professional officer corps, which had been a strong bastion of KMT loyalists and was hostile to Taiwan's independence movement. To neutralize the military, Chen Shui-bian introduced the most sweep-ing personnel reshuffling ever seen at the top echelon of the military through rapid turnover and the vigorous promotion of like-minded, na-tive Taiwanese senior officers. The reshuffling was so extensive, irregu-lar, and frequent that the military became very demoralized. In addition, its public image greatly suffered from recurring bribe-taking scandals.[11]

The only conceivable external threat to the survival of Taiwan's young democracy is a military invasion by the People's Liberation Army—most likely under a scenario of Taiwan declaring formal inde-pendence. In a sense, the 2000 election proceeded in the shadow of the military threat from the People's Republic of China. Beijing was deeply upset by Chen Shui-bian's victory, and Washington was prompted to exercise crisis management behind the scenes. To de-escalate the ten-sion in the Taiwan Strait, the United States cajoled Chen to pledge in his 2000 inaugural address the "four no's:" no declaring independence, no changing Taiwan's formal name from the Republic of China, no en-shrining a "state-to-state" relationship in the constitution, and no hold-ing a referendum on formal independence.

During his eight-year presidency, however, Chen could not resist pushing the Taiwanese independence agenda and stepping over the red line drawn by Beijing as these highly emotional issues always helped to galvanize his DPP constituency and divert people's attention away from the sagging economy. He pushed for holding a referendum to rede-fine the cross-Strait relations as "state-to-state," to change the name of the country, and to adopt a new constitution. Each time, he was forced to back down by an arm-twisting Washington that took Beijing's stern warnings very seriously and did not want to upset the strategic applecart in East Asia. Toward the end of Chen's tenure, the pro-independence constituency had grudgingly accepted the chilling reality that de jure in-dependence was simply not a realistic option and that the DPP's efforts could go no further in this regard.

In the 2008 election, the KMT candidate, Ma Ying-jeou, won a landslide victory with an agenda of resuming cross-Strait political dialogue and normalizing bilateral economic relations. In response, Beijing launched a series of peace overtures culminating in the signing of the Economic Cooperation Framework Agreement (ECFA) in July 2010. With the acceleration of cross-Strait economic integration and cultural exchange, the possibility for a head-on collision due to Taiwan's political provocation and mainland China's military retaliation has significantly, but not completely, diminished.

Avoiding Democratic Erosion

When examining the ability of Korea and Taiwan to avoid democratic erosion, we look for signs of any danger of slow decay—of more incremental and less transparent forms of regression. O'Donnell described this as "a progressive diminution of existing spaces for the exercise of civilian power and the effectiveness of the classic guarantees of liberal constitutionalism."[12] In both cases, we do not think there has been any systemic risk of slow regression. Yet there are pockets of gray areas that warrant vigilant scrutiny. In both countries, a witch-hunt for sympathizers of rival communist regimes could lead to serious violations of human rights. In Korea, the National Security Law—or anticommunist law—was used to crack down on democracy and human-rights activists and effectively curtail freedom of the press, freedom of assembly, and freedom of conscience. In Taiwan, this could be an even more serious issue in the midst of a national-identity crisis. Under the old martial-law regime, advocates of Taiwan's independence had been prosecuted on charges of treason. Under the new democratic regime, an impulse for reverse discrimination lurks under the rising tide of Taiwanese nationalism. We examine whether the two power rotations helped to arrest these undercurrents of human-rights backsliding.

In Korea, many worried that the outcome of the founding election that brought former army general Roh Tae Woo to power would be an omen for "silent regressions from democracy to semidemocratic rule."[13] Because many current and former military officers won key strategic posts in government—particularly national-security positions—and a broad domain remained reserved for the military and national-security apparatus, people feared that space for civilian power would remain narrow and the new democracy would slowly die.

Yet those worries of slow death or democratic erosion were not realized because the ruling party for the first time in history failed to receive a majority in the National Assembly. Instead, three opposition parties combined to win a solid majority. The policy coalition of these three parties possessed sufficient countervailing power to prevent authoritarian forces from attempting to erode democratic rule. The opposition majority persuaded, pressed, and compromised with President

Roh for more democratic reforms, the expansion of democracy in the socioeconomic arena, and the establishment of transitional justice for past wrongdoings, crimes, and violations of human rights.

President Roh tried to overcome his stalemate with the National Assembly by establishing a hegemonic party through the merger of three parties—the ruling Democratic Justice Party, Kim Young Sam's Reunification Democratic Party, and Kim Jong Pil's Liberal Democratic Alliance. The new party, the Democratic Liberal Party (DLP), had more than three-quarters of National Assembly seats. As a result, the process of pursuing transitional justice slowed down, violent attacks on radical labor and civil activists renewed, and electoral competition was suffocated in most regions except Kim Dae Jung's Cholla region.

The rise of the DLP might have made the new democracy regress gradually into a hybrid, semidemocracy. The experiment of a hegemonic party in posttransition Korea, however, was short-lived due to a family feud among the three party factions in the DLP. Kim Young Sam won the December 1992 presidential election by a plurality of eight percentage points over archrival Kim Dae Jung. The newly elected Kim Young Sam soon launched democratic reforms targeted mainly at the old establishment forces of the military and the *chaebols* (large, powerful, family-owned industrial conglomerates).

He pushed for the demilitarization of politics and civilian supremacy over the military, and he brought two former presidents to justice. He introduced "real-name financial accounts" to remove the possibility of black-money dealings between *chaebols* and corrupt politicians. These potential sources of democratic erosion were all removed during the Kim Young Sam presidency. Ironically, Kim Young Sam's reforms, coupled with his mishandling of the economy and the effects of the 1997 East Asian financial crisis, laid the groundwork for Korea's first peaceful power rotation, which helped put an end to the danger of regression to illiberal democracy.

Taiwan's potential sources of democratic erosion, on the other hand, are potentially more insidious. The island's national-identity crisis risks not only inviting external military intervention but also inducing intolerance, discrimination, and extremism at home, because by nature this crisis is a struggle between two seemingly irreconcilable emotional claims about Taiwan's statehood and the national identity of the people of Taiwan. During Chen Shui-bian's first term, there was a steady hardening over this issue by two competing power blocs, the "Pan-Green" alliance of the Democratic Progressive Party (DPP) and the Taiwan Solidarity Union (TSU) and the "Pan-Blue" coalition comprising the Kuomintang (KMT) and the People First Party (PFP).[14] Both sides feared that the other camp would use its governing power to impose its ideological agenda and introduce irreversible changes to the construction of national identity and the direction of cross-Strait relations.

Most unfortunately, there was no shortage of demagoguery from politicians, TV talk-show hosts, and bloggers, who willfully inflamed the politics of hate and fear. The zealots of the two camps paid little respect to civility, compromise, tolerance, due process, and rule of law—all essential elements in the workings of a liberal democracy. In this frenzied atmosphere, politicians were rewarded for their degrading language, unsavory political tactics, and unlawful practices.

The whole society became excessively polarized, and partisanship penetrated every aspect of social life as Taiwan approached the March 2004 presidential election, which was viewed by many die-hard supporters on both sides as the final showdown. In the end, the legitimacy of this election was seriously challenged by the losing camp and questioned by many skeptical voters.[15] The integrity and independence of the Central Election Commission was also cast into serious doubt, something that had never happened since Taiwan's democratic opening. The society was deeply divided over the "true" story behind the bizarre assassination attempt on Chen Shui-bian and Vice-President Annette Lu that took place on the eve of the election. The deep acrimony surrounding the 2004 election left Taiwan's democracy with a deep scar, as it seriously eroded popular faith in the openness and fairness of the political game.

Fortunately, Taiwan's democracy did not, in the end, lose its self-correcting capability. Passions finally reached the point of saturation by the time of the December 2004 parliamentary elections. Voter turnout dropped to 59 percent, a record low for parliamentary elections. Society gradually returned to a path of reconciliation, which paved the way for a much less stressful and tumultuous presidential race in 2008 and a smooth second power rotation.

Nevertheless, the national-identity crisis still precipitated endless debates and conflicts over legal discrimination against citizens who have family, social, cultural, or commercial ties with mainland China. Hundreds of thousands of Taiwanese expatriates and their dependents working and living in mainland China were de facto disfranchised due to the DPP's strong objection to absentee ballots. Telephone conversations across the Strait were regularly screened by Taiwan's security apparatus without sufficient legal grounds. Taiwanese students who graduated from the mainland's top universities could not get their diplomas officially accredited. Public-sector retirees who chose to live on the mainland were denied their monthly pension. Some of these issues have been steadily resolved after the second power rotation, but many more are still held up by skirmishes on the legislative floor and the inertia of the Council of Grand Justices, Taiwan's constitutional court.

Completing Democracy

While judging the effectiveness of Korea and Taiwan in attaining full democratic rule, we must establish to what extent the two power rotations helped to eliminate the residual authoritarian elements in the system. Residual authoritarian elements could include the constitution's birth defects, discrimination in electoral arrangements, reserved domains (beyond the scope of democratic accountability) enjoyed by the military and security apparatus, and a legacy of partisan control of the state bureaucracy, the judiciary, and the media. Another challenge is the handling of transitional justice, especially after the political force representing the victims of authoritarian suppression came to power for the first time.[16]

President Kim Young Sam completed democratic consolidation in the negative sense—that is, the elimination of antidemocratic forces and behavior—by instituting firm civilian supremacy over the military and purging politicized military officers from politics.[17] By the 1997 presidential election, there remained few antidemocratic forces to publicly veto democratically elected leaders. By preemptively removing potential veto forces, Kim Young Sam paradoxically paved the way for Kim Dae Jung to be elected president.

Producing the first peaceful transfer of power to an opposition-party candidate in Korean history, the 1997 election affirmed the maturity and effective functioning of democracy in Korea. The election was also historic because the power rotation took place in the midst of the Asian financial crisis, which almost caused a meltdown of Korea's financial and economic systems. The country avoided the worst scenario of state default through massive bailout loans (US$55 billion) from the IMF. The unexpected coincidence of the shared timing of the presidential election and the economic crisis tested the durability and accountability of Korea's new democracy. Faced with severe economic crisis, the Korean people did not defer to authoritarian nostalgia or populist demagogues. Rather, they went to ballot box to hold the ruling party accountable and elect the opposition candidate, giving him a strong mandate to overhaul the country's crony capitalism and restore its high-growth economy.

Taiwan's road toward completing democracy was a bumpy one, but there have been a number of positive developments on that path. The historic power rotation in 2000 opened up the opportunity to do away with the shady authoritarian practices that had been preserved, despite the transition to democracy, under continuous KMT rule. These practices constituted a sort of institutional fraud that had always loaded the political dice in favor of the incumbent and deprived the opposition of a level playing field. They also obstructed the creation of an unconstrained sphere for public discourse, an autonomous civil society and mass media, a politically neutral civil service, military, and security apparatus, and independent law-enforcement agencies and judiciary. Had the KMT remained in power, none of these lingering deficiencies would have been tractable.

Chen Shui-bian's overall record on removing these leftover practices was a mixed one and in certain areas rather disappointing. After the power rotation, the KMT had no choice but to sever its established organizational ties with the military, civil service, and government-sponsored business associations. The KMT relinquished its coveted television network to comply with new DPP-initiated regulations without a fight. However, the DPP government's initiative to clean up the KMT-owned enterprises and dubious business deals of the past was stalled by a feisty opposition on the legislative floor.

Being a longtime political underdog, facing an opposition-controlled parliament, and having won less than 40 percent in the presidential election, the DPP leadership came into office with a deep sense of insecurity. Chen and his top advisors were anxious to try everything conceivable to secure their hard-won but shaky hold on power, including using many of their predecessors' unsavory practices in order to turn control of executive power into political advantage. Chen and his top lieutenants did not ask the authoritarian watchdogs, such as the Attorney General's Office and the Bureau of Investigation, to kick their old habits. On the contrary, these watchdogs were ready to fulfill their new master's wishes with vigilance. They offered effective weapons for political intimidation by spying on the DPP's political enemies, applying selective prosecution and tax-auditing, and if necessary suppressing evidence of their master's own unlawful actions.

Chen and his top lieutenants also suspected that they were surrounded by senior bureaucrats with leanings toward the KMT. Instead of installing new mechanisms to enforce political neutrality, they set up a political academy and vigorously recruited midlevel bureaucrats to attend the training programs and formally join the DPP. Chen also encouraged the creation of a pro-DPP advertisement-buyers cartel to starve any unfriendly media. The government's advertisement budgets for various ministries and state-owned enterprises were substantially expanded, pulled together, and then strategically dispensed to reward friendly mass media. Most notoriously, Chen and his wife extorted business tycoons to hand over tens of millions of dollars in cash to be transferred to secret overseas accounts. In a sense, using such tactics was almost second nature to the DPP leaders, who had been victimized by these very practices in the past. In some instances, they even outdid their KMT predecessors.

Taiwan's first power rotation brought about three unexpected consequences, all largely conducive to the maturing of democracy. First, many weighty social actors—such as bureaucrats, academics, business executives, religious groups, trade associations, and NGOs—have learned to live with democratic uncertainty. These actors have tried to maintain an equal distance from both the Blue and the Green camps. Second, the political tug-of-war between the DPP-controlled executive and the KMT-controlled legislature inadvertently created more breathing room for other independent branches of the government. Some independent-minded prosecutors, judges, and auditors were able to crack down on corruption, embezzlement, vote-buying, and other criminal offenses committed by members of both political camps. As Chen Shui-bian's second term began, many of his top aides and protégés were indicted on corruption charges. Eventually, a few muckraking journalists brought to light the rampant corruption at the highest level. At the end of 2006, Chen's wife was indicted for corruption and forgery charges, and the president himself was also expected to be (and then was) indicted as soon as he stepped down and was no longer protected by presidential immunity.

Third, many of DPP's former allies in the progressive camp, such as liberal intellectuals and the labor, environmental, and gender movements, were able to maintain their antiestablishment propensity and scrutinize the new governing elite. In so doing, they helped to expand the sphere for nonpartisan public discourse. In response to the shocking revelation of rampant corruption and obstruction of justice by Chen and his family, the progressive camp collaborated with former DPP chairman Shih Ming-teh but rejected KMT involvement in organizing waves of large-scale demonstrations demanding the president's resignation. Altogether, close to a million citizens took part in this three-month-long demonstration at different points in time. For the first time ever, a political movement of this scale was able to transcend the Blue-Green divide. It also evidently reinforced prosecutors' resolve to press charges against the president and set a new hallmark for judicial independence.

By the time the KMT returned to power in 2008, the island's political soil had been thoroughly turned over. It is no longer possible for the KMT to recover its coveted political assets and old privileged ties, much less its overall political hegemony. Instead, the Ma Ying-jeou government has to cope with a less governable society featuring a very polarized, vulgarized, and overly competitive media sector that makes all public political figures look equally untrustworthy and incompetent; many more assertive, single-issue NGOs refusing to yield any ground; shortsighted business elites interested only in sector-specific issues and tax reduction; and overly cautious bureaucrats not ready to take on any new initiatives or responsibility. Without a quick fix to these symptoms of democratic malaise, the quality of democratic governance necessarily suffers.

Deepening Democracy

Have the two power rotations in Korea and Taiwan helped to institutionalize liberal democracy's basic ground rules and strengthen the legitimacy of the democratic form of government? For the former, we examine whether leaders of government, state institutions, and significant political parties respect the rule of law—in particular, whether they obey constitutional procedures, respect each other's legal rights, and up-hold constitutionalism. For the latter, we assess whether the democratic regime enjoys a "broad and deep" legitimacy in terms of popular beliefs and normative evaluations. We pay special attention to the moderating effect of power turnovers on the citizenry by asking if the gap in percep-tions of regime legitimacy between supporters of the winning and losing parties has narrowed.

A key indicator of the extent to which contending elites in a young democracy commit themselves to basic democratic rules is the deepen-ing of constitutionalism. This notion can be defined as a widely held belief that government can and should be legally limited in its powers and abide by the norms and procedures prescribed by the constitution and relevant statutes, and that its authority depends on its observing these limitations and rules.

Before 1987, Korea had been a notorious case of "weak constitution-alism" in which constitutions "were modified frequently and remained irrelevant."[18] Between 1948 and 1987, the constitution was amended nine times, and every president or prime minister gained greater author-ity with constitutional procedures that he drafted.

One of the post-1987 characteristics of Korean democracy is the strengthening and deepening of constitutionalism. Since the founding vote that year, Koreans have elected six different presidents and seven different National Assemblies. In 1991, local assemblymen were elected for the first time since Park Chung Hee ended local elections in 1961. The heads of local governments, governors, mayors, and county chiefs were added to the ballot in local elections in 1995.

Thus, since 1987, elections have been held regularly, and the over-whelming majority of Korean elites and average citizens believe that the only way to take power is through free and fair electoral competi-tion. Elections in Korea have become "the only game in town," and the constitution generates self-enforcing compliance with the outcome of an election from all relevant political actors.[19]

Nevertheless, while the constitution has become institutionalized and most Koreans have increasingly internalized the norms and values of constitutionalism, power mongers' efforts to politicize and manipulate the constitution in their favor have obstructed the deepening of con-stitutionalism. Since 1987, incumbent presidents and the ruling party's candidates have tried to revise the constitution. But they have failed without exception because of opposition from intraparty contenders and opposition parties.

Constitutionalism in Korea can be said to have been deepened and institutionalized in terms of longevity of the constitution, regularity of elections, and protection of human rights, political rights, and civil lib-erties. Yet the spirit of liberal constitutionalism and the rule of law, in particular, have not yet been deepened and institutionalized. In Korea, the "rule of man" rather than the "rule of law" continued to prevail even after the democratic transition, as Confucian patrimonialism persisted in the minds of politicians.[20] When democratically elected leaders applied laws in their protégés' favor and to their opponents' disadvantage, universal law-making, law-implementing, and law-adjudicating could not be routinized, and the rule of law could not be institutionalized.

Since its inauguration, the Lee Myung Bak government has emphasized the rule of law. When it talks about the rule of law, however, it is not actually speaking in the liberal constitutionalist sense, but rather according to the conceptions of the ancient Chinese legalists (*fa jia*), whereby the rule of law was a tool for the state and the emperor to rule efficiently and legitimately over their subjects. The true spirit of the rule of law is to limit and constrain the power of the state in order to guarantee civil liberties and the autonomy of civil society. In contrast, under the Lee government's legalist conception, politicians rely on politicized judicial institutions (courts and prosecutors), advocate the legitimacy of legal implementation of partisan government policies, and justify legal transgressions of civil liberties. In terms of the rule of law, Korean democracy under the Lee government has a long way to go.

The deepening of constitutionalism has also been a daunting challenge for Taiwan since the beginning of the island's democratic transition. Before the first power rotation, the ROC's constitution had undergone six phases of substantial revision. The basic design of the political system shifted from parliamentarianism to semipresidentialism. Over the course of the democratic transition, the process of constitution-making was complicated by a polarized conflict over national identity. For people who strongly believe in Taiwanese independence, all the revisions undertaken within the framework of the ROC's constitution were meant to be transitory. To them, the only acceptable final destination is the creation of a new constitution that declares the island's independent sovereign status. For people who vow to preserve and defend the existing state structure, the ROC's constitution and all the political symbols it carries constitute the cornerstone of their political identity. To them, all the amendments adopted during each round of constitutional revision were meant to be binding and lasting. They oppose any attempt to abolish the existing constitution through extraconstitutional means such as a plebiscite, the favorite tool of Taiwanese nationalists. Thus the emerging constitutional order was built on the fault line of two colliding nationalistic claims, and it did not enjoy the kind of broadly based legitimacy that one expects to find in a consolidated democracy.

The legitimacy of the emerging constitutional structure was further undermined by the strategic choices of some key players involved in the pact-making process, which had been littered with their unsavory hidden agendas, short-term political calculations, and improvised compromises.[21] There is no strong and widespread consensus among the contending political elites about the nature and logic of the government's structure defined by the current constitution. When the representatives of the two major political parties, the KMT and the DPP, coalesced to craft the current governmental structure during the fourth round of revisions (around late 1996 and early 1997), the newly amended system was sold to the public as an improved version of a semipresidential system modeled after the French Fifth Republic. But this bipartisan understanding of the moment is not shared by other political figures who were not directly involved in the constitution-crafting process.

After the first power rotation, these two inherited weaknesses of a fractured national identity and a lack of political consensus became sources of endless legal disputes and political stalemates between a combatant minority-party president and an aggressive parliament. A more serious conflict involved the very existence of the ROC's constitution. Chen Shui-bian made the adoption of a new constitution the top priority for his second term and openly pledged in his second inaugural speech to have the new constitution ready by the end of his term. He probably would have pushed this agenda to its realistic limit had it not been for the strong objection from Washington and the outbreak of political scandal, which dealt a fatal blow to his credibility and effectiveness. Nevertheless, as part of his ambitious agenda of constitutional overhaul, Chen Shui-bian managed to broker a deal with the KMT and coaxed through the seventh amendment, which slashed in half the size of the Legislative Yuan and changed the electoral rules for parliament to a more majoritarian system. At the same time, amending the constitution was made even more difficult by requiring the support of not just a three-quarters majority in the Legislative Yuan but also more than 50 percent of all eligible voters in a referendum.

After the second power handover, all major political actors on the island have finally come to a point where the possibility for further change to the constitution has been virtually exhausted. They have little choice but to live with this imperfect constitution. Making the existing constitution a living, active, and authoritative legal document seems to be the only feasible recipe for strengthening Taiwan's constitutional democracy. In this context, Ma Ying-jeou's solemn pledge in his first inauguration speech to reestablish a robust tradition of constitutionalism by affirming the authority of the ROC's constitution should be taken as a good starting point.

Public Attitudes in Korea and Taiwan

In each country, power rotation exerted the expected socializing and moderating effects in strengthening the legitimacy of democracy, but not without a bumpy ride. In both Taiwan and Korea, the first power rotations actually triggered a sharp decline in people's confidence about the superiority of democracy. Korean citizens' preference for democracy declined considerably from 54 percent in 1998 to 45 percent in 2001.[22] This sharp drop was probably mostly due to the extensive economic hardship that Koreans experienced in the wake of the 1997–98 regional financial crisis. At the same time, Korean voters were also disappointed by the antagonism between the ruling party and the opposition and the resultant legislative paralysis that stalled virtually all the political-reform bills initiated by the Kim Dae Jung government.

In Taiwan, citizens' confidence in democracy's superiority was also shaken by the extremely nasty, endless, and paralyzing political battles between the DPP-minority government and the KMT-controlled legislature. Citizens were shocked by the Chen Shui-bian government's mismanagement of the economy, which suffered from rising unemployment, a 2.2 percent negative growth rate in 2001, and a more than 40 percent loss in the stock market since the beginning of his tenure, just as the rest of East Asia was on the track of steady economic recovery. Taiwan's citizens' preference for democracy dropped from 57 percent in 1998 to only 40 percent in 2001.

After the subsequent power rotations in each country, however, popular confidence in the superiority of democracy rebounded. Citizens in both countries apparently have adjusted their expectations for and understanding of democracy, adapting to the noisy, messy, and even nasty aspects of real-life democracy. More important, the level of preference for democracy among supporters of the winning and losing parties has not only narrowed between 2001 and 2006 but even reversed after the second power rotation. In both countries, after the second power rotation the losers actually registered a much stronger commitment to democracy than did the winners. Thus, supporters of the DPP in Taiwan and the progressive camp in Korea have not only accepted their recent electoral defeats but have re-embraced their prodemocracy roots.

Organizing Democracy

One of the indicators of democratic consolidation is what Schedler calls "the organization of democracy" or what Schmitter terms the organization and institutionalization of "partial regimes" such as political parties, systems of interest intermediation, state bureaucracies, the judicial system, and legislative bodies.[23] For Korea and Taiwan, the question is whether the two power rotations in each case facilitated the strengthening of some key subsystems or partial regimes found in functioning liberal democracies. In the case of Korea, we focus especially on the transformation of political parties, political-finance reform, and how the Internet revolution has augmented transparency. In the case of Taiwan, we pay additional attention to the development of the mechanisms of horizontal accountability. In both cases, we ask

if the two power rotations helped to root out the single most important source of popular distrust toward democratic institutions in East
Asia—money politics.[24]

Among partial regimes in Korea, political parties have been the least
organized and institutionalized. During the "Three Kims Era" (1987–
2002), Kim Young Sam, Kim Dae Jung, and Kim Jong Pil acted as
feudal lords of their parties, founding, dissolving, reestablishing, and
renaming them at will. The three Kims reigned as imperial party presidents who monopolized the nomination of candidates, the appointment
of party secretaries, officials, and chairmen of National Assembly committees, and the allocation of party finances. They distributed political
money to their followers in return for their loyalty. Given that the parties
were organized along regional lines and that the three Kims maintained
unstinting loyalty from their home provinces, very few politicians could
challenge the Kims' hold over their parties.

Yet no regionalist political party could assemble a stable majority
in the National Assembly through the single-member, simple-majority
electoral system. Because every party was regionally based, a very loose
alliance with other regional parties had to be formed to win presidential
elections, and this alliance would break down one or two years after the
election.[25]

The volatile, short-lived, personal nature of political parties under
the three Kims was a major impediment to internal party democracy and
a responsive and accountable party system. These regionalist political
parties obstructed Korea from devising a policy-oriented party system.
The three Kims' parties were Confucian patrimonial parties in the sense
that leadership and rank and file were both defined according to personal relationships rather than rules or ideologies.

During the last days of the Three Kims Era in 2002, a party-reform
movement began in the ruling party. In the aftermath of a devastating defeat in the 25 October 2001 by-election, the ruling Millennium
Democratic Party (MDP) enacted a comprehensive reform in party governance and a new nomination system for party candidates. The new
party-governance system abolished the post of party president, separated the presidential candidate and the chief party representative, and
adopted a new nomination system in which presidential candidates were
to be chosen by a "People's Nomination System."

The new party reforms removed the personal, feudal, and autocratic
elements of party leadership and attempted to build a popularly based
party system. The new People's Nominating System, which was a mixed
system of open and closed primaries, was the turning point in the con-
version of the MDP from an elite party to a mass party. The Grand National Party felt compelled to follow this bottom-up process of nominating the presidential candidate.

At the same time, a "slimmed but more efficient political party" had become the catchphrase of party reform in the era of Internet-based, "neo-nomadic" democracy, which attempted to move governance from a sluggish, exclusionary bureaucracy toward an efficient, open, online community. The overdevelopment of the party secretariat and district-branch party organizations had been the major source of party bureaucratization, "high cost, low efficiency politics," and political corruption. Thus, the major parties slimmed down by virtually abolishing local party branches and by scaling down their central party secretariats. Now Korean political parties are transforming themselves into "neo-nomadic" parties that try to aggregate, represent, and respond to constituencies' interests quickly, efficiently, and responsively through online communications.

The second partial regime that has been reformed since the Roh Moo Hyun presidency is the political-finance system. In the 2002 election, major candidates relied less on outdoor campaigns in front of mobilized mass audiences and more on TV or radio, social media and text messages, and the organization and mobilization of supporters through online and offline means. The prominence of social media and mobile-phone campaigns reduced the necessary amount of campaign funds and led the presidential campaigns to emphasize the U.S. style of policy debates in the cyberspace. However, illegal political contributions did not disappear in the 2002 election. The disclosure of illegal campaign contributions to the conservative opposition GNP party by major *chaebol* groups reduced public trust in political society to its lowest level.

In 2003, President Roh Moo Hyun started a *mani pulite* (clean hands) campaign to end illegal money politics by ordering prosecutors to investigate illegal political funds of both the ruling and opposition parties. Together with the Office of the Prosecutor's investigation of illegal campaign money, public pressure for establishing a transparent political-finance system before the 15 April 2004 National Assembly election forced Korean political society to implement political-finance reform. The new political-finance laws obligated parties and candidates to report to the National Election Commission in a clear and verifiable manner by providing receipts, set new, more stringent limits on political contributions, and encouraged many small donations. Additionally, the government and the National Election Commission encouraged whistle-blowing on illegal campaign money and vote-buying by rewarding whistle-blowers with fifty times the amount of illegal money they reported and imposing fines of fifty times the amount of money transferred on both illegal donors and receivers.

With this reform of political finance, money played a less important role in the 2004 National Assembly elections than it had in any other Korean election. The polls that year were the cleanest in the country's history and a turning point for political transparency in Korea.

The third new partial regime has been the rise of Internet democracy.

Korea is a frontrunner in the IT revolution, and currently more than 30 million people out of a population of 47 million are "netizens." Korean netizens make use of the Internet as a revolutionary instrument to improve accountability and transparency in Korean politics. The Internet revolution has not only reformed representative democracy but also strengthened participatory democracy. Netizens have become "prosumer" voters, transforming themselves from passive consumers of political information that politicians and parties produced to active producers and providers of information.

Taiwan's Emerging Two-Party System

The political parties in Taiwan were more institutionalized than their counterparts in Korea even before Taiwan's first power rotation in 2000. Since then, the island's party system has moved steadily toward a two-party system. The introduction of new, more majoritarian rules for electing members of parliament in 2005 simply reinforced this trend. The two major parties, the KMT and the DPP, have increasingly become mirror images of each other, with the KMT undergoing a massive organizational downsizing after its humiliating defeat in 2000 and the DPP beefing up its party bureaucracy and local machine to match the KMT's organizational strength.

Both have experimented with a mixed system of closed and open primaries for the nomination of parliamentary and presidential candidates. Both have tried to countervail the weakening effect of primaries on the party center by consolidating the power base of the party chairperson through direct election by party members. With greater crystallization of partisanship, Taiwan's two major parties have been slower than their Korean counterparts to adapt to the explosion of social media and generate a more open, Internet-based democracy. So far, the Internet revolution has yet to strengthen accountability and transparency in Taiwan.

As with political parties, the mechanisms of horizontal accountability have provided both a site of contention within Taiwanese politics and a litmus test for the adequacy and coherence of the organization of democracy on the island. Well before the power rotation of 2000, many constitutional scholars had wondered how a non-KMT president could shape the cabinet and steer national policies without a power-sharing arrangement with the KMT, which most believed would (and did) continue its majority control of parliament for a long while. Under the revised constitution, the president is no longer obliged to appoint a premier with majority support in parliament, but parliament can unseat a sitting cabinet with a vote of no confidence. Furthermore, Taiwan's parliament is much more powerful than its peer under the French model in steering the legislative agenda (and crippling the government when it deems it necessary). The ROC's constitution does not recognize the priority of government bills. Instead, the legislature controls its own agenda. The cabinet can send back objectionable legislation and binding resolutions to parliament for reconsideration, but parliament has the final say if the same bill is passed again with an absolute majority.

After taking office in 2000, Chen Shui-bian overestimated his chances of pushing forward his agenda without a formal "cohabitation" arrangement with the KMT parliamentary majority. He refused the KMT's demand for party-to-party negotiations over a power-sharing scheme and insisted on exercising his authority to appoint the premier. The KMT chose to strangle the DPP government piece by piece, rather than unseating the sitting cabinet and forcing a political showdown. This inevitably sparked a fierce competition over the steering of the legislative agenda and national priorities between a combatant president and a hostile parliament. The opposition coalition of the KMT and PFP blocked virtually all the major legislative bills introduced by the DPP government.

Another major battle was over the confirmation of presidential nominees to three other branches of government: the Control Yuan, the Council of Grand Justices, and the Examination Yuan. The KMT-controlled parliament blocked nominees who it felt had suspicious track records, and Chen refused to nominate replacements and intentionally left many slots vacant. In 2005, the Legislative Yuan dramatically sent back the whole slate of Control Yuan nominees, citing the controversial backgrounds of many candidates, but Chen refused to nominate any other candidates. As a result, the Control Yuan, which performs the function of ombudsman and anticorruption watchdog, was left empty and dormant for three years.

The KMT's landslide victories in the January 2008 legislative election and the March presidential election brought eight years of political gridlock to a temporary end. Yet Taiwan's semipresidential system is still vulnerable to the recurrence of political gridlock under a scenario of divided government. In the future, the system needs to be augmented by reinstituting the old requirement of parliamentary confirmation to certify majority support for an incoming premier, either through formal constitutional amendment or by making this a convention to be adopted by all political parties.

Also, the last round of constitutional revision, which was engineered under an unholy alliance between the DPP and the KMT in 2005,[26] brought about many undesirable consequences when it was implemented for the first time in 2008. First, the new electoral rule, which carries a strong majoritarian bent,[27] dealt the DPP a crushing defeat. The DPP won 38 percent of the popular vote on the first (district) ballot and 36.8 percent on the second (party list), but it gained less than a quarter of the seats in parliament. The DPP caucus was so powerless that it was not able to mount any meaningful objection to KMT-initiated legislative proposals. When it came to the most controversial bills pertaining to cross-Strait relations, the DPP caucus simply tried to paralyze the parliamentary process with disruptive tactics.[28]

Next, since the size of the Legislative Yuan was cut in half to 113 seats, it takes only three or four MPs to block or manipulate a bill at the committee stage. On the surface, it appears as though the KMT-controlled cabinet has been given *carte blanche* under a Pan Blue–dominated parliament. Substantively, except on politically salient issues, decision-making power has become highly fragmented. Individual ministries have often become subservient to a few powerful MPs—including the Speaker, the party whips of both camps, and some ranking MPs—who broker legislative deals and fix the budget without much public scrutiny. As a result, the legislature is the most crucial decision-making arena for a wide range of issues, and the power of individual MPs makes it far easier for fat-cat donors or lobbyists representing special interests to exert undue influence.

Under strong popular pressure, the major political parties adopted a Lobby Law, which took effect in August 2008. But so far, the law has been mere window-dressing thanks to the complacency of virtually all the MPs. A great majority of MPs from both camps has shun any discussion on tougher rules for transparency that would allow the mass media and other public watchdogs to scrutinize the legislative logrolling process. It is no wonder that after the second rotation of power, popular trust in parliament has sunk to its lowest level. In a similar vein, the two major parties have shown little interest in making political donations more transparent and recipients and donors more accountable. While Taiwan's judicial branch has been more independent and vigorous since the first power rotation in hounding corrupt politicians, money politics remains an intractable problem that continues to erode public trust in the island's key democratic institutions.

In both Korea and Taiwan, the two power rotations to the political opposition were historic events, marking major steps forward toward democratic consolidation. In each case, the first power rotation also inaugurated a period of party realignment. Taiwan's first power rotation in 2000 ended an epoch of one-party dominance and opened the possibility of creating a level playing field for the two competing power blocs.

In both cases, the first power rotation went more smoothly and peacefully than many observers had expected. The presidential predecessors, Kim Young Sam and Lee Teng-hui, should be credited for removing some potential sources of democratic backsliding and paving the way for a smooth power turnover. Kim Young Sam launched democratic reforms targeted mainly against old establishment forces of the military and *chaebols,* while Lee Teng-hui marginalized the KMT old-timers and tamed the military.

The two cases show that passing Huntington's "two-turnover test" entails not just a confirmation of the behavioral acceptance of the rules of democratic competition by contending elites but also a deepening of the popular foundation of democratic legitimacy. The two power alternations also exerted positive socializing effects on the citizens of Korea and Taiwan, strengthening popular confidence in the mechanisms of democratic accountability and the public's sense of political empowerment. Most notably, after the second power rotation there was a convergence in levels of democratic support between the winning and losing camps in both countries.

In both Korea and Taiwan, the two power rotations have helped to strengthen constitutionalism, bringing a conclusive end to the saga of repeated attempts to amend the constitutional design. By the time of the second power rotation, after several rounds of aborted constitutional reform, both the current and former governing elites had depleted their reform credentials and political capital. All contending elites in each country have finally learned to live with the existing constitutions, despite their shortcomings and inadequacies. Last, but by no means the least, the two power rotations in each country have also strengthened the rule of law by dissuading future officeholders from repeating the mistakes of certain predecessors who, after the alternation in power, were brought to justice for their abuses and criminal offenses while in office.

NOTES

1. For an assessment of the democratic development in the two countries, see Yun-han Chu, Larry Diamond, and Doh Chull Shin, "Halting Progress in Korea and Taiwan," *Journal of Democracy* 12 (January 2001): 122–36; Yun-han Chu et al., eds., *How East Asians View Democracy* (New York: Columbia University Press, 2008); and Yun-han Chu and Doh Chull Shin, "The Quality of Democracy in South Korea and Taiwan: Subjective Assessments from the Perspectives of Ordinary Citizens," in Larry Diamond and Leonardo Morlino, eds., *Assessing the Quality of Democracy* (Baltimore: Johns Hopkins University Press, 2005).

2. According to Huntington, a nascent democracy is considered consolidated only after it has experienced two peaceful electoral alternations after the founding election. See Samuel Huntington, *The Third Wave: Democratization in the Late Twentieth Century* (Norman: University of Oklahoma Press, 1991), 266.

3. We adapted this useful analytical scheme from Andreas Schedler; see Schedler, "What Is Democratic Consolidation?" *Journal of Democracy* 9 (April 1998): 91–107.

4. Most scholars thought the election of Kim Young Sam in 1992 was not a real power rotation because in 1990 he had merged his Peaceful Democracy Party with Roh's ruling DJP. The "real" power rotation came only in 1997 when a whole slate of governing elites was replaced by people from the progressive camp.

5. Thomas Carothers, "Think Again: Democracy," *Foreign Policy*, Summer 1997, 11–12.

6. Hyug Baeg Im, "South Korean Democratic Consolidation in Comparative Perspec-

tive," in Larry Diamond and Byung-Kook Kim, eds., *Consolidating Democracy in South Korea* (Boulder, Colo.: Lynne Rienner, 2000), 23–26.

7. Guillermo O'Donnell and Philippe C. Schmitter, *Transitions from Authoritarian Rule: Tentative Conclusions About Uncertain Democracies* (Baltimore: Johns Hopkins University Press, 1986).

8. Larry Diamond and Doh Chull Shin, "Introduction," in Diamond and Shin, eds., *Institutional Reform and Democratic Consolidation in Korea* (Stanford: Hoover Institute Press, 2000), 10.

9. Terry Roehrig, "Putting the Military on Trial: The Consolidation of Democracy in South Korea and Argentina," Columbia International Affairs Online, March 1998, *www.ciaonet.org/conf/rot01*.

10. Hyug Baeg Im, "Development and Change in Korean Democracy since the Democratic Transition in 1987: the Three Kims' Politics and After," in Yin-wah Chu and Siu-lun Wong, eds., *East Asia's New Democracies* (New York: Routledge, 2010).

11. A series of scandals revealed that many senior military officers had to bribe their superiors (sometimes up to the presidential office) to get promotions.

12. Guillermo O'Donnell, "Transitions, Continuities, and Paradoxes," in Scott Mainwaring, Guillermo O'Donnell, and J. Samuel Valenzuela, eds., *Issues in Democratic Consolidation: The New South American Democracies in Comparative Perspective* (Notre Dame: University of Notre Dame Press, 1992), 19.

13. Schedler, "What is Democratic Consolidation?," 97.

14. The Pan-Blue camp also includes the majority of independents and the diminishing New Party.

15. According to the survey data, the freeness and fairness of the two previous presidential elections (in 1996 and 2000) were widely recognized even among the voters of the losing camp—82.6 percent and 80.7 percent of the electorate considered the 1996 and the 2000 elections, respectively, to be fair. After the 2004 election, only 46.4 percent of eligible voters felt the same way. Among the losing camp, only 11 percent of respondents thought the election was fair. See Yun-han Chu, "Taiwan's Democracy at a Turning Point," *American Journal of Chinese Studies* 11 (May 2005): 901–24.

16. Neil Kritz, ed., *Transitional Justice: How Emerging Democracies Reckon with Former Regimes*, vols. 2–3 (Washington, D.C.: U.S. Institute of Peace Press, 1995).

17. For the concepts of positive and negative consolidation, see Hyug Baeg Im, "Faltering Democratic Consolidation in South Korea: Democracy at the End of the 'Three Kims' Era," *Democratization* 11 (December 2004): 179–98.

18. Adam Przeworski, *Democracy and the Market* (Cambridge: Cambridge University Press, 1991), 35.

19. Przeworski, *Democracy and the Market*.

20. Confucian paternalism conceives of the state as an extended family wherein the leader acts in the paternal role. Personal relationships governing the subservient relationships of children or political subordinates to their fathers or political patrons take precedence over the law.

21. Jih-wen Lin, "Transition Through Transactions: Taiwan's Constitutional Reforms in the Lee Teng-Hui Era," *American Asian Review* 20, no. 2, (2002): 123–55.

22. See Chong-min Park and Yun-han Chu, "Trends in Attitudes and Values Toward Democracy and Liberalism in Korea and Taiwan," paper delivered at the "New Challenges for Maturing Democracies in Taiwan and Korea" conference organized by the Center on Democracy, Development, and the Rule of Law at Stanford University, 27–28 May 2011.

23. Schedler, "What Is Democratic Consolidation?"; Philippe C. Schmitter, "Organized Interests and Democratic Consolidation in Southern Europe," in Richard Gunther, P. Nikiforos Diamandouros, and Hans-Jürgen Puhle, eds., *The Politics of Democratic Consolidation: Southern Europe in Comparative Perspective* (Baltimore: Johns Hopkins University Press, 1995).

24. Eric Chang and Yun-han Chu, "Corruption and Trust: Exceptionalism in East Asian Democracies?" *Journal of Politics* 68 (May 2006): 259–71.

25. Byung-Kook Kim and Hyug Baeg Im, "Crony Capitalism in South Korea, Thailand, and Taiwan: Myth and Reality," *Journal of East Asian Studies* 1, no.1 (2001): 31–32.

26. Jih-wen Lin, "The Politics of Reform in Japan and Taiwan," *Journal of Democracy* 17 (April 2006): 118–31.

27. The old single-nontransferable-vote system for electing the members of the Legislative Yuan was replaced with a mixed system in which 75 percent of the members are elected through a single-member-district plurality system and the remaining 25 percent are elected from party lists under a PR rule.

28. The familiar repertoire includes using human chains to block the entrance, locking up the Speaker in his private chamber, or tearing down the Speaker's microphone and taking away his gavel. These disruptive tactics have made Taiwan's parliament infamous worldwide.

III

Southeast Asia

8

THE IRONY OF SUCCESS IN INDONESIA

Edward Aspinall

Edward Aspinall, *professor in the Department of Political and Social Change at the Australian National University, is the author of Opposing* Suharto: Compromise, Resistance, and Regime Change in Indonesia *(2005) and* Islam and Nation: Separatist Rebellion in Aceh *(2009). This essay originally appeared in the April 2010 issue of the* Journal of Democracy.

A dozen years ago, Indonesia looked like an unlikely candidate for democratic success. Born amid an economic collapse that has had few parallels in modern history, the country's new democracy faced at least three groups of potentially powerful spoilers. First, it inherited from President Suharto's regime (1967–98) a strong military that played an important political role and was seen by many observers as Suharto's natural successor. Second, in many regions of the country local actors stoked ethnic, religious, and separatist violence, prompting a serious crisis of "stateness" that, for a time, national leaders thought endangered the country's very survival. Finally, Islamist political forces—liberated after decades of repression—became more assertive, with some groups campaigning to transform Indonesia into an Islamic state, or at least to amend the constitution to oblige Muslims to obey *shari'a.*

Now, more than a decade after its democratic transition began, Indonesia has dealt effectively with these challenges to democracy. The military has retreated from the commanding heights of the political system. The most severe communal conflicts have receded, and the worst of the country's separatist insurgencies—in the Sumatran province of Aceh—has been resolved by a peace deal. Apart from a small fringe, Islamist forces have been absorbed into the political mainstream and no longer prioritize campaigning for a state based on *shari'a.* The neutralization of these threats has been accompanied by a host of other achievements—notably, a dramatic expansion of civil liberties, the emergence of a flourishing and pluralistic media market, and freely contested multiparty elections. The story of Indonesia's democratic success, in a decade that has witnessed worldwide democratic stagnation if not recession, presents valuable lessons for other countries.

There is, however, an underside to Indonesia's democratic accomplishments. The country has dealt with key challenges in ways that have come with costs. Spoilers have been accommodated and absorbed into the system rather than excluded from it, producing a trade-off between democratic success and democratic quality. This trade-off has not been an unfortunate side effect of Indonesia's democratic transition; rather, it has been central to its dynamics, and even an important ingredient in its success.

How and why this trade-off happened has much to do with the nature of Suharto's authoritarian regime, the path by which it was replaced, and its legacies. Suharto ruled only partly through coercion. His regime also tolerated a wide array of political and social forces so long as they generally obeyed the regime's rules and did not challenge it directly. This approach was reinforced by a system of patronage distribution from which political players who commanded sizeable social constituencies (for example, leaders of religious organizations) could benefit. The result was a widespread syndrome of "semi-opposition," in which many important political actors bridled at the regime's authoritarian controls yet adapted to the political culture of deal-making and compromise that it fostered.[1]

This background had important consequences for the nature of the democratic transition. Most of the key political forces and leaders who oversaw the transition after 1998 were either direct participants or marginal semi-oppositional players in the Suharto regime's power structure. As a result, Indonesia's democratic transition became like that of Brazil, which Guillermo O'Donnell once observed, "appeared to be the work of a coalition of anyone and everyone."[2] In Indonesia, few sharp dividing lines were drawn between the forces of the old regime and the new democrats. Rather, the tendency was to accommodate and absorb *all* major political forces, including those who in other circumstances might have challenged the new democratic dispensation. Patronage and corruption provided the oil to grease this arrangement.

Thus Indonesia's four post-Suharto presidents have all had some sort of background in the strongman's New Order regime. Bacharuddin Jusuf Habibie (1998–99) was a minister under Suharto and vice-president during his final term in office; Abdurrahman Wahid (1999–2001) was a leader of a prominent Islamic organization under Suharto, famous for the delight with which he played the regime's factional politics; Megawati Sukarnoputri (2001–2004), though she became a symbol of opposition in the late New Order years, was also the leader of one of the regime's three tolerated political parties and still articulates a political vision indelibly marked by that regime's mindset. The current president, Susilo Bambang Yudhoyono, was a senior military officer in the late Suharto years, albeit one with a reputation as a reformer.

More important, the cabinets of each of these presidents have represented broad coalitions in which all, or nearly all, of the major parties in the national legislature were represented, and they also have included a solid representation of former military officers and civilian bureaucrats—the two principal pillars of the Suharto regime. The ministers and their parties in turn often use cabinet posts as sources of patronage. National and regional legislatures are arenas in which members of different parties collude to share spoils that derive from the state budget and from business lobbyists.

Such phenomena have produced among scholars of Indonesia's democratic transition an almost obsessive interest in highlighting the degree to which authoritarian and corrupt forces have seized the new democratic institutions, giving rise to a distinctive range of terms to describe the results: "collusive democracy," "patrimonial democracy," "patronage democracy," and so on.[3] Whichever term one prefers, they all point to the manner in which Indonesian democracy has proven able to absorb, accommodate, and serve the interests of powerful elite groups, to the detriment of democratic quality. What the analysts sometimes neglect, however, is that this absorptive capacity has contributed greatly to the stability and achievements of the democratic transition.[4] Both the achievements and the costs are evident in the way that Indonesian democracy has neutralized its three main potential spoilers—the military, ethnoregional elites, and militant Islamism.

Buying Off the Military

Viewed in retrospect, perhaps the greatest achievement of Indonesian democratization has been the effective sidelining of the military from the commanding heights of political power. It was conventional wisdom among Indonesia specialists in the 1990s that the military would play a central role in any post-Suharto polity. The armed forces had been central to the Suharto regime for decades. Serving military officers occupied key posts in the cabinet, the bureaucracy, and the legislature. The doctrine of *dwifungsi* ("dual function"), implemented when Suharto came to power, reserved for the military a sociopolitical role in addition to its role of providing national defense. Its territorial command structure distributed troops throughout the country as part of a hierarchical structure that shadowed civilian government at every level, allowing the military to intervene in routine affairs of government from top to bottom on a daily basis. And, of course, the military provided the coercive muscle power that the regime needed to repress its critics.

After Suharto's regime collapsed in 1998, this situation changed rapidly. The senior officer corps suffered a crisis of political confidence. Many of the street protests that accompanied the regime change took a strongly antimilitary tone, and officers saw in them vivid evidence that the military's reputation as an institution had been damaged by political engagement. In response, they declared a "new paradigm" according to which the military would withdraw from direct involvement in political affairs: The police forces were separated from the armed forces and given primary responsibility for maintaining domestic security; the practice of allowing serving officers to occupy posts in the civilian bureaucracy was halted; and the seats in national and local parliaments reserved for military officers were phased out by 2004.

But another important part of this story was the reluctance of the civilian government to intrude on certain core military prerogatives, out of fear of antagonizing the institution. The military was eased rather than forced out of power, in a process marked by an urge to accommodate the military as much as to reform it. Thus little progress has been made in two key areas of military reform. One has serious consequences for the quality of Indonesia's democracy, and the other constitutes a potential threat to its future survival.

The first area is the culture of impunity that, to a large degree, the military continues to enjoy. Indonesia has failed to punish perpetrators of gross human-rights violations that occurred during the Suharto years or even seriously to examine these events. At the peak of the post-Suharto reforms, Indonesia's legislature passed new laws that allowed it to establish special ad hoc human-rights courts to try old cases and to set up new human-rights courts to try future ones. Several ad hoc courts were established, and trials were held for officers implicated in past abuses—notably, a 1984 massacre of protestors in the Tanjung Priok district of Jakarta and the violence that preceded and accompanied the 1999 East Timor independence referendum. There were even initial convictions, but all were eventually overturned on appeal. In some cases, crowds of uniformed soldiers attended the trials in what must have been intimidating displays of force for the judges. Other inquiries have been vetoed by Indonesia's parliament, the People's Representative Council (DPR).

The overall result is that the military's role in handling civilian dissent is much reduced, but when its soldiers do act against civilians they sometimes still behave brutally, and they run little risk of serious punishment. Thus when the military was given emergency powers and ordered to eliminate separatist insurgents in Aceh in 2003–2004, there were widespread abuses against civilians. The military claimed that it was investigating and punishing soldiers who committed breaches. Yet these processes were never seriously monitored, and it is likely that, at best, only very light punishments were given. A series of abuses in the province of Papua (formerly called Irian Jaya) has also gone almost entirely unpunished. In other cases, punishments have been imposed but

were very light: For example, when Marines fired on a crowd of protesting villagers during a land dispute in East Java in 2007, killing four of
them, fourteen of the Marines were tried but the heaviest penalty was a
three-year jail term and expulsion from the military. Equally important,
the culture of impunity extends into other institutions. Amnesty International recently concluded that "the use of torture and other ill-treatment
by police is still widespread in Indonesia."[5]

The second failure has been in the pursuit of institutional reforms that
would eliminate remaining reserve domains of military power. Many
examples could be cited here, including the failure to civilianize the defense bureaucracy, with the result that, as one observer pithily remarked
(with a little exaggeration for dramatic effect), "The only two people not
wearing military uniforms in the Ministry of Defense are the minister
and his driver."[6] Attempts to reduce the military's involvement in business—which acts as both a facilitator of and incentive for political involvement, especially at the local level—have largely stalled, although
the military budget has increased dramatically from US$1.2 billion in
2003 to over $7.5 billion in 2012. The main failing, however, has been
successive governments' inability to dismantle the military's territorial
system. According to military officers, this system maintains an essential early-warning system against internal security threats; however, it
also provides an infrastructure for the military to monitor and, should it
someday so choose, to intervene in civilian politics.

The result is that although the military is no longer an important direct player in day-to-day high politics, it retains the institutional capacity and the mindset that could allow it to intervene in the future.
The 2006 coup in nearby Thailand demonstrates that, even in apparently
consolidated democracies where the military has been sidelined, army
officers can take advantage of political turmoil to reassert themselves.
Indonesia's post-Suharto experience presents its own salutary lesson in
this regard: Efforts to reform the military reached their high point early
in the rule of President Abdurrahman Wahid, when a plan to gradually
dismantle the territorial structure was announced. But Wahid's chaotic
approach to government, by which he alienated most parties in the national legislature, triggered a political crisis. In response, the president
tried to enlist the military to back him against parliament, and shelved
his plans for major military reform as a payoff.

Since Wahid was removed from office in 2001, those plans have
never effectively been revived. Neither the major parties in the legislature nor successor governments have reopened the issue of abolishing
the territorial structure. During this period, Indonesia has also experienced democratic stability, providing few opportunities for military
intervention. The fact that since 2004 the president himself has been
a former military officer, able to exercise considerable personal authority over the armed forces, has helped to consolidate the institu-

tion's political marginalization. Yet as Marcus Mietzner concludes in his important study of the military in Indonesia's democratic transition, "Indonesia still cannot rely on sufficiently strong institutional mechanisms to fend off possible military interference in politics in the future."[7] Indonesia has all but eliminated the military's role in high politics, but future crises—whether precipitated by economic problems, electoral paralysis, or some other cause—could see a return to military intervention. Persuading Indonesia's military to accede to democratization by refraining from encroachment on its core interests may have been an effective strategy in the short term, but its long-term viability remains in doubt.

Resisting Disintegration

For many Indonesians, the most shocking feature of their country's democratic transition was the wave of communal unrest that accompanied it. After (and in some cases even before) the collapse of the Suharto regime in 1998, a series of bloody local conflicts broke out. Taken together, they caused approximately 19,000 deaths[8] (although nobody knows the exact figure), and provoked grave fears that Indonesia was on the verge of a process of national disintegration similar to that which destroyed Yugoslavia and the Soviet Union.

Most of the violence was highly localized. In some areas—notably, in Kalimantan—local "indigenous" groups launched pogroms against migrants from other parts of Indonesia. Elsewhere (Ambon, North Maluku, and Poso, in Central Sulawesi), there were virtual small-scale civil wars between rival religious and ethnic communities. In East Timor, Papua, and Aceh, long-suppressed separatist sentiments emerged explosively, leading to a UN-supervised independence referendum in East Timor, a powerful insurgency in Aceh, and a more peaceful but determined pro-independence movement in Papua. Very worryingly for some Indonesians, there were early signs of separatist sentiment in provinces where it had never been present historically, such as the oil-rich province of Riau in Sumatra.

In each of these conflicts, local people vented long-suppressed grievances about excessive central government control and neglect or violation of local interests. Most of these conflicts also involved competition among local elites for control of local government and the access to patronage resources that this provided. Although the violence was localized, the popular grievances and the elite competition were not: In every region throughout the country, there was vigorous competition among local elites to capture state power, often accompanied by a revival of local ethnic consciousness.

A decade on, Indonesia has survived intact. Rather than leading to a fiery spiral that could have consumed the nation, most of the violent conflicts of the early post-Suharto years have sputtered out or been extinguished by peace deals. Interregional conflict—such as the tension between Java and the "Outer Islands" that marked the early years of Indonesian independence—has hardly featured as an element in national politics. Secessionist movements have been defused. There were many reasons for this outcome, not all of which can be explored here, but three deserve particular note.

First, the design of the country's electoral system was important. Since 1999, Indonesia has used variants of proportional representation in which members of parliament are elected from multimember districts. Proposals by some reformers who wanted to improve accountability of elected representatives to voters by introducing single-member districts have always been rejected, often on the grounds that such an approach would introduce a winner-take-all attitude that could endanger Indonesia's ethnic and religious pluralism. Yet one important safeguard was built into this system: In order to register for and run in elections, parties had to show that they had a broad national presence with functioning branches in a large proportion of the country's provinces and districts, effectively excluding local political parties.

The exclusion of local parties has prevented Indonesia's national institutions from becoming a battleground for organized regional and ethnic interests, and limited the extent to which local institutions can be captured by ethnically exclusivist movements. At the same time, proportional representation has produced a highly fragmented party system in which no single party is able to dominate. In 1999, the largest five parties won a combined total of 87 percent of the vote; in 2004, the biggest seven won about 80 percent; and in 2009, the top nine together won a little over 80 percent. When added to the patronage-centered style of politics inherited from the Suharto years, this fragmentation has created a climate of cross-party alliance-building, flexibility, opportunism, and deal-making that, while not conducive to effective government, is positive for preserving pluralism and preventing the escalation of communal tensions.

Second, and most important, was a far-reaching policy of decentralization of political and financial power initiated by the Habibie government in 1999. In a "big bang" decentralization that is often described as one of the most dramatic the world has seen, considerable political powers were devolved to the country's districts, along with control over a good part of the state budget. Devolution had the effect of blunting regional-center tensions, as local political elites and activists immediately shifted from protesting about the depredations of the central government to organizing to capture political power at the local level. It also delivered a blossoming of local democracy that is rightly lauded as one of the signature achievements of Indonesia's reform. Around the country, local political office is now vigorously contested in open elections, and local governments make many of the key decisions about how best to use local resources.

This process has not been without tension. Early on in the transition especially, some local contests for political power triggered violence, with local elites mobilizing followers along ethnic lines to help them gain power. Yet by displacing political and resource competition to the regions, decentralization also fragmented it, reducing its impact as a first-order problem threatening the survival of the state. Moreover, the same inclusivist impulses that govern national politics came to determine local political dynamics too. Cross-party coalitions and opportunistic alliances are the order of the day, and in direct elections for subnational executive office, local politicians in ethnically plural districts and provinces have learned that they need to build cross-communal alliances if they want to win.

But there, too, lies the rub. As has by now been repeatedly demonstrated in a burgeoning scholarly literature on Indonesia's local politics, decentralization also fostered predatory behavior at the local level.[9] Local parliaments became sites of corrupt deal-making in which legislators colluded with officials and businesspeople to siphon off money from the state budget and to direct contracts and licenses to business allies. In some out-of-the-way districts, decentralization has produced a phenomenon akin to the "bossism" that characterizes neighboring countries such as the Philippines and Thailand, with local clans governing their districts like virtual private fiefdoms. "Money politics," in the form of vote-buying and bribery of electoral officials, has particularly damaging effects on the integrity of electoral processes at the local level.

These processes have been exemplified in the proliferation of new districts, a process known in Indonesia as *pemekaran* or "blossoming." When Indonesia democratized, it had 341 districts. By late 2009, the figure stood at 497 and the government declared a moratorium on the formation of more. This moratorium was withdrawn in early 2012 and proposals for yet more districts and provinces again began to be processed by the national parliament. Often the publicly stated rationale for creating a new district out of an old one is to provide an administrative home for a local ethnic or subethnic group who live in a concentrated area, and to ameliorate tension with other groups. The underlying motive, however, is often to provide a slice of patronage resources for the bureaucrats, political bosses, or networks that dominate these areas. A new district provides new seats in a new legislature, a new district budget, new opportunities to appoint family or friends to civil service positions, and lucrative construction contracts to build new government buildings. Indeed, sometimes *pemekaran* is driven by a candidate who loses election for political office in one district and so lobbies for a new district carved out of the old one.

In short, decentralization has greatly expanded the capacity of the political structure to absorb, neutralize, and buy off potential democratic spoilers. Virtually every locally influential political player can hope to be a winner in Indonesia's new local politics, due to the inclusivist and collusive pattern that predominates. Even losing candidates in races to become provincial governor or district head usually have political party allies with seats in local parliaments through whom they gain consolation prizes in the form of construction contracts, land deals, bureaucratic appointments, or other benefits. For a time at least, if that failed to satisfy them, they could also hope to create districts where they could dominate. Because many of these political bosses draw on ethnic constituencies, these arrangements help to diminish communal tension by drawing ethnic elites into the web of patronage distribution.

Third, in areas that experienced high levels of violent conflict during the transition years, peace deals have been cemented by the distribution of patronage. This pattern of "patrimonial peace," as I have called it elsewhere, has been most dramatic in the province of Aceh.[10] The site of Indonesia's bloodiest post-Suharto separatist insurgency, this region has become almost miraculously peaceful since 2005, when the guerillas of the Free Aceh Movement signed a peace agreement in Helsinki to bring their separatist war to an end. Crucial to their decision was the granting of concessions by the Indonesian government that allowed them to compete for power at the local level: What cinched the deal was a clause allowing local political parties in Aceh, the only place in Indonesia where this exception to the national legal framework applies. Former guerilla leaders or their close allies have now been elected as the governor and as heads of 12 of the province's 23 districts; they have also achieved a near-majority in the provincial parliament and are the largest party in 16 of 23 district parliaments. Yet despite their past rebellion having been partly motivated by grievances about corruption and neglectful government, some former guerillas since coming to power have been implicated in the predatory practices that they had previously condemned. Tellingly, many have almost overnight transformed themselves into wealthy construction contractors. Without skills or experience in construction, they have been able to access government-funded construction contracts by drawing on their new political connections.

Two other peace deals that helped to end communal violence in Poso and Maluku, respectively, have also been accompanied by the distribution of construction contracts and access to similar patronage resources to leading figures from the previously warring sides. A special autonomy law and direct elections in Papua, while being far less successful at ameliorating separatist sentiment, have partly succeeded in diverting the local indigenous elite of bureaucrats and aspiring politicians away from supporting independence (as they had in 1999–2000) and toward competition for patronage through elections and *pemekaran*.

To be sure, occasional outbreaks of communal violence have occurred in recent years (for example, in 2010 in the town of Tarakan in East Kalimantan, or in 2011 in Ambon, the capital of Maluku Province), though none on the scale of the earlier bloodlettings. In many respects, therefore, Indonesia's story is a dramatic and even inspiring testament to the capacity of democracy to curb ethnic and separatist conflicts. Indonesia is a supremely diverse society that has largely resolved the serious communal violence that threatened its early democratic transition. Yet it was the *style* of democracy as much as its form that was important in achieving this outcome. Instrumentalist analyses see ethnic conflicts as caused by the ambitions of communal elites who mobilize their followers to pursue material gain and political office. Indonesia has no shortage of ambitious and potentially violent ethnic elites, but its inclusivist and patronage-based form of democracy means that many of these elites can achieve their goals without having to resort to violence. The effects on conflict amelioration have been positive; the impact on corruption control and improving government performance has not been.

Absorbing Islamism

Indonesia also presents powerful lessons about the capacity of democratic rule to tame Islamism. The Suharto regime had repressed Islamist movements that campaigned for the establishment of an Islamic state. During the early years of the transition to democracy, such forces emerged into the public sphere and challenged the secular-nationalist assumptions that had long governed Indonesian political life. Several parties campaigned on an Islamic-state platform in the 1999 elections, and in the subsequent parliamentary debates they tried to introduce clauses into the constitution that would have made obedience to *shari'a* an obligation for all Muslims. On the streets, a more militant and violent fringe emerged, with some groups condemning democracy as an alien and Western-inspired imposition.

In fact, the potential of Islamism to dominate the Indonesian political scene, much less to threaten its new democracy, was never great. The majority currents in Indonesian Islam, represented by Indonesia's two great Islamic social organizations, the traditionalist Nahdlatul Ulama and the modernist Muhammadiyah, are politically accommodationist and moderate. During the New Order years, their leaders compromised with the regime and proclaimed their loyalty to *Pancasila*, the state philosophy that held that "Belief in One God," rather than Islam, was a core principle. After Suharto fell, the leaders of these organizations sponsored pluralist-oriented but Islamic-based political parties that tried to reach beyond their core constituencies to attract Chinese Indonesians, Christians, and other minorities. Moreover, Islamic politics in Indonesia is a minority rather than a majority tendency: The vote for all Islamic-based parties, including both Islamists and pluralists, was 36 percent in 1999 and 37.5 percent in 2004; it dropped sharply to 29 percent in 2009.

In part, this decline was a product of the way Indonesia's dominant political style has affected Islamic politics. Most Islamists in Indonesia are more interested in sharing in the fruits of power than overthrowing it. In Indonesia's early transition, the two most important Islamist parties were the United Development Party (PPP), one of only three parties allowed to participate in the tightly controlled elections of the New Order period, and the much smaller and ostensibly more puritanical Moon and Star Party (PBB). Both PPP and PBB proclaimed themselves in favor of reorganizing Indonesia's political, legal, and social order in line with *shari'a*, although PPP was always more pragmatic and less insistent than PBB. Both parties then went through the motions of advocating inclusion of a reference to *shari'a* in the constitution in a debate that they knew they would lose. Their leaders soon proved much more adept, however, at staking a claim to participation in government and enjoying the perks that this afforded them. Despite their claims to religious morality, leaders of these parties have included some of the most incompetent and corrupt cabinet ministers of the new democratic Indonesia. M.S. Kaban, the chairman of PBB, for example, has been linked to a string of high-profile corruption cases. Neither party has fared well electorally, with PBB's vote fluctuating around 2 percent, and PPP's declining from 10.7 percent in 1999 to 5.3 percent a decade later.

The fate of these two parties reflects a broader two-part political dynamic that has produced, one decade into Indonesia's political transition, a striking absence of a militant Islamist voice in electoral politics. No political party that openly proclaims—or at least emphasizes—a goal of dramatically overhauling Indonesia's social and political system in line with *shari'a* now represents a significant force. Two pressures have contributed to this outcome. The first comes from below, with polls repeatedly showing that voters are more interested in economic and welfare issues than in religiosity. The second involves cooptation and absorption from above. The first is a product of democracy itself, the second, of the particular variety of democracy practiced in Indonesia.

The clearest illustration of this dual dynamic is the evolution of the Prosperous Justice Party (PKS). This party was born out of a campus movement inspired by the Muslim Brotherhood in the Middle East. Its members pursued an incrementalist approach, hoping first to develop a true Islamic understanding and an all-encompassing Islamic lifestyle among the members of its study groups, then to gradually Islamize society through good works and *dakwah* (proselytization); and only then, at some unspecified time in the future, to Islamize the state itself. When the party made its electoral debut in 1999 (then it was known as PK, the Justice Party), it offered something that was otherwise virtually absent in Indonesia: an ideologically cohesive, disciplined, and programmatic party. Yet having won only 1.4 percent of the vote that year, the PKS also aspired to be more mainstream and influential. To that end, it decided to deemphasize its Islamist image and broaden its appeal. In the 2004 elections, it campaigned as being "clean and caring," stressing the reputation that many of its members enjoyed for incorruptibility, the social services that the party provided, and its plans for economic development, improved social welfare, and governance reform. It succeeded, dramatically increasing its share of the vote to 7.3 percent.

This stronger legislative result gave it greater weight in national politics. It took three posts in President Yudhoyono's first cabinet, and endorsed candidates in gubernatorial and mayoral races around the country, winning some key positions. Yet the absorption of the PKS into the political mainstream also did much to blunt its image. Among Islamists, including some of its core supporters, the party's new orientation—symbolized by its declaration that it was an "open party"—prompted fears that it was losing sight of its Islamization goals. On campuses, the party has begun to lose ground to the more militant Hizbut Thahrir (Party of Liberation), which condemns democracy and does not participate in elections. More significantly, the "party's 'clean' and reformist image has been tarnished by several of its prominent figures being implicated in corruption scandals," and some of its candidates for local executive office have been of "doubtful probity."[11] Such developments produced a decline of the PKS's electoral attractiveness as an outsider party concerned with cleaning up corruption. In 2009, the party's vote increased only slightly, up to 7.9 percent, far short of its goal of 20 percent. Since then, the party has been ever more mired in scandal, including an embarrassing incident in 2011 when a photographer captured images of a PKS legislator watching pornography on his tablet computer during a plenary session of the national parliament, as well as more serious accusations of corruption in the agriculture ministry, which is controlled by the party.

The absorption of Islamist political forces into Indonesia's governing institutions and the political mainstream has been accompanied by a partial Islamization of the public face of politics and of social policy. This process has partly been driven by ostensibly secular-nationalist parties and leaders seeking to win support from pious voters and Islamic social organizations. Islamist leaders now working from within state structures have played their part too, however. Some Indonesian Muslim leaders speak of Indonesia becoming a "Muslim democracy," comparable to the Christian democracy that they believe predominates in the West. Some of the implications of this trend have been negative, if not for democracy itself, at least for pluralism. For instance, the government failed to protect members of an Islamic sect, Ahmadiyah, when they were violently attacked by Islamist groups, and in 2008 it promulgated a decree prohibiting Ahmadis from promoting their beliefs. In the same year, the parliament passed an antipornography law that bans a wide variety of objects and actions "which contain obscenity or sexual exploitation which violates the moral norms in society"—a broad definition that many artists, intellectuals, and members of religious minorities feared could be used to restrict artistic expression and criminalize minority cultural practices (and indeed it has been used for such a purpose in some places). In some regions, local legislatures have passed even more restrictive *shari'a*-inspired regulations imposing dress restrictions, curfews for women, stricter Islamic education requirements, and the like. Former PBB chairperson Yusril Ihza Mahendra, when he was minister of justice and human rights and, later, state secretary, talked about revising Indonesia's criminal code to ensure that it contained more elements derived from Islamic law.

Such developments arguably point to the early stages of a long-term incremental struggle to Islamize the state from within. Overall, Indonesia is certainly not experiencing a process of "shari'aization by stealth," as some alarmist commentators suggest. State-sponsored religious conservatism lags far behind countries like Pakistan or even neighboring Malaysia. So far, the main effect of the cooptation of Islamic political forces has been to blunt their Islamic goals by integrating these forces into the system of patronage-based democracy and compelling them to compete for votes from a public that values performance more than piety. In the longer term, however, a gradual erosion of pluralism driven by forces inside government has now become a possibility in a way that it never was previously.

The Price of Success

Assessments of Indonesian democracy are often starkly contrasting. The international media, foreign governments, and Indonesia's own leaders frequently laud the country as a democratic success story, praising it for having institutionalized democratic freedoms, for having rolled back the military, and for having kept radical Islam in check. Comparativists point to the consolidation of Indonesia's democratic system in a period when the rest of the world has experienced democratic regression, as well as to polling data indicating high levels of satisfaction with democracy and support for democratic values.[12] Yet much of the scholarly literature, as well as commentary by Indonesian intellectuals and civil society activists, is full of gloomy assessments of Indonesia's low democratic quality, the capture of its democratic institutions by self-serving and authoritarian elites, the pervasiveness of corruption, and so on.

Both characterizations are correct. Indeed, they are intimately connected. The success of Indonesia's democracy and its poor quality are two sides of the same coin. It was precisely by achieving a low-quality outcome that Indonesian democratization proceeded so smoothly.[13] Key elites and potentially disruptive political forces such as the military were not starved out of Indonesia's new democracy. Instead, they were all given a piece of the democracy pie, reducing their incentive to resist and challenge the system from the outside. The price of this approach was that the potential spoilers were empowered to undermine the quality of Indonesian democracy from within and, more important, that patronage and corruption became means by which they—and everybody else who counted—were brought into the system.

The accommodation of spoilers and established elites produced a relatively smooth transition to democracy once the initial breakthrough was achieved in 1998. The transition became violent in some regions, but in most such places new dispensations were arrived at to accommodate local communal elites. At the national level, early fears in some quarters that there would be a repeat of the massive blood-letting that accompanied Indonesia's previous regime change (the demise of President Sukarno's Guided Democracy and the rise of Suharto's New Order in 1965–66, when approximately 500,000 alleged communists and their sympathizers were killed), were not realized. Ideological conflict never became bitter enough at the national level, and a winner-take-all dynamic was avoided by the design of the electoral and party system and by the capacity of the new political system to absorb all political forces.

Perhaps the trade-off between democratic success and democratic quality was worth it. Not only did Indonesia avoid nationwide social violence during the transition, it also successfully forestalled attempts by spoilers to destroy its new democracy, and it succeeded in building a functioning procedural democracy that is arguably the global democratic success story of the last decade. Even if I have not emphasized them much in this essay, Indonesia has made great strides in many areas of its democratic life, now having an open and plural political system that makes it the envy of many of its neighbors.

Moreover, this is arguably a story about sequencing. Up to 2004, the thrust of reform efforts was to establish new democratic institutions. Since then, Indonesia has moved into a phase of grappling with a series of second-tier reforms that aim to lock in its democratic success by improving governance. This has been evident above all in the dramatic work of the Corruption Eradication Commission (KPK), which has busted open a large number of corruption cases involving legislators, ministers, and other senior officials, delighting the public by broadcasting wiretaps of some of their more sordid dealings. A new Constitutional Court has made some important decisions that have extended political rights and resolved some potentially serious deadlocks, including in the administration of elections. In regional government elections, there is a high turnover rate of about 40 percent, with voters showing that they will not hesitate to oust local government heads whom they view as corrupt or incompetent.

But in a democratic system where "anyone and everyone" still has a stake, the dangers of erosion from within are real. Despite the reformist rhetoric of President Yudhoyono, both his first (2004–2009) and second (2009–) terms have seen few concrete achievements in deepening democratic reform. On the contrary, the president proved himself, above all, to be a consensus politician, captive to the array of interests in his rainbow cabinets and time and again willing to back down when opposed by them (perhaps most tellingly in 2010, when he allowed the sidelining of his reformist finance minister Sri Mulyani Indrawati after she had earned the ire of the Golkar party and its tycoon chairman, Aburizal Bakrie).

Much of the important progress was instead made by institutions established as part of earlier reforms, notably the KPK and the Constitutional Court. In some crucial areas, such as security-sector reform, there was paralysis. And for every success, there has been a sign of backlash—most dramatically demonstrated in late 2009 by a major conspiracy involving senior police officers and their allies in the business and political elite to undermine the KPK and even to frame two of its commissioners on corruption charges. The ensuing scandal shone a harsh light on the collusive and corrupt patterns of behavior that infuse the law-enforcement agencies, and has sparked fears among reformers of a backward slide toward the habits of the authoritarian past. In 2011 and 2012, the signs of malaise spread still further, with the eruption of a major corruption scandal in the president's own Democratic Party, which saw the arrest of party treasurer Muhammad Nazaruddin, who went on to make sensational allegations implicating a string of senior party officials.

Meanwhile, conservative forces in the national bureaucracy and legislature have periodically introduced, and sometimes passed, bills that threaten significantly to erode some of Indonesia's new freedoms. For instance, a draconian state-secrets bill and an amendment of Indonesia's electoral laws that reinserted political parties into the electoral administration organization have been thwarted only by campaigns by Indonesia's still highly combative civil society and media or by decisions of the Constitutional Court.[14]

Since 2004, Indonesia has been fortunate in having a president who values his public and global reputation as a democrat and has not actively tried to undermine his country's democratic achievements, even if he has not been the champion of reform that many of his supporters initially hoped he would be. Indonesia has also enjoyed economic growth rates exceeding 6 percent per year since 2007 (except for a dip to 4.6 percent in 2009 caused by the global financial crisis), helping its new democracy to stabilize.

Yet the legacies of a political transition that kept the old Suharto regime's ruling elite and patrimonial governing style largely intact continue to bedevil democratic governance. The signature theme of the protests that overthrew Suharto in 1998 was condemnation of "corruption, collusion and nepotism," yet these patterns of behavior still infuse political life, with serious consequences for how Indonesia's democracy delivers for ordinary people, and for how it is perceived by them. Poor governance is often the midwife of authoritarian reversals, and while Indonesia has yet to produce its Alberto Fujimori, Thaksin Shinawatra, or Vladimir Putin, Indonesian democracy is not yet out of the danger zone.

NOTES

The author would like to thank Marcus Mietzner for the discussions and input during the writing of this article and the organizers of the conference which preceded it for the invitation to participate

1. For elaboration of this argument, which draws on work by Juan Linz, see Edward Aspinall, *Opposing Suharto: Compromise, Resistance and Regime Change in Indonesia* (Stanford: Stanford University Press, 2005).

2. Guillermo O'Donnell, "Transitions, Continuities and Paradoxes," in Scott Mainwaring, Guillermo O'Donnell, and J. Samuel Valenzuela, eds., *Issues in Democratic Consolidation: The New South American Democracies in Comparative Perspective* (Notre Dame: University of Notre Dame Press, 1992), 50.

3. These three labels are taken from, respectively, Dan Slater, "Indonesia's Accountability Trap: Party Cartels and Presidential Power After Democratic Transition," *Indonesia* 78 (October 2004): 61–92; Douglas Webber, "A Consolidated Patrimonial Democracy? Democratization in Post-Suharto Indonesia," *Democratization* 13 (June 2006): 396–420; Gerry van Klinken, "Patronage Democracy in Provincial Indonesia," in Olle Törnquist, Neil Webster, and Kristian Stokke, eds., *Rethinking Popular Representation* (Basingstoke: Palgrave Macmillan, 2009).

4. In developing this argument, I acknowledge the influence of Howard Dick and Jeremy Mulholland, "Slush Funds and Intra-Elite Rivalry: The State as Marketplace," in Edward Aspinall and Gerry van Klinken, eds., *The State and Illegality in Indonesia* (Leiden: KITLV Press, 2011) and William Case, "Exemplar or Anomaly? Exiting the New Order in Comparative Perspective" in Edward Aspinall and Greg Fealy, eds., *Soeharto's New Order and Its Legacy: Essays in Honour of Harold Crouch* (Canberra: ANU E Press, 2010).

5. *Unfinished Business: Police Accountability in Indonesia* (London: Amnesty International, 2009), 26

6. Remark by Rizal Sukma at the Indonesia Update Conference, Australian National University, Canberra, 9–10 October 2009.

7. Marcus Mietzner, *Military Politics, Islam and the State in Indonesia: From Turbulent Transition to Democratic Consolidation* (Singapore: Institute of Southeast Asian Studies, 2009), 322.

8. Gerry van Klinken, *Communal Violence and Democratization in Indonesia: Small Town Wars* (London: Routledge, 2007), 4.

9. See for example, Edward Aspinall and Greg Fealy, eds., *Local Power and Politics in Indonesia: Decentralisation and Democratisation* (Singapore: Institute of Southeast Asian Studies, 2003); Vedi R. Hadiz, *Localising Power in Post-Authoritarian Indonesia: A Southeast Asia Perspective* (Stanford: Stanford University Press, 2010)

10. Edward Aspinall, "Combatants to Contractors: The Political Economy of Peace in Aceh," *Indonesia* 87 (April 2009): 1–34.

11. Anthony Bubalo, Greg Fealy, and Whit Mason, *Zealous Democrats: Islamism and Democracy in Egypt, Indonesia and Turkey* (Sydney: Lowy Institute, 2008), 50.

12. Larry Diamond, "Indonesia's Place in Global Democracy," in Edward Aspinall and Marcus Mietzner, eds., *Problems of Democratisation in Indonesia: Elections, Institutions and Society* (Singapore: Institute of Southeast Asian Studies, 2010).

13. In Indonesia we see, therefore, an echo of Philippe Schmitter's observation that democratization during the global third wave tended to be easier than he and other observers initially anticipated, in large part because it was also less consequential in its redistributional aspects than many thought it would be: Philippe C. Schmitter, "Twenty-Five Years, Fifteen Findings," *Journal of Democracy* 21 (January 2010): 17–28.

14. For a recent analysis of the threat of democratic regression in Indonesia, see Marcus Mietzner, "Indonesia's Democratic Stagnation: Anti-Reformist Elites and Resilient Civil Society," *Democratization,* 19 (April 2012): 209–29.

9

REVIVING REFORMISM IN THE PHILIPPINES

Mark R. Thompson

Mark R. Thompson is director of the Southeast Asia Research Centre (SEARC) and professor in the Department of Asian and International Studies of the City University of Hong Kong. He is author of The Anti-Marcos Struggle (1995) and Democratic Revolutions (2004). This is a substantially revised and updated version of an essay that originally appeared in the October 2010 issue of the Journal of Democracy.

Since his election in May 2010 by the largest plurality—42 percent of the vote—of any president since the overthrow of the Marcos dictatorship in 1986, Benigno Simeon Cojuangco Aquino III, known as "Noynoy," has based his presidency on the carefully scripted promise of political reform. With the late-2011 arrest of his unpopular predecessor, Gloria Macapagal-Arroyo, on charges of electoral manipulation and the May 2012 conviction and removal from office of Supreme Court chief justice Renato Corona for amassing "unexplained wealth" under Arroyo, Aquino has been able to keep this reform narrative at the center of Philippine politics.

Popular revulsion against the malfeasance of the Arroyo administration, despite its economic accomplishments, set the stage for the revival of "reformism." Although the country faces grave problems of poverty, economic inequality, unemployment, inadequate infrastructure, environmental degradation, armed insurgency (both by communists and Muslim secessionists), and general lawlessness, this venerable political discourse of clean government has made most Filipinos forgiving of Aquino's underperforming administration. In today's context, the appearance of good intentions seems more important than demonstrations of good governance.

During his 2010 presidential campaign, Aquino promised to uphold the legacy of his martyred father and saintly mother, "foundationalist" president Corazon "Cory" Aquino. Despite her administration's modest achievements (largely due to economic crisis and political instability), Cory Aquino embodied a powerful narrative of good governance after decades of cronyism and brutality under the Marcos dictatorship—her assassinated husband was its most prominent victim—and she became a political saint.[1] Her death in 2009 sparked nationwide grieving, paving the way for her son to revive reformism. Arroyo, by contrast, had a strong record of economic performance, but her presidency had been discredited by electoral manipulation and widespread corruption, making her deeply unpopular and transforming her into an "apostate" of reform.

Many of Noynoy's cabinet appointees served in his mother's administration. Most are well qualified with strong technocratic credentials. Some (such as Finance Secretary Cesar Purisma and Secretary of Social Welfare and Development Corazon "Dinky" Soliman) had resigned from Arroyo's government. Whatever the reality of Aquino's father's rough-and-tumble political career and the embarrassing scandals that marred his mother's administration, Noynoy successfully contrasted his dynastic credibility with his predecessor's unpopularity.

The tenor of Noynoy's presidency was set by his July 2010 state of the union address, which affirmed his commitment to clean government. Aquino pledged "no more influence-peddling, no more patronage politics, no more stealing . . . no more bribes." Symbolic of this commitment was the ban on siren-blaring presidential motorcades (*wangwang*) that snarled Manila traffic in what Aquino portrayed as an abuse of political power.[2] As of this writing in mid-2012, Noynoy remains the most popular post-Marcos president[3]—a sign that the reformist narrative still holds appeal in a country where most people are convinced that social ills stem mainly from poor governance. Noynoy's campaign slogan, "If there is no corruption, there will be no poverty," continues to resonate among Filipinos.

At the same time, Aquino's administration has been plagued by factional infighting and poor management, with the August 2010 bungling of a hostage crisis involving Hong Kong tourists in Manila being the most obvious example. The president's divided administration has put forward only a few major policy initiatives and has yet to systematically push serious institutional reform.

The Reformist Narrative

To date, the greatest accomplishment of Aquino's presidency arguably has been to put the Philippines back on the electoral path. The Philippines has a checkered electoral history that stretches back to its first national polls in 1907 and the days of "colonial democracy" under U.S. tutelage. Ferdinand E. Marcos, who was elected president in 1965, began manipulating voting in subsequent elections as part of a slide toward increasingly authoritarian rule. His theft of the 1986 presidential election triggered his overthrow, as the forces of the "people power" revolution rallied against him in the streets of Manila.[4] More recently, President Arroyo was accused of rigging the 2004 presidential vote. For the next several years, mass protests and coup attempts beset her presidency.

Despite a growing legitimacy crisis prompted by accusations of vote fraud and a series of corruption scandals, Arroyo consolidated power by coopting key players, including Roman Catholic bishops, top military officers, and major business interests. At the same time, civil society groups began to reconsider the wisdom of an insurrectionary approach that had replaced one problematic president (populist Joseph E. "Erap" Estrada, who was elected in 1998 and overthrown in a "people power coup" in 2001) with another (Arroyo). Instead of the "outside" game of street protests, Arroyo's foes began to focus on "inside" efforts to stop constitutional changes that they feared would keep her in power. In a conciliatory gesture, the Commission on Elections (COMELEC) ruled that Estrada's earlier "truncated" term meant that he could run again in 2010 despite a constitutional ban on second terms.

Filipinos—long used to having the "world's slowest elections"—were "shell-shocked" by the quick and fair reporting of the 2010 results. Despite worries about a fumbled or even a "failed" election, the Philippines' first-ever automated polls were conducted in a generally honest and orderly manner, surprising pessimistic Filipino and foreign observers alike. Fears of election-related violence—stoked by a horrific November 2009 incident in which 57 people (including several relatives of a gubernatorial candidate plus 32 journalists) were murdered in Maguindanao Province on the southern island of Mindanao—proved exaggerated. On the whole, the 2010 campaign was significantly more peaceful than the 2004 contest had been.[5]

The defining moment of the 2010 campaign was a "black swan": Cory Aquino's death of cancer on 1 August 2009, which brought millions of mourners onto the streets.[6] The groundswell of grief over his mother's death proved a political boon for Noynoy, who announced his presidential candidacy soon thereafter. One columnist observed that "there is something about the Aquino franchise that evokes magic." In other words, while pervasive political *dynasticism* is commonly criticized in the Philippines, familial *legacies* can be viewed positively. As another journalist explained, Noynoy benefited "from the public service record of his mother and his father, the martyred former Sen. Benigno S. Aquino, Jr., whose honesty and transparency appear to have been accepted by the Filipino public."[7]

Several leading NGOs affiliated themselves with Aquino's campaign under the auspices of the noncommunist Left. The moderate socialist Akbayan party, with its program of social reform, even formed an official alliance with Aquino's Liberal Party (LP). But rather than run as a social progressive, Aquino focused on his "reformist" credentials, a strategy that his mother also had adopted when running against Marcos in 1986.

Reformism is a "bourgeois" political narrative expressed by the direct media appeal "I will not steal from you." The problem with such a claim is making it credible in a country where government corruption is widespread. Many voters believed Noynoy's pledge in the 2010 election because he hailed from a "good dynasty" (his most successful campaign commercial showed him pledging honesty to Filipino voters in front of pictures of his iconic parents). Aquino was not even on the list of potential presidential contenders until his mother's death, when shrewd political operatives drafted him into the race. President Arroyo, though constitutionally barred from running for a second term, was suspected of plotting to keep power through a proxy candidate, spurring many opposition politicians to unite around Noynoy. Another major presidential contender, Manuel "Mar" Roxas, also of dynastic pedigree, yielded to Aquino, agreeing to become his vice-presidential running mate.

Like progressive movements in the early twentieth-century United States, Philippine reformism avoids direct class-based appeals and claims instead to act in the interest of the nation as a whole. In the Philippines, this narrative can be said to have originated with the writings of national hero and polymath Jose Rizal, whose 1887 novel *Noli Me Tangere* attacked the previously "untouchable" issue of Spanish-colonial corruption with bitter sarcasm and reformist intentions. In the years leading up to the Second World War, the "Great Dissenter," Juan Sumulong (Noynoy's maternal great-grandfather), criticized abuses of power during the U.S.-colonial-era presidency of Manuel Quezon (1935–44). Another famous reformist president was Ramon Magsaysay (1953–57), who ran (with secret CIA backing) against a corrupt incumbent in the early 1950s. Reformism peaked during the anti-Marcos struggle and Corazon Aquino's presidential campaign. It remains an influential line of discourse today, and several presidential candidates in the post-Marcos era have used it. Reformers' sincerity has been "tested" by their willingness to sacrifice their lives for the nation: The Spanish executed Rizal in 1896; the Marcos regime murdered Noynoy's father 87 years later; and Cory was willing to carry on her husband's struggle despite claiming to be but a "simple housewife."

Although reformism purports to transcend class, polls show that its strongest base of support lies among upper- and middle-income voters (known as the "ABC" classes in the Philippines), with significant but less support among the poor (the "D" class). The very poor (the "E" class, in local parlance) are least likely to be counted among reformism's supporters. The Catholic Church, and particularly the many bishops who have long backed campaigns seeking to promote "good governance," form an important source of reformist support. So does big business, which maintains close ties to the Church through the Bishop-Businessmen's Conference for Human Development, and which sees clean public administration as key to rapid economic development.

The problem facing would-be reformers is that once political "outs" gain power and become the new "ins," patronage can take on a corrosive attractiveness. But the promise of reform has gained more lasting political credibility through what can be termed "developmental reformism," carried out by technocrats. Marcos took pioneering steps toward such "technocracy" during the early years of martial-law rule in the 1970s, until growing cronyism undermined the whole effort. Fidel V. Ramos (1992–98) revived a strong technocratic emphasis during his presidency, but it lapsed under Estrada and compiled an ambiguous record under Arroyo (whose administration featured both capable technocrats and major corruption scandals). Another factor contributing to the durability of the reformist narrative is that it is now more clearly defined in opposition to a competing discourse—namely, populism.

Parrying the Populist Challenge

In 2010, two leading presidential candidates—Estrada and Senator Manuel "Manny" Villar—adopted a populist stance (with Estrada accusing Villar of stealing his colors by copying Estrada supporters' trademark orange clothing). In the Philippines, this narrative is of more recent lineage than reformism, going back to movie star Rogelio de la Rosa's successful 1957 Senate race and his abortive presidential bid four years later. It then became the basis of First Lady Imelda Marcos's "star power," prestige projects, and welfare programs during the Marcos dictatorship. In the post-Marcos era, it was exemplified by Estrada's "long" populist decade in which he bucked pro-Cory sentiment in 1987 to capture a Senate seat, defied presidential victor Ramos to take the vice-presidency in 1992, and outpolled his traditional political opponents to win the presidency by a landslide in 1998. In the 2010 presidential contest, he showed that even after being jailed for corruption he still could win about a quarter of the popular vote.

Far from imitating reformism's call for technocrat-led good governance, populism is explicitly anti-elitist. Even though its proponents themselves often come from the elite, they tend to have the air of outsiders. They emphasize popular sovereignty and, like reformists, rely on media-based appeals more than clientelist ties. But their message is different, with populists claiming "I am like you" and "I will help you." Populists customarily accuse self-proclaimed reformers of relying on privilege. Reformists return the favor by accusing populists of cynically vowing solidarity with the poor while enriching themselves.

The populist "rich-versus-poor" theme is kept intentionally vague by leaders who mobilize the masses without an extensive leftist organization. The decline of the Philippine Left after the overthrow of Marcos meant that would-be populist politicians enjoyed a greater political space in which to launch bids to woo the "unorganized masses"—the large informal sector of the urban poor and marginalized rural populations.

Estrada won over the *masa* (masses) with a persona forged during his years as a star of action movies in which he often played a downtrodden hero struggling for his rights against corrupt elites. He effortlessly transferred this celluloid image as a fighter for the poor to the political stage.[8] His nickname "Erap," the 1960s slang inversion of *pare* (friend), was the basis of his 1998 campaign slogan, *Erap para sa mahirap* ("Erap for the poor"), as he claimed to be a friend to the friendless poor. All the patron-client networks, bosses' bailiwicks, and oligarchs' wealth were not enough to stop the Estrada juggernaut in the 1998 presidential election. In 2004, Estrada's friend and fellow actor-turned-politician Fernando Poe, Jr. (known as FPJ), ran against Arroyo, who had served out the remainder of Estrada's term after his ouster. FPJ's appeals to the disadvantaged were so effective that Arroyo's win was overshadowed by strong suspicions of fraud—allegations that gained decisive credibility with the 2005 surfacing of an audiotape of Arroyo discussing electoral manipulation with a COMELEC official.

Villar, the richest presidential contender in 2010, proved to be no match for Estrada in terms of populist appeal. In the final election tally, Estrada finished in second place with 26.3 percent of the vote; Villar came in third with 15.4 percent; and pro-Arroyo candidate Gilberto Teodoro was fourth with 11.3 percent. Exit polls showed that voting varied according to class background. Although Aquino won support from rich and poor alike, his backing was strongest among the upper and middle classes (51 percent) and weakest among the very poor (35.1 percent). Estrada, by contrast, won many fewer ABC votes than votes from the poorer D and E classes.

Given Estrada's mass appeal in 1998 and Poe's popularity in 2004, how did Noynoy fend off the populist challenge in 2010? It was not due to changes in socioeconomic conditions, for these remained favorable to populism. Populism cannot be "read off" the social map of a country, but without friendly terrain populists have little chance of electoral success. Despite a decade of relatively high economic growth under Arroyo, socioeconomic inequality by some accounts actually become sharper between the beginning of Estrada's time in office and the end of Arroyo's mandate (with hunger among the impoverished on the rise).

Writing a year before the election, columnist Amando Doronila argued that "*masa* politics, or the rich-versus-poor theme, is not the game in 2010 . . . . The dynamics of the 2010 election are vastly different from those of 1998." He suggested that the "politics of transparency" would predominate instead.[9] This shift of focus caused image problems for the

156

populists, given the corruption that had marked Estrada's administration and the scandals surrounding Villar's alleged manipulation of legislation to benefit his housing business.

Arroyo had inadvertently set the stage for Aquino's revival of the reformist narrative by presiding over yet another administration dogged by charges of fraud and corruption. After evidence that she fixed the 2004 presidential election surfaced, Arroyo had to face down three impeachment efforts (which she crushed with her majority in Congress) and several feeble coup attempts (the most serious of which came in February 2006). Matters worsened as she found herself beset by a series of scandals, including a particularly embarrassing one that tied her husband, son, and brother-in-law to illegal gambling—the same offense that Estrada's foes had used to justify his ouster. Yet Arroyo's enemies seemed powerless against her. Some observers suggested that Filipinos suffered from "people power fatigue."[10]

Yet protests abounded during the Arroyo years. The catch is that in the Philippines mass rallies alone have never been enough to make "people power" succeed. Antigovernment demonstrations have also required the moral approval of the Catholic hierarchy, the backing of big business, and last but certainly not least, some form of military intervention in order to succeed. Arroyo not only generously rewarded her loyal generals, but allowed them to hunt down legal leftists (including journalists). One report states that more than nine-hundred leftists died in extrajudicial killings during her time in power.[11] The Catholic Church was on the defensive in the wake of sex scandals and weakened after the 2005 death of its leading prelate, Manila archbishop Jaime Cardinal Sin. Business interests generally felt satisfied amid robust economic growth, and Arroyo also enjoyed the support of many House members, most governors, and other local-government officials. Thus the allies that an opposition revolt would need were missing.

With the insurrectionist path closed, opposition to Arroyo began to focus on the 2010 elections. The problem, as had been the case in all post-Marcos polls, was the plethora of candidates. There was no clear frontrunner and no candidate who could harness anti-Arroyo reformist sentiment—until, that is, Corazon Aquino's death led to her son's anointing. Journalist Conrado de Quiros captured this Arroyo-as-foil-for-Aquino sentiment well: "But the 'Noynoy phenomenon' is not just about euphoria. It is also about tyrannyphobia . . . . Why has Noynoy become phenomenal? Simple: Because he is the opposite of Gloria."[12]

Interestingly, the vice-presidential race, which is contested on a separate ballot in the Philippines, saw the defeat of Aquino's running mate, Manuel Roxas, yielding a result that was in a sense the inverse of this "reformist" victory at the presidential level. As an accomplished technocrat and "good dynast," Roxas also had strong reformist credentials. Personally close to Aquino, he played a crucial role in managing the presidential campaign when organizational difficulties arose. Comfortably ahead in the polls for much of the race, Roxas seems to have underestimated the threat posed by the "stealth candidacy" of Estrada's running mate, Jejomar Binay.

Binay, a former human-rights lawyer who was mayor of Makati, the wealthy business district of Metro Manila, developed strong "populist" credentials with innovative welfare programs for the poor in his city. He cultivated ties with other mayors around the country, as well as with some members of the Aquino family who remained loyal to him due to his crucial support of Cory Aquino during several military coup attempts that nearly overthrew her government.

But the key to Binay's success was the poor showing of a third vice-presidential campaign, that of Loren Legarda. Legarda's credibility was undermined by her apparent opportunism in becoming Villar's vice-presidential candidate, despite not too long before having bitterly attacked him for corruption. While at the presidential level the populist vote had been divided between Estrada and Villar, in the vice-presidential race Binay squeaked to victory when Legarda, his rival for the populist narrative, fell precipitously in the polls. That the "populist" Binay edged out the "reformist" Roxas for the vice-presidency shows these narratives to be of similar electoral strength.

Cleavages and Clientelism

This analysis of the 2010 presidential election in terms of competing "narratives" does not fit easily into the prevailing paradigm for analyzing Philippine politics—clientelism. It claims that particularistic ties between patrons (often landlords) and clients (usually peasants) are the key to understanding the country's politics. This approach has been subject to much criticism. One critique emphasizes the impact of modernization as gentry politicians have given way to urban machines. Another points to the prevalence of coercion ("bossism") rather than consent in such relations.[13] But both of these modifications accept an underlying portrait of Philippine politics as a largely transactional, nonideological affair in which control over resources (material or coercive) is the key to "harvesting" the votes of peasants or the urban poor.[14]

Such a model seems to capture well the survival tactics employed by the Arroyo administration. Although by 2007 Arroyo's popularity had plunged, her clientelist networks, warlord allies, and electoral manipulators were strong enough for her to win a majority of seats in the lower house of Congress. But explanations that focus on clientelism cannot tell us why, in the years since Marcos was forced to step down, presidential candidates considered to have the best "political machinery" (such as Villar in 2010) nonetheless have failed if they suffered credibility problems (as Villar did when reports broke of his ties to Arroyo and his involvement in a series of corruption scandals). Although Arroyo used all the dark arts of clientelism in the 2004 presidential election, she still apparently felt compelled to cheat, even though her opponent had limited funds and organization. In this she resembled Marcos, who despite an overwhelming edge in resources had to steal the 1986 election from Corazon Aquino. What clearer illustration could there be of the limits to the politics of patronage and muscle even in the Philippines?

Social cleavages are generally understood to be societal divisions—often having to do with differences of class, religion, ethnicity, or region—that social movements and political parties actively politicize in order to win supporters and voters. Doubts about whether such cleavages shape politics in the Philippines begin with the country's weak party system, riven by factionalism and held together by clientelist ties. Supporters of Noynoy Aquino's Liberal Party claim that it has a long tradition as a progressive, reformist force. But it has also been home to plenty of old-school clientelist politicians. A similar but even less plausible case has been made for the ideological integrity of the Nacionalistas, the country's oldest surviving political party (founded in 1907) and one that Villar tried to revive for his populist campaign.

Despite clientelism's persistence within parties, Filipinos claim that what they see and hear via the media—especially television—affects their voting decisions more heavily than do the material promises that politicians make. In a February 2010 survey, for example, 68 percent of respondents said that a candidate's media image was the biggest single influence on their decision whether to vote for that candidate or not; only 1 percent said the same about the influence of local politicians. Although clientelism clearly weighs more heavily as a factor in local races, here too nontraditional "reformist" candidates have recently met with unexpected success.[15]

The post-Marcos rise of the populist and reformist campaign narratives means that voters can no longer be simply divided into incumbent "ins" and opposition "outs." Instead, they must also be seen as opposing camps that stress paternalistic promises to end corruption or that favor helping the poor. Opinion polls reveal strong support for both populist and reformist appeals. In a December 2009 Pulse Asia survey, a 27 percent plurality of all respondents listed "cares for poor" (a well-known populist code phrase) as their number-one reason for supporting a presidential candidate. Only 21 percent overall (and 17 percent of the E class) cited "not corrupt/clean record" as their main criterion for choosing whom to back. Yet another 12 percent (including 13 percent and 10 percent of the D and E classes, respectively) said that they would vote for a "good person." The words "clean" and "good" attached to candidates are reformist catchwords; their drawing power shows that there exists a strong basis for appealing to voters with claims of moral uprightness.

Aquino and Estrada offered differing diagnoses of the evils of the

Arroyo administration, with the former blasting its corruption and the latter its tolerance of inequality. But deep dislike for Arroyo was a common thread: She had Estrada tried and imprisoned on corruption charges, and she humiliated Corazon Aquino when the latter dared to call for Arroyo's resignation after allegations of electoral fraud were made against her. Pro-administration candidate Gilberto Teodoro, who tried to run as a reformist in 2010 but was unable to distance himself clearly from Arroyo, could gain little traction despite his impressive technocratic credentials, distinguished record of government service, and support from the "ruling" party. Villar, Estrada's rival for "ownership" of the populist narrative, also was hurt by his perceived closeness to the outgoing president—critics took to calling him "Villarroyo." The shared antipathy to Arroyo took some of the heat out of the race to replace her.

Aquino versus Arroyo

Arroyo made it clear that she had no intention of "going quietly" once she left the presidency. Rather than retire from public life, as unofficial protocol demands, she ran for and won a congressional seat in her native province of Pampanga on the large northern island of Luzon, seeking to hold onto her power base in the lower house and to gain immunity from prosecution. Just before leaving the presidency, she had made a series of "midnight" appointments of a kind not seen since outgoing president Carlos Garcia (1957–61) burdened his successor Diosdado Macapagal (Arroyo's father) with a plethora of unwanted officeholders. Arroyo circumvented an early-1960s court ruling against last-minute designations by backdating appointments to a time before election day, and by persuading the Supreme Court (whose fifteen justices were all her appointees) to hold itself exempt from the effects of these earlier rulings, much to the consternation of the country's legal community.

But upon assuming power Aquino quickly won control of the lower house, even though pro-Arroyo forces had a nominal majority. As has been common in the Philippines, many "opposition" legislators defected to the president's side to support his candidate for House speaker, Feliciano R. Belmonte, Jr., because of the executive's extensive patronage and appointment powers. But Aquino had to pay for his control of the lower house by stooping to old-school politics. Controlling the 24-member Senate has proved trickier, as presidential sway is not as great there. Although a compromise on the leadership question was reached with the reelection of Juan Ponce Enrile as Senate president, several of Aquino's political opponents remain influential senators.

Some key officials, including the military chief of staff, saw fit to resign rather than risk a conflict with Aquino. Others, however, showed little inclination to back down. The Supreme Court, packed with Arroyo appointees, soon became the chief battleground between the new administration and the *ancien régime*. Just days before she left office, Arroyo promoted Renato Corona from associate to chief justice. Displeased, Aquino refused to take the oath of office from him, and asked an associate justice to administer it instead. The High Court later struck down an executive order that Aquino had used to create a truth commission to investigate the corruption scandals of his predecessor's administration.

The Court dealt a blow to Aquino's family with a November 2011 ruling (reaffirmed in April 2012) that would force it to sell its huge sugar plantation, Hacienda Luisita, below market price for land redistribution. The court verdict overruled a stock-option scheme designed to preempt land reform as part of a bill passed during Cory Aquino's administration. The court's decision in favor of the land-to-the-tillers principle put Noynoy "on the spot," as it highlighted the "half-hearted social reform legacy of his mother."[16]

When Aquino's lower-house allies filed corruption charges and quickly impeached Chief Justice Corona at the end of 2011, Aquino's enemies denounced the move as vengeance. In the subsequent Senate trial, prosecutors portrayed the accused judge as benefiting from "un-explained wealth." Critics saw a political vendetta against Arroyo's most influential ally, but Corona's conviction and removal from office were widely perceived, both in the Philippines and abroad, as a "new paradigm" of good governance. The former president herself was arrested in late 2011 on charges of electoral sabotage in the 2004 polls, despite an earlier Supreme Court ruling allowing her to leave the country to seek medical care. (Her House seat did not provide immunity from "high crimes" such as plunder and vote fraud). By relentlessly pursuing Arroyo and her allies, Aquino reinforced his reformist credentials.[17]

Even the growing dispute between China and the Philippines over a potentially oil- and gas-rich area surrounded by fertile fishing grounds in the South China Sea (which the Aquino administration recently renamed the "West Philippine Sea") has been linked to the Aquino-Arroyo struggle. Toward the end of her administration, Arroyo had begun tilting the country's foreign policy away from the United States and more toward Beijing. Aquino's presidency has returned the Philippines to its traditionally pro-U.S. stance. The Chinese military mouthpiece, the *Liberation Army Daily,* criticized U.S. support for the Philippines, suggesting that Washington's "shift in strategic focus to the east and its entry into the South China Sea issue has provided the Philippines with room for strategic maneuver" and was "emboldening [it] to take a risky course."[18]

Divisions in Aquino's "reformist" administration have been evident from the outset of his presidency and can be traced back to the election. During the 2010 campaign, a rivalry emerged within the Aquino camp between Manuel Roxas, Aquino's vice-presidential candidate, and his rival Jejomar Binay of the Filipino Democratic Party–Laban. Despite Roxas's place on Aquino's Liberal Party ticket, key players in and close to the Aquino campaign not-so-secretly backed Binay instead due to old loyalties, leading to bitterness in the Roxas camp after Binay's come-from-behind victory.

The media have reported on the periodic administration infighting with gusto. Roxas's Balay group (named after Roxas's mother's house in Metro Manila, where his vice-presidential campaign was headquartered) relies on his clout as secretary of the Department of Transportation and Communications and president of the LP (nominally the party in power). Roxas is widely seen as the administration's preferred candidate in the 2016 elections, in which Aquino cannot seek reelection. The other group is Binay's Samar faction (named after the street on which his campaign headquarters sat). Binay is thought to be gearing up for a presidential run, although the election is (as of May 2012) still 48 months away. Set to sound the same populist appeals that led to his upset victory for the vice-presidency, Binay seems intent on running his own slate of candidates, separate from the president's, in the 2013 Senate elections—a move that is widely seen as a dry run for the 2016 presidential polls.

Factionalism within Aquino's administration has also been aggravated by other personalistic ties. Critics charge Aquino with the sin of the "three K's": surrounding himself with *kaibigan* (friends), *kaklase* (classmates), and *kabarilan* (shooting buddies—Aquino is a well-known gun enthusiast). Cronyism has long plagued the Philippine presidency, and the Aquino administration has proved no exception. Although no major scandals have yet come to light, purported favoritism within the administration may still prove damaging given the high moral standards that Noynoy has set for his government.

Administration officials have angrily denied that factional infighting and administrative incompetence contributed to the August 2010 Manila hostage-crisis fiasco that left eight Hong Kong tourists dead and six others injured (plus two bystanders). Aquino ignored most of the conclusions of a fact-finding commission headed by Justice Secretary Leila de Lima. The commission's final report recommended that administrative or criminal charges be filed against fifteen officials, many of whom were close allies of the president. The government's handling of the crisis itself and its unwillingness to file charges led to international embarrassment and a "black" travel alert from the Hong Kong government on trips to the Philippines.

Joining a growing number of developing countries and following international donor advice, the Aquino administration has expanded a conditional cash-transfer (CCT) program begun under Arroyo in 2007 known as Pantawid Pamilyang Pilipino (PPP). It gives cash to the country's poorest households conditional upon completion of health checks and keeping children in school. A 2011 report by the World Bank and the Australian Agency for International Development found that beneficiaries' annual income increased by 12.6 percent, with poverty incidence among them falling by 6.2 percent. Despite this success, a recent survey has shown hunger in the country at new highs, now affecting nearly a quarter of all Filipinos, and self-rated poverty up 10 percent to 55 percent of the population during the first two years of the Aquino administration. These figures reveal the limited reach of the CCTs and the administrative hurdles that they face. Militant groups have criticized the Aquino administration for failing to address hikes in the price of oil and basic commodities, the lack of basic services, joblessness, and low wages, while at the same time demolishing urban squatter communities. Aquino foes have dubbed these shortcomings "Noynoying."[19]

One area in which Aquino has demonstrated leadership despite substantial political risk is his support of the Reproductive Health (RH) bill, which the secretary of social welfare and development called a "keystone" of the Aquino administration's policy. Yet it remains bogged down in Congress due to strong opposition led by the Philippine Catholic Church, which has accused the Aquino administration of selling out the "Filipino soul" on this issue. Citing high maternal death rates and rapid population growth, RH proponents argue that the bill will encourage education on reproductive-health matters and increase access to family planning while not encouraging abortion, which is widespread but stigmatized in the heavily Catholic country. Department of Health estimates suggest the bill could reduce maternal deaths related to pregnancy and childbirth by a third—a substantial improvement in a country where, according to a recent UN study, eleven women die in childbirth each day and 22 percent have unmet family-planning needs.[20] Accusing the Catholic Church of holding the country hostage, RH advocates say that the long delay in passing the bill is contributing to poverty and preventing the Philippines from reaching its Millennium Development goals.

The Aquino administration has worked to achieve a final peace settlement with a Muslim secessionist insurgency, now entering its fourth decade, on the southern island of Mindanao. Although Arroyo had managed to reach a ceasefire with the Moro Islamic Liberation Front (MILF), the Supreme Court ruled the accord unconstitutional, and she lost interest in further negotiations. The Aquino government has thus far been unable to entice the MILF into signing a new agreement, but the relatively peaceful status quo has been preserved.

The government has likewise had little success in efforts to end a long-running insurgency by the Maoist New People's Army (NPA), which recently "celebrated" 43 years of guerrilla warfare. Despite the decline of communism worldwide, the NPA "movement" remains strong in several peripheral areas of the country. But unlike Maoists in Nepal, for example, the NPA has made only limited efforts to enter the political mainstream. Given bad blood and personality clashes between independent leftists, social democrats, and communists, there has been no sustained attempt to build a broad "legal Left" movement or party. Instead, Maoist fighters have continued a quasi-criminalized, largely localized insurgency, sometimes extorting food and money at gunpoint, killing reluctant donors, and even allying with provincial strongmen or big landowners.[21]

The anti-insurgency drive, in turn, continues to be marred by human-rights violations. Arroyo had launched a dirty war against communists, their civilian sympathizers, and other leftists as part of a deal that helped to secure military backing despite her loss of popular legitimacy. It was hoped that with a firm electoral mandate the Aquino administration would undertake a systematic overhaul of the military to curb such abuses. According to Human Rights Watch's 2012 World Report, however, the new government has made little progress in addressing impunity and ending extrajudicial killings by state-security forces.[22]

In assessing the first third of the Aquino presidency, the country's economic picture provides some basis for optimism. Despite the recent international financial crisis, the Philippine economy continues to perform reasonably well: It is expected to grow between 4 and 5 percent in 2012 after somewhat slower growth in 2011. While still below the 7.7 percent expansion of 2010, the economy seems to have returned to the solid growth trajectory it has enjoyed since 1999. Capable macroeconomic management practiced during the Arroyo years has been sustained under the Aquino administration, with the country's external debt-service burden continuing to ease and inflation remaining low. Exports have been a motor of growth, particularly in automobile assembly and parts, shipbuilding, electronics, mining, and natural resources. Fastest growing of all has been the outsourcing sector, primarily a rapidly burgeoning call-center industry that is now the largest in the world (although the foreign exchange it generates still trails behind remittances from Filipinos working abroad).

While the Aquino government deserves only limited credit for these successes, it has maintained macroeconomic stability. A rise in much-needed infrastructure spending with an emphasis on public-private partnerships is promising (including major renovations of the country's international airport, recently voted the world's worst). A small improvement in the country's corruption ranking by Transparency International has been interpreted as "a good indication that the government is doing something to fight corruption," which has helped to improve the country's image among potential investors and tourists and to maintain Aquino's popularity at home. But an Asian Development Bank report warns that red tape, the weak rule of law, and unpredictable policies, as well as high energy costs, poor infrastructure, and the high cost of doing business continue to limit foreign investment in the country.[23]

What Is to Come?

Noynoy Aquino won the presidency in a lopsided victory with promises of reform. By relentlessly pursuing the misdeeds of the previous administration, he has bolstered his reformist credentials and kept his opinion-poll ratings high. But what are the chances that the Aquino administration will bring significant, long-lasting changes to the Philippines? So far it has suffered from infighting, bungled a hostage crisis, put forward limited policy initiatives, and shown few signs of any systematic effort to undertake the fundamental institutional reforms that the country needs. In terms of corruption, not even Cory Aquino's administration was free from scandal. The younger Aquino seems to have learned a lesson from his mother's troubles, however, and has kept his close relatives at arms' length while in office. But even if Noynoy's administration turns out to be "cleaner" than usual, it is unclear whether this will lead to substantially higher economic growth or significant poverty reduction in a country where more than half the population considers itself poor.

Arroyo's presidency was a success in terms of the economy, even if few of her opponents care to acknowledge it. However corrupt her administration may have been, the economy suffered little as a result. One of Aquino's chief "accomplishments" has been simply to continue this sound financial management. Arroyo's real liability was her inability to reduce income inequality and help the very poorest. The Aquino administration has expanded Arroyo's much touted PPP conditional cash-transfer program, but so far it has made no dent in poverty and hunger. Meanwhile, the current government's efforts to control population growth and improve reproductive health have faced stubborn opposition from the Catholic Church, while peace initiatives have yet to entice either Muslim secessionists or Maoist rebels to sign agreements. Moreover, anti-insurgency campaigns are still plagued by military abuses.

Short of a major industrialization drive on the scale of the East Asian "tigers," there seems little prospect of rapidly expanding the middle class in the Philippines. Richard Doner's analysis of the economic troubles besetting Thailand—a country about twice as rich as the Philippines in per capita terms—is revealing.[24] Like Thailand, the Philippines has diversified economically, no longer relying primarily on agriculture. But even less than in Thailand, the Philippine economy has yet to be "deepened" through industrial upgrading. In the Philippines, one can point to successes in the automobile and electronics-assembly industries, mining, and the current boom in call centers as examples of diversification. Yet the Philippines' most important "export" remains its overseas foreign workers—Filipinos who labor abroad and send money home. The country remains weak in the production of major capital goods, with no "world-beating" companies that use local inputs and technical capacities. This weakness points in turn to a "human-capital" deficit that is due in large part to the disastrous state of education.

Thus, however clean government may become, most Filipinos will remain impoverished, with only about 10 percent of Filipinos considered part of the upper or middle classes. The poor will continue to suffer chronic problems in the areas of nutrition, housing, employment, healthcare, and education.

Electoral manipulations, corruption scandals, human-rights abuses, and the undermining of institutions discredited the Arroyo administration and led Freedom House to downgrade the Philippines from Free to Partly Free in its annual rankings for 2006—a ranking that seems likely to return to Free now that electoral stability has been restored and press freedom improved. Arroyo was also accused of cynically sacrificing the peace process in Muslim Mindanao to political expediency. The perpetrators of the November 2009 Maguindanao massacre on that island were her close allies, showing the potential for harm that lay in her ties to warlords.

That said, the opposition's abandonment of the insurrection strategy and the replacement of Arroyo via the ballot in what was probably the freest and fairest presidential contest since 1965 have together set the stage for fresh contentions between a reformist president and future populist challengers. While corruption charges are inevitable in a patronage-driven system, even a successful reformist president can be succeeded by a populist, as happened when Estrada took office following Fidel Ramos, whose time in office is generally thought to mark the golden age of political reform in the post-Marcos Philippines. Estrada's strong support among the masses of poor voters who swept him into the presidency in 1998 was a product of Ramos's failure, despite his reforms, to do much about poverty and inequality. But Estrada, who enjoyed strong backing from the poor throughout his presidency, was forced out of office in a middle-class–backed people-power coup in 2001, a severe setback to democratic consolidation in the Philippines.

But it now seems that the Philippine elite is prepared to tolerate populist challenges for power, with vice-president Binay preparing anew to present this alternative narrative for his 2016 presidential bid. If politicians who make populist appeals to impoverished Filipinos begin to place more emphasis on actually creating programs to help them, a pattern of electoral cycling may emerge in which greater efficiency and greater equality alternate as the main goals of public policy. In a country that faces challenges regarding both economic development and social inequality, a debate over the relative merits and drawbacks of pursuing these two goals seems like a sensible one to put before the electorate.

NOTES

The author wishes to thank Eric Batalla, Siegfried Herzog, Paul Hutchcroft, Yuko Kasuya, Ben Kerkvliet, Masataka Kimura, Howard Loewen, Francisco Magno, Diana Mendoza, Felipe Miranda, Michael Montesano, Alfred McCoy, Manuel Quezon, Nathan Quimpo, Temario Rivera, , Julio Teehankee, and Charles du Vinage for their suggestions and comments on earlier versions of this essay.

1. Filipinos hoped her sainthood would not be merely symbolic, with calls for her to be "fast tracked" to canonization, see Yolanda Sotelo, "Cory Sainthood? Wait 3 Years, Says Bishop," *Philippine Daily Inquirer* (Manila), 8 August 2009.

2. Paul Hutchcroft, "The Limits of Good Intentions: Noynoy Aquino One Year On," *Inside Story*, 30 June 2011, *www.inside.org.au/the-limits-of-good-intentions-noynoy-aquino-one-year-on.*

3. Although Aquino's satisfaction ratings for the first quarter of 2012 were down 10 percent over the last half of 2011 and 18 percent below the ratings with which he entered office, 46 percent of respondents remained satisfied: Social Weather Stations (SWS), "First Quarter 2012 Social Weather Survey: Net Satisfaction with National Administration at 'Good' +46," 30 April 2012 (*www.sws.org.ph*). SWS is one of the leading polling organizations in a country that has developed a highly sophisticated social-survey industry.

4. On how authoritarian cheating can spark popular uprisings, see Philipp Kuntz and Mark R. Thompson, "More Than Just the Final Straw: Stolen Elections as Revolutionary Triggers," *Comparative Politics* 41 (April 2009): 253–72.

5. Cecille Suerte Felipe, "Ten People Killed in Poll-Related Incidents," *Philippine Star* (Manila), 10 May 2010.

6. A "black swan" is an event that is both significant and hard to predict. See Nassim Nicholas Taleb, *The Black Swan: The Impact of the Highly Improbable* (New York: Random House, 2007). I wish to thank Siegfried Herzog for bringing this concept's relevance to the 2010 election to my attention.

7. Alexander Magno, "Game Changer," *Philippine Star*, 20 August 2009; and Amando Doronila, "Transparency Now a Defining Issue in Campaign," *Philippine Daily Inquirer*, 16 September 2009.

8. Eva-Lotta E. Hedman, "The Spectre of Populism in Philippine Politics and Society: *Artista, Masa, Eraption!*" *South East Asia Research* 9 (March 2001): 5–44.

9. Amando Doronila, "Damaged Goods," *Philippine Daily Inquirer*, 3 December 2009.

10. Patricio N. Abinales and Donna J. Amoroso, "The Withering of Philippine Democracy," *Current History* 105 (September 2006): 290–95.

11. Agence France-Presse, "EU to Help RP Tackle Extra-judicial Killings," *Philippine Daily Inquirer*, 8 October 2009.

12. Conrado de Quiros, "The 'Noynoy' Phenomenon," *Philippine Daily Inquirer*, 1 October 2009.

13. See Carl Landé, *Leaders, Factions, and Parties: The Structure of Philippine Politics* (New Haven: Yale University Southeast Asia Monographs, 1965); Kit G. Machado, "Changing Patterns of Leadership Recruitment and the Emergence of the Professional Politician in Philippine Local Politics," in Benedict Kerkvliet, ed., *Political Change in the Philippines: Studies in Local Politics Preceding Martial Law* (Honolulu: University Press of Hawaii, 1974); and John Sidel, *Capital, Coercion, and Crime: Bossism in the Philippines* (Stanford: Stanford University Press, 1999).

14. Benedict J. Tria Kerkvliet, "Toward a More Comprehensive Analysis of Philippine Politics: Beyond the Patron-Client, Factional Framework," *Journal of Southeast Asian Studies* 26 (September 1995): 401–19; and Kerkvliet, "Contested Meanings of Elections in the Philippines," in R.H. Taylor, ed., *The Politics of Elections in Southeast Asia* (Cambridge: Cambridge University Press, 1996): 136–63.

15. Jennifer Conroy Franco, *Elections and Democratization in the Philippines* (London: Routledge, 2001).

16. Amando Doronila, "Ruling Puts Noy, Cory Legacy on the Spot," *Philippine Daily Inquirer*, 30 April 2012.

17. Floyd Whaley, "Philippine Chief Justice Removed over Omission on Report on Assets," *New York Times*, 29 May 2012, called it "a landmark conviction that could strengthen the president's hand in cracking down on the endemic corruption that has long been a drag on the economy." One Philippine journalist rhapsodized that this was the "best time to be a Filipino" and that the "future was full of hope" due to the high governance standards demonstrated by Corona's conviction; Jose Ma Montelibano, "Best Time to Be Filipino," *Philippine Daily Inquirer*, 8 June 2012. It is worth recalling in this context the very different reactions provoked by the jailing of former Ukranian prime minister Yulia Tymoshenko. Aquino's success has been to frame his campaign against Arroyo and her allies as being waged in the name of good governance rather than for mere revenge.

18. Manuel Mogato, "China Criticizes Philippines on South China Sea Protest," *Reuters*, 11 May 2012. The most recent maritime skirmish between the Philippines and China occurred in April 2012 over an island located near Scarborough Shoal (known as Huangyan Island in China and as Panatag Shoal or Bajo de Masinloc in the Philippines). Chinese fishing and surveillance vessels were pitted against Philippine naval warships. Supposedly resource-rich and a fertile fishing ground, Scarborough Shoal is located a little over 200 km from the Philippines, but China, using historical precedent, claims it as part of its far-flung maritime territory.

19. "Philippines Conditional Cash Transfer Improves Health and Education," *Microfinance Focus*, 7 September 2011; Mahar Mangahas, "Painful statistics," *Philippine Daily Inquirer*, 11 May 2012; and Leila B. Salaverria, "Dip in Aquino's Rating Due to 'Noynoying,' Says Militant Group," *Philippine Daily Inquirer*, 2 April 2012.

20. Elizabeth Angsioco, "Arguments for the Reproductive Health Bill," *Manila Times*, 10 August 2008, Diana Mendoza, "Criminal Ban, Stigma Drive Unsafe Abortions," *Ipsnews.net*, 2 September 2010, and Dona Pazzibugan, "UN Study: 11 RP Women Die of Childbirth Each Day," *Philippine Daily Inquirer*, 15 January 2009.

21. Jennifer C. Franco and Saturnino M. Borras, Jr., eds., *On Just Grounds: Struggling for Agrarian Justice and Citizenship Rights in the Rural Philippines* (Quezon City, Philippines: Institute for Popular Democracy, 2005); and Benedict J. Kerkvliet, "A Different View of Insurgencies," in Human Development Network, *In Search of a Human Face: 15 Years of Knowledge Building for Human Development in the Philippines* (Manila: Human Development Network, 2010): 268–79.

22. Tetch Torres, "New York-Based Group Calls on Aquino, Army Chief to Act on Human Rights Violations," *Philippine Daily Inquirer*, 2 April 2012.

23. Tina G. Santos, "Naia 1 is Rated 'World's Worst Airport'," *Philippine Daily Inquirer*, 19 October 2011, Ritchie A. Horario, "Philippine Rank in World's Most Corrupt Improves," *Manila Times*, 2 December 2011, and Agence France-Presse, "Foreign Business Still Cool on the Philippines," *Philippine Daily Inquirer*, 20 July 2011.

24. Richard Doner, *The Politics of Uneven Development: Thailand's Economic Growth in Comparative Perspective* (Cambridge: Cambridge University Press, 2009).

10

THAILAND'S UNEASY PASSAGE

Thitinan Pongsudhirak

Thitinan Pongsudhirak *teaches international political economy and directs the Institute of Security and International Studies at Chulalongkorn University in Bangkok. His essay "Thailand Since the Coup" appeared in the October 2008 issue of the* Journal of Democracy. *This essay originally appeared in the April 2012 issue of the* Journal of Democracy.

Few countries struggling to emerge as democracies have undergone bouts of "democratic rollback"[1] as dramatic as those that Thailand has endured over the last several years. Since a September 2006 military coup deposed deeply flawed but popularly elected premier Thaksin Shinawatra and forced him into exile, the Thai body politic has been battered and torn as never before in its already tumultuous history. Street protests and violent faceoffs between red-shirted Thaksin backers and yellow-shirted Thaksin foes have continued year after year and show no sign of stopping. Although Thaksin himself was banned from actually appearing on the ballot in the 3 July 2011 parliamentary elections, he emerged as the big winner when a new electoral vehicle known as the Pheu Thai Party (PTP, or "For Thais") gained a decisive victory with his younger sister Yingluck at its head.

As twilight settles over the 65-year reign of King Bhumibol Adulyadej (b. 1927), Thais find themselves caught in a national stalemate. Those who favor maintaining the monarchy-centered hierarchy as the ultimate source of political power are arrayed against others who want to reform the monarchy and reconcile it with a fuller and more mature form of democracy. With Cold War imperatives now obsolete, with international norms increasingly favoring democracy and human rights, and with new media technologies and demographic realities making themselves felt, Thailand's monarchy-based establishment finds itself hard-pressed to maintain the status quo. Yet it has too much at stake to simply give way to the challenges that Thaksin (in his faulty and not-always-democratic way) spearheaded during a premiership that began with his election in 2001 and was cut off by the coup five years later.

The two imperative or pressing questions are: Can and will an entrenched monarchy reconcile itself with an irreversible trend toward democracy? And can that democracy be kept safe from the usurpations, manipulations, and abuses of power that marred the Thaksin years and put all Thais on notice that getting democracy is one thing, but getting it *right* is another?

The Rise of Thaksin

The last decade of Thai politics has featured volatility and contention in abundance. In the wake of the 1997–98 Asian financial crisis, Thaksin rode his Thai Rak Thai (TRT, or "Thais Love Thais") party into office in the January 2001 election. He enacted unprecedented policy innovations and a broadly populist platform designed to appeal to the rural voters left behind by the long economic boom that ended in 1997. He suspended rural debts while offering microcredit schemes and cheap healthcare. He launched development projects and niche industries to promote food, fashion, tourism, healthcare, and automobiles.[2] He revamped policy making to give elected politicians more sway than bureaucrats. He also tinkered with military promotions in order to elevate trusted associates (including a cousin) to the high command, and undermined the 1997 Constitution by politicizing and coopting its intended checks and balances. In August 2001, he was narrowly found not guilty of hiding assets in a trial marred by charges that Constitutional Court judges had been pressured or paid off.

Thaksin continued to enact policies that won majority support among voters, but accompanied these successes with corruption, conflicts of interest, human-rights violations, abuses of power, and displays of an authoritarian bent. When he was reelected by an overwhelming margin in February 2005, he came to feel virtually invincible.[3] His problems with the palace date from this time. Already an outsider, with a vast fortune springing from a stock-market boom rather than from the traditional realm of protected state concessions, Thaksin further alienated himself from the establishment by deciding that he no longer needed to consult with General Prem Tinsulanond, the former premier and army chief who runs the Privy Council, the king's nineteen-member advisory body. As a former officer in the police service, moreover, Thaksin favored it over the military and used the police to wage a war on drugs that claimed close to 2,300 lives, many by extrajudicial killings.

While Thaksin's populism was winning at the polls, his abuses were rousing his foes. By mid-2005, they had formed a coalition that included the Democrat Party (DP), the military, senior bureaucrats, some private business elements, the urban middle class, and palace insiders as well as royalists in society at large (yellow-shirts wear that color because of its association with the Thai monarchy). When Thaksin's Shinawatra Corporation (Shin Corp) conglomerate was sold, tax-free, for US$1.9 billion to Singapore's Temasek Holdings in January 2006, cries went up for his resignation. His response was to call a snap election (later nullified by the courts) for April 2006. The DP and two smaller allies boycotted the vote, setting up a constitutional crisis. The widening coalition against Thaksin kept up the pressure, eroding his legitimacy and filling the streets with protesters in the weeks leading up to the 19 September 2006 putsch.

Thaksin, out of the country on official business, decided to remain abroad. The coupmakers, who later styled themselves the Council for National Security, were meanwhile careful to publicize a photo that they had taken with the king and queen on the night of the putsch. But if the plotters thought that they had turned back once and for all the challenge to the established order represented by Thaksin and his redistributionist platform, they were mistaken.

The military installed a caretaker government under a retired general, saw to the judicial dissolution of Thaksin's TRT, and arranged for the drafting of a new constitution that would elevate bureaucrats and judges at the expense of elected politicians, political parties, and parliament. Yet in the ensuing election, held in December 2007, the TRT's successor, now called the People's Power Party or PPP, thrashed the DP by 233 to 165 seats in the revised 480-member assembly. By January 2008, Thaksin was back on top through a proxy prime minister. Thaksin's adversaries, led by the yellow-shirted People's Alliance for Democracy (PAD), replied with sit-ins, taking over Government House (which holds the prime minister's office) in May 2008 and then Bangkok's main international airport for a week in late November and early December. Thus a crisis of governability erupted even as the Constitutional Court was disbanding the PPP and two smaller allied parties after a vote-fraud conviction.[4]

With the weight and influence of the military behind it, the DP took power in early 2009 under the premiership of the Eton- and Oxford-educated Abhisit Vejjajiva. Then it became the pro-Thaksin red-shirts' turn to hit the streets in protest. In April 2009, and then from March to May 2010, they staged demonstrations that the army dispersed. In 2010, the death toll from these confrontations reached 91. The strife partly set the stage for the early dissolution of parliament and the July 2011 elections, with the PTP as Thaksin's third-time-around vehicle after the banning of his previous two. Yingluck—whom her brother has called his "clone"— and the PTP brought the pro-Thaksin forces even more success at the polls than they had experienced in December 2007, winning 265 of 500

seats and dwarfing the DP with its 159 seats. Once again, a clear majority of Thailand's electorate has made its pro-Thaksin preferences clear.

The 44-year-old Yingluck allows her much-older brother (Thaksin
is 62) to present as his proxy a youthful and attractive new figure with
no baggage—she had previously worked in the family real-estate business and has no background in politics. Thaksin picked nearly her entire
cabinet.[5] As she began her mandate, she was greeted by a crisis not of
human making: The worst flooding in decades swept large parts of Thailand starting with the monsoon season in July 2011. Her government
emerged from the flood crisis in a much weaker position due to inter-
agency conflicts and lack of policy coordination among cabinet members. But for Yingluck herself, the floods constituted a political baptism.
Her day-to-day devotion to flood management and disaster relief earned
her public sympathy and allowed her to emerge from the crisis with
heightened stature and confidence.

In the wake of the disastrous floods, 2012 began in an atmosphere of
stalemate. Yingluck's government has been upholding the monarchy's
sanctity by strictly enforcing Article 112 of the Criminal Code, otherwise
known as the *lèse-majesté* (LM) law, and its related Computer Crimes
Act. In return, debilitating street protests, party dissolutions, and politician disqualifications have abated. Neither side seems capable of a decisive move. The government lacks the will to amend the repressive laws
that stifle freedom of expression. Establishment forces, for their part,
cannot muster the strength for more rounds of party dissolutions, street
demonstrations, and changes of government, let alone a military coup.
When the ban on former TRT politicians that accompanied the party's
dissolution expires in May 2012, Thaksin (acting through Yingluck) will
have more political talent to pick from.

As long as the monarchy remains sacrosanct and the symbiotic relationship between it and the military remains untouched, Yingluck may
be able to muddle along with a reheated populist agenda of higher wages
and subsidies for the urban poor and upcountry farmers. Should the palace begin to perceive a clear and present danger, however, the Yingluck
government and anyone who actively aspires to a basic reform of the
monarchy will likely face stepped-up pressure and perhaps even the
specter of violence from royalist and conservative quarters.

Contemporary Electoral Patterns

This brief narrative of Thailand's political dynamics and Thaksin's
durable impact over the past decade is supported by a review of election
results. Despite the 2006 coup and protracted political turmoil, elections have proceeded with substantial regularity since November 1996.
Over that time, the party system has gravitated toward bigger parties.
The introduction of party lists to fill a portion of seats in the legislature

TABLE—THAI ELECTION RESULTS BY REGION, 2001–11

Party	Total Seats[1]	Constituency Seats	Bangkok	Central	Northeast	North	South
July 2011							
Pheu Thai*	265	204	10	41	104	49	0
Democrat	159	115	23	25	4	13	50
Others	76	56	0	30	18	5	3
Total	**500**	**375**	**33**	**96**	**126**	**67**	**53**
December 2007							
People's Power*	233	199	9	39	102	47	2
Democrat	165	132	27	35	5	16	49
Others	82	69	0	24	28	12	5
Total	**480**	**400**	**36**	**98**	**135**	**75**	**56**
February 2005							
Thai Rak Thai*	377	310	32	80	126	71	1
Democrat	96	70	4	7	2	5	52
Others	27	20	1	10	8	0	1
Total	**500**	**400**	**37**	**97**	**136**	**76**	**54**
January 2001							
Thai Rak Thai*	248	200	29	47	68	55	1
Democrat	128	97	8	19	6	16	48
Others	124	103	0	29	63	6	5
Total	**500**	**400**	**37**	**95**	**137**	**77**	**54**

Source: Election Commission of Thailand.

[1] "Total Seats" includes party-list as well as constituency seats. "Constituency Seats" equal the sum of all regional seats.

* Thaksin's party.

dates from the 1997 Constitution and has had the effect of weeding out smaller parties. The party-list system also provided the basis for a gerrymandering scheme—enacted as part of the military-backed postcoup constitution of 2007—that is meant to dilute the power of Thaksin's movement. In the December 2007 balloting, the gerrymandering did help the DP to nearly match the PPP in party-list seats (with a final tally of 33 to 34), but otherwise it has not been the game-changer that its backers in the establishment had hoped that it would be.

Since 2001, Thaksin's party (under whatever label) has won each of the four national elections by a large margin. During that time, the DP and the forces behind it have succeeded in engineering various systemic changes—including party-list gerrymandering and a switch from single- to multi-member constituencies—to improve DP chances, but none have stripped Thaksin or his populist platform of their ability to win elections. His biggest margin of victory came in February 2005, which makes it puzzling that before the year was out he would face major street protests in Bangkok that swelled into a broad-based movement by early 2006.

Part of the explanation lies in the capital's status as a bastion of anticor-ruption sentiment and its disproportionately prominent voice in national politics. In February 2005, TRT nabbed 32 of Bangkok's 37 lower-house seats. But the shady Shin Corp sale and the rising tide of anti-Thaksin protests in the capital throughout the period from 2005 to 2007 (years punctuated by the coup and the new constitution) reversed this situation. In December 2007, the DP won 27 Bangkok seats, leaving the PPP with a mere 9 seats from the capital. In July 2011, the score was 23 seats for the DP versus just 10 for the PTP.

Northern and Northeast Thailand, which together are home to slightly more than half the electorate, show a very different pattern. Thaksin (or his stand-in) swept those regions in 2005, 2007, and 2011. He saw some shrinkage of support in 2007, after the protests and coup against him and the passage of a new constitution, but his wide margin of vic-tory returned in 2011. The DP has fared consistently poorly in these two populous regions while Thaksin's electoral appeal there has proven highly resilient.

The South, however, has gone for the DP time and again. None of Thaksin's electoral vehicles has been able to penetrate the DP bastion there, where Thailand's territory extends down the northern neck of the long Malay Peninsula. Yet this region, which has its own distinct dialect and customs and has been the scene of a deadly Malay-Muslim insurgency in the provinces bordering Malaysia, accounts for just 11 percent of the seats in parliament. Central Thailand has been more like the North: It voted for TRT in 2005, saw the DP make up some ground in 2007, and then witnessed the PTP reopen a lead on Thaksin's behalf in 2011. As about a quarter of parliament comes from the central region, it is traditionally an area of fairly intense competition between the two main parties, with smaller parties joining in as well. Although the DP still ran well behind there in 2011, it has palpably expanded its presence in the Central region.

These regional trends mirror the larger conflict. Rural folk from the North and Northeast are the mainstays of the pro-Thaksin red-shirts. They ran amok in the capital after the PPP was dissolved, rioting in April 2009 and then staging a sustained sit-in at a major street intersec-tion in Bangkok's central business district. Thaksin has won all Thai elections in the early twenty-first century by comfortable margins, yet his parties have lost substantial support in Bangkok since the coup and have never been able to penetrate the South. The DP has gained considerable ground in Bangkok and the Central region since 2005, and has held its southern base over the entire past decade. But even after being hoisted into office with help from the military in December 2008 and holding power for thirty months, the DP could not solve the electoral challenge posed by Thaksin's populism. Over this same period, parts of the country's court system became politicized and, at times, willing to ban entire parties and large numbers of politicians. This added to the Thai party system's already considerable institutional shortcomings and constitutes a thread of the story that warrants attention.

The Failure of "Judicialization"

Until recently, Thailand's judiciary was rarely in the political spotlight. That began to change when the framers of the 1997 Constitution, seeking improved governmental stability, effectiveness, transparency, and accountability, mandated a clutch of agencies to oversee the Thai body politic. The new constitutional entities included the Election Commission, the National Anti-Corruption Commission (NACC), the Administrative Court, and the Constitutional Court.

Given this last court's jurisdiction over all matters related to constitutional interpretation, it did not take long for it to become politicized. For the first few years after it opened its doors in 1998, the Court invariably endorsed corruption indictments brought to it by the NACC. In December 2000, the NACC handed down, by a vote of 8 to 1, an indictment of Thaksin for having hidden assets under the names of his housekeeper, maid, driver, security guard, and business colleague.[6] Shortly thereafter, Thaksin emerged triumphant in the January 2001 election, nearly securing an outright majority in the lower house for his Thai Rak Thai party.

The pressure on the Court was immense, and intensified as the verdict drew near. Should Thaksin be convicted, his supporters swore, they would wreak havoc in the streets. On 3 August 2001, a divided Court narrowly acquitted him on a technicality by an 8-to-7 vote. Four judges ruled that the Court had no jurisdiction, while four more accepted jurisdiction but held Thaksin to have been "honestly negligent" regarding financial records that his wife had been handling. The seven minority judges, by contrast, were united in holding that Thaksin had deliberately hidden and falsely declared his assets in knowing contravention of constitutional stipulations. One dissenting jurist has said that senior figures including a four-star general and a former Supreme Court chief justice had lobbied the Constitutional Court on Thaksin's behalf.[7] Other heavy hitters such as Privy Council chairman Prem Tinsulanond had dropped public hints while the case was pending about the need for "giving [Thaksin] a chance."

Plainly, Thaksin was no ordinary defendant. His party had just won eleven million votes plus the right to form a government, and his platform of economic nationalism and new growth strategies seemed as if it might be suited to pulling the Thai economy out of the doldrums in which it had been languishing since the 1997–98 crisis. Indeed, many of those who would oppose Thaksin after the coup, including media tycoon and yellow-shirt leader Sondhi Limthongkul, lined up firmly behind him during his early legal troubles. Yet whatever might have been the merits of influencing the course of justice for the sake of democracy and prosperity, this episode hopelessly compromised the new Constitutional Court's ability to build a reputation for independence and impartiality.

Before and after Thaksin's overthrow in the 2006 coup, the Court's politicization went from passive to active. Letting him off in 2001 had been a *passive* politicized decision because it maintained rather than changed the course of electoral politics: The winner of the election was allowed to take power, make policy, and build political momentum. In 2006, however, the Court turned activist and tried to set new political directions. The boycotted snap election of 2 April 2006 led to an impasse that the king exhorted the judiciary to resolve. As the monarch told the Administrative Court judges in a televised address on 26 April 2006:

> You must find ways to solve the problem. . . . Should the election be nullified? You have the right to say what is appropriate or not. If it is not appropriate, it is not to say the government is not good. But as far as I am concerned, a one-party election is not normal. The one-candidate situation is undemocratic.[8]

In the ensuing weeks, the chiefs of the Supreme Court, the Administrative Court, and the Constitutional Court met and agreed to adjudicate "in the same direction." The key ruling came from the Constitutional Court, which annulled the April balloting. Later, the chiefs of the three courts would demand that the Election Commission's three remaining members (two members had already stepped down) resign to make way for the naming of a new commission. When the three commissioners refused, they were ignominiously jailed for a night before bail was granted. A public intellectual described this at the time as the "judicialization" of Thai politics, implying that the judiciary was Thailand's way out of crisis.[9] Judicial decisions, in other words, aspired to actively set political directions in view of the prevailing impasse.

Among the lessons of 2011 is judicialization's failure. Put in motion by the king's 26 April 2006 speech, it was seen by some analysts as royal interference in politics.[10] After the coup, the Constitutional Court was disbanded and replaced by a smaller, nine-judge Constitutional Tribunal. The DP and TRT charged each other before this body with having resorted to illegal electoral practices. On 30 May 2007, the Constitutional Tribunal absolved the DP and found TRT guilty. The penalties included dissolution and a five-year ban on officeholding by any of its 111 executive-board members, including Thaksin and many of those who had served in his cabinets. But by election time in December 2007, the TRT remnant had managed to regroup under the PPP label, and came out on top in the voting. In September 2008, the Constitutional Tribunal ousted PPP prime minister Samak Sundaravej on a technicality—his acceptance of an honorarium for hosting a televised cooking show, the Tribunal ruled, made him a private-sector "employee" and hence disqualified him from holding the premiership. Samak, aged 73 at the time, left politics for good and died of cancer a year later. Thaksin's brother-in-law, Somchai Wongsawat, stepped in as premier and came under immediate pressure from yellow-shirt protests. On 7 October 2008, police were ordered to disperse demonstrators who had surrounded Parliament House, where Somchai was slated to announce his policy agenda. (The army chief had earlier refused to obey government instructions and had gone on television to urge Somchai's resignation.) In the clashes that ensued between police officers and yellow-shirts, several hundred were injured and two protesters died. In an unusual step, the queen presided over the funeral of one of those killed.[11]

As December began, yellow-shirts were in the midst of their weeklong occupation of Bangkok's largest airport while the Constitutional Tribunal was convicting the PPP and two smaller allied parties of vote fraud and banning their leading figures from running for or holding office. These bans are set to expire later in 2012, an event that will probably give a broad boost to the Yingluck government and may be a boon to Thai politics in general. (Whatever talent Thai politicians have to offer, much of it has been systematically kept off the playing field for the past half-decade.) Looking back over the last few years, it is obvious that judicialization has come to nought. The TRT party was shuttered but reorganized itself as first the PPP and then the PTP, which secured a thumping majority in the July 2011 election. Thaksin remains in charge from abroad. His sister rules in his name, and his TRT lieutenants are to be reinstated on 30 May 2012, with his banned PPP supporters to follow in December 2013. The failure of judicialization carries far-reaching implications.

Challenge and Pushback

The monarchy is associated with the launch of the judicialization strategy, and that strategy's failure appears to have compromised the monarchy up to a point. If the bans and dissolutions, the postcoup seizure or freezing of Thaksin's assets, and his 2010 Supreme Court conviction *in absentia* on "policy corruption" charges had succeeded in ending the challenge that he represented, then perhaps Thai politics might have stabilized and returned to something like its pre-Thaksin form, led by a

weak party system and a strong military-monarchy-bureaucracy trium-
virate. But Thaksin with all his strengths and weaknesses—the innovative efforts to increase economic competitiveness, the offer of greater
upward mobility to those on society's bottom rungs, and also the corruption, the conflicts of interest, and the human-rights violations of the
war on drugs—became "indestructible."[12] The failure of judicialization
marked the monarchy's failure to extinguish the political awakening and
the runaway expectations that Thaksin's TRT years had ignited. Moreover, when a senior general left the Privy Council to head the coup-
appointed government, then rejoined the king's advisory body after the
December 2007 poll, it reinforced the popular perception that the putsch
had been carried out to protect and promote the crown (and the military-
bureaucratic establishment long associated with it) at the expense of a
democratically elected government.

That perception gained force when Chanchai Likitjitta, justice minister for the coup government, was named to the Privy Council on 8
April 2008. Similarly, Air Chief Marshal Chalit Pookpasuk, a core
coupmaker who had headed the Council for National Security after
September 2007, was appointed to the Privy Council on 18 May 2011.
Many also noted the queen's conspicuous attendance at the October
2008 funeral of the yellow-shirt protester. The *lèse-majesté* law may
deter public discussion, but it cannot prevent people from taking private notice.[13] Then there were the televised comments in which top
army general Prayuth Chan-ocha effectively endorsed the DP just
weeks before the 2011 election, urging viewers not to vote for the
same politicians but to elect "good people" who would defend the
monarchy. This could not help but tarnish the revered institution when
Pheu Thai won handily.[14]

Unsurprisingly, challenges to the established order have grown since
the military coup. According to a letter that eight royal descendants
sent to Prime Minister Yingluck urging amendment of the *lèse-majesté* law, cases involving Article 112 went from zero in 2002 to 165 in
2009.[15] They have ranged from the convictions of an Australian writer
and a Thai-American who translated an unauthorized biography of the
king[16] to the twenty-year sentence handed to a 61-year-old man who
was charged with sending four SMS messages deemed in violation of
Article 112.[17]

Many studies of Thailand's state and society published since the coup
have reflected this challenge to established centers of power. Although
it was greeted with mixed reactions when it came out, journalist Paul
M. Handley's controversial royal biography *The King Never Smiles*
eventually reverberated far and wide, and is now a staple for anyone
intent on understanding contemporary Thailand.[18] Prior to Handley's
work, scholarly scrutiny of the Thai establishment was scant and not
widely available,[19] especially during the Cold War. But since the mili-

tary coup, what used to be droplets have swelled into a steady flow of critical expositions. Less than a year before Handley's account of the king was published, Duncan McCargo's analysis of the Malay-Muslim insurgency taking place in southernmost Thailand identified a "network monarchy" that revolved around Privy Council chairman and army general Prem Tinsulanond.[20] In early 2008, the *Journal of Contemporary Asia* offered a special issue on Thai politics that challenged much of what had been the conventional wisdom regarding the putsch and its backers.[21] An influential international weekly followed suit the same year.[22] Other critiques focused on the king's deification through propaganda and popular culture.[23] In 2010, two major edited volumes further challenged the establishment's political role, economic interests, and popular image.[24] In terms of the scholarly literature on Thai politics, the genie was irreversibly out of the bottle.

As intimidation, coercion, and suppression through the *lèse-majesté* and Computer Crimes laws began to draw increasing attention at home and abroad, the establishment pushed back with the publication of a new and more positive scholarly biography of the king, *King Bhumibol Adulyadej: A Life's Work*,[25] which comes across as an implicit antidote and indirect rebuttal to Handley's *The King Never Smiles*. Other manifestations of the royalist pushback have been available online and all across the state-owned airwaves, including some vigilante threats against dissenters. When a set of Thammasat University law professors known as the Nitirat Group tried to suggest amendments to the *lèse-majesté* law, a broad array of royalist groups castigated them.

Reconciling Monarchy and Democracy

As of early 2012, no other reformist groups or individuals had appeared on the scene possessing anything like what it will take to reconcile monarchy and democracy in Thailand. All the same, however, it appears that Thailand cannot escape the challenge of reaching a new consensus that will root the monarchy more squarely within the constitution of an emerging democracy, but in a way that reconciles conservative royalists. The desire of the rural lower classes to have their voices heard and their numbers felt is legitimate, but so is the desire for a government that does not simply replace the lack of accountability that characterized the old military-bureaucratic power centers with a similarly unaccountable populist strongman.

Yingluck Shinawatra may head the new government, but her brother continues to bestride Thailand's political landscape like a colossus. Currently, his adversaries' shortcomings loom larger in the public eye than do his own glaring defects and wrongdoings. The intellectual hegemony of a hierarchical social and political order centered on the monarchy is no longer tenable and offers no path to a viable future. The superstructure of this old order can sense the ground shifting beneath it and is maneuvering hard to maintain the status quo. Its maneuvers will not always be pretty to watch, and they must all take place in the long shadow cast by Thaksin, who even after being deposed by a coup, convicted of corruption, and banned from office keeps winning at the polls, with no serious challenger in sight.

Thaksin's name is synonymous with divisiveness. In deeply polarized Thailand, mentioning him seems to rouse either love or hate; few are lukewarm. His supporters may outnumber his detractors in the voting booth, but in the public square the voices crying out against him are louder and more potent than those that speak in his defense. In bygone eras, elections and coups came and went. Voters sold their votes like commodities, and legislators went to Bangkok seeking pork and patronage via graft and corruption, hardly bothering even to acknowledge (much less consult) their constituents. Elected officials, not surprisingly, enjoyed scant legitimacy, thereby making coups more thinkable and more feasible. Coups sometimes issued in new constitutions, but these were just more turns of the wheel, not true departures pointing the way to sounder models of governance.

While the Cold War imposed its exigencies, the pillars of the Thai state—the nation, its Buddhist religion, and its hereditary monarchy—kept communism at bay, brought unity, and underwrote stability. Challenges to the order represented by the army, the monarchy, and the bureaucracy were invariably put down, as left-wing students discovered in the 1970s. Thai schoolchildren sang martial songs and the national anthem each morning. Thais knew what to expect and where their places lay in their country's sociopolitical hierarchy, thanks to socialization via the classroom and the living room, where the state-run media were ever-present to drive home the lesson. Dissenting views of what it meant to be Thai gained little traction.

All this undergirded rapid development. Yet this economic growth and the benefits that it brought became distributed in increasingly uneven ways, and thus set the stage for Thaksin's rise as a tribune of populism and the less well-off. The rise of TRT put an end to the old clubby-yet-distant world of Thai politics. The party pursued a scientific approach to electioneering complete with expensive polling carried out by foreign experts, clear and deliverable platforms, and strong leadership. Judicial bans notwithstanding, TRT and its successors became household names. Thaksin's was the first post–Cold War party to capture the collective imagination. The voices of once-marginalized voters began to count. Vote-buying, long a staple of Thai politics, remained necessary but was no longer sufficient. Whatever else can be said about it, TRT did introduce to Thailand the idea of close ties between a party, its policies, and its voter base.

By 2001, the Cold War was long over. Political leaders dissenting from the status quo could not so easily be jailed on communism-related charges. The Internet and new media were making it harder for official sources to mold minds uncontested. Information became more widely diffused and media outlets multiplied even as state propaganda continued to make its influence felt. New international norms came to the fore. Foreign powers that had once turned a blind eye to coups and repression now put more emphasis on democracy and human rights. The passage of time, meanwhile, has ensured that most university students today cannot even recall the Cold War, for it ended before they were born.

Thaksin was well positioned by circumstance and insight to take advantage of this new and more open political environment. Given an opportunity, he overhauled the bureaucracy, delivered on his populist pledges to do more for poorer Thais, mapped out plans to upgrade the country's industrial base, and even pursued an ambitious foreign-policy agenda in pursuit of Thai regional leadership. Yet there was to all this an underside of corruption, conflicts of interest, cronyism, human-rights violations, abuses of power, and other sins of misrule. Such is Thaksin's mixed legacy. The wider opportunities that he opened for the downtrodden and his ambitious plans for Thailand's future were inextricably entangled with his self-dealing, his penchant for corruption, and his habit of abusing the powers of his office. Thaksin Incorporated went hand-in-hand with Thailand Incorporated.

Yet Thaksin's enemies have shown their own limits in refusing to admit that there is more to him and what he stands for than graft and corruption. They should have weighed his policy innovations and put forward their own ideas for assisting the impoverished and marginalized. In the end, they came up with the Abhisit government and its programs for "welfare" and fostering a "sufficiency economy" that most voters find insufficient. For Thaksin's establishment foes, conceding to his spectacularly successful populism would have been tantamount to admitting that most people in the hospitable, smiling, conspicuously tourist-friendly Kingdom of Thailand have been—and have been kept—poor.

Wittingly or not, Thaksin has been the catalyst for propelling Thailand into the twenty-first century while his adversaries have stayed stuck in Cold War times. Although he committed many infractions, Thaksin's most egregious crime and gravest sin were that he changed the way Thais see themselves and their country. Some see this change as usurpation and manipulation by Thaksin and his cronies. Others see it as Thailand's overdue deliverance from the Cold War era. Those who have ruled in the past must accept this new reality, just as those who are atop the polls now must accept the legacy of the past.

NOTES

1. Larry Diamond, "The Democratic Rollback: The Resurgence of the Predatory State," *Foreign Affairs* 87 (March–April 2008): 36–48.

2. Thitinan Pongsudhirak, "Thailand Since the Coup," *Journal of Democracy* 19 (October 2008): 140–53; Thitinan Pongsudhirak, "Thaksin: Competitive Authoritarian and Flawed Dissident," in John Kane, Haig Patapan, and Benjamin Wong, eds., *Dissident Democrats: The Challenge of Democratic Leadership in Asia* (New York: Palgrave Macmillan, 2008); Thitinan Pongsudhirak, "Thailand: Democratic Authoritarianism," *Southeast Asian Affairs 2003* (Singapore: ISEAS, 2003), 277–90.

3. In the February 2005 general election, Thaksin's TRT party won 75 percent of the national assembly, or 377 of 500 contested MP seats. The literature on Thaksin's abuse of power is voluminous. See, for example, William Case, "Democracy's Quality and Breakdown: New Lessons from Thailand," *Democratization* 14 (August 2007): 622–42; and Thitinan Pongsudhirak, "Thaksin's Political Zenith and Nadir," *Southeast Asian Affairs 2006* (Singapore: ISEAS, 2006), 285–302.

4. See James Ockey, "Thailand in 2008: Democracy and Street Politics," *Southeast Asian Affairs 2009* (Singapore: ISEAS, 2009): 315–33. For Thaksin's latent policy impact and the larger challenge that he posed, see Kevin Hewison, "Thaksin Shinawatra and the Reshaping of Thai Politics," *Contemporary Politics* 16 (June 2010): 119–33.

5. Author's interview with a Pheu Thai adviser on condition of anonymity, 11 August 2011.

6. For an excellent analysis of the judiciary's role in politics, see Björn Dressel, "Judicialization of Politics or Politicization of the Judiciary? Considerations from Recent Events in Thailand," *Pacific Review* 23 (December 2010): 671–91.

7. Author's interview with former Constitutional Court judge Suchit Bunbongkarn, 23 January 2012.

8. "H.M. the King's April 26 speeches (unofficial translation)," *Nation* (Bangkok), 27 April 2006.

9. Theerayuth Boonmee, *Tulakarn Piwat* [Judicialization] (Bangkok: Winyuchon, 2006).

10. See, for example, Michael Montesano, "Thailand: A Reckoning with History Begins," *Southeast Asian Affairs 2007* (Singapore: ISEAS, 2007), 311–40.

11. Ockey, "Thailand in 2008."

12. "The Indestructible Mr. Thaksin," *Economist,* 1 November 2007.

13. Part of the law states: "Whoever defames, insults or threatens the King, Queen, the Heir-apparent or the Regent, shall be punished with imprisonment of three to fifteen years."

14. "The Army Chief Issues Veiled Election Endorsement," *VOA News,* 15 June 2011.

15. "Royal Kin Call for *Lèse-Majesté* Law Overhaul," *Bangkok Post,* 12 January 2012. Other accounts suggest a much higher number of cases. See, for example, David Streckfuss, *Truth on Trial in Thailand: Defamation, Treason, and* Lèse-Majesté (London: Routledge, 2010).

16. Paul M. Handley, *The King Never Smiles: A Biography of Thailand's Bhumibol Adulyadej* (New Haven: Yale University Press, 2006).

17. Ampon Tangnoppakul, an unemployed grandfather whose only occupation was tending to his grandchildren after school hours, sent the four SMS messages to an assistant of Prime Minister Abhisit Vejjajiva during the May 2010 army crackdown on red-shirt protesters. Ampon's case became a *cause célèbre* as an instance of authority running wild and lashing out at an obviously harmless citizen. See "Ampon Gets 20 Years for *Lèse-Majesté* Text Messages," *Bangkok Post,* 24 November 2011.

18. Handley, *The King Never Smiles.*

19. There were notable exceptions, including Kevin Hewison's chapter titled "The Monarchy and Democratisation" in Kevin Hewison, ed., *Political Change in Thailand: Democracy and Participation* (London: Routledge, 1997); and Roger Kershaw, *Monarchy in South-East Asia: The Faces of Tradition in Transition* (London: Routledge, 2001), 136–54.

20. Duncan McCargo, "Network Monarchy and Legitimacy Crises in Thailand," *Pacific Review* 18 (December 2005): 499–519.

21. See the essays by Thongchai Winichakul, Michael K. Connors, Kevin Hewison, and others that appeared in the special issue on Thailand which was the first of Volume 38 of the *Journal of Contemporary Asia* in 2008.

22. "Thailand's King and Its Crisis: A Right Royal Mess," *Economist,* 4 December 2008, 29. The magazine's critical coverage of the coup and its aftermath drew threats, and as of 2010, the *Economist* began basing its Southeast Asia correspondent in Singapore rather than Bangkok.

23. See, for example, Peter A. Jackson, "Markets, Media, and Magic: Thailand's Monarch as a 'Virtual Deity,'" *Inter-Asia Cultural Studies* 10 (September 2009): 361–80.

24. Marc Askew, ed., *Legitimacy Crisis in Thailand* (Chiang Mai: Silkworm, 2010); Søren Ivarsson and Lotte Isager, eds., *Saying the Unsayable: Monarchy and Democracy in Thailand* (Copenhagen: Nordic Institute of Asian Studies, 2010).

25. Nicholas Grossman and Dominic Faulder, eds., *King Bhumibol Adulyadej: A Life's Work* (Bangkok: Editions Didier Millet, 2011).

11

STRONG-STATE DEMOCRATIZATION IN MALAYSIA AND SINGAPORE

Dan Slater

Dan Slater *is associate professor of political science at the University of Chicago. He is author of* Ordering Power: Contentious Politics and Authoritarian Leviathans in Southeast Asia *(2010) and coeditor of* Southeast Asia in Political Science: Theory, Region, and Qualitative Analysis *(2008). This essay originally appeared in the April 2012 issue of the* Journal of Democracy.

Malaysia and Singapore have long had authoritarian regimes that looked like no others in the world—except for each other. These neighbors' shared distinctiveness begins with their dogged defiance of the correlation between economic development and democracy. As Adam Przeworski and Fernando Limongi put it, "Singapore and Malaysia are the two countries that developed over a long period, became wealthy, and remained dictatorships until now."[1] Similarly dominated for decades by a seemingly invincible ruling party, these two regimes also long seemed distinctive by virtue of being "hybrid regimes," where elections at times appear meaningfully competitive yet meaningful amounts of power never change hands. A third reason to group Malaysia and Singapore as a distinctive pair has been the centrality of ethnic considerations in all matters political, given the historically fraught relations between Malay Muslims and ethnic Chinese—the former being the power-wielding majority in Malaysia, and the latter holding that position in Singapore.[2]

Since the Cold War's end, however, Malaysia and Singapore have become less globally distinctive along all these dimensions. For starters, the notion that development and democracy do not naturally go together has become utterly unremarkable. Authoritarianism endures in countries with rapidly growing economies (China and Russia, for example), while democracy survives in some of the poorest corners of Africa and Latin America, and struggles to be born in deeply impoverished corners of the Middle East. Second, although "hybrid regimes" used to be thought of as curiosities, "competitive authoritarianism"—or, more broadly, "elec-

toral authoritarianism"—is now one of the world's most common regime types.[3] Finally, ever more countries are now struggling, as Malaysia and Singapore long have, to reconcile electoral politics with ethnic
tensions. The apparent contribution of electoral competition to ethnic
conflict in cases ranging from Iraq to Kenya to Serbia has vividly shown
how the fate of regimes hinges on their capacity to preserve the peace.
In all these respects, Malaysia and Singapore increasingly look like the
global rule rather than the exception.

To be sure, Malaysia and Singapore differ in degree along all of these
dimensions; they have the resemblance (and rivalry) of siblings, not of
identical twins. Yet the shared distinctiveness of Malaysian and Singaporean authoritarianism has always run much deeper than their elections, economies, and ethnic politics in any event. It is the extraordinary
strength of the state apparatus in both countries that most sharply distinguishes their similar brand of authoritarianism, and that best explains
why it has proved so stable and enduring on both sides of the Johor
Causeway. State strength is the most important feature of Malaysia's
and Singapore's politics to keep in mind when pondering whether they
might democratize—and if so, what might follow.

Understanding where these extraordinarily durable regimes might be
headed requires understanding where their extraordinarily strong states
came from. It is most significant that ruling parties in Malaysia and Singapore did not so much *build* their powerful state apparatuses as build
them *up*. These powerful Leviathans were initially a product of unusu-
ally intense forms of counterrevolutionary collaboration between British and local elites under late-colonial rule during the 1940s and 1950s.
Strong states thus *preceded* the rise to dominance of Malaysia's United
Malays National Organization (UMNO) and Singapore's People's Action Party (PAP). It follows that impressive levels of state power would
also *outlast* these ruling parties were they to loosen their authoritarian
controls or even lose power altogether.

State power is a far more reliable source of political stability than
authoritarian rule, though it is also immeasurably harder to build.[4] Once
constructed, state power does not depend on regime type; democracies
can have strong states as surely as dictatorships can. Since democratization would not debilitate the Malaysian or Singaporean Leviathans,
neither would it destabilize politics, as these countries' rulers often as-
sert. Authoritarianism is at its strongest when it is widely perceived as
a necessary stabilizer, and authoritarian durability in both Malaysia and
Singapore has always rested upon this perception. The prospects for instability *after* democratization are thus critical to whether Malaysia and
Singapore will democratize *at all*.

Northeast Asia offers valuable comparative lessons in this regard.
The particularities of Malaysian and Singaporean politics notwithstanding, regime change in both cases would constitute new instances of a

more general historical process that I call "strong-state democratization." Apart from Western Europe, Northeast Asia has been the world's trailblazer on this front. Japan underwent strong-state democratization in the 1940s, South Korea followed suit in the 1980s, and Taiwan did likewise in the 1990s. In each case, inherited legacies of state power endured after authoritarianism ended, as did underlying political stability and effective governance. Decades of state-sponsored development and poverty reduction under authoritarian conditions produced moderate, middle-class-dominated electorates that have eschewed radical policies and favored conservative, formerly authoritarian ruling parties at the polls. When strong-state dictatorships foster democratization at times of relative prosperity and stability, as in Korea and Taiwan, stability and democracy coincide. Loosening authoritarian controls does not mean losing Leviathan.

Yet herein lies the irony. The same state strength that facilitates stable transitions to democracy also empowers rulers to forestall democratization for much longer than plausible concerns about stability would dictate. Thus the main reason that democratization would go smoothly in Malaysia and Singapore is also the main reason that it might not happen at all.

Hobbesian Origins

To call the state apparatuses in Malaysia and Singapore "Leviathans" is fitting, given the Hobbesian dynamics that drove their formative years.[5] Japan's short-term occupation of Southeast Asia during World War II decimated the region's minimalist prewar colonial state structures, whereas longer and more intensive Japanese colonization in Korea (from 1910 to 1945) and Taiwan (from 1895 to 1945) yielded much stronger administrative and coercive infrastructures. Japanese occupation gave rise to state-building in Southeast Asia as well, but indirectly, by sparking the mobilization of communist-inspired armed resistance movements. After Japan surrendered, these movements presented returning Western colonialists with major challenges, spurring a range of state-building efforts to cope with explosive threats from below.

More than anywhere else in Southeast Asia, Malaya[6] and Singapore saw wartime anti-Japanese resistance metamorphose into powerful and radical postwar labor movements. Urban militancy sparked extensive state-building efforts by the British and their local collaborators. This initially took the form of reorganizing both states' coercive apparatuses for purposes of labor control and, in Malaya, full-blown counterinsurgency. By the early 1950s, both British colonies had literally become police states, with effective civilian institutions of coercion to bridle endemic communalism and leftist radicalism.

British authorities also responded to leftist and communal unrest by pushing through major reforms in civilian administration and imposing direct taxation on economic elites. This put both states—and any regime that would subsequently run them—on solid fiscal ground. State-builders scored their greatest success on this front with the introduction in 1947 of direct taxes on individual and corporate incomes in Malaya and Singapore. This entailed a dramatic shift in fiscal strategy in what had been, before World War II, the only two states in Southeast Asia *not* to have significant systems of direct tax collection. It was during this immediate postwar period that Malaya and Singapore began to surpass neighbors such as the Philippines and Thailand in their capacity to collect direct taxes: a capacity that has distinguished Malaysia and Singapore ever since.

In 1951, leftist unrest also afforded colonial officials the political opportunity to introduce Malaya's Employees' Provident Fund (EPF), the first fund of its kind in the developing world. British authorities responded similarly to the worsening of Chinese labor and student unrest in Singapore in 1955, implementing a compulsory-savings scheme known as the Central Provident Fund (CPF). These funds subsequently ensured that the preponderance of national savings would remain in public rather than private hands, complementing the fiscal power of highly extractive tax states. State apparatuses that had abundant revenue and were skilled at a wide array of interventions thus emerged *before* the ruling parties that would later commandeer them.

British success in crafting new institutions in late-colonial Malaya and Singapore always depended on the active support of powerful local elites. Such support was grounded in shared elite perceptions that stronger state institutions were necessary to check the considerable combined threat posed by communalism and the radical Left. Because that threat from below persisted into the postindependence period, state power was not only *inherited* in both cases, but would be *intensified* after UMNO and the PAP rose to power.

Although they have governed in highly authoritarian ways, both parties initially gained power democratically. As the bureaucratic politics of late colonialism gave way to the electoral politics of decolonization during the 1950s, both parties cultivated mass support with promises to leverage state power to supply public goods. Since political stability in Malaysia and Singapore is the joint product of robust ruling parties as well as highly effective states, it is noteworthy that these parties first won their stabilizing cross-class backing through the pressures of intense democratic competition and not from a position of authoritarian hegemony.

Malaysia's UMNO gained its dominant position before the PAP, but saw its performance and popularity slacken more quickly. After securing power in a series of decolonizing elections, the UMNO-led multiethnic Alliance maintained parliamentary supermajorities in the postindependence votes of 1959 and 1964. Yet its unresponsiveness to pressures for redistribution from the Malay and Chinese communities led to a nasty shock in the 1969 elections. The Alliance lost its two-thirds majority as populist challengers made surprising inroads among Malay and, especially, Chinese voters. Postelection riots pitting Chinese working-class oppositionists against pro-UMNO Malays prompted UMNO leaders to declare martial law and suspend Parliament for more than two years. What emerged from this electoral interregnum was a far more authoritarian political arrangement, with the Alliance expanded into a wider party coalition, the Barisan Nasional (BN, or National Front), thereby restoring the government's two-thirds majority (an advantage it would not lose again until 2008).

The PAP similarly had to traverse democratic shoals in order to reach the placid shores of authoritarian dominance. Initially a cross-class movement embracing radical leftists as well as more conservative quasi-nationalists, the PAP romped to victory in the 1959 elections that ushered in Singaporean self-rule. The party quickly began leveraging state power to reward labor for its support. Yet state provision under capitalist conditions was not what the PAP's radical rank and file had in mind. The party's noncommunist elites were vastly outnumbered by its procommunist masses. PAP leaders thus precipitated the party's breakup in 1961 by using draconian security laws to crack down on radical trade unionists. The left-wing Socialist Front split from the party, leaving the PAP without its key mass constituency, organized labor.

Despite divorcing its most powerful constituency in society, the PAP was nonetheless able to flourish through its marriage with the state. By crafting "a coalition between political leadership and the civilian bureaucracy,"[7] the PAP accrued ample coercive and administrative power with which to overwhelm the opposition. Systematic coercion was the bluntest instrument in the party-state's arsenal, most fearsomely deployed when 24 opposition leaders and more than a hundred leftist activists were detained in Operation Coldstore in February 1963. Subsequent elections delivered 37 of 51 parliamentary seats to the PAP. With their position secured, PAP leaders quickly ordered more rounds of arrests and deportations to further decimate the opposition's prospects. Yet the PAP's dominance was still only at the local level. With Singapore's impending incorporation into the Malaysian federation, the PAP was forced to continue cultivating mass support to compete in democratic national elections.

Singapore's brief period of incorporation into Malaysia (1963–65) went badly. Tensions between the PAP and the UMNO ran high, and communal conflict spiked again. Singapore was ultimately expelled from the federation, making the island an independent city-state in which the PAP could freely pursue authoritarian single-party rule. Thus in Singapore in 1965, as in Malaysia in 1969, a party that had first gained dominance democratically became the authoritarian ruling party that the world knows today. Like their colonial predecessors, both the PAP and UMNO took advantage of destabilizing leftist and communal conflicts to build the kind of political institutions that best promised to prevent the recurrence of such clashes.

The upshot of these parallel Hobbesian origins was that authoritarianism in Malaysia and Singapore was founded on "protection pacts"— broad elite coalitions unified by shared support for heightened state power and tightened authoritarian controls as institutional bulwarks against especially threatening types of contentious politics.[8] Yet state power had been heightened long before the two parties' authoritarian controls had been tightened. While these ruling parties' sharp authoritarian turns signified regime changes in kind, the state-building that followed only increased state power by a matter of degree.

In processes reminiscent of the mid-to-late 1940s, outbreaks of leftist unrest and communal contention led to new bouts of state-building in Singapore in the mid-1960s and Malaysia in the late 1960s. In Malaysia, the shock of sectarian rioting in 1969 caused the political center to tighten its grip on the periphery, ushering in an era of "unequivocal centralization."[9] Malaysia's political leaders have never since been effectively constrained by countervailing power centers at the state level, even when they lose state-level elections.

In both Singapore and Malaysia, the intensified deployment of inherited coercive and extractive institutions was at the heart of authoritarian state-building. On the fiscal side, both UMNO and the PAP expanded their already impressive extraction of revenue. Most notably, the EPF and CPF have provided ideal mechanisms for both states to sink their fiscal claws into the burgeoning middle class. Both regimes have used compulsory contributions to lessen their financial dependence abroad and to cultivate political quiescence within. Rates of contribution from both employers and employees in Singapore and Malaysia have been described as "the highest in the world."[10] Since decades lapse between collection and payout, regime leaders always possess a large surplus of fungible reserves that can be put to political use with maximal flexibility and minimal accountability.

State power was inherited and intensified on the coercive side as well. Both governments' policing powers were initially expanded to cope with the combined threat of communal and leftist unrest, but have long been more than adequate for countering any perceived threats to the regimes as they define them. Authoritarian turns after 1965 in Singapore and 1969 in Malaysia gave the PAP and UMNO the authority on paper to do what they had long been able to do in practice, thanks to the propitious legacies of late-colonial state-building.

In sum, the Malaysian and Singaporean states have served as ideal power apparatuses for the authoritarian regimes that have controlled them. This largely explains why neither UMNO nor the PAP has ever lost political control or even come close to doing so. Since their original *raison d'être* was to preserve political stability in what were widely thought to be endemically unstable polities, prospects for democratization in Malaysia and Singapore hinge on the popular perception that democracy and stability can coincide.

Strong-State Democratization

In Malaysia and Singapore alike, state power has served as the cornerstone of ruling parties' cherished record of political stability. Concerns with ethnic conflict and redistributive radicalism initially motivated authoritarian rule and state-building in tandem. How, then, might authoritarianism and state power become disentangled, and with what consequences for political stability, if Malaysia and Singapore were to undergo strong-state democratization?

None of the *state* institutions discussed above would lose their impressive capacity if Malaysia and Singapore were to undergo a change of *regime*. This includes extractive fiscal institutions such as the EPF, CPF, and ministries devoted to collecting direct taxes. Equally important, democratization would not prevent coercive institutions from preserving public order. Even democracies conduct surveillance and police their citizens, and few new democracies would be better equipped to do so as expertly and effectively. This is not only because coercive institutions in Malaysia and Singapore are efficient, but because they are *civilianized*. Whereas military regimes often see their main institution for repression crumble during democratization, authoritarian regimes with powerful parties and civilian police apparatuses need not suffer any serious hiccup in public order when undergoing regime change.

Of course, Malaysia and Singapore would not be the first strong-state dictatorships with long-ruling dominant parties to democratize in recent Asian history. Taiwan and South Korea present informative regional parallels. In Korea, rising popular pressures for democratization were met with preemptive steps toward liberalization in 1987 by Roh Tae Woo, the designated presidential successor from the ruling Democratic Justice Party (DJP). At virtually the same historical moment, Taiwan's government loosened authoritarian controls even more preemptively, as President Chiang Ching-kuo lifted martial law and abolished single-party Kuomintang (KMT) rule amid weaker popular pressures for regime change. A quarter-century after ruling parties began loosening authoritarian controls in Taiwan and Korea, what lessons might their experiences offer for strong-state democratization in Malaysia and Singapore?

The overarching lesson is that strong-state democratization has not meant political destabilization. Korea and Taiwan's relative stability has had three primary sources. First, by democratizing politics on their own terms and in a constitutional manner, Taiwan's KMT and Korea's

DJP ensured that they would remain major forces—indeed, *the* major forces—in national politics during the new democratic era. Belying the conventional wisdom that ruling parties hold onto power tenaciously to avoid obsolescence under democracy,[11] Korea and Taiwan show how authoritarian parties that initiate democratization can thrive under it. Not only did the KMT and DJP and its successors easily win initial democratic elections in the 1980s and 1990s. They came back to power in the 2000s after triumphant opposition parties failed to govern as effectively as their authoritarian predecessors.

This points to the second key source of continuing stability under strong-state democratization. After decades of state-sponsored industrialization and poverty reduction, the Taiwanese and Korean authoritarian regimes each had incubated a vibrant middle class with moderate and even conservative political leanings. Especially in Taiwan, democratization was more a matter of widening political inclusion than of imposing radical redistribution. When democratization seemingly fostered rising labor unrest and steeply increased wages in Korea, middle-class voters became more conservative, abandoning their support for "reforms and democratization . . . in the face of real or perceived threats to economic and political stability."[12] This has been as true in the 2000s as it was in the 1990s, as the Grand National Party (a successor to the DJP) roared back into control of the presidency and parliament in 2008 after the rocky term of President Roh Moo Hyun (2003–2008) of the Uri Party. This parallels developments in Taiwan, where the relative populism of Democratic Progressive Party rule in 2000–2008 was countered by a decisive electoral return to conservative KMT control.

The recurrent alternations of power and bouts of scandal that have characterized Korean and Taiwanese democracy might seem to support the notion that democracy equals destabilization. Yet beneath the frothy waves of scandal and partisan rancor, Korea and Taiwan possess a deeper source for enduring political stability—an inherited strong state. Herein lies the third reason for continuity after strong-state democratization. The iron cages of authoritarian Leviathans have been redeployed for democratic purposes in Korea and Taiwan, but they have by no means been dismantled. Qingshan Tan's observation about democratic Taiwan has also proven true of democratic Korea: "The bureaucratic state has not withered away."[13]

One can identify a shift in both Korea and Taiwan from developmental states to welfare states,[14] but not from strong states to weak ones. Like their richer Western counterparts, these Asian democracies confront the chronic challenge of controlling public spending and debt, but not radical challengers to a conservative model of capitalist development. With relatively strong fiscal institutions in place, Korea and Taiwan have been better equipped to manage pressures to expand the welfare state than countries in Latin America or Southern Europe. Since Malaysia and Singapore enjoy institutional strengths similar to those of authoritarian-era Korea and Taiwan, democratization in Southeast Asia's strongest states would be accompanied by the same sort of party-system continuity, electoral conservatism, and persistent state capacity that we have seen after democratization in Northeast Asia's strongest states.

Strengthening Oppositions, Slackening Regimes?

For strong-state democratization to occur, authoritarian incumbents must be willing to restrain their use of coercion. Such coercive restraint may well depend, in turn, on the capacity of opposition forces to muster a sufficient challenge to press leaders to reconsider their patterns of rule. Yet Malaysia and Singapore have long had exceptionally weak and divided oppositions alongside their exceptionally strong states. This means that both countries have not only been safe *for* democratization; they have been safe *from* it.

Recent years have seen opposition parties become somewhat stronger and more unified in both Malaysia and Singapore. Yet UMNO and the PAP still hold power advantages over their respective rivals that are wide enough to let them forestall democratization for the foreseeable future should they so wish. Only if Malaysian and Singaporean leaders eschew the kind of coercive tactics that have served them so well for so long can the playing field become level and strong-state democratization get truly underway.

Predicting whether and when UMNO and the PAP might countenance an opposition victory is more a task for a soothsayer than for a social scientist. What is much clearer is that state-led development has helped to spawn moderate oppositions. This suggests that, as in Taiwan and Korea, regime-initiated processes of liberalization in Malaysia and Singapore would not prove destabilizing, even if freer and fairer elections were to deliver power into the hands of leading oppositionists.

What is much less clear, however, is whether opposition parties in Malaysia and Singapore are either well-positioned or well-prepared to assume the mantle of power. This could convince UMNO and PAP leaders that liberalization is unnecessary. Yet it should also deepen their confidence that democratization would not necessarily bring their own electoral defeat anytime in the near future.

Political opposition has made greater headway in recent decades in Malaysia than in Singapore. During the first 25 years of BN rule, Malaysia's ruling coalition rhythmically romped to a landslide win every five years, never relinquishing the two-thirds majority it had lost momentarily in 1969. A dramatic 1987 split within UMNO seemed briefly to threaten BN dominance, but the rift made little difference at the voting booth. From the early 1970s to the mid-1990s, the BN faced fragmented opposition from two parties that had little more in common with each other than with the BN: the mildly Islamist, mostly rural Pan-Malaysian Islamic Party (PAS) and the mildly leftist, mostly Chinese Democratic Action Party (DAP). As ethnicized parties in a multiethnic polity, they could occasionally win a state or two in national elections. But they could never come close to threatening the multiethnic BN's stranglehold on national power.

Malaysian politics would undergo its first dramatic turn of the BN era in 1998, when the Asian financial crisis sparked a serious political crisis. Prime Minister Mahathir Mohamad responded to the economic crash (and the specter of Suharto's overthrow in neighboring Indonesia) by sacking and imprisoning his popular but untrusted deputy, Anwar Ibrahim. Anwar's dismissal and subsequent beating while in police custody sparked *reformasi,* the largest protest movement in Malaysia's postindependence history, demanding legal justice for Anwar and democratic reforms more generally. Whereas previous prime ministers had tended to mix repression and responsiveness in their reactions to popular protest,[15] Mahathir showed little compunction about using coercion alone, ordering the crushing of *reformasi* by force in late 1998 and early 1999.

Mahathir's heavy-handed treatment of Anwar, the *reformasi* movement, and the People's Justice Party (PKR) that emerged under the imprisoned Anwar's banner had mixed consequences. On the one hand, widespread resentment toward Mahathir generated a significant protest vote among Malays in the 1999 elections. UMNO's parliamentary-seat advantage over PAS shrank from 89-7 to 72-27. On the other hand, the BN's support among non-Malays remained practically unshaken, and Mahathir's jailing of Anwar along with five other leading PKR figures prevented this potentially potent multiethnic upstart from making electoral inroads. As long as the main opposition parties were ethnic in character, the BN could not be seriously threatened at the polls. After Mahathir resigned in 2003 and handed power to his less aggressively authoritarian deputy, Abdullah Badawi, the Malay protest vote disappeared, and UMNO and the BN inflicted their biggest-ever rout on the Malaysian opposition in the 2004 elections. Malaysia's UMNO and BN seemed to have returned to their golden era of hegemony.

Singapore's PAP marched from the 1960s through the 2000s with even fewer political bumps and bruises. The PAP won a monopoly of parliamentary seats in the 1968 national elections, thanks to the Socialist Front's understandable but self-defeating decision to boycott the authoritarian election process. The PAP then proceeded to win every single parliamentary seat in the elections of 1972, 1976, and 1980. When the PAP finally lost a single parliamentary seat in a 1981 by-election, it was seen by some as "a demonstration that from then on not only was opposition possible but that it would not inevitably break the nation's will and ability to survive; a threat commonly touted by the PAP."[16] This gave the opposition little momentum, however. Ongoing legal and political intimidation of oppositionists (and the districts that looked primed to back them) ensured that the PAP would not even face an opponent in more than half of Singapore's districts until 2006. The opposition finally fielded enough candidates that year to force the PAP to wait until election day to declare victory, yet captured only two seats.

Only in the most recent Malaysian and Singaporean elections has the tide seemed to turn. Malaysia in 2008 provided the biggest shock. With Anwar Ibrahim released from prison, his fledgling People's Alliance (PR) coalition (uneasily grouping the PKR, PAS, and DAP) denied the BN a two-thirds majority for the first time since 1969 and prevailed outright in an unprecedented five of thirteen states. Equally important, Anwar's multiethnic PKR resurrected itself to become the largest party in the opposition coalition, winning 31 parliamentary seats to outstrip the DAP's 28 and PAS's 23.

The multiethnic character of the opposition's leading party means that a BN electoral defeat has gone from pipe dream to real possibility. This has had a moderating effect on both the DAP and PAS, which standing alone could never become more than fringe parties but can hope to share national power on the coattails of the multiethnic PKR. To be sure, the PR opposition coalition has struggled mightily to maintain its shaky footing and cohesion since its 2008 successes, and remains perilously dependent on Anwar's personal leadership. Such is the typical fate of parties and coalitions fighting to break out of the "wilderness" of opposition in dominant-party settings. Be that as it may, recent opposition gains represent a sea change in Malaysian politics, if not necessarily an irreversible one.

An imminent electoral defeat of the PAP remains a pipe dream, but a bit less so after the 2011 elections. Though the opposition won only six parliamentary seats (one of them a first-ever PAP defeat in an especially hard-to-win Group Representation Constituency), the 2011 campaign in Singapore bore interesting resemblances to Malaysia's coercion-light election under Badawi in 2008. First, the vibrancy of new media beyond the government's chokehold helped opposition parties to gain more voter attention and generate larger campaign rallies. Second, opposition parties made headway in coordinating their candidacies across constituencies, avoiding debilitating three-cornered races. Finally, the themes of the 2011 campaign in Singapore (like the 2008 campaign in Malaysia) centered on bread-and-butter issues of government accountability and performance, and voters increasingly gravitated toward the notion that checks and balances would be conducive to better governance. Guided by its cleverly unobjectionable slogan ("Towards a First World Parliament"), the Singaporean opposition ironically presented itself as extreme in only one respect—its pronounced moderation.

There is no easy way to predict whether Malaysian and Singaporean leaders will allow these increasingly robust and organized oppositions to flourish. Yet there are several useful ways to analyze the issue. One can start by gauging how repressive or responsive rulers have been in dealing with opposition thus far. On this score, there are ironically greater grounds for optimism in the more closed case (Singapore) than in the case where opposition has had more historical success (Malaysia). In Malaysia, the reduction of repression witnessed under Prime Minister Abdullah Badawi (2003–2009) has been reversed under his successor, Najib Razak, who appears more inclined to follow Mahathir's than Badawi's playbook for handling opposition. This is best indicated by the renewed judicial harassment of Anwar (whose acquittal on a new round of sodomy charges is currently under government appeal) and the crackdown on the peaceful "Bersih 2.0" protests for cleaner elections in July 2011. Perhaps because the opposition challenge remains so much weaker in Singapore, and because the Singaporean state's battery of everyday authoritarian controls remains so much harder to crack, PAP leaders seem to be responding to opposition gains with relative equanimity. Whether this will remain the case is an open question.

Yet it is not an entirely unanswerable one. Beneath the ebb and flow of particular leaders and their proclivities for repression, both Malaysia and Singapore have undergone a much deeper historic shift. In short, there is strong reason to believe that these countries' eras of "protection pacts" might finally be a thing of the past. The Radical Left has long ceased to be a meaningful factor, and there is no longer reason to suppose that freer democratic competition would produce either a minority-group takeover or a radicalization of communal politics. Since the strongest justification for authoritarianism in Malaysia and Singapore has always been as a necessary bulwark against destabilization, the moderate and multiethnic character of the emergent opposition in both countries gives grounds for hope that repression will not be seen as necessary to prevent a return to the Hobbesian days before authoritarian rule. The paradox is that these more moderate and credible oppositions pose a bigger electoral threat to the BN and PAP, perhaps convincing party leaders that repression will be necessary to protect their own political power, if not to preserve social order.

Loosening Authoritarianism, Not Losing Leviathan

An important debate has recently emerged in academic and policy circles over how best to "sequence" democratization and state-building. One perspective holds that strong states must be built before democratization can proceed smoothly. The top priority in the world's many weak states is thus to strengthen the state, not to install or deepen democracy. Other analysts see no reason to delay democratization until state-building has been accomplished, arguing that the two can go hand-in-hand.[17] Since building a state is harder than changing a regime, waiting for the former to be accomplished before pursuing the latter is as fruitless as waiting for Godot.

For Malaysia and Singapore, more than any other authoritarian regimes on earth, this "sequencing debate" is utterly irrelevant. Even the
most democracy-shy observers would be hard-pressed to make the case
that Malaysia and Singapore need more state-building before becoming
safe for greater democratic competition. To be sure, overall government
performance has been far more deeply compromised in Malaysia than
in Singapore in recent years, especially since Mahathir's personalization of power in the 1980s and 1990s worsened official corruption and
partisan abuses of authority. Yet one must not confuse any particular
regime's *performance* with the underlying character of state *power*.
Corruption and personalization indicate the abuse and exploitation of
the state by political leaders, not a state incapable of doing its job if
politically supported in doing so. Like its Singaporean counterpart, the
Malaysian Leviathan remains sturdy enough to withstand the disrup-
tions of regime change.

With no credible Hobbesian case to be made for continuing authoritarianism, backers of the current regimes' repressive practices must resort to a more particularistic defense: Democracy is not the regime type
that Malaysians and Singaporeans prefer. Such arguments typically rest
on culturally relativist, even essentialist notions of political attitudes in
East Asia. Yet one need not tar the entire region with the same essentialist brush to conjure a credible argument that, in Malaysia and Singapore
specifically, leveling the playing field between regime and opposition
might actually make government less representative of popular desires
in several critical ways.

According to one line of thinking, Western liberal democracy is simply ill-fitted to conservative societies such as Malaysia and Singapore.
This argument falters because democracy does not necessarily entail
less conservative policy outcomes—as the policies of many U.S. states
amply attest. Democratization is simply a loosening of authoritarian restrictions so that the political opposition can compete on a nearly level
playing field without fear of targeted repression or restrictions. This
entails broader freedom to organize and express alternative views in
public spaces, but it does not require the full battery of human-rights
protections that international critics of these regimes understandably
prioritize. For instance, Malaysia and Singapore can democratize while
preserving their extensive use of the death penalty and nonrecognition
of same-sex relationships. Continued illiberal policies on such issues
would keep both countries politically conservative, but not make them
less procedurally democratic.

A second concern centers on the issue of communal difference, particularly in the realm of religion. One of the most enduring tensions
within democracy is that it requires both majority rule and minority protections. To the extent that minorities cannot expect protection from majorities after elections are held, the procedures of democracy threaten to

yield the substance of ethnocracy. A democracy that cannot preserve the peace is not a democracy that most people (Asian or otherwise) would consider worth having. More than forty years after Malaysia and Singapore underwent their respective authoritarian turns, however, there is no reason to believe that democratization would produce physical insecurity of any sort in either country. The frequent PAP refrain that authoritarianism is necessary in Singapore due to external threats appears laughable in comparative perspective: Taiwan and South Korea face immeasurably greater and more immediate geopolitical foes, yet each was able to democratize without compromising national security. As for internal threats, no party seeking to overturn longstanding ethnic bargains represents a credible threat to capture power in either Malaysia or Singapore.

A third and final possibility may be that voters broadly perceive authoritarianism to be better than democracy at producing prudent economic policies. But economic policies are made by governing parties and implemented by the state apparatus, not by the regime type. Voters who believe that the BN or PAP can best handle the economy could continue to vote for them after democratization. If the experiences of South Korea and Taiwan are anything to go by, most Malaysian and Singaporean voters would come to precisely this conclusion and stick with the BN and PAP in droves. To the extent that rising popular discontent currently focuses on these parties' repressive practices, loosening those controls would not only be good for democracy. It would be good for the BN and the PAP themselves.

NOTES

1. Adam Przeworski and Fernando Limongi, "Modernization: Theories and Facts," *World Politics* 49 (January 1997): 155–83. Malaysia's and Singapore's total GDP are virtually even, but Singapore's per capita GDP is approximately five times larger.

2. Lest one take the categories of "Malay" and "Chinese" or the divisions between them as eternal or inevitable, see Anthony Reid, *Imperial Alchemy: Nationalism and Political Identity in Southeast Asia* (New York: Cambridge University Press, 2009), chs. 3–4, for a masterful historical account.

3. On "competitive authoritarianism," see Steven Levitsky and Lucan A. Way, *Competitive Authoritarianism: Hybrid Regimes After the Cold War* (New York: Cambridge University Press, 2010). On "electoral authoritarianism," which more clearly encompasses both Malaysia and Singapore, see Andreas Schedler, ed., *Electoral Authoritarianism: The Dynamics of Unfree Competition* (Boulder, Colo.: Lynne Rienner, 2006). For an argument that Singapore has recently transitioned from "closed" to "competitive" authoritarianism by Levitsky and Way's definition, see Stephan Ortmann, "Singapore: Authoritarian but Newly Competitive," *Journal of Democracy* 22 (October 2011): 153–64.

4. On the state-regime distinction in authoritarian settings and the role of state power in sustaining durable authoritarianism, see Dan Slater and Sofia Fenner, "State Power and Staying Power: Infrastructural Mechanisms and Authoritarian Durability," *Journal of International Affairs* 65 (Fall–Winter 2011): 15–29.

5. The following historical analysis draws upon Dan Slater, *Ordering Power: Contentious Politics and Authoritarian Leviathans in Southeast Asia* (New York: Cambridge University Press, 2010), chs. 4 and 8.

6. Malaya was not renamed Malaysia until 1963.

7. Cho-Oon Khong, "Singapore: Political Legitimacy Through Managing Conformity," in Muthiah Alagappa, ed., *Political Legitimacy in Southeast Asia: The Quest for Moral Authority* (Stanford: Stanford University Press, 1995), 115.

8. Slater, *Ordering Power*, 5.

9. Robert O. Tilman, "The Centralization Theme in Malaysian Federal-State Relations, 1957–75," Institute for Southeast Asian Studies (Singapore), Occasional Paper No. 39, May 1976, 63.

10. Mukul G. Asher, "Issues in Forced Savings and National Economic Development: The Management of National Provident Fund Systems," in Al' Alim Ibrahim, ed., *Generating a National Savings Movement* (Kuala Lumpur: Institute for Strategic and International Studies, 1994), 238.

11. Barbara Geddes, "What Do We Know About Democratization After Twenty Years?" *Annual Review of Political Science* 2 (1999): 115–44.

12. John Kie-Chiang Oh, *Korean Politics: The Quest for Democratization and Economic Development* (Ithaca: Cornell University Press, 1999), 114, 115. I am very grateful to Sofia Fenner for her insights on voter conservatism in the wake of strong-state democratization.

13. Qingshan Tan, "Democratization and Bureaucratic Restructuring in Taiwan," *Studies in Comparative International Development* 35 (June 2000): 48–64.

14. Stephan Haggard and Robert R. Kaufman, *Development, Democracy, and Welfare States: Latin America, East Asia, and Eastern Europe* (Princeton: Princeton University Press, 2008); and Joseph Wong, "Democracy's Double Edge: Financing Social Policy in Industrial East Asia," in Yin-wah Chu and Siu-lun Wong, eds., *East Asia's New Democracies: Deepening, Reversal, Non-Liberal Alternatives* (New York: Routledge, 2010).

15. On Malaysia's "repressive-responsive regime," see Harold Crouch, *Government and Society in Malaysia* (Ithaca: Cornell University Press, 1996).

16. Beng-Huat Chua, *Communitarian Ideology and Democracy in Singapore* (New York: Routledge, 1995), 174.

17. For the more optimistic argument, see Thomas Carothers, "How Democracies Emerge: The 'Sequencing' Fallacy," *Journal of Democracy* 18 (January 2007): 12–27. On the more pessimistic side, see Edward D. Mansfield and Jack Snyder, "The Sequencing 'Fallacy,'" *Journal of Democracy* 18 (July 2007): 5–9.

12

ELITES VS. REFORM IN LAOS, CAMBODIA, AND VIETNAM

Martin Gainsborough

Martin Gainsborough *is a reader in development politics in the School of Sociology, Politics, and International Studies at the University of Bristol. His publications include* Vietnam: Rethinking the State *(2010) and* Changing Political Economy of Vietnam: The Case of Ho Chi Minh City *(2003). This essay originally appeared in the April 2012 issue of the* Journal of Democracy.

Taken together, Vietnam, Cambodia, and Laos present something of a puzzle. While Vietnam and Laos have remained one-party communist states, Cambodia underwent a democratic transition in 1993 under the supervision of the international community. Yet all three countries have ended up with remarkably similar politics characterized by a lack of commitment to liberal values. In seeking to explain this, we should weigh the importance of political culture and "money politics" while noting as well that civil society activism and spontaneous protest are becoming more common.

Vietnam, Cambodia, and Laos are often grouped together for the purposes of analysis. There are some obvious reasons for this. All are former colonies of France—once known collectively as "French Indochina"—located next to one another on the Southeast Asian mainland. All witnessed the rise of communist parties to nationwide power in the mid-1970s. Also relevant is Vietnam's ill-fated attempt during the Cold War to sustain a special leadership role in Indochina, incorporating Cambodia and Laos after the Vietnamese invasion of Cambodia in 1978. Since the Cold War's end, Vietnam, Cambodia, and Laos have been grouped together because they are among Southeast Asia's poorest states; because they are linked through what is known as the Greater Mekong Subregion; and because they are among the newest members of the Association of Southeast Asian Nations (ASEAN). All three have also seen fast-rising economic growth and falling poverty since the 1990s, and are viewed as undergoing a process of "reform" involving a shift from central planning to a market economy.

Yet Vietnam, Cambodia, and Laos are independent sovereign states with different histories and precolonial influences. Each had a different experience under French colonial rule, and the character of the postcolonial state in each is different too, often in quite subtle ways. Nor can it be said that the three states have followed the same trajectory since the Cold War ended. Vietnam and Laos have seen no democratic transition and remain one-party communist states. Cambodia, by contrast, did experience such a transition (overseen by the international community) in 1993, though many of its democratic advances have since been reversed.

Furthermore, as the three have integrated more fully into both the economy of their Southeast Asian region and the global economy, their varying circumstances are causing them to respond in varying ways to external economic, political, and cultural forces. These circumstances include questions of size and location. Vietnam, with 86 million people, dwarfs Cambodia (with 15 million) and landlocked, mountainous Laos (the poorest and smallest of the three, with only 7 million). Vietnam's economy is also some eight times larger than Cambodia's and fifteen times larger than that of Laos. The three countries remain comparable but distinct, in short, with trajectories that do not and will not match.

Regional specialists are used to thinking of all three countries as having embraced—by virtue of a conscious elite decision—a "reformist" (market-oriented) national economic policy. Vietnam and Laos are usually thought to have done so in 1986, at respective national party congresses held that year by the ruling Communists. Vietnam adopted a policy called *doi moi* (which literally means "new change" but is usually translated as "renovation"), and Laos announced a "new economic mechanism" based on "new thinking."[1] Cambodia is generally said to have more or less followed suit in 1989, after Vietnamese troops left.

In terms of what elites are said to have done, the general consensus is that in each case the changes have had a significant political as well as economic dimension, even if the latter looms larger than the former. This consensus, however, overemphasizes change, formal policy, and elite initiative while underrating the significance of economic and political continuity and the extent to which factors *other than* elite-led policy initiatives have shaped events in these three states.

Relevant here is the extent to which elites in all three countries have often merely formalized spontaneous, "bottom-up" initiatives or experiments, whether by officials, enterprise directors, city dwellers, or farmers. Generally speaking, elites prefer to seem as if they are in charge and will not admit that they are reacting rather than acting. Yet as has been said regarding the related case of China, any account that neglects the role of informal or unsanctioned initiatives is a "highly sanitised" one, which "distracts us from the real dynamics of the reform process."[2] This is not to deny that elites have initiated changes, but only to plead for a balanced assessment that notes the role of the informal as well as the

formal, and considers continuity as well as change. Such balance, moreover, is just as important when weighing political change—even where
it falls short of full-blown democratic transition—as when examining
reforms to the economy.

The Limits of Formal Political Reform

Within the bounds of their respective one-party regimes, Vietnam and
Laos have taken similar steps to reform their political systems. Cambodia's trajectory has been different, though it has wound up in much the
same place politically as its neighbors, despite having experienced a
democratic transition in the early 1990s.

Although the reforms launched at the Sixth Communist Party Congress in Vietnam and the Fourth Congress of the Lao People's Revolutionary Party in 1986 are often seen as being primarily economic, in
both cases they had a clear political component. In Vietnam, the key
policy statement from that year highlighted problems that included poor
coordination between the Communist Party and the government and
Party officials' tendencies to operate outside the law and ride roughshod
over electoral procedures. This critique set in train formal moves by
the Party to build a state "ruled by law," to strengthen the role of the
National Assembly, and to clarify the relationship between the Party,
the government, and the citizenry. These issues remain current: Exactly
how the Party views the "rule of law" and the "correct" relationship
between citizens and the state are open questions.

The reforms in Laos also focused on the rule of law, and included
enactment of the country's first postcolonial constitution in 1991, along
with an emphasis on strengthening the bureaucracy. In both countries,
there was also a loosening up in relation to the social sphere through the
"destalinisation of everyday life."[3] Restrictions on domestic and even
foreign travel were eased; day-to-day surveillance became less pervasive and intense; and new media outlets were allowed to emerge along
with informal associations and groups, including religious groups. Although none of this added up to a democratic transition in either Vietnam or Laos—Communist Party control remained and the security forces were still formidable—in both countries the atmosphere did become
considerably freer.

In the late 1980s and early 1990s, as popular protests in Tiananmen
Square, the tearing-down of the Berlin Wall, and the collapse of communism across Central and Eastern Europe and the former Soviet Union
sent shock waves across the world, debate broke out over the future of
the Vietnamese and Laotian political systems. Much of the discussion
went on behind the scenes in these closed regimes, however, so it is hard
to know exactly what was said. Yet the basic verdict was clear. As the
1990s began, both Vietnam and Laos moved to silence what appeared to

be minority voices calling for political pluralism. In Laos, two former vice-ministers and a Justice Ministry official were jailed for allegedly plotting to overthrow the regime.[4] In Vietnam, a Politburo member was sacked prior to the Seventh National Party Congress in 1991, apparently because he advocated multiparty politics.

Reinforcing their opposition to democratic politics, both ruling parties issued statements decisively rejecting what they called "extreme liberal demands" (Vietnam) or "a multi-party system" (Laos).[5] Since then, neither party has budged. Both continue to talk about developing "democracy," but by this they do not mean liberal democracy. Instead, they mean things such as widening the number of ruling-party members who are allowed a role in choosing the top leaders, raising the number of directly elected local-government posts, and ensuring that the Communist Party listens more attentively to state officials, legislators, and citizens.

Since the early 1990s, Vietnam and Laos have both opened their doors to a wide range of bilateral and multilateral donor organizations and international nongovernmental organizations (NGOs), receiving high levels of aid and technical assistance in the process. The donors are both Asian and Western. In Laos there is a heavy Chinese, Thai, and Vietnamese presence. Vietnam's big Asian donor is China, but the Chinese presence is carefully managed (the two countries fought a short but bitter border war in early 1979, and carried on armed frontier clashes until 1990). Western donors have worked with both the Vietnamese and Laotian governments on governance-related areas such as public-administration and legal-system reform, the fight against corruption, and civil society development. None of this, however, has had much effect on the two countries' politics.

Cambodia's trajectory has been somewhat different. Following the Vietnamese invasion in 1978 to oust the murderous Khmer Rouge, Cambodia was ruled by a Hanoi-backed regime led from 1985 by Prime Minister Hun Sen. During the 1980s, a civil war raged as a coalition of royalists and the Khmer Rouge battled the Hanoi-backed regime. Peace became possible only when Vietnam, for its own domestic political reasons, decided that it could no longer sustain its military presence in Cambodia. Following the peace accord (signed in Paris in 1991) came a major UN operation that culminated in the 1993 elections, contested by 19 parties.

In the short term at least, the UN had a major impact. Cambodia acquired some of the formal underpinnings of liberal constitutionalism, including a new basic law consistent with its tenets. There was also a surge in civil society activity, and more vocal and diverse media emerged as well. Yet this liberal flowering soon began to wither. Elections have continued to go forward at regular intervals, but the gains of the early 1990s have suffered steady reversal at the hands of Hun

Sen and his ruling Cambodian People's Party (CPP), which are determined to maintain a tight grip on power. The result has been the systematic emasculation of the political opposition, including the royalist
party known as FUNCINPEC (the CPP's former coalition partner) and
the Sam Rainsy Party. The government's critics in the media, trade
unions, and civil society at large have often been bought off or si-
lenced through a mixture of patronage, intimidation, violence, changes
to electoral laws, and recourse to politically biased courts.[6]

In the most recent election, held in July 2008, the CPP captured 90
out of 123 seats, and for the first time since 1993 was able to form a government on its own. The CPP also controls 90 percent of all commune or
local-government committees.[7] This is a remarkable transformation for
a party that—as many tend to forget—finished second behind FUNCIN-
PEC in the 1993 balloting.

Like its counterparts in Vietnam and Laos, the Cambodian government has permitted the international donor community to operate,
working with it on a wide range of governance reforms since the 1990s.
Again, donors are Asian as well as Western, with China and Vietnam
predominating among the former. And as with Vietnam and Laos, the
effect that outside donors have had on Cambodia's basic political direction has been distinctly limited.

The Formidable Forces of Continuity

Why have these three neighboring countries—Cambodia after the
interlude of the 1993 transition and the other two more or less continu-
ously—hewed so firmly to a nondemocratic path? The answer may lie
in the strikingly similar elite political cultures found in all three. Tracing
this similarity to its origin lies beyond the scope of this essay,[8] but we
can document the common characteristics that these political cultures
share, and outline their effects.

At the heart of Vietnamese, Cambodian, and Laotian political cultures alike lie heavy doses of elitism and paternalism. Under their influence, cultural assumptions about the proper relationship between the
state and its citizens, or between rulers and the ruled, contrast starkly
with what is taken for granted in the West. In these Southeast Asian societies, there is a strong implicit belief that the goodwill and high moral
capacity of those in authority—and not the impersonal checks and balances favored by the liberal tradition—should serve as the key restraints
on power.[9] The relevance of this cultural mindset can also be glimpsed
in the emphasis placed on family (or to be more precise, on who your
parents are) in all three countries.

Taking political culture into account makes it easier to understand
why all three ruling parties reject pluralism and feel deeply uneasy about
civil society or indeed any form of organization that operates outside

state or ruling-party structures. In this respect, it is worth noting that regulations legalizing NGOs and their dealings have advanced only slowly and often with much controversy in all three states.

A focus on political culture also sheds light on the character of elections in Vietnam, Cambodia, and Laos. In each country, the powers that be treat voting less as a contest of alternatives than as a chance for the citizens to confirm the intrinsic merits of their leaders.[10] Thus in Vietnam and Laos the state seeks to control who is elected to parliament, and in Cambodia Hun Sen has moved as if by instinct to shut down any notion of elections as a serious contest.

Furthermore, giving political culture its due weight raises profound questions about what is going on when the ruling parties work with the international donor community in areas such as public-administration reform or anticorruption. The reforms that the donor community pushes typically involve institutional checks and balances that host-country elites view with deep ambivalence. Whatever donors think they are doing, the reality is that local elites either lack seriousness about instituting liberal reforms or insist on interpreting and applying them in nonliberal ways. Finally, a focus on political culture makes it easier to understand (although not to condone) the rulers' tendency to treat dissidents and other critics harshly. Rights, the rulers' thinking seems to run, derive from buying into this elite-centered, paternalistic mindset. No buy-in, therefore, means no rights.[11]

In addition to an unfriendly political culture, the other major obstacle that liberal politics faces in Vietnam, Cambodia, and Laos can be attributed to the rise of "money politics" and the resulting commercialization of the state. The conventional account of Southeast Asian reform associates it (whether implicitly or explicitly) with economic liberalization and the retreat of the state. But this is not what has happened. The reform years in Vietnam, Cambodia, and Laos have indeed seen marketization, but also a form of state advance rather than retreat as politicians, officials, and those with close ties to them have seized on their "insider" access to business opportunities associated with marketization and globalization in order to enrich themselves.

In Vietnam, this process was first documented in relation to the rise of new state business interests from the 1980s as those with political connections began to accumulate capital by engaging in market transactions even under central planning. In Laos, the commercialization of the state is evident in frequent references to politicians and relatives of politicians who are known to occupy the commanding heights of the Laotian economy. In Cambodia, the process began in the late 1980s with the selling-off of state assets, particularly by the CPP, as Hun Sen sought to win friends and influence people in anticipation of changes to come in the political climate.

The characteristics of this "reform era" political economy are similar across Vietnam, Cambodia, and Laos. First, as has been suggested, political connections and relationships are key. These are necessary for political protection as well as accessing land, capital, and contracts, or obtaining (if not bypassing) needed permits. Conflicts of interest are common, with officials (often acting through friends or relatives) operating in sectors of the economy that they are charged with regulating. Speculation and profiteering based on inside information gained under cover of public office are frequent as well. Land speculation—or, in Cambodia, outright land-grabbing—is ubiquitous in all three states, and has proved a well-greased path to instant riches for many an officeholder, particularly since land began to recover its status as a tradeable commodity toward the end of the 1980s.

In many minds across these three societies, there exists a close connection between the holding of public office and the acquisition of private wealth. As with the elitist political culture, we are here in the presence of a phenomenon that has deep historical roots, but which has also received fresh impetus from new circumstances—in this case, those associated with market-based economic reform. In Vietnam, Cambodia, and Laos alike, public salaries are low but aspirants will pay dearly for office and the easy access to private gain that it offers. Thus a bribe offered to gain preferment appears to its payer as an investment that can be readily recouped with the rents and other opportunities that a well-placed bureaucrat can lay hands on.[12]

In all three countries, this political economy is having profound consequences for politics. Inequality is high, not only in terms of income but also in terms of concentrated land ownership. In Cambodia, for example, where the process of accumulation has been the most rapacious, a tenth of the populace owns almost two-thirds of the land, and the top tenth of that tenth—or 1 percent of all Cambodians—owns an estimated 20 to 30 percent. One out of every five rural households is landless, and the figure is climbing by two percentage points each year.[13] Business interests are exerting a growing influence on politics, sometimes to the point of state capture. Behind-the-scenes lobbying of government grows intense as businesses try to shape regulations in favorable ways. The ruling communist parties now allow businesspeople to join, and prominent figures from the private economy sit in parliament. Finally, the tightening bonds between government and business are prompting a state bias in favor of capital when commercial disputes arise, and are compounding the political elite's instinctive feelings of hostility toward independent labor unions.

Finally, direct links run between the "reform era" political economy and the failure of liberal governance to make much headway. In the area of public-administration reform, long a mainstay of donor efforts across Vietnam, Cambodia, and Laos, attempts to winnow out unneeded bureaucracies continually fail to achieve overall reductions, as positions or offices eliminated here are replaced by new posts or bureaus over there. This often puzzles outsiders, but it makes perfect sense to anyone who understands how closely public officeholding and private moneymaking are linked in these societies. Closing down government departments or clarifying job descriptions strikes at the heart of the discretionary behavior on which officials depend to supplement their income, and hence must be subverted.

Spontaneous Protest and Civil Society

As powerful as may be the forces of culture and interest that bar the way to liberal politics, they have not been able to prevent the emergence of new kinds of protest and citizen activism in communist-ruled Southeast Asia. In the 1980s, popular protests, or indeed any forms of organization outside the ambit of the party-state, were extremely rare. This began to change during the 1990s. Although the regulatory environment governing civil society activism remains uncertain and restrictive, there has been no re-Stalinization of everyday life, and things have not stood still. Small-scale protests have become commonplace and larger ones are not unknown, as citizens take to the streets or camp outside government offices demanding redress of grievances.

In Vietnam, Cambodia, and Laos alike, most protests have to do with land disputes or complaints about corruption. Yet Vietnamese Catholics have demonstrated for freedom of worship while citizens in Cambodia have protested over a temple dispute with Thailand. Vietnam has also seen citizen protests against Chinese actions in the South China Sea, where the uninhabited but hydrocarbon-rich Spratly Islands are the subject of a Sino-Vietnamese territorial dispute.

In Cambodia, the opposition held political rallies in the late 1990s, but the space for this is now circumscribed and the risks are high. In Vietnam and Laos, some individuals and groups have sought to organize against the state despite bans on opposition parties. There was a one-off protest by Laotian students and teachers in 1999, and in 2006 Vietnamese dissidents launched Bloc 8406, but in both cases the hammer of official repression came down hard and ended the outbreak of free speech and assembly.

As a force for political change, dissident or opposition activity is outweighed in all three countries by a new and quieter form of behind-the-scenes activism on the part of the countries' emerging middle classes. Working through various networks and NGOs, Vietnamese, Cambodians, and (to a lesser extent) Laotians with some means and education at their disposal are beginning to lobby their respective governments on issues ranging from resource protection to safeguards for the rights of women and the disabled. For the most part, the process is thinly institutionalized at best and relies heavily on activists' personal connections as well as the willingness of state organs to engage civil society. Nevertheless, there is a sense of progress being made, as well-connected NGOs are able to "work the system" and get results. Here one should stress that this civil society activism often has a fiercely nationalist cast and is not (or at least not yet) pushing to replace the one-party system, but only seeks to reform a party-state to which some activists profess fervent loyalty.

The emergence of civil society would not have been possible without the many social changes that have occurred in Vietnam, Cambodia, and Laos since 1986. Citizens, including especially those belonging to the urban middle class, are for the most part richer and better educated than previously. They travel more, are more likely to have worked for international organizations, and hence have more experience of how things are done in other countries. They are exposed to a wider variety of media both old and new, including international media. They are more confident and less willing to tolerate state excesses or abuse. This does not necessarily mean that they are demanding the end of the one-party system, but they are conscious of their rights and want a greater say in matters that affect them.

There is of course a tension between this emerging middle-class mindset and the change-averse elite political culture discussed earlier. Yet the tension is less severe than one might think, in part because the middle classes and elites influence each other. Much of the Southeast Asian middle class has emerged at not too far a remove from the state and remains tied to it, often via family members who serve as state officials. Conversely, officeholders too travel, take in foreign media, and interact with international organizations—social changes affect state employees as well as other citizens. Thus the character of the Vietnamese, Cambodian, and Laotian ruling elites is changing in a process that can be expected to affect the ruling parties as well, even if the pace of change within the elite establishment lags behind what one sees in society (and especially urban society) at large.[14]

Looking to the Future

What does the future hold for the politics of Vietnam, Cambodia, and Laos? Regime collapse is unlikely in any of the three—those who rule in Hanoi, Phnom Penh, and Vientiane do not have their backs against the wall. The party-state in each country derives legitimacy from a variety of sources: economic performance, nationalism, concerns about order, and the personal charisma of top officials, for instance. Saying precisely how much regime support exists or how strong it runs is tricky, however, since people are reluctant to speak openly and there is no objective and scientific opinion polling. As for elections, in Vietnam and Laos all candidates must be vetted by the

Communist Party, and most are Party members. Cambodia has elections in which opposition parties run, but vote-buying and intimidation are major concerns. All three states, moreover, have imposing security forces. The Hun Sen regime in Cambodia is arguably the least stable because of the more brutal and rapacious manner in which its elites go about piling up private wealth. Yet it is also the fiercest of the three states when it comes to stamping out opposition.

The collapse of communism in China would be likely to have repercussions for all three countries, much as the collapse of communism in Vietnam would affect Cambodia and Laos. Yet few scholars expect such an outcome in the near future. Cambodia's CPP could face trouble when Hun Sen leaves the scene, but he is 60 years old and could rule for some while yet. The party-states in Vietnam and Laos, by contrast, rely on collective leadership and so have less need to worry about a succession crisis.

The matter of Hun Sen aside, our analysis leads us to anticipate the continuation of the existing regimes in all three states for some years, yet combined with a gradual evolution of the underlying political system. This evolution has been taking place over the last fifteen or twenty years. It means that while there has been no change in the ruling parties (even in Cambodia, where the CPP was able to strongarm its way back into power fairly quickly despite losing the 1993 election), society as a whole has not stood still and its ferment has had an effect on the ruling elite itself. In time, this will widen the scope of what is possible.

In the long term, we would not rule out the possibility that the Vietnamese and Laotian communist parties could decide to allow other political parties to form, or that the CPP in Cambodia might allow existing opposition parties to operate more freely. Yet the elitist, nonliberal political cultures of these three countries are changing only slowly, and control over public offices still means big money, so the "long term" may be a long way off indeed. Much the same could be said regarding other countries in Southeast Asia as well. Perhaps things might evolve into a situation not unlike that in South Korea, which about a quarter-century after its transition is a functioning democracy, but one where traditional ways (such as the tendency of everything to revolve around the person of the president) persist and lend a distinctive character to political life there.[15]

Will such an evolution occur in our three Southeast Asian countries? With regard to Cambodia, one cannot say so with much confidence. Such (currently enfeebled) opposition forces as do exist there neither stand apart decisively from the authoritarian values of traditional political culture nor stand firmly on the ground of classic constitutional liberalism. Thus if some version of the opposition were to ever find its way into office, which is not likely in the short term, it would take along elitist and paternalist assumptions about how political life is to be conducted.

Turning to Vietnam and Laos, one can applaud the growth of civil so-ciety activism while also soberly recognizing that while it reveals some liberal influences, it is also less than thoroughly liberal in outlook. Thus with regard to none of the three countries would it be fair to assume that a regime change in the direction of multipartism will in and of itself betoken the triumph of liberal values.

Still, such a shift away from one-party rule would represent great progress, so it is worth considering how it might come about. If the experience of other states is any guide, one possible scenario is that the ruling party itself will come to see the existing political system as a li-ability and move to change it. Widespread protests might be involved, as they were in South Korea during the second half of the 1980s. Or the process might be a more placid affair of the sort that unfolded in Taiwan at around the same time. There, the ruling Chinese Nationalists began dialoguing with the opposition in 1986 not due to popular pressure, but rather as part of a strategic bid to ease the Republic of China's grow-ing marginalization on the world scene as Beijing reengaged.[16] In South Korea, change came in 1987 when Roh Tae-woo, the presidential candi-date of the ruling Democratic Justice Party, broke ranks with incumbent Chun Doo-hwan by agreeing with opposition demands for direct presi-dential elections in the face of massive social and labor unrest.[17]

Of course, crisis-generated splits within elite ranks are common driv-ers of political change in many places. In both the Korean and Taiwan-ese cases, the ruling party won time for itself insofar as it was some years into multipartism before the opposition won office. It is not hard to imagine a similar situation playing itself out in Vietnam, Cambodia, or Laos in years to come.

Another scenario envisions ruling parties scheming to undercut any emerging opposition by forming regime-friendly "loyal" opposition groups. The long-ruling People's Action Party of Singapore has done something similar with its "nominated members of parliament."[18] Such an approach might seem appealing to old-line ruling-party elites made nervous by the prospect of real opposition politics. Yet it is hard to see how setting up a "tame" opposition can generate legitimacy or mollify those who want far-reaching change. Nevertheless, it is not out of the question that elites in Vietnam or Laos might choose to go this route to avoid what they fear would be a divisive and destabilizing process of political-party formation. Whichever of these routes Vietnam, Cambo-dia, and Laos eventually take, what is certain is that a sudden and whole-sale ascendancy of liberal politics is the least likely outcome.

NOTES

1. Borje Ljunggren, ed., *The Challenge of Reform in Indochina* (Cambridge: Harvard University Press, 1993).

2. Barry Naughton, *Growing Out of the Plan: Chinese Economic Reform, 1978–93* (Cambridge: Cambridge University Press, 1995), 22.

3. Adam Fforde, "The Political Economy of 'Reform' in Vietnam: Some Reflections," unpubl. ms., 1991, 8.

4. Søren Ivarsson, Thommy Svensson, and Stein Tønnesson, *The Quest for Balance in a Changing Laos: A Political Analysis*, NIAS Reports 25, 1995, Nordic Institute for Asian Studies, Copenhagen, 51–52.

5. Communist Party of Vietnam, *Seventh National Congress: Documents* (Hanoi: Vietnam Foreign Languages Publishing House, 1991), 104; and Ivarrson et al., *Quest for Balance*, 38–39.

6. Caroline Hughes, *The Political Economy of the Cambodian Transition, 1991–2001* (London: Routledge, 2003).

7. David Chandler, "Cambodia in 2009: Plus C'est la Même Chose," *Asian Survey* 50 (January–February 2010): 229.

8. Without being deterministic or forgetting the mutability of culture, I would posit that the resistance to democracy in these societies lies at the intersection where something uniquely Southeast Asian meets a legacy of longtime communist rule. The notion of "something uniquely Southeast Asian" refers to the influence of India over China—or a coming-together of Indian and Chinese influence—in the precolonial era and the way in which this influence worked its way differently through Vietnam, Cambodia, and Laos, respectively, with the upshot in each being a legacy that endures to this day. For more on this, see Alexander Woodside, *Vietnam and the Chinese Model: A Comparative Study of Nguyen and Ching Civil Government in the First Half of the Nineteenth Century* (Cambridge: Harvard University Press, 1971); Robert S. Newman, *Brahmin and Mandarin: A Comparison of the Cambodian and Vietnamese Revolutions*, Centre of Southeast Asian Studies, Working Papers, Monash University, 1978.

9. Geir Helgesen and Li Xing, "Good Governance—Democracy or *Minzhu*," in Hans Antlöv and Tak-Wing Ngo, eds., *The Cultural Construction of Politics in Asia* (Richmond, Surry: Curzon, 2000), 175–202.

10. R.H. Taylor, ed., *The Politics of Elections in Southeast Asia* (Cambridge: Cambridge University Press, 1996).

11. Antlöv and Ngo, *Cultural Construction of Politics*.

12. Martin Gainsborough, Dang Ngoc Dinh, and Tran Thanh Phuong, "Corruption, Public Administration and Development: Challenges and Opportunities as Viet Nam Moves Towards Middle-Income Status," in Jairo Acuña-Alfaro, ed., *Reforming Public Administration Reform in Vietnam: Current Situation and Recommendations* (Hanoi: National Political Publishing House, 2009), 377–427.

13. Caroline Hughes, "Cambodia in 2007: Development and Dispossession," *Asian Survey* 48 (January–February 2008): 71.

14. Although reliable comparative data are hard to come by, all three countries have seen high levels of rural-to-urban migration during the reform years. The cities in Vietnam and Cambodia are much larger than those in Laos, but there too the process of urbanization and its effects have been no less significant. Masses of rural migrants strain urban infrastructure and bring new social pressures to bear. In terms of the urban middle class, there are signs of its growth in all three countries as evidenced by conspicuous consumption, foreign travel and education, and increased leisure time. Middle-class political activism, generally of a reformist nature, is most pronounced in Vietnam, though Cambodia

and Laos have nascent networks of middle-class activists as well. For background, see Sarthi Acharya, "Labour Migration in the Transitional Economies of South-East Asia," *Economic and Social Commission for Asia and the Pacific*, December 2003, 1–21; and Lisa Drummond and Mandy Thomas, eds., *Consuming Urban Culture in Contemporary Vietnam* (London: RoutledgeCurzon, 2003).

15. Tat Yan Kong, "Power Alternation in South Korea," *Government and Opposition* 35 (July 2000): 370–91.

16. Laurence Whitehead, "Afterword: On Cultures and Contexts," in Antlöv and Ngo, *Cultural Construction of Politics*, 234.

17. Han Sung-Joo, "South Korea in 1987: The Politics of Democratization," *Asian Survey* 28 (January 1988): 52–61.

18. Michael Barr, "Perpetual Revisionism in Singapore: The Limits of Change," *Pacific Review* 16, no. 1 (2003): 77–97.

13

BURMA:
THE DEMOCRATS' OPPORTUNITY

Min Zin and Brian Joseph

Min Zin is a doctoral student in political science at the University of California, Berkeley. Brian Joseph is senior program director for Asia and Global Programs at the National Endowment for Democracy. This essay originally appeared in the October 2012 issue of the Journal of Democracy.

For a half-century after the military took over in 1962, the prospects for political change in Burma appeared remote at best. The regime was one of the world's most rigidly authoritarian, and it oversaw one of the world's least developed countries. On virtually every index by which human development is measured, this country of 56 million people has lost ground and now sits near the bottom of world rankings. As if to make the picture even gloomier, Burma's soldier rulers have long followed isolationist policies that have guaranteed continuing economic and political stagnation, even as many other nondemocratic countries in Asia have embraced economic reforms and foreign policies that have helped to integrate them into the global community and in some cases made them less authoritarian. Despite the efforts of a prodemocratic opposition movement and its best-known figure, Nobel laureate Aung San Suu Kyi, Burma seemed fated to remain unfree and poor in the military's iron grip.

Much to the surprise of observers, however, that picture began to change in early 2011. Despite retaining a firm hold on power and facing no urgent domestic or international threats, the military began to shift course. Oddly, what turned out to be the curtain-raiser to the new direction was more of the "same old same old": On 7 November 2010, presidential and parliamentary elections had taken place under highly fraudulent conditions, and had produced resounding wins for 65-year-old premier and former general Thein Sein and the military-backed Union Solidarity and Development Party (USDP).

In his 30 March 2011 inaugural address, Thein Sein's tone was conciliatory but still paternalistic. He praised the role that the military had played, but noted the need for economic and political reform. The introduction of a reform agenda was even more remarkable given that those driving the process were all ex-generals, that the regime continued to exert near-total control over civic and political life, and that the system it ran came complete with a massive and constitutionally built-in role for the military in what the regime touted as Burma's new "democratic" order.

Within half a year, the transformation was unmistakable. The government freed most political prisoners, including prominent figures such as Aung San Suu Kyi, who had been held under house arrest for most of the two previous decades; revised political-party laws in ways that allowed Suu Kyi and her National League for Democracy (NLD) plus other opposition parties to take part in politics; entered ceasefire negotiations with a number of ethnic groups; relaxed press censorship and control of civil society; and permitted leading dissidents to return.

The democratic opposition responded to the openings favorably and energetically. Aung San Suu Kyi re-registered the NLD, which performed superbly in the 1 April 2012 by-elections, contesting 44 of the 45 seats available and winning all but one race. Suu Kyi was among the 43 winners, and now sits in the Union Parliament. These were the first elections in Burma in more than fifty years in which the results reflected the people's will and were honored by the government. Although less than a tenth of the seats in Parliament were at stake in these by-elections, they marked a break from the rigged or stolen elections of the past and underlined the government's new and more accepting attitude toward political opposition.

To make the most of the opening, prodemocracy activists are launching new think tanks, training centers, and publications. The international community has responded as well. In the last year, Burma has hosted British prime minister David Cameron, UN secretary-general Ban Ki Moon, and U.S. secretary of state Hillary Clinton. ASEAN awarded Burma its 2014 chairmanship. The United States restored full diplomatic relations after 22 years, and then followed the EU and Britain by easing investment and financial sanctions in May 2012.

Despite the excitement that the reforms have sparked at home and abroad, Burma remains a military dictatorship. Serving or retired generals control every important institution, and the constitution guarantees military domination. Yet something profound is changing, even if this is not—or not yet—an outright transition to democracy. What is driving the changes, why are they happening now, and where will they lead? What is the government's goal, and why does it think it can stay in charge of the process? What are the chances that reform will continue and that the next general elections, currently set for 2015, could lead to democratic breakthrough and consolidation?

Under whatever official name, acronym, or general turned premier or president, Burma's military rulers have long been known for their ruthlessness and ability to withstand pressures both foreign and domestic. When the military regime held elections in November 2010, there was little sign that any course change was coming. Why did the shift come, and why now? For light on these questions, we can look to five interrelated reasons. They are: 1) an internal timeframe governed by the regime's "seven-step roadmap" and the retirement of longtime top general Than Shwe; 2) a recognition that Burma had become too reliant on China politically, economically, and militarily; 3) fear of another popular uprising; 4) a recognition of the need to engage the West; and 5) a desire to address Burma's lack of development.

The regime's seven-step roadmap. The roadmap dates to 2003 and is supposed to lead to "discipline-flourishing democracy." The plan laid out seven steps that involved reconvening the National Convention (called in 1993, suspended in 1996) and allowing it to complete its work of drafting a new constitution to be put to a referendum. After that, the plan called for holding legislative elections and building what the regime calls a "modern, developed, and democratic state."

In the event, the reconvened Convention dragged on without the NLD (which boycotted), without legitimacy, and without much result. When at last the new constitution appeared, it featured democratic window-dressing on a frame of strengthened rule by the military, which among other things was guaranteed a quarter of all seats in Parliament. The referendum took place on 10 May 2008, barely a week after Cyclone Nargis had killed more than 130,000 Burmese and displaced millions more (official sources nonetheless claimed 98 percent turnout and a near-unanimous "yes" vote). Then came the bogus 2010 parliamentary elections and a lopsided majority for the USDP.

The first six steps of the roadmap were completed under Than Shwe, a general well known for his personal dislike of Suu Kyi and a figure who appears on the list compiled by Reed Brody of Human Rights Watch of ex-dictators who deserve to be called to account for their crimes.[1] When he retired on 30 March 2011, he felt confident that he had not only solidified military primacy but had also ensured that none of his successors could amass enough power to turn against him the way that he had turned against his predecessor Ne Win. The constitution's distribution of power across a number of "democratic" institutions seemed cleverly calculated to allow Than Shwe to play potential successors against one another. In addition to arranging for Thein Sein to become president, Than Shwe installed his third-in-command, Thura Shwe Mann, as speaker of the lower house. Hard-line second-tier leaders headed the USDP while General Min Aung Hlaing, a relatively junior officer, was named to the once all-powerful post of military commander-in-chief.

The seventh and hardest step is now at hand. It is too soon to say precisely what the generals mean when they talk of building a "modern, developed, and democratic" state. Likewise, it is also too soon to say how many hard-liners remain in posts from which they can undermine reforms. But it increasingly appears that the government's goal is to set up a system—run by a military-backed dominant party—that will bring all political and ethnic forces within a single constitutional framework and pursue economic development more or less in the style of Malaysia or Singapore.

The China factor. In the wake of the August 1988 democracy uprising, the May 1990 elections, and the regime's refusal to respect the verdict of those elections, the United States and other Western countries imposed sanctions, denied multilateral loans and assistance, and increased international political pressure on Burma. Facing all this, Burma's military rulers tacked away from their usual nonaligned policy and turned to China for military, political, and economic support. Over the next two decades, not only did Burma become more dependent on China, but Burma's importance to China in terms of natural resources, regional economic integration, and security grew.

In 1988, total trade between China and Burma had been worth a mere US$9.5 million. A year later, it exploded, octupling to $76 million. By 2009, China had displaced Thailand as Burma's largest trading partner. In 2010 and 2011, trade with China was worth $4.7 billion, or slightly more than a third of all Burma's trade. Burma sells China lumber, gems, seafood, marble, coal, nickel, and other natural resources, while China floods the Burmese market with cheap finished products from foodstuffs to electronics.

Investment has followed a similar path. From 1988 to 2012, Burma received about $41 billion in Chinese investment. China has now passed Thailand as Burma's biggest investor. If all the Chinese investments and business ventures hidden from public accounting were included, China would have an even more commanding lead as Burma's largest single source of trade and investment.

The sector that draws more foreign investment than any other is oil and natural gas. According to EarthRights International, 69 Chinese-owned multinational corporations are involved in more than ninety hydropower, mining, oil, and natural-gas projects in Burma.[2] In August 2007, the Burmese junta confirmed the sale of natural gas from the lucrative Shwe gas reserves, the largest field in the Bay of Bengal off the Arakan coast of Burma, to a Chinese state-controlled company.[3] A number of well-informed analysts have speculated that the regime selected the company controlled by the Chinese government (over Indian and South Korean companies) for the lucrative contract in return for the support that Burma received from China at the UN, including the use of its veto in 2007 to block a U.S.-led resolution on Burma. This was the first time since 1973 that Beijing had vetoed any matter not related to Taiwan.[4]

In 2009, China began to build a twin pipeline for oil and natural gas that will run from Burma's west coast through ethnic-minority areas in the northeast all the way to the southern Chinese provinces of Yunnan, Guizhou, and Guangxi. The pipeline will allow China to obtain oil and gas from the Middle East and Africa as well as natural gas from Burma itself without having to worry about shipping it through the strategically vulnerable Malacca Strait.

Burma's dependence on China reaches beyond economics to security relations. After the military's bloody August and September 1988 suppression of the so-called Four Eights Uprising (it began on 8 August 1988) and the subsequent Western arms embargo, China became Burma's major supplier of weapons, on credit and at low "friendship" prices. The Burmese junta provided China with resources and other concessions in exchange for cash, supplies, and armaments. China's military also began to train Burmese officers both in China and in Burma. China's investment in the Burmese military is closely tied to Beijing's goal of building a world-class bluewater navy by 2050: Burma offers China the possibility of a direct window on the Indian Ocean.[5]

Even though Burma's generals knew that their country's international-pariah status made Chinese political and diplomatic protection crucial, they showed signs of worry. They began seeking military equipment and training from India, Russia, Pakistan, and even North Korea.[6] Burma's military relationship with North Korea was publicly noted as early as the 1990s but did not capture headlines again until it was exposed in a 2010 documentary titled *Burma's Nuclear Ambitions*. On 12 June 2011, the U.S. Navy turned back a North Korean ship with military cargo headed for Burma.[7]

Just as China sought to expand its economic influence in Burma, so did Burma's other neighbors. In 1991, Indian prime minister Narasimha Rao began a "Look East" policy that sought to link India's recently liberalized economy with the dynamic "tiger" economies of Southeast Asia. Six years later, Burma and Laos became the last two of Southeast Asia's ten countries to join ASEAN. Burma's rulers, though not directly challenging Chinese influence, were cautiously moving to dilute it with additional allies and greater regional economic integration.

Such a direct challenge to Beijing would become one of the more striking developments of 2011, however. On September 30, President Thein Sein announced the suspension of work on the Chinese-built, Chinese-funded Myitsone Dam. The dam is the largest of eight that China had been planning to build on the Irrawaddy River. The vast hydroelectric project, begun in 2006, involved the creation at Myitsone of a reservoir with a surface area larger than that of Singapore.

Earlier in 2011, researchers, activists, and media organizations in

Burma had started ringing alarm bells about the dam's environmental, economic, and human costs, capturing the country's imagination and prompting a sense of public urgency around the need to protect the Irrawaddy River, the country's largest and most important waterway. Although few of the reform measures had yet to take effect, it was already apparent that public mobilization around the dam presented a challenge to the new government's commitment to reform, or at least the public-relations aspect of it. In part due to public concern, but more likely driven by strategic and economic considerations, including the potential harm to the important downstream agrarian economy, President Thein Sein's decision to suspend work on the dam was a clear indication of concern within the government about Chinese influence in Burma.

The Myitsone Dam decision signaled a change in attitude toward China's role in Burma, but not a break in relations. The Burmese government still depends heavily on its giant neighbor economically, politically, and strategically, and has expressed no desire to confront it. The NLD has been equally tactful in discussing the role of China. "So it is not true that we can't have good relations because of different systems," Aung San Suu Kyi has stressed. "Burma and China have enjoyed very warm and friendly relations, and problems were peacefully settled whenever they arose."[8]

For Thein Sein and the new generation of military leaders under him, it seems that the reform opening offers a chance to begin steering their country cautiously away from overreliance on China, which they believe has taken advantage of Burma's isolation, and to interact more closely with the West.

Fear of another uprising. During the military's time in power, it has felt pressure not only from abroad but from at home as well. Although the military had long dealt harshly with public expressions of discontent—most recently in September 2007, when it brutally suppressed the Saffron Revolution—by 2010 the soldiers seemed to grasp that something fundamental had changed. Were they worried and wearied by the thought of more international opprobrium and sanctions? Had they finally realized that a prosperous and modern, not to say a democratic state is unlikely to be built with clubs? For whatever reason, Burma's rulers appear to have understood—even before the Arab Spring came along and reinforced the lesson—that they could no longer simply lash out with force against protest as they had in the past.

As in 1990, when the junta of the day had underestimated the NLD's public support, the soldier-rulers failed in 2007 to understand the breadth and depth of discontent that lay behind early signs of unrest. The NLD was not the only source of organized domestic opposition. Recently released leaders of the Four Eights Movement led protests over oil and gas price hikes. In early September 2007, the regime met a peaceful demonstration by Buddhist monks in Pakokku with brutal tactics that quickly turned a small protest movement into a nationwide uprising. Before the month was over, hundreds of thousands of monks and others would take to the streets in a direct challenge to military rule.

The Saffron Revolution was the first uprising in Burma to be shown on television. The Democratic Voice of Burma, a Norway-based satellite station, relied on a network of underground video journalists who offered something close to real-time coverage. The sight of legions of monks marching through the streets of Rangoon and other cities with their alms bowls turned upside down in a gesture of protest presented a direct and unmistakable challenge to a regime that had long tried to use Buddhism to legitimize its rule.

Eight months later, on 8 May 2008, Cyclone Nargis ripped through the Irrawaddy Delta. The massive storm and the flooding that it brought killed more than 130,000 people and left another 1.2 million homeless and desperate. The regime's initial response was to downplay the disaster and refuse international aid. Within a month, as Burmese citizens mobilized to respond and as international pressure mounted, the regime finally gave in, allowing in international aid and relaxing some restrictions on local civil society groups.

Little is known about the deliberations within the military that led to the decisions to meet the Saffron Revolution with brutal force and the aftermath of Cyclone Nargis with a ban on outside aid despite the suffering of millions of ordinary Burmese. It seems likely, however, that these episodes bred tensions within top military circles.

Reengaging the West. The regime wanted to reengage with the West as a way of lessening its dependence on China and gaining help in meeting its deep economic challenges, but it also recognized that it could not achieve this goal without engaging with its domestic opposition. For twenty years, the junta had sought to discredit, delegitimize, and decimate any opposition, no matter how peaceful. Not only did the regime's efforts fail, they had the unintended consequence of helping to ensure that popular support for the NLD-led opposition never waned. As is evident from the Saffron Revolution and the April 1 by-election, public support for the opposition has remained consistently high. The endurance, commitment, courage, and sacrifice of the activists have bolstered the legitimacy of prodemocracy groups, forcing the regime to accept that their acquiescence was essential to the successful rollout of a reform agenda.

President Thein Sein signaled as much when he met with Aung San Suu Kyi in the regime's new capital of Naypyidaw on 19 August 2011. Neither Burma nor the world at large, he knew, would be sold on his opening unless she approved it. The centrality of her role in legitimizing the process and, by extension, giving the international community a green light to reengage Burma was underlined again when U.S. president Barack Obama sought her opinion prior to sending Secretary of State Hillary Clinton to Burma in December 2011.

Worries about falling behind. Closely related to the government's concern with containing public discontent was a growing recognition that Burma was falling ever farther behind its neighbors. Despite their country's relative isolation, Burmese officials were painfully aware of Burma's economic and social failings. As one of the world's least developed countries, Burma lags even the poorer Southeast Asian countries, and trails especially badly when compared to such nearby economic powerhouses as Malaysia, Singapore, and Thailand. In 2010, the UN Development Programme's Human Development Index ranked Burma 132nd out of 169 countries, the lowest in Southeast Asia.

Although Burma's exposure to trade and foreign direct investment (FDI) is expanding, its economy remains among the region's slowest-growing. Trade and investment mostly revolve around the extraction of natural resources, while the labor-intensive agricultural and manufacturing sectors go begging with just 1 percent of FDI. What is worse, the regime has wasted the country's natural-resources windfall on white elephants such as the new capital at Naypyidaw—a project that the International Monetary Fund estimates may have cost Burma as much as 2 percent of its annual GDP for 2006.[9] By the government's own official statistics, it allocated 23.6 percent of its 2011 budget to military spending, while spending a mere 5.4 percent on education and health combined.[10]

Tough international sanctions—including targeted financial measures enforced by the United States—have compounded the disastrous effects of Burma's poor economic policies. Although it is difficult to measure the impact of the sanctions, President Thein Sein has made lifting them a key goal in discussions with Western leaders, UN officials, and his ASEAN counterparts.

Managing the Transition

The shift that now appears to be underway in Burma raises questions not only of motivation and timing but also of management. In other words, how did Burma go from a military-dominated authoritarian state to a quasi-civilian government so quickly while avoiding a backlash by hard-liners and recruiting oppositionists into legitimating the reforms? Key to the reforms' success (or at least survival) have been constitutional guarantees for the military and hard-liners combined with a series of shrewd personnel assignments that have placed ex-generals in competing positions of institutional authority.

Those competing positions exist because Thein Sein's predecessor Than Shwe had been anxious to forestall the kind of power concentration and palace intrigues at levels just below the top that had led to the imprisonments and eventual deaths of both his immediate predecessors, Senior General Saw Maung (the 1988 coupmaker) and General Ne Win (the original 1962 coupmaker), who died in 1997 and 2002, respectively. Than Shwe thus left behind a political system still under military tutelage, but without many opportunities for any one new figure to consolidate power beyond challenge by fellow generals.

The 2008 Constitution contains a number of provisions that protect military prerogatives. In addition to setting aside a quarter of the seats in Parliament for serving officers, it establishes a National Defense and Security Council with powers to declare states of emergency (a power the president also has) and name the commander-in-chief. The six fundamental constitutional principles, moreover, include the dictum that the military should "be able to participate in the national political leadership role of the state." Amending any of these provisions requires a parliamentary supermajority of 75 percent as well as a national referendum.

The constitution provides for a number of new (or newly empowered) democratic institutions that include not only Parliament but executive and judicial bodies as well. The manner in which these institutions have been filled—whether by appointment or election—has been meant to ensure both that military men remain in charge and that no one senior officer can amass too much power vis-à-vis his peers. The effect has been less to democratize these institutions than to ensure that power is spread more broadly than before throughout the upper ranks of a military establishment that still calls the shots.

The 2008 Constitution requires that the president and the cabinet ministers, all of whom are elected MPs, resign from Parliament as well as their respective political parties during their executive-branch service. Since March 2011, this provision, meant to minimize the appearance of partisanship among national officials, has had the effect of putting distance between these officials and the ruling USDP. This is significant because the USDP leadership has generally appeared to be more cautious and conservative than President Thein Sein and his team. Thus the USDP, correctly foreseeing that the NLD would do well in the 2012 by-elections, had opposed holding them. It also pushed unsuccessfully to amend the constitution to allow executive officials, most of whom were USDP members, to retain their party affiliation. According to one of Thein Sein's advisors, the president regards himself and certain other reform-minded leaders as one-termers.[11] If that is so, their lack of concern with staying in office should tend to put even more space between them and their party.

The success of the reform process hinges on opposition cooperation, particularly that of the NLD and the major ethnic nationality parties. Although the changes of the last eighteen months are often said to have been driven "from the top," the opposition's role in both pressing for reform and making reforms work has been critical. As noted above, President Thein Sein's course change appears to flow in part from an understanding that there is no moving forward—whether politically, economically, or strategically—without support from Aung San Suu Kyi and the NLD. Her backing both eased domestic pressure and made it acceptable for the United States and the broader international community to resume engagement with Burma.[12]

Civil Society, the NLD, and the Ethnic Groups

The reforms have altered the political climate in Burma. For the first time since the soldiers took over in 1962, the opposition is playing a formal and significant role in Parliament. Press censorship is easing, politically engaged independent organizations are forming, and exiles are coming home or at least pondering return. The military's hold on power is more diffuse and perhaps weaker. Yet as David Steinberg notes, the reforms appear driven in part by the soldiers' concern with retaining power.[13] As long as reforms do not impinge on the military's political veto or its economic interests, the military and other hardliners are likely to tolerate a degree of political liberalization, including the incorporation of dissidents and ethnic leaders into the political process.

Prior to the 2011 reforms, there was little free space for the political opposition or civil society. Oppositionists remained largely underground, with only a few individuals able to work openly. Organized civil society groups were limited in size, scope, and mandate.

Yet as they have even during the most repressive eras of modern Burmese history, citizens continued to engage in the political life of their country. As the Four Eights Movement gave rise to important new forces including the NLD, student groups led by Min Ko Naing and others, and the once-important multiethnic Democratic Alliance of Burma, so the aftermath of the Saffron Revolution almost twenty years later inspired the formation of a number of new organizations and initiatives inside Burma that sought to operate in public and outside state control. By definition, these efforts were small-scale, informal, and quiet. Yet much as the 88 Student Generation Group had kept on organizing throughout the 1990s and 2000s, the groups that emerged during the Saffron Revolution sought to expand and strengthen their efforts, linking diverse communities in an effort to sustain and build on the momentum that the Saffron Revolution had generated.

Political space for civil society was at its tightest in late 2007 and early 2008, between the crackdown on the Saffron Revolution and the coming of Cyclone Nargis. The latter's devastating effects called forth an outpouring of citizen-led and international efforts to relieve the severe and widespread suffering born of the monster storm. While the

Nargis response helped to carve out a space in which NGOs could operate, it was largely confined to the storm-ravaged zones along Burma's southern coast and was limited to humanitarian assistance and basic development efforts. It extended neither to more politically sensitive sectors nor to conflict-prone ethnic areas.

When Thein Sein introduced reforms and relaxed controls on political organizations and civil society, political activists responded quickly and began to work more openly. The media began to test the waters by publishing photos of Aung San Suu Kyi and carrying material that had once been banned. Within months, activists opened training centers, organized to make their voices heard on environmental issues, publicized human-rights violations, and demanded improvements in labor standards. Democracy activists were also essential to the mass mobilization of support for Aung San Suu Kyi, who drew crowds numbering in the tens of thousands as she toured the country for the first time since 2003.

In addition, leading exiles were allowed to visit Burma for the first time in nearly two decades. Although civil society, including the media, is increasingly able to operate openly, it still faces tremendous pressures. These include the lack of a legal operating environment as well as a lack of clarity and consistency at different levels of government coupled with unchecked authority in the hands of various officials. To highlight one example of what this can mean, the Special Branch Police in Rangoon arrested at least 27 student activists on 6 July 2012. All went free the following day, but the authorities had made their point about how tenuous the operating environment for activists really is.

Just as civil society has learned to adapt to the new environment, the NLD has sought to position itself to exert maximum leverage on the reform process. Under Aung San Suu Kyi's direction, the NLD has pursued a strategy that seeks to embed the opposition within the current system without giving up the ability to contest any aspects of that system which need changing. The embedding process inevitably involves being at least conditionally coopted into the existing political framework, and necessarily focuses more on building institutions than on asserting autonomy vis-à-vis the military.

During this delicate phase, the opposition has chosen to work with the government to develop institutional capacity (whether legislative, bureaucratic, or judicial); to differentiate the functions of various institutions from one another; and to increase institutional complexity and professionalism. By choosing *not* to demand steps that would directly threaten the military—such as immediate constitutional changes meant to curb the soldiers' role or establish a federal union—the NLD has shown itself committed to gradualism. Its leaders realize that their odds of success will improve if they can find a way to strengthen reformers without antagonizing hard-liners, a group that is marginalized now but which could cause serious trouble down the road.

Embedding—claiming a place within the system—does not mean that Suu Kyi and her supporters must resign themselves to its failings or avoid all contestation. As a sign that she grasps this, Suu Kyi has refused official requests to drop the name "Burma" in favor of the regime's preferred "Myanmar."[14]

Even as the NLD's MPs work within the tight constraints of the non-democratic Parliament, the NLD will be able to use its presence in civil society and the media to challenge the regime's poor governance practices. To cite but one example, fighting endemic corruption (a form of contestation) and working to establish the rule of law (a form of institution-building) are really two sides of the same coin. If the NLD can manage to find and stick to the right mix of participation and contestation, it could succeed in gradually steering Burma away from Thein Sein's updated version of authoritarianism—what he calls "disciplined democracy"—and toward genuine democratization.[15]

The Challenge of Ethnic Relations

Although conditions in Rangoon have improved for the political opposition and other activists, life remains dire in the ethnic-minority areas where more than two of every five Burmese citizens reside.[16] Sixty years of civil war have left the country prey to further violence, exploitation, and conflict. Since independence, the military has ensured the territorial integrity of the state through violence, repression, and political opportunism. If the military recedes from power and democracy begins to take hold, resolving the political divide between the ethnic minorities on the periphery and the ethnic-Burman majority that predominates in the center of the country will take on a new urgency. Unsettled ethnic conflicts and fragile ceasefire agreements are perhaps the most likely source of friction between the army and the current government, as well as any possible future civilian governments.

With serious fighting continuing in Kachin State in the far north and the human-rights situation still poor in the other ethnic areas, Thein Sein has publicly acknowledged that in order to mean anything his reforms must tackle the intensely troubled matter of interethnic relations.[17] The twelve-member peace committee that he formed in May 2012 and tasked with talking to the armed nationalities movements includes himself, his two vice-presidents, the speakers of both houses of Parliament, the minister of home affairs, and the uniformed armed-forces commander. Over the past year, the government has secured ceasefire deals with a dozen armed ethnic groups. The government and the Kachin Independence Army continue to talk in the midst of ongoing fighting.

As the June 2012 outbreak of communal violence in Arakan State on the west coast has made clear, outbursts of violence not tied to the ceasefire talks could yet derail the reform process. Tensions between the state's Arakan (and mostly Buddhist) majority and the Muslim Rohingya minority are far from novel. What is new is the government's public handling of the matter. The violence in Arakan State erupted following the rape of a Buddhist Arakan girl by three Rohingya men and a retaliatory mob attack on a group of Muslims in another town that left ten dead. Dozens more have since died in full-blown communal violence. Facing pressure to respond, President Thein Sein tried to stop the mayhem by declaring a public emergency in Arakan State. Although his declaration was widely applauded at home even as looting, arson, and mob clashes (not to mention alleged state-sponsored abuses) continued to spread in that strife-torn part of Burma, his proposal to the UN to resettle the Rohingya drew sharp international criticism.

The political transition—if that is what it is—in Burma remains tension-wracked and far from complete. The reforms have liberalized the political environment to a degree, but they cannot lead to democratization absent major constitutional reforms.

The government faces immense challenges. Its ability to meet them is less likely to be undermined by open hostility from within the military (it seems that everyone is a reformer in Burma these days) than by such ills as dire poverty, a broken health-care system, a poorly educated populace, and civil war in ethnic areas. The state itself, moreover, is hobbled by institutional incompetence, bureaucratic dysfunction, pervasive corruption, a lack of funds for even the most basic public services, and an authoritarian political culture.

Saddled with a corrupt and weak government and deep-rooted animosities, Thein Sein will need to do what he can to manage the elite and institutional rivalries that go on behind the scenes within official and military ranks. His goals must be to improve the provision of basic public goods; to end the civil war in Kachin State and shore up fragile ceasefire deals elsewhere (they are all currently military rather than politically negotiated agreements); to expand cooperation with Aung San Suu Kyi and various opposition forces; and to begin the sorely needed process of building up institutions to face the future.

The success of the reform effort will depend in part on how those who stand to lose the most respond. Thein Sein has so far faced surprisingly little opposition—that we know about—from within the military or the USDP. Yet the prospects for a backlash remain real. To help guard against this, the government should revisit the electoral system to steer it away from the dangers of plurality voting.[18] The NLD's sweeping win in the April 2012 by-elections hints at an NLD landslide in 2015. The adoption of a mixed system that combines proportional and majoritarian representation might reduce the threat of a regime backlash against an NLD that has "run the table" and hence appears highly threatening.

The current plurality system, moreover, may serve to dilute the strength of smaller democratic parties, most importantly ethnic-minority parties, thereby creating tension between the NLD and its allies among these groups.

The success of the reform effort will also depend in large measure on how Burma's political leadership—including the current government, the military, the NLD, and ethnic leaders—handles the structural and political issues that have eroded any sense of national unity or identity and led to a highly contested state. The old question of the state's fundamental nature cannot be avoided. Is it a Burmese-speaking Buddhist country with a large minority population but with ethnic Burmans more or less in the driver's seat? Or is it a multiethnic country in which everyone has an equal claim on what it means to be Burmese? Failure to face this question will not only guarantee more human-rights abuses in the ethnic areas, but also undermine any prospect of creating a just and enduring democratic state.

The main challenge now, therefore, is less democratization per se than the building of a state in which democracy can take root and grow. For the substantive democratization process, the real test will be how the transition proceeds in the aftermath of the 2015 elections.

Looking Toward 2015

Those elections, unlike the April 2012 by-elections, have the potential to significantly alter Burma's basic power structure. Thus they represent a far greater threat to the military and other hard-liners than the by-elections did. If free and fair, the 2015 vote would be the first time in more than six decades that Burmese citizens would have a say in how and by whom they are to be governed—a voice that is unmistakably aligned against continued military rule. The patterns and trends of the past quarter-century strongly suggest that the NLD will win a majority of the popular vote, as it did in 1990 and 2012. The regime-backed USDP will lose heavily, even in military strongholds. The ethnic-nationality parties, the largest and most important of which are allies of the NLD, will remain dominant in their respective constituencies. Other, smaller prodemocracy parties will continue to draw support but will not likely be in a position to challenge the NLD.

Although the military will continue to hold a quarter of the seats in Parliament and will retain power via constitutional provisions meant to block the establishment of a true democracy, a resounding victory for the NLD and its allies will mark an even starker divide between the new reform era and the past sixty years of military rule. Moreover, if free voting under the current electoral system leaves the USDP—and hence the military—with few parliamentary seats, the NLD and the ethnic nationalities will be in a strong position to push for greater democratization. If reformers predominate within the government, this could indeed lead to deeper democracy. But if hard-liners come to have the upper hand, there could be a repressive backlash.

Election results aside, constitutional issues and unresolved questions of ethnic autonomy will ensure that the political climate in Burma remains tenuous. As in other postconflict or transitional states, no one should expect the first elections to resolve all issues, but instead should see them as setting the table for what one must hope will be the smoothest possible "pacted" transition, premised on power-sharing agreements negotiated among the broadest array of forces that can be included in talks. Electoral-system reform may reduce the risk of a backlash by giving the old guard a stake in the new system and by granting fairer representation and voice to minority parties.

At the end of the day, the military will have to be persuaded to accept the outcome. For this, public contestation and free balloting alone will not suffice. The 2015 elections loom as a turning point in Burma's political life, but all will depend on skillful deal making between the military and the democratic (including the ethnic) opposition. Burma needs the rostrum and the ballot box, but it needs the bargaining table too.

NOTES

1. Reed Brody, "The Dictator Hunter's Wanted List: 9 Former Autocrats and Bad Guys That Should Be Made to Pay for Their Crimes," *Foreign Policy Online*, 18 June 2012, available at *www.foreignpolicy.com/articles/2012/06/18/the_dictator_hunter_s_wanted_list*.

2. EarthRights International, "China in Burma: The Increasing Investment of Chinese Multinational Corporations in Burma's Hydropower, Oil and Gas, and Mining Sectors," September 2008, available at *www.earthrights.org/publication/china-burma increasing-investment-chinese-multinational-corporations-burmas-hydropower-o*.

3. Anupama Airy, "Myanmar Prefers China as Gas Buyer; India Sees Red," *Financial Express* (Delhi), 29 May 2007, available at *http://m.financialexpress.com/news/myanmar-prefers-china-as-gas-buyer;-india-sees-red/194197*.

4. Stephanie Kleine-Ahlbrandt and Andrew Small, "China's New Dictatorship Diplomacy: Is Beijing Parting with Pariahs?" *Foreign Affairs* 87 (January–February 2008): 38–56.

5. Poon Kim Shee, "The Political Economy of China-Myanmar Relations: Strategic and Economic Dimensions," *Ritsumeikan Annual Review of International Studies* (2002): 33–53, available at *www.ritsumei.ac.jp/acd/cg/ir/college/bulletin/e-vol1/1-3shee.pdf*.

6. Anton Khlopkov and Dmitry Konukhov, "Russia, Myanmar and Nuclear Technologies," Center for Energy and Security Studies, 29 June 2011, available at *http://ceness-russia.org/data/doc/MyanmarENG.pdf*.

7. Bertil Lintner, "Burma's WMD Programme and Military Cooperation Between Burma and the Democratic People's Republic of Korea," March 2012, available at *www.asiapacificms.com*.

8. Aung Thet Wine, "Suu Kyi Looks to 'Good Neighbor' China," *Irrawaddy,* 4 July 2012, available at *www.irrawaddy.org/archives/8346.*

9. "As Myanmar's New Capital Emerges, Analysts Question Its True Cost," *Channel News Asia,* 7 April 2007, available at *www.channelnewsasia.com/stories/afp_asiapacific_ business/view/268959/1/.html.*

10. "Myanmar Allocates 1/4 of New Budget to Military," *Real Clear Politics,* 1 March 2011.

11. Flavia Krause-Jackson and Daniel Ten Kate, "Myanmar's Leader May Step Aside After 2015 Elections, Aide Says," *Bloomberg News,* 3 May 2012, available at *www. bloomberg.com/news/2012-05-03/myanmar-s-leader-may-step-aside-after-2015-elec- tions-aide-says.html.*

12. "Reuters: Suu Kyi to Meet Burma President," BurmaNet News, 10 April 2012, available at *www.burmanet.org/news/2012/04/10/reuters-suu-kyi-to-meet-burma-presi- dent.*

13. David Steinberg, "The Arab Spring and Myanmar," *Asia Times Online,* 21 October 2011, available at *www.atimes.com/atimes/Southeast_Asia/MJ21Ae01.html.*

14. Min Zin, "Burma or Myanmar? The Name Game," *Foreign Policy Online,* 5 July 2012, available at *http://transitions.foreignpolicy.com/posts/2012/07/05/burma_or_ myanmar_the_name_game.*

15. Min Zin, "Aung San Suu Kyi's Strategy for Change," *Foreign Policy Online,* 10 April 2012, available at *http://transitions.foreignpolicy.com/posts/2012/04/10/aung_san_ suu_kyis_strategy_for_change.*

16. See Bill Davis, "Under Siege in Kachin State, Burma," Physicians for Human Rights report, 2011, available at *https://s3.amazonaws.com/PHR_Reports/Burma-Kachin- Rpt-full-11-30-2011.pdf.*

17. "Burma's Economic Development Requires Peace: Thein Sein," *Mizzima,* 4 July 2012, available at *www.mizzima.com/news/inside-burma/7446-burmas-economic-devel- opment-requires-peace-thein-sein.html.*

18. See Alfred Stepan et al., "How Burma Could Democratize," *Journal of Democracy* 12 (October 2001): 105.

14

MINDING THE GAP BETWEEN DEMOCRACY AND GOVERNANCE

Donald K. Emmerson

Donald K. Emmerson *is director of the Southeast Asia Forum at the Walter H. Shorenstein Asia-Pacific Research Center at Stanford University. His many works include "The Problem and Promise of Focality in World Affairs," in* Strategic Review: The Indonesian Journal of Leadership, Policy, and World Affairs *(2011). This essay originally appeared in the April 2012 issue of the* Journal of Democracy *along with the essays by Dan Slater, Martin Gainsborough, and Thitinan Pongsudhirak.*

The eleven countries of Southeast Asia vary widely by type of regime and quality of governance. Those that are the most democratic are not always the best governed, and the reverse is also true. Recently in these pages, an essay about Indonesian democracy cautioned against confusing the quality of democracy with the quality of governance.[1] Anyone who has traveled on the London Underground, or used mass transit in Singapore or Hong Kong, will have read a sign saying "MIND THE GAP." This admonition to "mind the gap" is helpful when considering the relationship between democracy and good governance in Southeast Asia.

Based on evidence from these countries, this essay explores two propositions—one normative, the other empirical. The normative argument is this: Good things *ought* to go together. Because democracy is more humane than dictatorship, democracy in Southeast Asia should also do a better job delivering security, welfare, and other public goods. The empirical argument, whose validity would bolster the normative one, is this: Good things *do* go together.

To the extent that a polity is democratic and the quality of governance is high, other things being equal, democracy is more likely to be legitimated and institutionalized. Conversely, if governance is poor in a democratic polity, the legitimacy—and thus the future—of democracy is more likely to be jeopardized. The same logic would apply to the legitimation and institutionalization of authoritarian regimes. Good governance in an autocratic polity would strengthen authoritarian rule, just as bad governance would weaken it.

The empirical proposition implicates the normative one. If a democratic regime provides worse governance than an authoritarian one, the moral case for democracy is harder to make absolutely. To the extent that an authoritarian regime effectively fosters life-enhancing outcomes for its population, a relativist might argue, the ethical case against autocracy should be reconsidered—not abandoned necessarily, but qualified to take performance into account. On the other hand, if more democracy and better governance really do go together, if good governance is necessarily democratic and democracies necessarily govern well, then the moral argument is empirically vindicated. The advice to "mind the gap" between democracy and governance makes sense only if the gap exists.

The analytical separation of democracy from governance begins with the specification of terms. Two decisions are crucial. First, the scope of democracy must be limited to the political process and its openness to inputs from society, leaving governance to denote the performance of ruling authority and its outcomes for society. Second, accountability must be considered an aspect of democracy and not of governance. An effective official performance need not be accountable, either vertically through elections or horizontally by balancing executive, legislative, and judicial powers, but an unaccountable government cannot be democratic. To make accountability a requirement of both "good democracy" and "good governance" would prevent their analytic separation. That separation is further served here by construing democracy as more or less liberal and governance as more or less effective, in keeping with my understanding of how these variables are measured, respectively, by Freedom House and the World Bank, whose data are used here.[2]

Deng Xiaoping's Cat

Indonesia was the sole country in Southeast Asia that Freedom House ranked as Free in 2010[3]—or, in my terms, as more liberally democratic than any other state in the region. Of the ten other Southeast Asian countries, five were classified as Partly Free (Malaysia, the Philippines, Singapore, Thailand, and Timor-Leste) and five as Not Free (Brunei, Burma, Cambodia, Laos, and Vietnam). Freedom House also designated three countries as "electoral democracies": Indonesia, the Philippines, and Timor-Leste. These are useful taxonomies, but they combine into a few large bundles what for my purpose here must be disaggregated and reconceived as a spectrum of incremental gradations.

Those gradations were obtained for the measure of liberal democracy simply by adding the component Freedom House score for 2010 that each Southeast Asian country received on civil liberties (from 1 to 7, best to worst) to the score that it received on political rights (similarly 1 to 7, best to worst) in order to create a scale from most to least liberal-democratic (2 to 14, best to worst) along which all eleven countries could be ranked. On this continuum, Burma was the region's least liberal-democratic country, with the worst possible combined score of 14 (7 on political rights plus 7 on civil liberties). No Southeast Asian country was a full-fledged liberal democracy. Indonesia did better than any of its neighbors, but its score of 5 fell short of perfection on both political rights (at 2) and civil liberties (at 3). The region's remaining states were distributed between these extremes.

Thinking in gradations along two separate variables does complicate the analysis. If a government is neither fully democratic nor wholly undemocratic, how can we be sure that when it engages in better governance, and thereby improves the lot of its people, the legitimacy of democracy will benefit? The answer depends on the extent to which accountability is a feature of the political process in question. The less accountable a nevertheless effective government is, the more convincingly can its leaders keep democracy at bay by arguing, however speciously, that political competition would only undermine performance. A government that is both accountable and effective, on the other hand, can be rewarded at the polls, further validating democratic rule.

Note the dilemma faced by someone who wants to see more countries become more democratic—a *democratist*. If, as I argue, good governance tends to legitimate the regime under which it occurs, regardless of how democratic or autocratic that regime may be, should the democratist wish for *bad* governance in the five Not Free countries of Southeast Asia in the hope that these regimes will thereby lose legitimacy and be replaced by democracies? Or should the democratist hope instead that better governance in such places will somehow stimulate public demand for a government that is not only effective but also accountable? Or should the democratist yield to the *pragmatist*, for whom the effectiveness of a regime (what it manages to accomplish) is more important than whether or not it is democratic? Such a pragmatist would have no qualms about wanting a Not Free state to do the right things—ensuring security, spreading education, protecting health, and raising welfare. One can even imagine such a results-focused person quoting Deng Xiaoping's famous remark: "I don't care if it's a white cat or a black cat. It's a good cat as long as it catches mice."

Two aspects of the pragmatist's position warrant emphasis: It is *disconnective* in distinguishing effective governance as a matter of performance outcomes from democratic governance as a matter of participant inputs; and it is *instrumental* in making approval of democracy conditional on proof of its ability to deliver public goods. These viewpoints stand in contrast, respectively, to a *connective* understanding of good governance as necessarily democratic, and to an *intrinsic* conception of democracy as a naturally superior end-in-itself.

Table—Liberal Democracy and Effective Governance in Southeast Asia: Rankings for 2010

Country	Liberal Democracy (LD)	Effective Governance (EG)	The Gap (LD minus EG)
Timor-Leste	3	10	-7.0
Indonesia	1	6	-5.0
Philippines	2	5	-3.0
Cambodia	7.5	8	-0.5
Burma (Myanmar)	11	11	0.0
Laos	10	9	+1.0
Thailand	5.5	4	+1.5
Malaysia	4	2	+2.0
Vietnam	9	7	+2.0
Brunei	7.5	3	+4.5
Singapore	5.5	1	+4.5

Note and sources: To ensure the comparability of the rankings across columns, countries whose summary scores were tied were assigned identical fractional ranks. For the scores underlying the rankings, see Freedom House, "Table of Independent Countries," Freedom in the World 2011, 12–16; and World Bank Group, "Worldwide Governance Indicators," 2011, *http://info.worldbank.org/governance/wgi/mc_countries.asp.*

The Table below is disconnective. It ranks the countries of Southeast Asia from best to worst (1 to 11) in the region along two variables: degrees of liberal democracy based on the Freedom House scores and degrees of governmental effectiveness according to the World Bank.

The Table has limitations. Like Freedom House's trichotomy, it trades subtlety for simplicity. Because it offers a slice in time, not evidence over time, change cannot be inferred from its static contrasts. Its Southeast Asian frame obviates wider generalizations. The patterns that the Table conveys do, nevertheless, warrant notice and interpretation.

By the evidence in the Table, liberal democracy and effective governance do not go hand in hand in Southeast Asia, but neither are they consistently inimical. If they were perfectly and positively related, the sum of the absolute values—the differences, ignoring minus and plus signs—in the last column would be zero. If liberal democracy and effective governance were perfectly and negatively related, that total would be 60. At an actual sum of 31, Southeast Asia is an in-between region.

Timor-Leste, Indonesia, and the Philippines

Although the Table is not about change, we may still speculate about what, in that regard, its column of differences—"The Gap"—might imply. The greater and more negative the gap is for a given country, the larger the gulf between higher-quality democracy and lower-quality governance, and (if other things are equal) the greater the chance of instrumental disappointment—that democracy is not delivering the goods. By this admittedly narrow measure and based on this instrumental logic, democracy would appear to be at greatest risk in Timor-Leste.[4]

Timor-Leste is poised on the cusp between extreme individual poverty and extreme collective wealth. Among Southeast Asian countries, only Burma ranks lower on the Human Development Index—a summary measure of health, education, and living standards. More than four-fifths of Timor-Leste's 1.1 million people rely on subsistence agriculture, yet no country depends more on revenue from oil and gas; hydrocarbons account for nine-tenths of the republic's GDP. At the end of 2011, the Petroleum Fund of Timor-Leste—the country's nest egg for the future—was worth US$9.3 billion, not to mention anticipated revenues from reserves still beneath the Timor Sea. Stoked by government spending, inflation for 2011 was expected to exceed single digits. Timor-Leste's ranking on Transparency International's Corruption Perceptions Index worsened between 2010 and 2011, falling from 127th to 143rd.[5] (Among Southeast Asian states in 2011, only Laos, Cambodia, and Burma, in that downward order, were seen as more corrupt.)

A presidential election in Timor-Leste was scheduled for March 2012, with a second round in April if needed, followed by parliamentary polls in June. One hopes there will not be a repetition of the factional violence that swept the country in 2006. But if the quality of governance does not improve, Timor-Leste could become a poster child for the resource curse. Overdependence on rents from extraction could distort the economy and undermine democracy as well. If ably and honestly managed, the returns from oil and gas could be used to lift the population from poverty, thereby ensuring stability and preserving a reasonably high-quality democracy. If mismanaged, however, such revenues could disproportionally fatten the accounts of a self-interested elite in Dili, the capital. Should this happen, we might anticipate the eventual rise of an authoritarian populist able to appeal to a populace disillusioned by the instrumental failure of democracy to deliver a better life.

According to the evidence in the Table, the disconnect between laudable democracy and underwhelming governance is less severe in neighboring Indonesia than in Timor-Leste. Nor are resource rents so important. Indonesia's once-dominant energy sector—oil, gas, and mining—today accounts for a mere tenth of GDP.[6] That said, extractive activity still provides ample opportunity for corruption, both nationally and in those parts of the country where mineral wealth is concentrated. Mining is especially controversial in the eastern province of Papua—the site of labor unrest at a huge copper and gold mine, and political unrest linked to a movement for independence from Indonesia.

Aburizal Bakrie is Indonesia's one-time "king of coal," although his conglomerate—the Bakrie Group—has also done business in agriculture, banking, construction, insurance, manufacturing, media, real estate, shipping, and trade. His estimated $5.4 billion family fortune in 2007 made him the richest man in Indonesia that year. By 2011, his worth had shrunk to a "mere" $890 million, but that did not stop him from declaring in 2012 his readiness to run for the presidency in 2014.[7] As the head of Golkar, the second-largest party in the national legislature, he is his country's wealthiest politician—a personification of the "money politics" that so many Indonesian democrats lament.

If he does become Golkar's presidential candidate, he will carry a lot of baggage into the race.[8] The Indonesian government bailed out Bakrie after his conglomerate defaulted during the Asian Financial Crisis of 1997–98. When his overleveraged empire again suffered losses during the financial crisis that originated in the United States a decade later, Bakrie pressed the government for a second bailout. Then–finance minister Sri Mulyani, a highly regarded economist who personified good governance, refused. Her investigation of Bakrie for possible tax fraud had already put the two at odds. Bakrie proceeded to mount a political campaign in the legislature, accusing Mulyani of malfeasance in the handling of the financial crisis.

Like Mulyani, Bakrie was at the time a minister in the cabinet of President Susilo Bambang Yudhoyono, whose Democrat Party was—and, technically, still is—allied with Bakrie's Golkar in the ruling coalition. In 2010, SBY accepted Mulyani's resignation. She then took up a position with the World Bank in Washington, D.C. If Bakrie was the winner of his battle with Mulyani, arguably the loser was good governance in Indonesia.

In the meantime, Yudhoyono's campaign to make public authority less corrupt and more effective has lost momentum. He is becoming a lame duck. Elected in 2004 and reelected in 2009, both times by wide margins, he is constitutionally barred from running for a third term in 2014. The reputation for bold reform that he acquired in the earlier years of his presidency has been tarnished by evidence of corruption inside his own party. Human rights have suffered because of his passivity in the face of violent acts of vigilante "justice" perpetrated by militant Islamists against religious minorities.

In January 2012, a respected nonpartisan Indonesian think tank asked 2,220 Indonesians in 23 of the country's 33 provinces what they thought of Yudhoyono's performance. Most respondents regretted his lack of leadership in improving the economy, curbing corruption, enforcing the laws, and reducing poverty—precisely the issues an effective government might be expected to address. While some 60 percent of all respondents voted for Yudhoyono in 2009, only 17 percent said that they would do so in 2014 even if the constitution allowed him to run. Less than a fifth thought that Indonesia's economy had improved over the previous three years.[9]

The survey results did not impugn the systemic legitimacy of democracy. But they did reveal political apathy and a "none-of-the-above" inclination to dismiss all political parties as scandal-ridden and conflict-prone. None of the prospective candidates for president garnered much support among the respondents. It is hard to know how much of this indifference to attribute to outright alienation, how much to the media's preoccupation with controversy, and how much to the election's still being more than two years away. But if the legitimation of democracy presupposes an instrumental belief that it can improve people's lives through better governance, and governance worsens instead, how long will democracy remain "the only game in town"?

The country most similar to Indonesia in the Table is the Philippines. Relative to the rest of Southeast Asia, the quality of governance lags the quality of democracy in both countries; they are "governance-short." Asked about this gap, a knowledgeable source inside the government of Philippine president Benigno Aquino III replied in scathing terms. Corruption, he said, is "like a hydra." Kickbacks are common and law-enforcement agencies are themselves compromised. "Money politics" is rife. Elections are not decisions between policy alternatives, but popularity contests between charismatic leaders.[10]

Despite long-running communist and Islamist insurgencies, however, the Philippine political system is not ripe for revolution. In no other Southeast Asian country have people historically had greater faith in elections, which were introduced and took root at the local level early in the course of U.S. colonial rule. The country has never had a strong state. To put the matter abstractly, the legitimacy of procedural democracy in the Philippines limits the potential for systemic change that disappointment with performative democracy—the quality of governance—might otherwise entail.

Indochina and Burma

The prevalence of continuity over change is also a main theme of Martin Gainsborough's treatment, on pages 198–210 in this volume, of the very different conditions prevailing in Vietnam, Cambodia, and Laos. There, he argues, the commercialization of the state in combination with a patrimonial political culture tends to reinforce the status quo. His point has relevance for Indonesia and the Philippines insofar as the power of "money politics" to coopt opposition could have stabilizing effects in those countries too.

Gainsborough does acknowledge that social changes of possible significance are underway in each of the three countries that he covers. The ruling party could decide to loosen the reins. A crisis could split the ruling elite. Incumbents could incubate an ersatz opposition in order to preempt a real one. Should any of these things occur, unintended consequences could follow.

These scenarios for near-term change originate inside the state, and that is precisely where the extraordinary developments now underway in Burma also began. One might expect that popular uprisings in Southeast Asia would be most likely to occur in countries that are simultaneously most deficient in both liberal democracy *and* effective governance—Vietnam, Cambodia, Laos, and especially Burma. Burma does have a history of political ferment from the bottom up. Witness the uprising of 1988 and the Saffron Revolution of 2007, both brutally repressed. But the economic and political opening currently in progress in Burma is a ruler's move.

The Burmese authorities have released some political prisoners, reduced media censorship, widened electoral competition, and welcomed foreign assistance and investment. The regime appears also to want to lessen or balance its dependence on China, and finally to defeat or demobilize the ethnic insurgencies in outlying areas.

There are as many explanations of this "Burmese spring" as there are generals in the regime, active or retired. Among the latter is the ostensible reformer-in-chief himself, President Thein Sein. The most generous among these accounts imputes to the army leadership a sincere change of heart upon realizing that the modern world was passing Burma by. A more skeptical hypothesis has the generals hoping to trade the country's pseudo-socialist autarky for a personally lucrative version of crony capitalism.

A third view features nationalist pushback against overdependence on China. This explanation cites Thein Sein's September 2011 decision to suspend construction of the Chinese-funded $3.6 billion Myitsone Dam being built by Chinese labor in northern Burma. But like so much else going on in Burma, the suspension can be read in different ways. Nine-tenths of the power to be generated upon the dam's planned completion in 2019 was meant to meet China's energy needs, not Burma's. Poor people in the area, including restive ethnic minorities, had protested their impending displacement and the impact downstream on Burma's main artery, the revered Irrawaddy River. Was the project suspended to assert sovereignty against China, to placate disaffected ethnic groups, or to respond to the concerns of the poor? Or, in opaque proportions, all of the above?

Whatever the answer, it is striking that, by the evidence in the Table, reform in Burma has occurred in the absence of any gap at all between abysmally authoritarian rule and woefully ineffective governance. The advice to "mind the gap" must not be taken to imply that change can result only from a discrepancy between the quality of democracy and the quality of governance. Nor are the quality of democratic politics on the input side and the degree of effective governance on the output side ineluctably driven toward each other's level. The lesson of the Table is not thermostatic; smaller gaps are not necessarily more stable than larger ones; and matching rankings do not preclude change. If that were true, the reforms in Burma would never have begun.

Nor is it likely that Thein Sein's reforms (if they continue) will move both the polity and its governance—process and policy—simultaneously up the quality scale, notch by notch in tandem, neatly maintaining a zero gap between the two. More plausibly, one will lead or lag behind the other, opening a gap that could even widen over time.

A vital aspect of democracy is the institutional accountability implied by free and fair elections. The polls in Burma in 2010 were neither free nor fair. Not least among their purposes was the entrenchment of military rule in civilian guise. The success of that exercise in political engineering probably helped to convince the long-ruling dictator, senior general Than Shwe, that he could afford to pass the reins to Thein Sein and risk a controlled measure of reform.

As of this writing in March 2012, much was being made of the scheduled April by-elections for 40 seats in the lower house of the Burmese legislature and the government's willingness to permit their contestation by the iconic opposition leader Aung San Suu Kyi and her National League for Democracy. Yet even if she and her party's other candidates were to win all 40 seats, they would still be outnumbered ten-to-one by the other 400 more or less proregime legislators in the lower house, including a 110-strong military bloc appointed by Than Shwe. Some have speculated that, if she wins her by-election, Suu Kyi might even be invited to join the cabinet, although probably not with a key portfolio.[11] Should this happen, and were she to accept, she and her party would be visibly gambling on their ability to obtain, in return for their participation, accountability rather than cooptation.

Thailand, Singapore, and Malaysia

The Table locates both Thai democracy and Thai governance in or near the middle of the spectrum from best to worst, and the gap between their rankings is only slightly more than zero. Yet over the last five years, political life in Thailand has been more polarized and tumultuous than in any other Southeast Asian country.

Thailand's political travail is rife with irony. It took the corrupt and sometimes brutal tycoon Thaksin Shinawatra to instrumentalize Thai democracy. He transformed the abstract and encapsulated democracy favored by a Bangkok elite that was largely indifferent to the rural poor. He promised and delivered welfare to millions of needy Thais, who elected and reelected him by landslides. His ouster at the hands of royalist officers in 2006 ushered in a prolonged partisan struggle that continues to this day.

On the input side, since the 2006 military coup, Thai democracy has been degraded by the refusal of losers to accept the verdicts of the voters. On the output side, as discussed in this issue by Thitinan Pongsudhirak on pages 168–82, the politicization of judicial decisions has undermined governance. If Thailand is to recover, he argues, a consensus must be found that can sustain a transition to a fully constitutional monarchy whose institutions are simultaneously more accountable and more effective.

Different still are the cases of Singapore and Malaysia, as analyzed by Dan Slater on pages 183–97. His essay underscores the historic strength of these two states—the most effective in Southeast Asia according to the Table. Without using the phrase, Slater explicitly minds the gap. In his words, "one must not confuse any particular regime's *performance* with the underlying character of state *power*."

State strength for Slater is Janus-faced. The relative effectiveness of the Singaporean and Malaysian states on the output side—their capacity to decide and execute policy—has equipped these ruling elites to constrain purportedly destabilizing voices and movements on the input side. Yet precisely because the state is so strong, the regime can afford to loosen its grip without losing control. The chance of democratization hangs in the balance.

In Singapore and Malaysia, the quality of governance exceeds the quality of democracy. No other countries in Southeast Asia are, in this relative sense, more democracy-short. By the logic of promiscuously instrumental legitimation, effective governance—the provision of public goods—should legitimate even an illiberal state. By this reasoning, Singapore's and Malaysia's rulers should be sleeping well, comfortable in the belief that their prowess at performance is continuing to forestall dissatisfaction.

But people do not live by bread (or rice) alone, especially not in countries as prosperous as these. The electoral gains achieved by the oppositions in both places—incremental in Singapore in 2011, dramatic in Malaysia in 2008—were wake-up calls to these ruling elites not to take their own entrenched incumbencies and legitimating performances for granted.

In sum, democracy and governance do not co-vary in Southeast Asia. These two good things do not go together. Gaps exist, and they are worth minding, in theory and in practice. From these disjunctures, however, consistent causal inferences are hard to draw. Are large gaps destabilizing? Potentially, to an extent, yes, and that is not at all necessarily a bad thing. In the most governance-short cases—Timor-Leste and Indonesia—rulers are being challenged to perform better on the outcome side. In the most democracy-short countries—Singapore and Malaysia—the ruling parties must deal with pressures for political reform.

Burma is different. In that country relative to the rest of Southeast

Asia, on the eve of Thein Sein's changes, democracy and governance were equally abject. But an analyst would have been dead wrong to think that since bad things in Burma had gone together for so long, they would keep on doing so—that 2011 would turn out to be just another worst-case no-gap year. Thailand's gap in 2010 was only modestly greater than Burma's. Yet Thais are hardly assured of future political stability—not if the politics of the upcoming royal succession interact with factional conflict in a country that has suffered more political turbulence in recent years than any other in the region.

In discussions of democracy, it is normatively satisfying but empirically unhelpful to weld adjectives to the nouns that they modify. That democratic governance is desirable does not make it the only kind available. The gap exists, and it should be minded. That said, however, a narrowly instrumental or results-focused view of democracy as legitimated solely by its ability to deliver public goods omits far too much. Southeast Asians do care about human rights, civil liberties, electoral fairness, and political representation—democracy as a political process rather than a policy performance. The ostensibly reformist generals in Burma could have gone the Chinese route, opting for economic but not political reform. They did not—or, more cautiously put, they have not so far. To acknowledge that democracy and governance are not, in fact, synonymous is not a reason to ignore the color of Deng Xiaoping's cat.

NOTES

1. Danielle N. Lussier and M. Steven Fish, "Indonesia: The Benefits of Civic Engagement," *Journal of Democracy* 23 (January 2012): 71.

2. Freedom House (FH) does not claim to be scaling "liberal democracy." Yet, taken together and applied to any given country, the 27 questions that they ask—12 about "political rights" and 15 on "civil liberties"—do measure the extent to which that country is both democratic (including the accountability of its government vertically in elections and horizontally in a separation of powers) and liberal (including freedoms of speech and association). FH "does not rate governments or government performance per se"; see FH, "Methodology," *www.freedomhouse.org/report/freedom-world-2012/methodology.* In contrast, the measure of "government effectiveness" devised by the World Bank (WB) "captures perceptions of the quality of public services, the quality of the civil service and the degree of its independence from political pressures, the quality of policy formulation and implementation, and the credibility of the government's commitment to such policies"; see *http://info.worldbank.org/governance/wgi/pdf/ge.pdf.* The closest that these two measures come to overlapping is in FH's inclusion of an independent judiciary among the elements of liberal democracy and the WB's inclusion of an independent civil service among the elements of effective governance.

3. Freedom House, "Table of Independent Countries [2010]," available at *www.freedomhouse.org/sites/default/files/inline_images/TableofIndependentCountries-FIW2011.pdf.*

4. A systematically causal analysis over time would need to assess the contrary logic as well: that faced with such a large negative gap, the country's people would remain satis-

fied with their high-quality democracy as a moral end in itself and not expect it to improve bad governance. The population might also not know how abysmally its government was performing relative to good governance in neighboring states, despite the likely erosion of such ignorance by the globalization of information and communication.

5. UN Development Programme, "Human Development Index (HDI)—2011 Rankings," *http://hdr.undp.org/en/statistics/*; "High Inflation Threatens East Timor: IMF," Agence France-Presse, 2 February 2012; Petroleum Fund of Timor-Leste, Quarterly Report no. 26, 31 December 2011, 1, available at *www.bancocentral.tl/Download/Publications/Quarterly_report26_en.pdf*; Transparency International, "Corruption Perceptions Index 2011," *http://cpi.transparency.org/cpi2011/results/*, and "Corruption Perceptions Index 2010," *www.transparency.org/policy_research/surveys_indices/cpi/2010/results*.

6. Hanan Nugroho, "Energy and Economic Growth," *Jakarta Post*, 15 July 2010, *www.thejakartapost.com/news/2010/07/15/energy-and-economic-growth.html*.

7. Justin Doebele, "Indonesia's 40 Richest," 24 December 2007, *www.forbes.com/global/2007/1224/049.html*; "Indonesia's 40 Richest: #30 Aburizal Bakrie," Forbes.com, *www.forbes.com/lists/2011/80/indonesia-billionaires-11_Aburizal-Bakrie_0J8F.html*; "I'm Ready for 2014: Bakrie," *Jakarta Globe*, 19 February 2012, *www.thejakartaglobe.com/politics/im-ready-for-2014-bakrie/499072*.

8. An ongoing instance of such baggage is the world's biggest mud volcano, which erupted in East Java in 2006. Apparently triggered by negligent drilling for gas by a Bakrie family–owned company, this catastrophe has already rendered unusable a 3-square-mile area, killed 13 people, and displaced 13,000. Homes, schools, and croplands have been buried to depths as great as 60 feet. Despite the judgment of experts that Bakrie's company was probably responsible for the disaster, he blames an earthquake that occurred 174 miles away. The flow of muck is expected to continue and remain unmanageable until 2037. "Mud Volcano Eruptions Likely to Continue for a Quarter of a Century," News and Events, Durham University, 28 February 2011, *www.dur.ac.uk/news/newsitem/?itemno=11636*. Arguably related to the weight of such baggage was Bakrie's philanthropic decision to endow a chair in Southeast Asian studies at the Carnegie Endowment for International Peace in Washington, D.C.

9. Keyko Ranti Ramadhani, "Fed Up with Politicians, More Indonesians Won't Vote: CSIS," *Jakarta Globe*, 13 February 2012, *www.thejakartaglobe.com/news/fed-up-with-politicians-more-indonesians-wont-vote-csis/497834*. Indonesians express rising confidence in their own personal economic circumstances, however; see Debnath Guharoy and Roy Morgan, "Analysis: 240 Million Reasons for a Confident Future," *Jakarta Post*, 21 February 2012, *www.thejakartapost.com/news/2012/02/21/analysis-240-million-reasons-a-confident-future.html*.

10. Interviewed by the author on 2 February 2012.

11. "Is Suu Kyi Heading for a Cabinet Position?" *Irrawaddy*, 29 February 2012, *www.irrawaddy.org/article.php?art_id=23125*.

15

THE SHADOW OF CHINA

Benjamin Reilly

Benjamin Reilly *is professor of political science in the Crawford School of Public Policy at the Australian National University. His books include* Democracy and Diversity: Political Engineering in the Asia-Pacific *(2006). He has been a Reagan-Fascell Democracy Fellow at the National Endowment for Democracy and a visiting professor at the Johns Hopkins School of Advanced International Studies (SAIS) in Washington, D.C. This essay originally appeared in the January 2013 issue of the* Journal of Democracy.

In the April 2012 edition of the *Journal of Democracy*, four leading political scientists cast critical eyes upon the progress (or lack thereof) that democracy has been making in Southeast Asia. Thitinan Pongsudhirak looked at the troubled prospects for democracy in his home country of Thailand; Martin Gainsborough asked why democracy has failed to flower in Cambodia, Laos, and Vietnam; Dan Slater analyzed "strong-state democratization" in Singapore and Malaysia; and Don Emmerson surveyed the region more generally. A common theme—seen especially in Slater's and Gainsborough's contributions—was the roles that domestic elites, state structures, and money play in explaining the unevenness of democratic development across the region.

Each author alluded to but did not solve a core problem that bedevils all discussions of democracy in Southeast Asia. As a region that has experienced vast political and economic advances in recent years, Southeast Asia should be a showcase displaying the positive link (so long a political-science staple) between development and democracy. In nearby Northeast Asia, South Korea and Taiwan both offer good examples of this link between economic and political modernization: Each country went through a long stretch of economic development overseen by an authoritarian regime that clung to power even as rising prosperity spawned a large and increasingly restive middle class. Then, in the late 1980s, each regime launched a process of political liberalization that led in fairly short order to democracy. Along with Japan, East Asia's oldest democracy, South Korea and Taiwan are among the richest and most developed countries in the world. Their stories thus lend support to a central tenet of modernization theory.

In Southeast Asia, however, this neat relationship between economic and political development is missing. Throughout the region, the "Lipset thesis" (named for social scientist Seymour Martin Lipset), which holds that democracy is more likely in well-off countries than in poorer ones, is being stood on its head. Democracy is weak or absent in the region's richest states (Brunei, Singapore, and Malaysia), but present to at least some degree in three of its poorer ones (Indonesia, the Philippines, and Timor-Leste). Moreover, these three democracies all feature relatively high amounts of ethnolinguistic or religious diversity, defying the conventional wisdom that sees divided societies as unfriendly soil for democracy. Indonesia, moreover, is the world's largest Muslim-majority country, countering the thesis that democracy is incompatible with Islam. Finally, none of the three ranks high according to such well-known indices of human development as educational levels, literacy, maternal health, and the like—all usually held to correlate strongly with democracy.[1]

Compounding this problem is the region's most developed state, Singapore, which represents a huge anomaly for scholars of democracy. Despite a per capita GDP of $54,000 a year (higher than that of the United States), this city-state at the southern tip of the Malay Peninsula has long been a soft-authoritarian "semidemocracy." Larry Diamond calls it "the most economically developed nondemocracy in the history of the world."[2] Singapore's neighbor Malaysia also represents a significant challenge for democratic theory, combining as it does high levels of human development and per capita income (more than $15,000 a year) with an illiberal competitive-authoritarian regime. Despite allowing a degree of opposition contestation, neither Singapore nor Malaysia has yet come close to experiencing a democratic turnover of government. By contrast, Indonesia, the Philippines, and Timor-Leste have all experienced successive handovers of power following competitive elections, an important threshold of democratic development according to some political scientists.[3]

Nor are these countries the only democratic anomalies in Southeast Asia. The former French colonies of Cambodia, Laos, and Vietnam have seen rapid economic growth and rising middle classes, but remain de facto or de jure one-party regimes with strikingly illiberal political climates, as Gainsborough well explains. In Thailand, which has only recently returned to civilian rule following the 2006 military coup, the Bangkok-based middle classes have confounded democratic theory by turning actively hostile toward majority rule since the rise of populist politician Thaksin Shinawatra rewrote the rules for winning elective

Map—Freedom House "Electoral Democracies" in the Asia-Pacific, 2006–2012

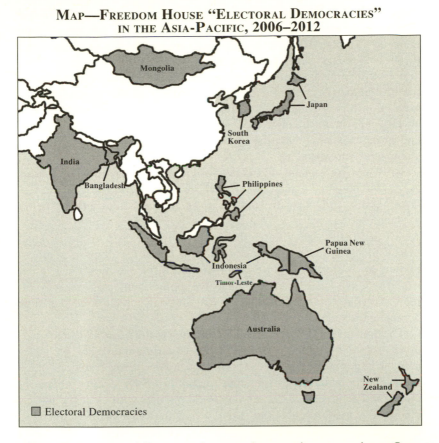

office. Burma, too, fails to conform to democratic expectations: Once the richest Southeast Asian state with widespread literacy, it has over the past forty years dropped almost to the bottom on nearly every measure of political, economic, and human development, although hopeful changes are now occurring with the election to parliament of Aung San Suu Kyi and other opposition members.[4]

A Geographical and Historical Explanation

Southeast Asia thus presents a profound puzzle to students of democracy and democratization. How to solve it? Here, I want briefly to raise the possibility of an alternative explanation for the presence or absence of democracy across Southeast Asia. This explanation looks not to domestic sociological or even political factors, but rather to geography, international influences, and history.

First, there is the matter of geography. The distribution of civil liberties and political rights across Southeast Asia (as measured by Freedom House) follows a striking spatial pattern: All the maritime states (save

Brunei) are democratic, all the mainland states that border China are autocratic, while the region's semidemocracies are geographically in-between (see Map). If we divide the region more simply between "electoral democracies" and nondemocracies, then the picture is even clearer.[5] This mainland-maritime democratic divide has been stable since the Philippines became an electoral democracy in the "people power" revolution of 1986, the Suharto regime fell in Indonesia in 1998, and an independent East Timor (now Timor-Leste) emerged following the end of Indonesian domination in 2001, with only Thailand changing its status over this period.

How can we explain this clear geographic demarcation of regime type? One potential explanation is that a country's location—especially its proximity to China, the core East Asian state—may offer a better explanation than more conventional analyses for what could be called Asia's distinctive "geography of democracy." The deep historical legacy of China's "tributary" relations with the countries along its southern border, in contrast to China's more limited influence over the remoter island realms of the Indonesian and Philippine archipelagoes, may offer a pathway to understanding Southeast Asia's pattern of maritime democracies and mainland autocracies.

To summarize: Throughout their changing history as traditional kingdoms, colonial fiefdoms, or modern single-party autocracies, the states along China's southern border have never been democracies. Today, Laos and Vietnam remain standout examples of the "China model" of closed and nominally communist political systems with open and mostly competitive market economies. Cambodia practices a different but analogous model of partly competitive elections under what is effectively single-party rule. Burma is currently undergoing a political opening but shares aspects reminiscent of Cambodia's system as well as Suharto's Indonesia. This is one reason that the political openings in Burma since 2010 have so disturbed the Chinese: Burmese president Thein Sein's process of liberalization is seen as having undermined not just a close partnership between authoritarian systems but China's core strategic interest in retaining like-minded regimes around it.

As one moves further from China, the modal regime-type also starts to loosen. The core state in mainland Southeast Asia, Thailand, has lurched between competitive democracy, military rule, and civilian quasi-democracy over the past decade. Currently, Freedom House classifies it as Partly Free. By virtue of both its geographical location and its uncertain political future, Thailand can be seen as the key "swing state" in Southeast Asia, not just in terms of the region's democratic prospects but also China's growing influence. Moving south, soft-authoritarian systems remain in Malaysia and Singapore, two of the world's most resilient semidemocracies, combining parliamentary government with enduring single-party dominance. These two states have been described as geographically "amphibious"—half in mainland and half in maritime Southeast Asia. Their semidemocratic political models mirror this spatial positioning.

A related explanation for the durability of authoritarianism in Cambodia, Laos, Vietnam, and (at least until very recently) Burma compared to the relative success of democracy in maritime Southeast Asia stresses the impact of Chinese foreign policy. Traditionally, China sought to coopt its Southeast Asian neighbors through assimilation into China's sphere of influence—in sharp contrast to the centuries of wars fought against the Mongols and other northern invaders, the impetus for the Great Wall of China. There was no Great Wall in the south. Rather, over centuries, the southern kingdoms were assimilated into the Chinese sociocultural order. This happened first via the expansion of China's own borders to include Yunnan, Fujian, and Guangdong, and then via the coercion of latter-day Burma, Laos, and Vietnam into a China-focused "tributary" system that enmeshed these neighboring states in a growing web of Sinitic influence.[6]

The tributary system evolved under the Ming dynasty (1368–1644) as a way to formalize China's imperial authority over its southern neighbors. Only countries that acknowledged Chinese suzerainty were permitted trade relations, through officially sanctioned entry ports in Canton and Kunming. "Near countries" on China's border, such as Vietnam, were required to send tribute every three years. More distant countries were required to send tribute only infrequently.[7] The tribute itself, usually consisting of local luxury items, was less important than the symbolism of ritual submission to the Chinese empire, which after all stood at the center of the world and enjoyed the mandate of heaven. Acknowledgement of the supreme status of the Middle Kingdom was thus at the heart of this profoundly unequal and hierarchical worldview.

The tributary system was further reinforced by the designation of the various tributary kingdoms as "pacification superintendencies" whose responsibility was to keep the peace along China's southern frontier. These included the Tai principalities of Luchuan and Cheli in present-day Yunnan, the Lao kingdom of Lan Xand, the Kingdom of Lan Na in northern Thailand, and the Kingdom of Ava in present-day Burma, all of which were designated as "pacification commissioners" and made to conduct their formal relations with China via Yunnan.[8] Nothing like this highly institutionalized sphere of influence covered the Malay Peninsula or the maritime sultanates of island Asia.

In more recent decades, this sphere of influence has been manifested via China's support for communist revolutions and Leninist political structures in 1960s Laos and Vietnam, Beijing's assistance to the Khmer Rouge in 1970s Cambodia, and China's current nervousness about the possibility of democracy (and potentially U.S. engagement) in Burma. The rapid economic integration of southern China with Vietnam, Laos,

Burma, and, increasingly, Thailand and Cambodia is another important part of this story. "Not only do China's geographic size and proximity to Southeast Asia make China more difficult to ignore for those who exist in its shadow," notes Alice Ba, "but they also make China relatively more interested in what happens in Southeast Asia as part of its 'backyard.'"[9]

The situation of the three "China-lite" states of Cambodia, Laos, and Vietnam is a good example. All are former colonies of France, located next to one another. Laos and Vietnam border southern China. All witnessed the violent rise to power, culminating in the mid-1970s, of communist parties that enjoyed active or passive Chinese help. Such parties have ruled Laos and Vietnam ever since. In Cambodia, the communists rebranded themselves as the Cambodian People's Party. Despite a 1993 UN electoral intervention, they have ruled that country more or less unchallenged for decades. All three countries have also seen rapid recent economic growth fueled by outside aid and investments that come mainly if not solely from China. All tend to support China in international forums to a greater (Cambodia) or lesser (Vietnam) extent.

China has dangled the carrots of economic engagement (in larger states such as Thailand and Vietnam) and aid (in smaller states such as Cambodia and Laos) and brandished the stick of military threats or assaults (Beijing actually invaded Vietnam in 1979) to advance its interests and build a ring of protective borderland partners. Support for Leninist political models is one element of this partnership. Beijing finds it easier to relate to familiar nondemocratic regimes, particularly if they share China's quasi-communist model. Democracies are not only more alien to current Chinese authorities, but could also pose the threat of "demonstration effects" by giving the Chinese public what its rulers would see as dangerously close examples of open political competition and self-government.

Gainsborough's explanation for the resilience of autocracy in Cambodia, Laos, and Vietnam features internal factors such as colonial legacies, a hierarchical and paternalistic elite culture, and deeply held antipathies to pluralism.[10] A simpler explanation may be that each of these states once formed part of China's "tributary" system, and hence developed a political culture different from what one finds in states that sit farther from Chinese influence. This was an inherently and explicitly unequal bilateral relationship, in which smaller neighbors had to swear fealty to Chinese imperial power.

The tributary system fell apart once the West began aggressively penetrating East Asia, including China itself after the two Opium Wars (1839–42, 1856–60). As Martin Stuart-Fox recounts, China had traditionally used a combination of trade and armed force to get its way along its southern and western borders. But this system broke down amid the European scramble for Asia. Sniffing the wind, once-loyal tributaries such as the Thai kingdom rejected repeated Chinese demands for tribute and in 1882 repudiated all tributary obligations. The colonization and annexation of Indochina by the French and of Upper Burma by the British in the second half of the nineteenth century added to Beijing's losses. "For the first time," as Stuart-Fox notes, "a serious security threat existed along previously peaceful, if poorly defined, frontiers with cooperative tributary states."[11]

The Afterlife of Tributary Relations

Yet even though the formal tributary system collapsed, its legacy lived on. With Japan's defeat in the Second World War and the victory over the Nationalists a few years later of Mao Zedong and his Chinese Communist Party (CCP), China began to reestablish the form if not the content of a tributary system in its neighboring "buffer states." One illustration of this was Chinese support to the nondemocratic systems of its near neighbors. Under Mao, China tried to protect friendly (North Korea, North Vietnam) or neutral (Burma, Laos) buffer states in order to keep challenges at bay. Even during the partial political opening of the post-Mao era, China continued to actively support communist parties in Laos and Vietnam while also giving military and financial aid to first the Khmer Rouge and then the People's Party in Cambodia. The historical roots of such behavior are deep: For at least six *centuries*, Beijing has consistently sought, by means diplomatic or otherwise, to line its frontiers with friendly supplicant powers.

A current consequence of this approach is the present-day prevalence along China's southern border of single-party socialist systems complete with the same rhetorical commitments as the CCP. As Alice Ba notes:

> Chinese power has greater significance for continental states that are more affected for better and worse by their proximity to [China]. For countries like Vietnam, proximity to China has critically shaped its evolution and . . . offered Vietnam a model of governance, of revolution and of post-socialist development.[12]

Similar observations could be made about Laos and, in a rather different way, Cambodia as well. Even the state-sponsored socialism of Ne Win's Burma was closer in form and spirit to the CCP than to anything emanating from the West.

China's active support for Southeast Asia's communist parties throughout the 1960s and 1970s, and its ties to them since, have also informed key aspects of Chinese foreign policy. Following the end of the Cold War, China attempted to fashion its politically like-minded neighbors into an Asian Socialist Community (ASC) in which "each regime seeks to preserve one-party rule based on the legitimacy of the party in

the struggle for national independence, resistance to foreign intervention, and commitment to building socialism," on the understanding that
all members face "a common external threat—pressure to democratize
society, to allow political pluralism and to implement internationally
acceptable standards of human rights."[13] While in formal terms nothing
came of the ASC, its core vision of resolutely nondemocratic governments standing together against international pressures has remained a
common touchstone for China and its socialist neighbors.

By contrast, Southeast Asian countries situated farther from the Chinese orbit, particularly those off the Asian mainland, were much less
susceptible to such arrangements. Again, this follows the historical pattern, in which "differences in geographic proximity also help explain
variations in substance, and especially intensity, in China's relations
with Southeast Asian states."[14] Maritime Southeast Asia posed a much
greater barrier to the extension of Chinese influence, in large part because China's bilateral relations with island Asia were historically much
less developed. Of all the countries of Southeast Asia, Indonesia and the
Philippines stand out in recent history as least likely to accept Chinese
hegemony. As Stuart-Fox notes:

> Indonesia could look back on no long historical kingdom-to-empire bilat-
> eral relations regime of the kind developed between China and Vietnam,
> or Thailand, or Burma. Even less could the Philippines, whose significant
> trade relations with China (apart from Sulu) post-date the arrival of the
> Spanish and were conducted under their auspices.[15]

A final piece of the puzzle is the divergent way in which Southeast
Asian states have reacted to the communist threat in the contemporary
era. Communism, as both a doctrine and a program of political action,
polarized Southeast Asia for several decades following the end of the
Second World War. While communists tried to seize power in almost
every Southeast Asian state, they were ultimately successful only in Indochina. Communist victories in Laos, Vietnam, and (indirectly) Cambodia were balanced by sustained and in some cases brutal resistance
to communist movements in Indonesia, Malaysia, Singapore, and the
Philippines.

Indonesia's 1966 crackdown on communism after a coup attempt the
previous year not only brought Suharto to power but resulted in the
deaths of as many as half a million communists and communist sympathizers and their families (most of them Indonesians of Chinese heritage). Communist movements were similarly suppressed, often brutally,
in Malaysia and Singapore. Communist parties were banned in all three
countries and in the Philippines, which is still waging a rural guerrilla
war against a nominally communist insurgency, the New People's Army.
Explicitly anticommunist laws remain on the books in several Southeast
Asian countries, and the specter of communism has been evoked and at

times exaggerated to justify the continuance of internal-security laws and other political controls.[16]

In sum, history and geography offer alternative, and possibly more convincing, path-dependent explanations for the current distribution of democracy and autocracy across Southeast Asia than conventional political science can provide. Southeast Asia's mainland states, particularly those nearest China, were the subject of repeated demands for tribute in the precolonial era, and have received consistent support from China for their nondemocratic political models in the postcolonial era. This support helps to explain their resilience today. By contrast, more distant maritime states like the present-day democracies of Indonesia and the Philippines were much less subject to historical demand for tribute, much less willing to accept Chinese hegemony in the eighteenth and nineteenth centuries, and violently resisted communist movements in the postwar period. Understanding the interplay of history and geography is thus critical to understanding the contemporary contours of democracy and its alternatives in Southeast Asia, and helps to explain what democratic theory cannot.

NOTES

1. The classic work on the relationship between democracy and development is Seymour Martin Lipset, "Some Social Requisites of Democracy," *American Political Science Review* 53 (March 1959): 69–105. For a more recent analysis, see Adam Przeworski et al, *Democracy and Development: Political Institutions and Well-Being in the World, 1950–1990* (New York: Cambridge University Press, 2000).

2. Larry Diamond, "China and East Asian Democracy: The Coming Wave," *Journal of Democracy* 23 (January 2012): 7.

3. Samuel P. Huntington, *The Third Wave: Democratization in the Late Twentieth Century* (Norman: University of Oklahoma Press, 1991).

4. Brian Joseph and Min Zin, "Burma: The Democrats' Opportunity," *Journal of Democracy* 23 (October 2012): 104–19.

5. As Freedom House explains in its "Freedom in the World" survey for 2012: "Freedom House's term 'electoral democracy' differs from 'liberal democracy' in that the latter also implies the presence of a substantial array of civil liberties. In the survey, all Free countries qualify as both electoral and liberal democracies. By contrast, some Partly Free countries qualify as electoral, but not liberal, democracies." See *www.freedomhouse.org*.

6. For an outstanding synthesis of scholarship on relations between China and Southeast Asia, see Martin Stuart-Fox, *A Short History of China and Southeast Asia: Tribute, Trade and Influence* (Sydney: Allen and Unwin, 2003).

7. Stuart-Fox, *Short History,* 75.

8. Stuart-Fox, *Short History,* 80.

9. Alice D. Ba, "A New History? The Structure and Process of Southeast Asia's Rela-

tions with a Rising China," in Mark Beeson, ed., *Contemporary Southeast Asia,* 2nd ed. (London: Palgrave Macmillan 2009), 193.

10. See Martin Gainsborough, "Southeast Asia: Elites vs. Reform in Laos, Cambodia, and Vietnam," *Journal of Democracy* 23 (April 2012): 34–46.

11. Stuart-Fox, *Short History,* 122.

12. Ba, "A New History?" 193.

13. Carlyle A. Thayer, "Comrade Plus Brother: The New Sino-Vietnamese Relations," *Pacific Review* 5, no. 4 (1992): 402.

14. Ba, "A New History?" 193.

15. Stuart-Fox, *Short History,* 238.

16. Justus M. van der Kroef, *Communism in South-East Asia* (Berkeley: University of California Press, 1980).

INDEX

Burma *(cont'd)*
quality of, xxviii, 222, 230*t*,
234–237; labor unions in, xvi;
liberalization in, xxvii, 18, 48,
212, 218–222; political culture
in, 223; re-engagement with
West, xxvii, 217–218; rule of
law in, 222; seven-step roadmap
in, xxvii, 213–214; uprisings
in, xxvii, 216–217. *See also*
Myanmar

Cambodia, x*t*, xxvi–xxvii, 16, 18,
20–21, 22*t*, 228, 230*t*, 239–240,
242, 246; 1993 democratic transition in, 28, 48, 194, 198–199,
201–202, 207, 244; China
and, xxviii, 19, 243–245; civil
society in, xxvi–xxvii, 198, 202,
205–206; corruption in, 205,
231; democratization in, 48,
199–200; economic growth and
democratization in, 198, 240;
elections in, 18, 201, 203, 207,
242; governance, quality of,
202, 230*t*, 234; labor unions in,
204; patronage in, 202; political
culture in, xxvi, 198, 202–204,
206–207, 233, 244; PR in, 22*t*
CCP (Chinese Communist Party),
xvii, xxi, xxvii, 9–10, 75–89,
245; economic growth and,
xxii, 80, 86–87; and KMT,
xxii–xxiii, 90, 93–97, 99–103;
political cooptation by, 80–83,
85; political repression and,
xxii, 76, 80–81, 86–87; popular
discontent and, xvii–xviii, 78
censorship, in Burma, xvi, 212, 220,
234; in China, xvii–xviii, 81; in
Singapore, xiv; in Taiwan, 97
Chen Shui-bian, 92–93, 107*t*, 108,
111, 113, 117, 120–121, 125
China, ix, x*t*, xii, xiv*t*, xvi–xix, xxi–
xxiii, xxvii–xxix, xxx*n*, 3–15,

19–21, 48, 75–76, 78, 81, 84–85,
183, 199, 207, 209*n*; accountability in, xix, 10–12, 93, 99;
authoritarian resilience in, xxi,
75–78, 80, 87; bureaucracy in,
xix, 4, 8, 10–11, 96; censorship
in, xvii–xviii, 81; civil society in,
xviii; corruption in, xvii, 9–11,
78, 84, 86, 96, 101; crony capitalism in, xxvi, 81, 101; democratization in, xvi–xviii, 10–12, 21,
90, 102–103; demography of,
xviii; dynastic, 4, 8, 11; economic growth in, xvii–xviii, 76, 84,
86–87, 94, 96, 102; elections in,
10, 92, 101; governance, quality
of, xix, 12, 77, 92, 96; Internet
in, xvii, 11, 91, 97; modernization in, xvi–xvii, xxii–xxiii, xxix,
97; patronage in, 9–10, 81–82,
84–85; the Philippines and, 160,
167*n*; repression in, xxii, 80; rule
of law in, 4, 8; social media in,
97; Taiwan and, xvi–xvii, xxii,
35, 90–104, 111–112, 114; Vietnam and, 201–202, 205
"China factor," ix, xii, xviii, xxix,
239–248; in Burma, xxvii,
19, 213–216, 234, 242–243,
245–246; in Cambodia, 19,
243–244; in Laos, 18–19, 48,
207, 242–245; in Malaysia,
xxviii, 239–242, 246; in Taiwan,
111–112; in Thailand, 246; in
Vietnam, 18–19, 242–246
civil society, xx, xxvii, 52; in
Burma, 212, 217, 220–222; in
Cambodia, xxvi–xxvii, 198,
202, 205–206; in China, xviii;
in Indonesia, 145, 147; in Japan,
39–40; in Korea, 39–40, 107,
119; in Laos, xxvi–xxvii, 198,
201–202, 205–206, 208; in
Malaysia, xv; in the Philippines,
152; in Taiwan, 39–40, 107,

KMT (Kuomintang), x, xvii, xxii,
    34, 37–38, 40–41, 44–45,
    90, 93–100, 102, 103*n*, 107,
    110–111, 113, 115, 125–126,
    189–190; DPP and, 105, 108,
    116–117, 120–121, 124–125,
    190. *See also* Taiwan

labor unions: 1986 economic
    reforms in, 199; bureaucracy
    in, 201; in Burma, xvi; in Cam-
    bodia, 204; "China factor" and,
    18–19, 48, 207, 242–245; civil
    society in, xxvi–xxvii, 198,
    201–202, 205–206, 208; corrup-
    tion in, 203–205, 231; economic
    growth and democratization in,
    198, 240; elections in, 203, 206;
    governance, quality of, xxviii,
    201, 230*t*, 234; in Laos, x*t*, xiv*t*,
    xxvi–xxvii, 198–210, 215, 228,
    233, 239–240, 246; political
    culture in, xxvi, 198, 202–204,
    206–207, 233, 244; rule of law
    in, 200; suppression of dissent
    in, 200–201; in Taiwan, 95
LDP (Liberal Democratic Party),
    32–33, 38–39, 41, 44–45
Lee Teng-hui, 92, 107*t*, 108–109,
    111, 126
Leninism, xxii, xxviii, 9, 19, 77,
    93–94, 99, 243–244
Lipset, Seymour Martin, 240, 247*n*

Ma Ying-jeou, 93, 107*t*, 111, 117,
    120
Malaysia, x*t*, xiv*t*, xv, xvi, xxv,
    xxix, 18, 20*t*, 21, 22*t*, 27, 49,
    77, 145, 214, 218, 228; accoun-
    tability in, 188; "China factor"
    and, xxviii, 239–242, 246; civil
    society in, xv; corruption in,
    195; democracy, faith in, 61*t*,
    61–62; democracy, quality
    of, 236; democracy, support

for, xiii, 51*t*, 52, 53*t*, 53, 55*t*,
    55–56, 57*t*, 57–58, 59*t*, 59–60,
    61*t*, 61–62, 195; democratiza-
    tion in, xv, xxv–xxvi, 16, 25,
    48, 183–197; elections in, xv,
    183–184, 186–188, 191–194;
    governance, quality of, 230*t*,
    236; Internet in, xv; opposition
    in, xv, 192–194; rule of law in,
    53*t*, 59*t*; social media in, xv;
    strong-state democratization in,
    183–197
Marcos, Ferdinand, xi, 150–151,
    153–158, 165
Mexico, xi, xiv*t*, xv–xvi, 43, 77
mixed-member electoral systems,
    xx, 16, 18, 25. *See also* MMM
MMM (mixed-member majorita-
    rian electoral systems), xx, 17,
    20–21, 22*t*, 23, 26; in Japan, 17,
    20–21, 22*t*, 28; in Mongolia,
    17, 22*t*, 23–24, 28; in Taiwan,
    21; in Thailand, 18, 26. *See
    also* mixed-member electoral
    systems
modernization 5; in China, xvi–
    xvii, xxii–xxiii, xxix, 97; in Ja-
    pan, 13; in Korea, xxvi, 239; in
    the Philippines, 157; in Taiwan,
    xxvi, 97, 99, 102; in Thailand,
    xxii, xxix
modernization theory, xxviii–xxix,
    8, 85; accountability in, 60;
    corruption in, xi; democracy,
    faith in, xii, 61*t*, 61; demo-
    cracy, quality of, 59*t*, 59–60;
    democracy, support for, 51*t*,
    52, 53*t*, 53–54, 55*t*, 55–56, 57*t*,
    57–58; democratization in, x,
    xii, 48; elections in, 28, 48; in
    Korea, 240; in Malaysia, xv;
    MMM in, 17, 22*t*, 23–24, 28;
    in Mongolia, ix, x*t*, x, xii, xx,
    xxix, 16, 20*t*, 21, 49, 241*m;*
    multiparty system in, 48; rule